Guide to Greece

by Michael Haag and Neville Lewis

MICHAEL HAAG

Other books about Greece published by Michael Haag:

Delphi and the Sacred Way by Neville Lewis
The Traveller's Journey is Done by Dilys Powell
An Affair of the Heart by Dilys Powell
The Villa Ariadne by Dilys Powell

Please send for our complete list:
Michael Haag Limited, PO Box 369, London NW3 4ER

Guide to Greece, third edition

Cover design by Colin Elgie

Photo credits: Lawrence Durrell, page 35; Michael Haag, pages 23, 65, 127, 285; Neville Lewis, page 159; NTOG, the remaining.

Copyright © 1986 by Michael Haag and Neville Lewis

Typeset, printed and bound in Great Britain by The Bath Press, Lower Bristol Road, Bath BA2 3BL

Published by Michael Haag Limited, PO Box 369, London NW3 4ER, England

ISBN 0 902743 51 1

CONTENTS

About This Guide	4
Background	5
Athens	36
Around Attica	76
The Islands of the Argo-Saronic	84
The Argolid	95
The Central Peloponnese	106
The Southern Peloponnese	117
The Road to Delphi	136
Euboea and the Northern Sporades	164
Central Greece	172
Northern Greece and the Islands of the North Aegean	187
Northwest Greece	214
The Ionian Islands	230
The Cyclades	245
The Eastern Sporades	267
The Dodecanese	275
Crete	293

Maps, Plans and Elevations

Greece	7
Greek Temple	25
Doric and Ionic Orders	27
Athens	39
Acropolis	45
Ancient Athens	55
Daphni Church	77
Citadel of Mycenae	101
Olympia	111
Ancient Delphi	155
Delphi Museum	158
Thessaloniki	191
Delos	251
The Dodecanese	277
Crete	295
Palace of Knossos	297

Practical Information sections follow each chapter, and there is an index at the rear.

ABOUT THIS GUIDE

This is a new, entirely revised and expanded edition, packed with the latest practical information on travel, accommodation and so on. The Guide covers the whole of Greece, including the islands. As well as giving extensive descriptions of the better known places, it also includes a number of select and undiscovered spots for those who are tired of mere 'tourist Greece'.

At the end of each chapter is a *Practical Information* section full of helpful details for that area. These sections make it easy for the traveller to plan his journey, get the most for his means, and enjoy his stay. The information is for all price ranges and degrees of adventurousness.

The *Background* chapter provides the information you need before you go; explains in general terms what you can expect when you arrive; and also serves as a reference section on the spot.

This is a complete Guide to Greece. But while the *Practical Information* sections and the *Background* chapter were up to date when going to press, inflation and changing circumstances have their effect. New hotels may be built, sea and air services may extend (or vary with season), and, annoyingly, museum times and days of opening may alter (winter openings are usually shorter than the summer openings stated here). Also the traveller might like to add his own recommendations of places to visit, things to do, where to stay, for inclusion in the next edition. The reader is asked, therefore, to help with the next edition of this Guide by sending information and comments to the *Area Editor for Greece, Michael Haag Limited, PO Box 369, London NW3 4ER, England*. Thank you.

BACKGROUND

Greece reaches down into the Mediterranean like a sweeping hand that has sown a thousand islands upon the sea. The sea is everywhere, not on three sides only, but at every turn, penetrating the broken phalanxes of the coastline. You cannot travel very far across country without meeting the sea and you cannot sail for long upon the sea without an island rising off your bows. Greece is a tough cloth woven from the contrasting textures and colours of rugged mountain land and blue water.

There is a dignity to this land and in the people who live upon it. It is not that Greece was ever simply great in her monuments, in her intellect or in her power, but that her people expressed through these things their hard discovery of the proportions of their existence. Amidst a landscape of stark brilliance where the mountains stand in razor-sharp clarity against the sea and sky, with the hot sun at his neck and the stony soil resisting at his feet, the Greek forces the elements to meet and give him life. The clear, slightly resinated wine is the synthesis of his labours. He drinks life in all its contradictions and knows joy.

The Greek lives out so many contradictions that one suspects he deliberately creates them, partly to nourish his inborn scepticism, partly to make the world more complicated. He will place his lips upon an ikon and then emerge into the sunlight with a sly smile which says that in there we believe, out here we know better. He will open a taverna, stand outside, and you will sit down and wait an hour before he bothers to serve you. Then he will insult you into the bargain and finally, having decided that he likes you, will give you a bottle of wine on the house.

He is as passionate about women as any Italian but in the villages anyway does his best not to show it. He will say to foreigners, why do you talk with women? Why do you dance with women? Women are for making love to and nothing else. At the same time, you will find no more proud, assured or independent woman in all the Mediterranean than a Greek woman. That Greece was the 'cradle of democracy' is a cliché. It is no less true that the country has been a nursery for tyranny and anarchy. Sometimes the government abuses the people; other times the people abuse the government; and when both the government and the people are abusing each other simultaneously, that is democracy. The cradle is rocked vigorously and the Greek comes through it all with anything but complacency: he is tough and resilient, sharply intelligent and inquisitive; he is his own man, independent of spirit and free.

*

When Perithoos, king of the Lapiths, invited the neighbouring Centaurs on the slopes of Mt Pelion to his wedding feast, these creatures, half man, half horse, attracted by the unfamiliar fragrance of wine, pushed their bowls of sour milk aside and drank the wine-skins dry. Drunk and lecherous, they dragged the bride off by her hair and raped the nearest women and boys. Theseus, legendary founder of Athens and friend of Perithoos, joined the Lapiths in their day-long fight to drive the savage guests away.

One more outrageous tale of Greek mythology it seems, but an exceptionally popular one in classical times. With events like the defeat of the Persians to celebrate, the Athenians chose instead to depict the battle between Lapiths and Centaurs on the metope reliefs of the Parthenon, and the same theme appears on the interior frieze of the Temple of Apollo Epikouros at Vassae, high up in the wild mountains of the Peloponnese, and again on the west pediment of the Temple of Zeus at Olympia.

For all the exhilaration the Greeks felt after their victories over Darius and later Xerxes at Marathon, Salamis and Plataea, they understood that these momentous episodes were also only momentary episodes in their struggle for civilisation, a struggle that would have to be waged for endless centuries to come. The battle between Lapiths and Centaurs, between men on the one hand and on the other men who are yet half beasts, expresses a larger, timeless struggle. Sophocles' 'moderation in all things' is not the motto of a moderate people – for whom it would be superfluous. It is a warning against the beast in man, a warning that destruction arises from within as well as from without. The Greeks of Pericles' time could be an immoderate people. It was their awareness of this and the prizes they won in their struggle with themselves that was their glory.

This is a guide to the land and its people, and inevitably a guide through time. Even if one shunned the Parthenon and could somehow avoid not stumbling upon a broken column, a Mycenaean wall, a Byzantine chapel, the land itself has that awesome dawn-of-creation clarity and the people that naked response to it that cannot have changed since Homer's day. Greece today is the same Greece as when man first surveyed the savage landscape about him and within him and dared pit reason and justice against what he found. Time weaves back upon itself. Mycenaean, classical, Byzantine, modern are not eras within a chronology but each designs upon an ever-present tapestry that portrays the continuing struggle.

Tourist Information
The National Tourist Organisation of Greece (NTOG) is

NTOG offices abroad

extremely helpful both inside and outside the country, supplying maps, brochures (in English, German, French and Greek) and travel information sheets. Their offices are found in principal cities abroad, including:
Britain: 195-7 Regent Street, London W1 (Tel: 734.5997).
USA: 654 Fifth Avenue, New York, NY 10022 (Tel: 421.5777); 611 West Sixth Street, Los Angeles, California 90017 (Tel: 626.6696); 168 North Michigan Avenue, Chicago, Illinois 60601 (Tel: 782.1084).
Canada: 1233 de la Montague, Montreal QC, H36 1Z2 Quebec (Tel: 871.1535).
Australia: 51–57 Pitt Street, Sydney, NSW 2000 (Tel: 241.1663).
Netherlands: Leidsestraat 13, Amsterdam (Tel: 25.42.12).

Belgium: Blvd de l'Imperatrice 62-66, 1000 Brussels (Tel: 513.02.06).
France: 3 Avenue de l'Opera, Paris 75001 (Tel: 260.65.34).
Germany: Neue Mainzer Strasse 22, 6 Frankfurt/Main (Tel: 23.65.62); Pacellistrasse 2, 8000 Munich 2 (Tel: 22.20.35).
Italy: Via L. Bissolati 78–80, 00187 Rome (Tel: 4744.249); Piazza Diaz 1, Milan (Tel: 860.470).
Austria: Kartner Ring 5, 1015 Vienna (Tel: 52.53.17).
Sweden: Grev Turegatan 2, Box 5298, 10246 Stockholm 5 (Tel: 21.11.13).
Switzerland: Gottfried Keller Strasse 7, 8001 Zurich (Tel: 2518.487).
Japan: 11 Mori Building, 2-6-4 Toranomon Minato-Ku, Tokyo 105 (Tel: 5035001).

Tourist assistance in Greece

The NTOG's head office in Greece is at 2 Amerikis Street, Athens (Tel: 3223.111), and there are information desks inside the National Bank of Greece at 2 Karageorgi Servias Street, Syntagma Square, Athens and at the East Main Airport. In Thessaloniki the office is at 34 Mitropoleos Street (Tel: 271.888). Regional offices are located in other major towns and at the border, while the Tourist Police all over the country can be relied upon for their courtesy and efficiency in supplying information and finding rooms.

Entry regulations and documents

No visas are required of Western European, American, Australian and New Zealand nationals, amongst others. A valid passport is sufficient to gain entry for 3 months. If you wish to extend your stay, contact the nearest police station or the Aliens Bureau, 9 Halkokondyli Street, Athens (Tel: 3628.301). Personal belongings such as clothing and camping gear may be brought through customs duty-free, as well as one each of the following: cameras, cine cameras, projectors, binoculars, musical instruments, record players (with up to 20 records), radios, typewriters, tape recorders, bicycles and sports gear such as skis and sporting rifles. It is forbidden to export any work of art dating from before 1830 without permission. 'Works of art' can include old coins and potsherds. Penalties are severe. Cars and motorcycles brought into the country are entered on your passport to ensure that they are taken out again at the end of 4 months, though this period can be extended to 8 or even 12 months. The importation of foreign currency is free and unlimited, but sums in excess of the equivalent of US $500 should be declared to ensure free exportation. No more than 3000 drachmas in Greek currency may be brought into or taken out of the country. There are no special vaccination or inoculation requirements except that cholera and yellow fever certificates are required if coming from an infected area. Dogs and cats require health and inoculation certificates issued in the country of origin.

Climate

Hot summers and mild winters are the rule for all of Greece

except in the north, and at higher elevations in the mountain regions, where winters are cold. The highest summer temperatures are usually found in the Peloponnese, Rhodes and the Dodecanese and Crete. July and August are the hottest months. Athens is then stifling, but the islands of the Aegean are cooled by the meltemi which indeed can make them positively windy at times. Crete and Rhodes are the warmest parts of Greece during the winter though certainly do not count on being able to swim, especially in January and February. The very best time to come to Greece is in April and May when it is not too hot, the land has not yet been parched, and all is green and brilliant with wildflowers. Second best is October; most of the vegetation has dried up but the sun has released a herbal scent amongst the hills, and for some plants there is a second flowering.

Travel Notes

Getting there by air Athens is served by major international airlines and charter operators from all over the world, and from within Europe it is also possible to fly directly to Thessaloniki, Corfu, Kos, Rhodes and Heraklion. APEX fares to Greece are inexpensive, but you need to fix your dates of departure and return at the time of purchase, and if travelling in the summer you should purchase your ticket as far in advance as possible.

By sea Piraeus is the port of Athens and the major port of Greece, but you are only likely to arrive there if coming from major European ports like Venice, Trieste, Genoa or Marseille. The more usual sea approach to Greece is from one of the more southern Adriatic ports, ie Ancona or Brindisi, and perhaps Bari and Otranto, calling variously at Corfu, Igoumenitsa on the mainland, and Patras in the Peloponnese. There are connecting coaches to Athens. If you buy a ticket for Patras but want to spend some time on Corfu enroute, insist that this be noted on your ticket. Car ferries operate year-round from Venice, Ancona and Brindisi; the best is the Karageorgis Lines service from Ancona: their ships are comfortable, their fares no greater than those from the more southerly ports, and you save yourself a half to full day's drive down Italy's boring east coast.

By land Coming to Greece by train means passing through Yugoslavia, a hot, crowded, unpleasant journey. It is better to go by train to an Italian port and continue on by boat. The cheapest way of getting to Greece is by bus, but this is recommended only to those with a sense of humour.

Youth discounts The new low-fare APEX tickets (see above), available to all, have by now probably killed off the once privileged student discount flight market, but enquire at your local student travel office all the same. Anyone under 26 can buy discounted rail passes for travel through European countries including Greece: either Interail, available from British Rail or travel agents and valid one month, or the slightly more expensive Transalpino ticket available from Transalpino, 214 Shaftesbury Avenue, London WC2 (Tel: 836.0087) or travel agents and valid two months. Interail and International Student Identity Card holders can obtain discounts on some of the trans-Adriatic shipping lines.

Travel within Greece by air Olympic Airways is the exclusive operator within Greece and has a network of routes connecting Athens with Thessaloniki and a few other mainland cities, but is most valuable for getting out to some of the major islands in a hurry: Chios, Corfu, Crete, Karpathos, Kos, Kythera, Lemnos, Rhodes, Samos, Skiathos, Thera, Zakynthos and a few others. Some of these routes may be dropped during the winter months; during summer you should book far in advance, before leaving home if possible. Olympic's head office is at 96 Syngrou Avenue, Athens (Tel: 92.921) and there is a booking office in the Athens Hilton (Tel: 9292.445) as well as on Syntagma Square. One flight over the Aegean is worth it for a god's eye view of that ancient blue sea speckled with scores of islands – you can almost see the square sails of Odysseus, Theseus or the Argonauts down below. Air fares compare favourably with first class boat fares. For example, flights from Athens to Kos and Thera (Santorini) cost about 3600 and 3250 drachmas respectively.

By sea Voyaging by sea is what Greece is all about and always has been. A mountainous country making overland communications difficult, hundreds of boats still bob along the coastline or from island to island at very low fares. Piraeus is the hub of Aegean routings. For weekly information sheets on sailing times, routes and fares, go to the NTOG office in Syntagma Square. Also you can scan the shipping page of the English-language *Athens News*. Car ferries operate over many routes, and there is a fast but relatively expensive hydrofoil service (for passengers only) in the Argo-Saronic gulf and down to Monemvasia, and between some of the Cyclades. However the majority of the routes are served by ordinary passenger boats, on which there is a wide range of fares from first class to deck class. Cabins are available for those paying the higher fares on the longer runs.

The joys of a sea voyage Deck class on a steamship is the cheapest way to travel (some 2000 and 1600 drachmas respectively from Piraeus to Kos and Thera) and for the young or adventurous the most enjoyable. For daytime voyages, like the early morning sailings from Piraeus through the Cyclades, deck class means nothing more than that you may freely wander above and below deck but not into the first-class restaurant and bar.

But for overnight voyages, like the one to Crete, the question of where to sleep arises. Down below, on every available bunk, chair or sheet of newspaper, the Greek passengers have staked out their claims, but first they sit around talking, smoking, drinking, sharing out food from vast parcels (better and cheaper than the food you buy on board). Gipsy women despatch their children to maraud the ship, and themselves sit on beautifully woven cloths selling dresses, blouses, trinkets. Hawkers stand by doorways with trays of nuts, chocolates and honey-cakes. There is a man with a lamb slung over his shoulder who presses through the pandemonium selling raffle tickets.

The soldiers are drunk, the old men are laughing and slapping their knee boots when not playing vicious games of cards, mothers are breast feeding their babies, and then by 2am, amidst a clutter of paper, bread crusts, bottles and cans, everyone is sprawled out fast asleep in their reserved positions. The air is choked with smoke, damp with sweat, hot with sufficient snoring bodies to sink a ship twice the size of the one you are on, the engine thuds against the floor, the wind chops against the half-open port holes.

Greeks rarely like sleeping on deck, but every foreigner with a sleeping-bag is up there (even in mid-summer, sun and wind compete for the sea and by the time the first star appears in the sky, the sea breeze has taken cold possession of the night). Cigarettes glow in windless corners, thick borrowed novels are read beneath the deck lights, life-boats sway with the sea and the copulating travellers who have made their beds inside them. Dark islands slip by in the black Aegean night.

Some Greeks do appear on deck before passing out below. One time, sailing to Heraklion, several were attracted by the noise of a ukelele and the voices of a dozen Germans singing *Gaudeamus Igitur* as though on the deck of a sinking U-boat. One Greek had a flute, another a violin, a third expropriated the ukelele and the rest began dancing with the Germans to wild Cretan music. Several bottles of wine later, the frenzy declined, the moment had come for an older Greek to come forward and dance in that proud measure of a toreador before the horns and soft eyes of a breathless bull.

This old mountain man with stubble on his chin, high boots, threadbare jacket flicked by the wind, danced with a power that held all eyes, and gesturing towards a young and muscular soldier who could have knocked half of us off deck with one sweep of his arm, these two then danced, shoulder to shoulder, the old man's every step a mastery of grace, the soldier following, prettily, deferentially, like a young girl dancing with her father on her wedding night.

There is a sexuality in this dance, perhaps a homosexuality, though really it is a dance of another passion, a challenge to disorder, destruction and death (the Spanish bullfight is a bastardised bull dance, common in the Aegean 3500 years ago), the older men showing the younger the way. Anyway, they dance on these ships, they sing, they sell and trade and drink and argue, and you fall asleep on the deck, and if you have not rolled off during the night you wake with the sun in your face, and the old Venetian walls of Heraklion loom close leaving only enough time for a quick coffee.

Yachting Probably the most exciting way to see Greece is in your own boat, perhaps pottering around the islands. However it is not for the inexperienced (except possibly in flotilla), nor is it cheap to hire a craft. Uncrewed sailing yachts will vary between $175 and $450 a day (four to ten berths), crewed yachts will be at least double. Information from Yacht Brokers Association, 36 Alkionides Street, Alimos, Athens: a suburb near the airport, by the sea (Tel: 9816.582). Several British tour operators specialise in sailing holidays for the experienced and right down to beginners, even offering learn-to-cruise holidays. Prices range from £375 to £850 per person for two weeks, flight from London to Greece included, but not food. Consult a travel agent or the NTOG for further information.

Bus and train Both buses and trains are cheap, though of the two trains are mostly cheaper. Buses are usually faster and more comfortable and reach nearly every nook and cranny of the country, whereas the railway system is far more limited. The bus fare from Athens to Delphi is about 500 drachmas and to Mycenae about 400. Be sure to be in good time for buses, as they sometimes leave early.

By car Greece is among the most expensive countries in Europe for car rentals, with summer rates from about 2000 drachmas a day and 20 drachmas a kilometre upwards. There are car hire companies, including Hertz and Avis, in most tourist centres. The great advantage to having a car, your own or rented, is being able to get to inaccessible spots, indeed being able to discover places miles from nowhere which you probably would not have chanced seeking out had it meant waiting hours for a bus or hiking for miles in the mid-day sun. On the other hand, there is the danger of shutting yourself off from the country, in particular missing the lively society of the Greek bus. Taxis remain relatively cheap. A 10-kilometre ride might cost 700–800 drachmas, and you can usually strike a reasonable bargain if you want the driver to wait for you, like at a museum, or to return and collect you later.

Tours There are numerous coach tours of varying duration from the main centres to ancient and other sites. The leading operator is CHAT, 4 Stadiou Street, Athens (Tel: 323.4444), but there are many others, usually less expensive. There are also organised cruises or sea excursions from Piraeus, Kos, Chalcidici, Crete, Corfu, Rhodes, Santorini and many of the other islands. Details can be obtained from local travel agents.

Maps Maps available in Greece are usually poorly produced and inaccurate. The maps and plans in the free NTOG leaflets are usually as good as anything you will buy, although on some of the islands you can buy passable local maps (and guides). The best maps are those produced for each nome (county region) by the National Ministry of Statistics, 14 Likourgou, Athens (scale 1:200,000), where they may be bought with some difficulty if you take your passport – or they may be bought very easily in London, at Edward Standford, 12 Long Acre, WC2.

Further details
For further notes on internal travel see the *Practical Information* section at the end of each chapter.

Living Notes

The alphabet
The first thing you should do is learn the Greek alphabet. Greek is not nearly as strange as it looks on first sight: once you know that an upside down L is really a G, that a P is an R and that a B is a V, you're on your way to seeing through the camouflage of peculiar letters which reveals words not all that more difficult than the ones you easily make sense of in French, Italian or Spanish. After all, a fair part of the English language has grown up from Greek as well as from Latin roots.

The more assiduous alphabet-learners among you may want to grapple with the lower-case letters as well, but they make less initial sense than the upper-case ones, and fortunately street names, names of hotels and so on are usually written entirely in upper-case letters.

In the columns below from left to right is the Greek alphabet in upper-case and in lower-case letters, the names of the letters in Greek, and their approximate pronunciation.

Α	α	alfa	a
Β	β	vita	v
Γ	γ	ghama	gh or y (depending on what follows)
Δ	δ	dhelta	dh
Ε	ε	epsilon	e
Ζ	ζ	zita	z
Η	η	ita	i
Θ	θ	thita	th
Ι	ι	iota	i
Κ	κ	kapa	k
Λ	λ	lamdha	l
Μ	μ	mi	m
Ν	ν	ni	n
Ξ	ξ	ksi	ks
Ο	ο	omikron	o
Π	π	pi	p
Ρ	ϱ	ro	r
Σ	σ	(ς at the end of a word) *sighma*	z or s (depending on what follows)
Τ	τ	taf	t
Υ	υ	ipsilon	i

Φ	φ	*fi*	f
Χ	χ	*khi*	kh
Ψ	ψ	*psi*	ps
Ω	ω	*omegha*	o

A few words

A number of excellent phrase books cum dictionaries are available both in Greece and abroad. For making a start at learning the language, try the well known *Teach Yourself* series which has a book on Greek.

The French, Spanish and Italians are all used to foreigners knowing a few words of their languages, but the Greeks seem not to expect it and are therefore all the more gratified if you can utter the simplest greeting. So it is very much worth your while to get a phrase book, or even just to learn the following words: *parakaló* = please, *efcharistó* = thank you, *kaliméra* = good morning, *kalispéra* = good afternoon or good evening, *kalinikta* = good night. *Kala* alone means good, and you can use it when you pat children on the head, comment on a meal, or in any situation where you want to convey approval. One of the most common words you will hear is *endáxi*: it means okay. And as a general greeting or farewell, as when you encounter a goatherd on a hillside, there is *yia-sou* (though that is the familiar singular; the formal – best used initially – and the plural is *yia-sas*). Yes is *ne*; no is *óhi*.

And gestures

Here you might run into some trouble. When a Greek says no he also tilts his head back. Sometimes he says nothing at all but just accompanies this gesture with a clicking of the tongue. And sometimes he does not even click his tongue. The result is that you ask at a kiosk for a certain newspaper and the Greek cocks his head back. At first you think this means 'I beg your pardon?', so you say it again, and again the head flicks back. After you have asked for your newspaper seven times, each time raising your voice, simultaneously trying to enunciate more clearly and to gesticulate fiercely in the appropriate manner, you realise that he has been saying 'no' all along and you feel like a numbskull. So along with learning the alphabet and a few words and phrases, you should also learn some gestures. There is a very funny book (all the more funny for being so true to life) by Papas called *Instant Greek* which illustrates this aspect of communication. It is published in Greece and readily available throughout the country.

A few more words

There are a few other words worth being able to recognise when walking around: *odós* = street, *plateía* = square, *leofóros* = avenue, *stásis* = bus stop, *xenodochío* = hotel. Also, using the following two phrases together with some gestures or some English thrown in can get you a long way: *thélo* (I want, eg *Thélo* . . . and point); also *pou eínai*? (where is?, eg *Pou eínai* museum, or toilet? It is pidgin Greek but often works.).

And an apology This is a good place to apologise for any inconsistencies in our transliteration of Greek words and place-names into English. There is no standard formula. We write odos as odos because it seems simpler to do so, though its pronunciation in Greek is more like 'odhos' (the 'd' in Greek being pronounced like the 'th' in 'that'). We do not overly-mimic the phonetic subtleties of Greek. On the other hand, we have often written place-names as they are pronounced in Greek (indicating how they are stressed both at their principal entry and in the index), partly for flavour, partly so that you can be more immediately understood. Epidauros, for instance, is Epídavros to a Greek and that is the way we have written it. Eleusis is pronounced Elefsís. (A 'u' after 'a' or 'e' is pronounced either 'v' or 'f' depending on what follows.) It may seem incredible that Greeks should speak of Zeus as 'Zefs', but after all, he was their god and it is their language. But then we have not always gone so far. Thebes we commonly write as Thebes, noting the Greek 'Thivai' only in brackets. Names of people have usually been written in their Greek form, but occasionally, in recognition of popular usage, Sophocles, for example, might appear instead of Sophokles. Writing leoforos with an 'f' but Phaleron with a 'ph' when both could be either the one or the other can only be explained as an aesthetic idiosyncrasy and our small contribution to furthering the spirit of contradiction which the Greeks themselves, in other matters, are so good at promoting.

Accommodation Depending on your preferences and on what you are prepared to spend, there is a choice of hotels from luxury to fifth class (denoted in this Guide as L and A, B, C, D and E), rooms in private homes, youth hostels and organised camping grounds. Hotel prices are controlled by the government and despite huge increases in recent years they remain relatively good value. During the summer you might expect to pay some 5000 drachmas for an air-conditioned double room with bath in a B hotel in Athens (less elsewhere). Or you can pay as little as 2000 drachmas for a basic (and usually clean) double room in a private house. It can be worthwhile to bargain, especially out of season. Remember that the Tourist Police will usually help you find accommodation if necessary.

Hotel reservations can be made by writing directly to the hotels or to the head office of the Hellenic Chamber of Hotels, 6 Aristidou Street, Athens (Tel: 323.3501). Or in person go to 2 Karageorgi Servias Street in Athens (near Syntagma Square) or reserve on arrival at Athens airport.

For place-by-place listings of hotels see the *Practical Information* sections at the end of each chapter.

There are numerous camping grounds, some organised by

the NTOG (write to the National Tourist Office of Greece at 2 Amerikis Street, Athens, for a list), some by the Hellenic Touring Club and many run by private individuals under licence. Prices vary with the facilities, and the NTOG camping grounds which are often of a better standard and in better positions tend to be the more expensive.

There are comparatively few youth hostels (some 27 in all Greece) and in summer it may be necessary to book in advance. There is usually a maximum stay of five days (ten in Athens). Membership of any association affiliated to the International Youth Hostels Federation will entitle you to use the youth hostels in Greece on production of an IYHF card. Details of hostels are available from the Greek Youth Hostel Association, 4 Dragatsaniou Street, Plateia Klafthmonos, Athens (Tel: 3234.107).

Places with camping grounds and youth hostels are indicated in the *Practical Information* sections.

Roof-tops, monasteries and freelance camping

It is also possible at many tavernas around the country to get free or very cheap roof space. Monasteries and convents may offer beds (usually to males and females respectively), especially in out-of-the-way places where there is no alternative accommodation, and though these are free, and though an offer of some payment will usually be refused, something should be left in the chapel upon leaving. Freelance camping is no longer allowed; but the law was introduced to stop people from sleeping out in the middle of Athens or along resort beaches (there was considerable abuse, litter and lack of hygiene), so that if you are out of the way and not making a nuisance of yourself it is less likely that this restriction will be enforced. The air is warm, the nights are brilliant with stars, and all of Greece could be yours for the price of a sleeping-bag.

Eating places

If there is much distinction to be made between a restaurant (estiatorion) and a taverna, it is that the latter is less formal, at least partly outdoors and its fare uncompromisingly Greek. A taverna meal can be inexpensive and delicious, though the menu will be limited in variety. Greece is not renowned for its cuisine, and though some eating places will serve better food than others, it is probably as much if not more worthwhile basing your choice of where to eat on atmosphere. Greeks themselves frequently dine out as the large numbers of tavernas attests; lunchtime is from 1 to 3, dinner from 9 to 1am (though earlier outside Athens) and at least half the point of going to a taverna for dinner at all is the convivial evening spent talking and drinking.

Like hotels, restaurants and tavernas are officially graded and their prices fixed accordingly. Menus will show the basic price against each item, and then the price with service added. When served by the owner of a small taverna, it is not necessary to tip as the service charge covers this. But in larger places something should be left on the change dish for the employee-waiter, and if a boy has been helping out with the water and retsina, a coin can be left for him under your eating plate. In Athens and major towns and resorts the menu is likely to be in English or French as well as in Greek, though wherever you are it is quite acceptable to go into the kitchen and see for yourself what is there.

Food   A meal might start with soup, pasta or an hor d'oeuvre such as the pink fish roe paste called *táramosaláta* or stuffed vine leaves (*dolmádes*). Fish, common on the islands or by the coast, rare inland, is usually served as a main course and is often expensive. Red mullet (*barboúnia*) and whitebait (*marídes*) are fairly standard; also octopus (*ktapódi*) and squid (*kalamári*) which largely depend for their taste on the wine sauce in which they are prepared. Foreigners might prefer the more tender baby squid (*kalamarákia*), crisply fried. Meat (*kréas*) is most usually veal (*moskári*), lamb (*arnáki*), or increasingly pork (*chirinó*); also shish kebab, skewered chunks of grilled meat as often called *sou̇fláki*. Each person might order his own main fish or meat course, but the usual practice is to share vegetables and salads from common plates. The selection will be determined by the season. In spring you should try *chórta*, or greens – in fact dandelion and other leaves plucked from the slopes of the Acropolis, by the roadside, or in someone's back garden – which are served cold in plenty of lemon and oil. Salad (*saláta*) can be all tomato (*domáta saláta*), all lettuce (*maroúli*) or mixed, popularly known as Greek or country salad (*choriátiki*), served with goat's milk cheese (*féta*). Old standbys include *moussaká*, a layered pot-pourri of peppers, tomatoes, minced meat, cheese, potatoes, etc. – its flavour and quality varying from day to day, place to place – and macaroni casserole (*makarónia*). If there is any chance of oil (*ládi*) being added to anything it will be. So if you do not want oil you had better be fast with '*óhi ládi*'. But anyone spending any time in the sun should welcome all the olive oil they can get: it finds its way to the skin, lubricates you against the heat and works with the sun to give you a beautiful colour.

Wine   Wine (*krasí*) comes either resinated or not. The mouth-puckering retsina, flavoured with resin from pine trees, may seem strange at first taste, but in combination with Greek food it is perfect. Retsina is sometimes still served from the cask in cans and so there are local variations in quality and taste; more often and less interestingly it comes standardised in bottles. Unresinated wine almost always comes bottled, Hymettos and Demestica being two of the most widely available labels. White wine is *áspro*, red is *mávro* (literally 'black') and rosé is *kókkino* (literally 'red').

17.

Cafés Sweets are not usually served at tavernas, nor coffee. For coffee you go to a café or *kafeneíon*, where you might find sweets too though you might have to go to a patisserie (*zakaroplasteíon*). The coffee is usually Greek-style, thick and black in small cups and comes without sugar (*skétto*), with sugar (*métrio*) or with loads of sugar (*variglikó*). If you want Western-style coffee, ask for Nescafé. The favourite kafeneion aperitif is ouzo, colourless and flavoured with aniseed, and traditionally served with *mezé*, little snacks of cheese, nuts, olives or fish. The most popular sweets are *baklavá*, layered pastry filled with honey and nuts, and *kataífi*, shredded wheat filled with sweetened nuts.

Shopping In Athens, the department stores are found mostly around Omonia Square and the smartest shops are in Kolonaki, Imports are likely to be expensive. The yellow kiosks (*períptero*) throughout Athens and in other cities and towns of Greece are open for as much as 18 hours a day and are extremely handy for obtaining a myriad of small items. Not only can you purchase newspapers (Greek and foreign), cigarettes, postcards, chocolate and other items on display, but somehow tucked away within are toothpaste, shampoo, lightbulbs, combs, aspirins, film, razor blades, glue, watchstraps, needles, worry beads, men's contraceptives and still more. Also the periptero will have a public telephone or two for local calls.

Crafts Craft items are found at markets, villages and monasteries as well as in many shops. In Athens, to avoid wasting time searching from one nasty souvenir place to another, go directly to the National Organisation of Hellenic Handicraft, 3 Mitropoleos Street, where craft goods are displayed but none sold: when you've found what you want you are given the address of the shop or artisan where purchase may be made. Different towns, islands and regions around Greece have their specialties. Some of the most famous are:

Arta and **Trikala**: kilimi, hand-woven rugs, shoulder bags.
Corfu: jewellery, embroidery, woodwork.
Heraklion (Crete): onyx and alabaster work.
Ioannina (Epirus): jewellery, metalwork, silver.
Kastoria: furs.
Metsovo: weaving, woodwork.
Mykonos: woven fabrics, clothes.
Pelion: pottery.
Rhodes: jewellery, pottery.
Sifnos: pottery.
Skyros: pottery, embroidery, woodcarving.
Vitina (Peloponnese): woodwork.

Shopping hours Shopping hours for general trade stores and pharmacies are from 8am to 2.30pm, Monday, Wednesday and Saturday; from 8am to 1pm and again from 5pm to 8.30pm on Tuesday,

Thursday and Friday. There may be variations for foodstores and hairdressers. Gift shops are generally open from 8am to 9pm from Monday to Saturday; in the Monastiraki area of Athens they remain open on Sunday morning too. There is a move to abolish siesta and keep stores open all day. This may yet succeed, at least in winter. Tavernas, kafeneions, etc., are usually open seven days a week.

Health There is a national health system in Greece, but it remains inferior to many other European health services. If you are a UK citizen entitled to UK benefits you may obtain national health treatment in Greece, but you should take with you Form E111 from the DHSS (other EEC countries have similar arrangements). Alternatively obtain medical insurance to allow for private treatment. In Athens a list of doctors and dentists may be obtained from your embassy (see embassy addresses in the *Practical Information* section following Athens). Urgent cases are dealt with by the roster of hospitals which stay open day and night (dial 166 for the hospital on duty) and by the Hospital Control Centre (Rythmistikon Kentron) of the State Hospital on Leoforos Mesoghion, Athens (Tel: 7701.211). For pharmacies open 24 hours dial 107.

Freelance campers and those hiking around the countryside should consider inoculation against tetanus. Gastric disorders can be countered by abstaining from food for a while, though drinking plenty of water against dehydration; also a standard preparation can be obtained from any pharmacist. Their advice in all matters is usually knowledgeable.

Banks and changing money Banks are normally open Monday to Friday from 8am to 2pm, though some branches open longer hours to cater for tourists, and the National Bank of Greece in Syntagma Square is open seven days a week until at least 8pm. Money may also be changed at port of entry, hotels and travel agencies. A Eurocheque card will usually allow personal cheques to be cashed. Many of the better hotels, car rental agencies, etc., will accept credit cards, but sometimes an additional charge is made. Certain banks (eg The Commercial Bank of Greece in the case of Visa) will make cash advances against credit cards.

Greek currency The drachma is the unit of currency in Greece. It is allowed to float and therefore its value is changeable. In recent years its value has declined both against the dollar and the pound, indeed it has almost halved, which is why Greece has remained relatively good value for visitors despite its internal inflation. Notes come in denominations of 50, 100, 500, 1000 and 5000 drachmas; coins in 20, 5, 2 and 1 drachmas.

Post office Post offices (ELTA) are open usually Monday to Fridays from 8am to 1pm and then again in late afternoon. The central post office in Athens (100 Eolou) is open from 8am to 8pm Monday to Friday, and the post office (*to takhidromío*) in Syntagma Square has similar hours. In addition you can buy stamps from kiosks and post card shops, and you may post letters in the yellow letter boxes to be seen hanging on walls outside shops, etc. Correspondence marked 'Post Restante' may be addressed to any post office (write the surname in capitals) and collected by the addressee on proof of identity. Parcels are not delivered by the post office, but must be collected. Postage is slow both out of Greece and within the country.

Telephone and telegrams OTE is the Greek telephone and telegraph service with offices in all large towns. Though local calls can be made from coin-operated phone boxes and from kiosks, long distance and international calls should be made at an OTE office. It is possible to dial directly to most countries in Europe, also to the USA – though you have to be patient at busy times; it is cheaper after 9pm. Telegrams can be sent from OTE offices or larger post offices. In Athens the telegraph office in Athinas Street is open all the time, and that in Stadiou until about midnight.

Electricity Electricity is 220 volts AC except in the most outlying places where it is still 110 DC.

Time, calendar and holidays Greek time is two hours ahead of GMT: noon in London is 2pm in Greece. All movable festivals are governed by the fixing of Easter according to the Orthodox calendar. The Greek and Western Easters occur on the same day only once every four years. Public holidays are 1 January; Epiphany on 6 January; Shrove Monday; Independence Day on 25 March; Good Friday, Easter and Easter Monday; Assumption on 15 August; *Óhi* day (when the Greeks said no to the Italian ultimatum in 1940) on 28 October; Christmas Day on 25 December and St Stephen's Day on the 26th.

Tourist police The Tourist Police operate a 24-hour phone service for any kind of problem affecting tourists. If you have lost your wallet or cannot find a hotel, need urgent medical attention or just want information, give them a ring. Their office in Athens is at 7 Leoforos Syngrou (Tel: 171).

Weights and measures The metric system of weights and measures was adopted by Greece in 1958, along with its familiar terms: metro for metre, kilometro for kilometre, etc. However, some liquids, including wines, are measured by weight, not volume, thus a kilo of retsina rather than a litre. The standard unit of land measurement is the stremma, about $\frac{1}{4}$ of an acre.

Temperature		
Fahrenheit	=	Celsius
122		50
113		45
110		43.3
107.6		42
104		40
102.2		39
100		37.8
98.6		37
96.8		36
95		35
93.2		34
91.4		33
90		32
87.8		31
86		30
84.2		29
80		26.7
75		23.9
70		21
65		18.3
60		15.6
55		12.8
50		10
45		7.2
40		4
32		0
23		−5
14		−10
00		−17.8

Fahrenheit into Celsius: subtract 32 from Fahrenheit temperature, then multiply by 5, then divide by 9.
Celsius into Fahrenheit: multiply Celsius by 9, then divide by 5, then add 32.

Linear Measure

0.39 inches	1 centimetre
1 inch	2.54 centimetres
1 foot (12 in)	0.30 metres
1 yard (3 ft)	0.91 metres
39.37 inches	1 metre
0.62 miles	1 kilometre
1 mile (5280 ft)	1.61 kilometres
3 miles	4.8 kilometres
10 miles	16 kilometres
60 miles	98.6 kilometres
100 miles	160.9 kilometres

Square Measure

1 sq foot	0.09 sq metres
1 sq yard	0.84 sq metres
1.20 sq yards	1 sq metre

Weight

0.04 ounces	1 gram
1 ounce	28.35 grams
1 pound	453.59 grams
2.20 pounds	1 kilogram
1 ton (2000 lbs)	907.18 kilograms

Liquid Measure

0.22 imperial gallons	1 litre
0.26 US gallons	1 litre
1 US gallon	3.79 litres
1 imperial gallon	4.55 litres

Nude bathing   Until recently nude bathing has been prohibited throughout Greece, with the occasional arrest, fine, even deportation of offenders. Nevertheless, nude bathing – partial or total – has become fairly prevalent with the police turning a blind eye to the law (and a glad eye to the beaches). Now with the approval of the NTOG, nudist centres are being established in remote seaside areas, with the understanding that 'nudists are not lacking in morals but are people who are entitled to practice their way of life undisturbed by perverts'. This could however mean a crackdown on other areas, so care should be taken – particularly not to offend people in traditional localities.

Cultural Notes

Artistic events

The National Tourist Office of Greece (NTOG) sponsors a number of artistic events throughout Greece. The following are presented annually:

Athens Festival: From July through September ancient drama, opera, music and ballet are included in the programme of the Athens Festival at the Odeon of Herodes Atticus against the southern base of the Acropolis. Both Greek and foreign companies of international repute are invited to perform.

Epidavros Festival: Through July to mid-August ancient Greek drama is performed in the famous theatre of Epidavros whose perfect acoustics permit attendance by 14,000 people at a time. Similar festivals, usually in August, take place in the ancient theatres of Dodoni, Thassos and Philippi.

Sound and light: Sound and light shows in several languages bring the history of the Acropolis to life from your vantage point at the Pnyx, and similar shows take place at Rhodes and Corfu. They are presented from early April to the end of October.

Information and tickets for the Acropolis sound and light shows, as well as the Athens and Epidavros festivals, can be obtained at 4 Stadiou Street (Tel: 322.3111) or before the performances (which usually start at 9pm). However it is wise to buy tickets for the festivals several days in advance if possible.

Song and film festivals: During the Thessaloniki Trade Fair (September) a Festival of Greek Light Song is held in the Palais des Sports within the fairgrounds; and immediately after the fair there is a festival of Greek and foreign films.

Demetria Festival: A series of theatrical, musical, ballet and operatic performances follow the Thessaloniki Trade Fair in October, reviving the tradition of Byzantine festive events.

Folk dancing: The Dora Stratou ballet and song troupe present a programme of Greek folk dancing at the open-air theatre on Philopappou Hill, Athens, in the evenings from May to September. Similarly in Corfu from May to September there is a dance drama at the Venetian castle, and on Rhodes the Nelly Dimoglou troupe presents Greek folk dancing in the theatre of the old city from May to October. And from November to March, folk dance performances move indoors to the Aliki winter theatre, 2 Amerikis Street, Athens, home of the Greek Lyceum company.

Wine festivals, saints' days and Easter

There are well-known wine festivals at Daphni (outside Athens) and Alexandroupolis in the evenings from July into Stepember. The modest entrance fee allows unlimited tasting, and there is folk dancing. Nearly every town and village holds a festival at least once a year in honour of their patron saints, and after the church service there is frequently

The electric railway ploughs through the Athenian agora

feasting and dancing. Many of these festivals (*panigíria*) fall during the summer. Visitors are generally welcome if there are not too many. Easter is the major event in the Orthodox calendar and almost anywhere in Greece it is a moving and finally exuberant occasion (for example, see Hydra).

Museums and archaeological sites

Museums and most archaeological sites throughout Greece require tickets of admission costing from 50 to 150 drachmas. Student admission is reduced upon presentation of an ISIC. Additional fees are charged for filming or photographing inside Museums, or filming at archaeological sites. Still photography at sites (provided no tripod is used) is free.

There is considerable variation in opening hours of sites and museums, so that it is difficult to generalise. However sites are usually open from Monday to Saturday for most of the daylight hours with shorter hours on Sundays and public holidays. The same applies to museums though some (like the National Archaeological Museum) close early in the afternoon and most are closed on Tuesdays (some minor museums close on Mondays instead). All sites and museums are closed on 1 January, 25 March, Good Friday and Easter Sunday, and 25 December.

For hours of particular sites and museums see under the relevant *Practical Information* section.

Architecture   In the 8th and 7th C BC the Doric temple developed the features that were to achieve their greatest refinement in Periclean times. The entire structure stood upon a stylobate. The cella housed the image of the god and was at first built of mud brick and timber. To protect the cella from the rain a verandah was added on all sides supported by columns (the peristyle). The pronaos led to the cella and for symmetry's sake the opisthodomos was added at the opposite end.

The Doric temple   During the 6th C BC mud brick and wood were replaced by limestone, the thatched roof by tiles. Stucco covered the limestone to improve its appearance, though towards the end of the century the Athenians improved upon both the strength and beauty of their temples by building them of marble quarried from Pentelikon. The Parthenon, completed in 438 BC, with its fine proportions enhanced by subtle optical effects, marked the perfection of the Doric temple.

The Ionic order   Stagnation following upon perfection was avoided by the introduction to mainland Greece of the Ionic order from across the Aegean. Within a few years of the Parthenon's completion, Athenian architects were complementing Doric maturity with the slenderness and the restrained elaboration of the Erechtheion and the Temple of Athena Nike, both of the Ionic order; while already the Parthenon itself and, soon after, the Propylaia successfully combined elements of both orders.

Church architecture   Christian architecture at first borrowed classical forms, the earliest churches employing the basilical plan of the pagan temples, when not actually taking over the temples themselves. But it was the dome that became the most distinctive feature of later Byzantine churches. Its considerable outward thrust required buttressing: buttresses external to the basilical plan of Western churches supported high Romanesque and Gothic vaults; the Eastern church solved the problem more neatly by setting the dome upon a vaulted superstructure in the form of an equal-armed Greek Cross and then enclosing the cross at the lower level within a square. The structure was entirely self-supporting, the thrust of the dome extending down through the vaulted arms of the cross, the arms in turn bolstered by the square that contained them. The churches at Daphni and Osios Loukas are mature expressions of this cross-in-square style.

Glossary of terms
Amphora: tall, two-handled jar with narrow neck.
Anta (plural **antae**): projecting front portion of a cella's side wall in a temple, often forming an enclosed porch.
Apse: semi-circular domed recess, most frequently at the east end of a church.
Architrave: horizontal supporting beam across columns of temple, stoa, etc., supporting the pediment or roof-front.

GREEK TEMPLE (hexastyle)

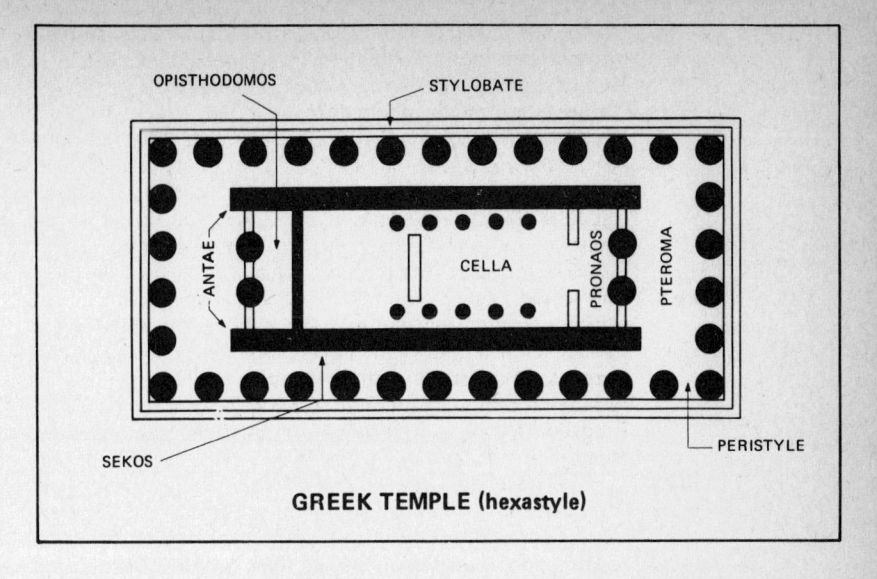

Atrium: court in front of an early Christian church.
Basilica: church in the form of a long colonnaded hall, usually with one or more apses at the east end, and a narthex at the west end.
Cavea: concave auditorium of seats in a theatre.
Cella: enclosed inner 'house of the god', central room of a temple.
Chthonic: dwelling in or under the ground, of the earth.
Crysobul: document containing decree of Byzantine emperor.
Entasis: slight swelling in a column to counteract the optical illusion of a straight column appearing pinched.
Exedra: semi-circular, recessed structure with seating.
Exo-narthex: outer vestibule of a church.
Frieze: horizontal band of sculpture comprising either metopes and triglyphs (Doric order) or continuous figures in relief (Ionic order), usually placed above the architrave on the exterior (sometimes also on an interior wall) of a temple.
Hexastyle: having six columns along the end of a temple, etc.; octostyle, eight columns; etc.
Ikonostasis: screen carrying ikons between the main part of a church and the sanctuary or choir.
Kore: archaic statue of standing clothed young woman.
Kouros: archaic statue of standing nude young man.
Loggia: covered portico on the side of a building.
Megaron: central main room of Minoan or Mycenaean palace, sometimes also applied to an old temple.
Metope: square space between triglyphs in a Doric frieze, used for relief sculpture.

Naos: cella, though sometimes referring to the entire temple.
Narthex: entrance vestibule at west end of a church.
Nave: main body or central aisle of a church.
Odeon: concert hall, roofed over.
Orchestra: flat circular area of theatre stage where chorus moved and sang.
Pediment: triangular area below gabled roof of a temple, usually filled with sculpture.
Peristyle: row of columns round the outside of a temple.
Pithos (plural **pithoi**): large storage jar.
Polygonal: form of masonry in which large blocks of stone, cut in irregular shapes, have been fitted together like a jigsaw.
Poros: a soft, coarse limestone (same as tufa).
Pronaos: a columned porch, leading to the cella.
Propylon (plural **propylaia**): entrance gate to a temenos.
Rhyton: drinking vessel terminating in the shape of an animal's head.
Rotunda: circular building, sometimes domed.
Skene: back scene structure behind theatre stage.
Skete: a community of monks, smaller or of less importance than a monastery.
Squinches: small arches across the corners of a square, enabling support of a circular dome.
Stele: upright stone slab or pillar with an inscription or design, used as a monument or grave marker.
Stoa: portico, usually in the market-place of an ancient Greek city, used for shops, discussion, etc.
Stylobate: top step or platform on which temple or stoa columns rest, loosely applied to all levels beneath the columns.
Temenos: sacred enclosure, for temples, etc.
Tholos: round building with conical roof, particularly a Mycenaean 'beehive' tomb.
Transept: northern or southern arm of a cruciform church.
Triglyph: decorative element of Doric frieze above architrave or temple or stoa, imitating primitive wooden beam ends, with two vertical grooves between three raised vertical panels.
Tufa: same as poros.

DORIC ORDER   IONIC ORDER

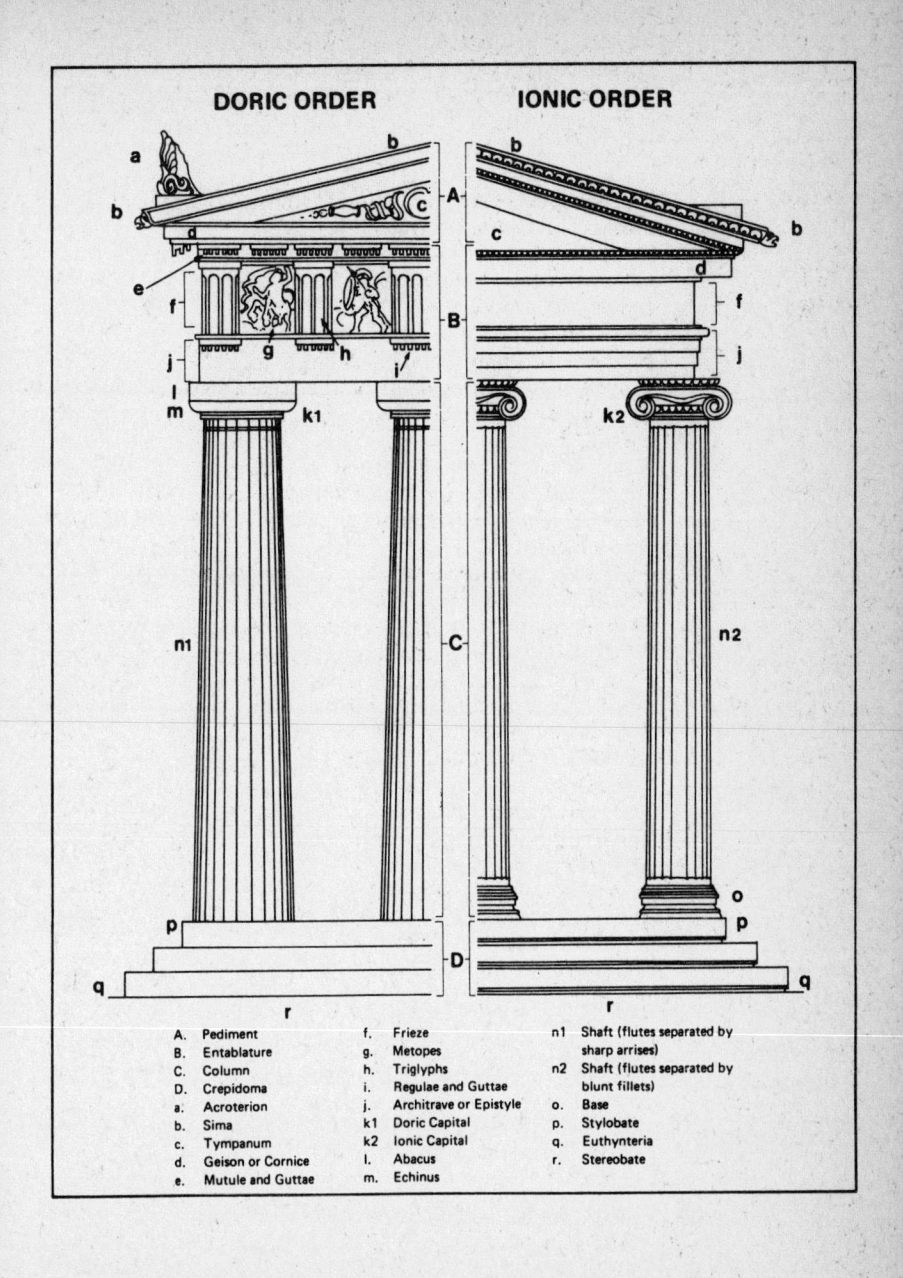

- A. Pediment
- B. Entablature
- C. Column
- D. Crepidoma
- a. Acroterion
- b. Sima
- c. Tympanum
- d. Geison or Cornice
- e. Mutule and Guttae
- f. Frieze
- g. Metopes
- h. Triglyphs
- i. Regulae and Guttae
- j. Architrave or Epistyle
- k1 Doric Capital
- k2 Ionic Capital
- l. Abacus
- m. Echinus
- n1 Shaft (flutes separated by sharp arrises)
- n2 Shaft (flutes separated by blunt fillets)
- o. Base
- p. Stylobate
- q. Euthynteria
- r. Stereobate

ANCIENT GREECE

NEOLITHIC PERIOD			6000 BC	Early settlement at Nea Nikomedia, northern Greece. Later settlements in Thessaly at Sesklo and Dimini and on Crete.
B R O N Z E A G E	Mainland	Crete	2800	Invaders from Anatolia, with pre-Greek language, settled near Corinth and in Argolid, eg Lerna. Flourishing settlements in eastern Crete. Worship of Earth Goddess prevalent.
	Early Helladic (Pre-Hellenic)	Pre-Palatial		
	Middle Helladic	Proto-Palatial: first palaces at Knossos, Phaestos and Mallia.	2000	First Greeks invade mainland (? Achaeans). Significant settlements at Mycenae, Tiryns and Argos.
	Late Helladic (Mycenaean) Palaces at Mycenae, Tiryns, Athens, Gla, etc.	Neo-Palatial: palaces rebuilt, palace at Zakros.	1700 c1600 c1550	Shaft graves at Mycenae Acme of Minoan civilisation: 'colonies' in Aegean, eg Thera. Linear A script on Crete.
			c1450 c1400	Eruption of Thera. Devastation of Cretan palaces except Knossos. Linear B (Greek) script on Crete. Final destruction of Knossos.
		Post-Palatial	1400 c1350	Palace at Mycenae enlarged, Cyclopean walls built. Mycenae predominant in Greece: beehive tombs (1500–1300).
			c1300–1200 c1200–1100	Tiryns rebuilt. Linear B tablets at Pylos. Trojan expedition (c1250). Mycenae and other palaces destroyed
IRON AGE commences Geometric period (from style of pottery, notably at Athens)			1100 c850 c800 776	Dorian invaders occupy most of mainland. Male gods now dominant. Invention of Greek alphabet. Birth of Greek city-state. Athens leader of unified Attica. First Olympic Games *Iliad* and *Odyssey* by Homer sometime during this century.

Rise of HELLENIC CIVILISATION Archaic Period (Early representational art)	750	Period of increasing commerce and colonisation throughout Mediterranean, and development of city-states through tyrannies towards democracy.
	c600	Invention of coinage spurs economic activity.
	600–500	Statues of Kouroi and Korai. Attic Black Figure style on vases.
	561–510	Peisistratid tyranny at Athens; Festival of Great Dionysia instituted.
	c540	Doric Temple of Apollo at Corinth.
Classical Period	500	Democracy at Athens (instituted 507)
	490–479	Persian Wars. Marathon (490), Salamis (480), Plataea (479).
	c475	Delphi Charioteer. Acme of Red Figure vases.
	c454	Delian Confederacy becomes Athenian Empire. Age of Pericles (died 429). Parthenon completed (438). Sophocles' *Oedipus Tyrannus*.
	431–404	Peloponnesian War between Sparta and Athens ends in Athenian defeat.
	399	Death of Socrates.
	371	Thebans defeat Sparta at Leuktra.
	c370	Fortifications at Messene.
	c360	Hermes of Praxiteles.
	c350	Temple of Apollo at Delphi rebuilt. Aristotle, pupil of Plato at Athens.
	338	Macedonian victory over Greek states at Chaironeia.
	c330	Alexander the Great's conquest of Persia.
	323	Death of Alexander. Lamian War (323–322): Athens' revolt against Macedonia fails.
Hellenistic Period	323 4th C	Death of Demosthenes (322). Wars of Alexander's successors result in rule of Antigonids in Macedonia. Formation of Greek states into leagues against Macedonian interference.
	280–	Invasion of Gauls repulsed by

Hellenistic Period	278	Aetolian League.
	c220	Boy Jockey from Artemision.
	220–217	War between Achaean and Aetolian Leagues.
	197	Romans defeat Macedonians at Kynoskephalae, Flaminius proclaims Rome 'protector of Greek freedom'.
	168	Romans end Macedonian Empire after Pydna.
	c150	Stoa of Attalos.
	148	Macedonia becomes Roman province.
	146	Greece becomes part of Roman Empire; Corinth destroyed.
ROMAN GREECE	146	Pax Romana.
	88–86	Mithridatic War. Sulla sacks Athens.
	48–31	Battles of Pharsalus (48), Philippi (42) and Actium (31).
	31 BC–AD 14	Reign of Augustus. Greece separated from Macedonia into province of Achaea, capital at Corinth.
	AD 54	St Paul visits Athens and Corinth.
	c130	Temple of Olympian Zeus dedicated by Hadrian.
	c160	Odeon of Herodes Atticus.
	c170	Pausanias writes *Description of Greece*.
	267	Goths pillage Athens.
	c325–330	Under Emperor Constantine, Christianity becomes official religion of Roman Empire, its capital at Constantinople.
	393	Last Olympic Games.
	395	After further Goth invasion, on Emperor Theodosios' death (395) Roman Empire is divided; eastern half, including Greece, ruled from Constantinople.

BYZANTINE TO MODERN GREECE

BYZANTINE GREECE

	AD 395	On division of Roman Empire, eastern half including Greece is ruled from Constantinople (Byzantium).
	5th C.	▲ Church of Agios Dimitrios, Thessaloniki.
	529	▲ Emperor Justinian abolishes pagan University of Athens.
Period of Slav invasions of Greece. Athens sacked c580	Early 6th–mid 8th C.	Ikonoclast movement (726–843)
Slav settlers subjected to Byzantine Empire.	783	
Saracens possess Crete.	826–961	Renaissance under Macedonian dynasty (867–1059)
Saracens sack Thessaloniki.	904	
Bulgars expand into northern Greece.	10th C.	
	963	▲ Foundation of Great Lavra on Athos.
Northern Greece recovered by Empire.	1018	
	c1020	▲ Church of Osios Loukas
	1054	▲ Final schism between Eastern Church and Rome.
	c1080	▲ Church of Daphni.
Normans occupy Corfu, penetrate Thessaly.	1081–1084	
Roger of Sicily loots Thebes.	1146	
Normans loot Thessaloniki	1185	
Increasing influence of Venetians.	12th C.	

FRANKISH AND VENETIAN GREECE

EPIRUS	MACEDONIA	THESSALY	ATTICA/C. GREECE	PELOPONNESE (except Venetian Ports)	ISLANDS		
Despotate of Greek Angeli	Frankish Kingdom of Salonika 1223		Frankish Duchy of Athens	Frankish Principality of Achaia	1. Frankish County of Cephalonia (Ionian Is.) 1194–1479	1204	Sack of Constantinople by Fourth Crusade.
	Despotate of Epirus 1246				2. Frankish/Venetian Duchy of Archipelago (Aegean Is.) 1207–1566	1204–1261	Latin Empire of Romania
	Byzantine Empire (1186–1258 Bulgars in northern part)	Duchy of Neo Patras or Great Wallachia		1262 Monemvasia, Mistra, Mani	3. Venetians held i. Crete 1204–1669 ii. Euboea 1209–1470 iii. Aegina 1451–1537, 1654–1718 iv. Most Ionian islands from 1483–1797 v. Tinos to 1715	1261	Constantinople recaptured by Byzantine Empire of Nicaea.
1318 Orsinis of Cephalonia		1318 Byz. Emp. Neo-Patras in north 1349	1311 Catalan Duchy of Athens (Sicilian rulers)	1318 Angevins		c1312	Church of Holy Apostles, Thessaloniki.
1336 Byz. Empire –1349	1349 Serbians (except Thessaloniki) 1375	Serbians 1393	1388 Florentine Duchy of Athens		4. Genoese held (periodically) Eastern Sporades 14th & 15th C (Chios to 1566)	14th C.	Renaissance under Palaeologan dynasty. Macedonian School of Painting
Serbians/ Albanians	TURKS (except Thessaloniki, taken in 1430)	TURKS		1383 Navarrese Company	5. Knights of Rhodes 1309–1522 (Kos 1315–1522)	14th/15th C.	Development of Mistra as Byzantine centre.
1418 Toccos of Cephalonia 1449	I o a n n i n a 1430		1456–60 TURKS	1432 Byz. Empire 1461 TURKS	1453–1797 TURKS acquire all islands (but Ionian Islands only from 1479–1482 except Levkas and Kythera	1453	Fall of Constantinople.
TURKS							

Mid 16th C	Theophanes the Cretan paints frescoes at Meteora and Athos.
1571	Venetians defeat Turks at Lepanto.
1821–1832	War of Independence. Allied fleets destroy Turkish & Egyptian fleets at Navarino, 1827.
1833	Kingdom of Greece, with Capital at Athens.
1881	Treaty of Constantinople cedes Thessaly and District of Arta to Greece.
1913	War with Turkey ends with Treaty of London. War with Bulgaria for Macedonia.
1922	Greek-Turkish war in Asia Minor ends in disaster, and exchange of populations.
1924–1936	Republic
1936–1941	Metaxas dictatorship
1941–1945	German and Italian occupation. Athens liberated October 1944.
1946	Monarchy restored.
1947–9	Civil war
1967–	Dictatorship of Papadopoulos and Ioannides.
1974	
1974	Democracy and Republic.

Venetians abandon coastal areas by 1573 (Navplia 1540)

Venetians 1685–1715

Venetians occupy Athens 1687–1688

1832

Ionian islands under British protectorate 1815–1864.
Freedom from Turks:
Euboea and Cyclades 1832.

Crete in 1898 (united with Greece 1912).

Eastern Sporades in 1912.
Dodecanese freed from Italians 1947.

MODERN GREECE

—1788
Rule of Ali, Pasha
—1822

1881
District of Arta free

1881

—1913—
Bulgarians occupy eastern area 1916–18.

1913

| Germans/Italians | German and Italian Occupation 1941–5 | Bulgarian occupied 1942–4 |

Key: ▨ Byzantine ▨ Turks

33

Suggested Reading

A wide selection of books on Greece, in English, is available in several Athens bookshops (see the Athens *Practical Information* section), and the most popular titles will be available throughout the country. Most, perhaps all, of the books below can be purchased there. All are in print in Britain and most are probably in print elsewhere, eg the United States. The name of the British publisher (in one case the Greek publisher) of the cheapest (usually paperback) edition is given in brackets following the title.

Andrews, Kevin: *The Flight of Icaros* (Penguin). Travels through Greece during the civil war; along with Durrell, Miller, Fermor and Dilys Powell, one of the outstanding writers on Greece.

Bury, J B and Meiggs, Russell: *History of Greece* (Macmillan). An excellent and authoritative history up to the death of Alexander the Great.

Byron, Lord: *Letters* (John Murray). Edited by Leslie Marchand, this is the complete letters in 11 volumes, plus a further volume of letters selected from the whole. There is rarely a dull line among them.

Cavafy, Constantine: *Collected Poems* (Chatto). Edmund Keeley and Philip Sherrard have provided the best translation of the Alexandrian's poetry which reaches throughout the time and space of the Greek world, and comes home with Cavafy's famous *Ithaka*.

Dubin, Marc: *Greece on Foot* (Cordee). This is for anyone wanting to get off the beaten path and follow the old and now often disused tracks of a largely undiscovered Greece.

Durrell, Lawrence: *Prospero's Cell* is about Corfu where Durrell lived before the war; *Reflections on a Marine Venus* is about Rhodes during its still pristine days immediately after the war (both Faber); some say these island books are the finest he has ever written.

Fermor, Patrick Leigh: *Mani* is a classic piece of travel literature about one of the least-known parts of Greece; *Roumeli* covers the dying ways of central Greece, including its Sarakatsani nomads and monks of the Meteora (both Penguin).

Gage, Nicholas: *Eleni* (Fontana). A Greek-American returns to the village of his birth to track down the Communist guerillas who executed his mother during the civil war; a true and gripping examination of unromantic Greece.

Graves, Robert: *The Greek Myths* (Penguin). An essential reference work, remarkably comprehensive and erudite; in two volumes.

Holst, Gail: *The Road to Rembetika* (D Harvey, Athens). Underlying all that awful bazouki music is the strong, gutsy, blues-like music that flourished in Greece between the world wars and was reborn again after the fall of the recent dictatorship – the songs of Greeks thrown out of Turkey, of criminals and dope-smokers; the soul music of Greece. A delightful book, with translations.

Kazantzakis, Nikos: *Zorba the Greek*, *Christ Recrucified*, etc (Faber). Novels by the great Cretan writer.

Levi, Peter: *The Hill of Kronos* (Arrow Books). A beautiful account of Greece before, during and immediately after the dictatorship, a book of self-discovery and encounters with some of the country's greatest poets, writers and composers.

The young Lawrence Durrell with a priapic stone at Delphi

Luce, J V: *The End of Atlantis* (Paladin). The theory that Thera, and Minoan civilisation with it, was blown to bits by the most tremendous volcanic explosion known.

Miller, Henry: *The Colossus of Maroussi* (Penguin). Miller finally succumbed to Durrell's invitation to visit Greece – just before the war; and indifferent to the country's classical history but with his genius for friendships and joy in the spirit of place, Miller wrote what Durrell called 'probably his best book . . . and one of the best books about modern Greece'.

Pausanias: *Guide to Greece* (Penguin). Translated and annotated by Peter Levi, this is the famous 2nd C AD *Description*, invaluable today for resurrecting the past in your mind's eye.

Powell, Dilys: *An Affair of the Heart* is a lovely work of personal evocation, both a travel book and an exploration through the mind and memory as the author surmounts the tragedy of death and civil war in Greece to renew her affair with the country she loves; also *The Villa Ariadne*, which weaves the story of Knossos with the modern exploits of such men as Patrick Leigh Fermor who during the Second World War secretly landed on Crete and kidnapped the German commander; finally *The Traveller's Journey is Done*, recalling her first experience of Greece, in the 1920s and 1930s, with her archaeologist husband Humfry Payne until his death in 1936 – this is the background to *An Affair of the Heart* (all Michael Haag).

Renault, Mary: *The Bull from the Sea* about the Hippolytos legend, *Fire from Heaven* about Alexander (both Penguin), *The King Must Die* about Theseus (New English Library), and other historical novels – all very readable and generally respected by scholars.

Seferis, George: *Collected Poems* (Anvil). In literature and particularly poetry, Greece is one of the modern (let alone ancient) superpowers of the written word, and Seferis is one of the reasons why.

ATHENS (Athínai)

At the time of Greek independence, centuries of Turkish occupation had left Athens no more than an unhealthy village of narrow dirt alleyways, huts and jumbled houses huddled beneath the Acropolis. Ruins poked out of the ground like broken bottles in a rubbish dump, of no interest to the mixture of its few thousand Greek, Turkish, Slavic and Levantine inhabitants. It was left to foreigners like Byron and Chateaubriand to see or care or know anything of Athens' glorious past, and probably only in deference to this outside feeling was the city chosen as the capital of the new kingdom.

The adopted capital was almost entirely contained within that tiny area which today is the Plaka, and at a distance was surrounded by wild hills and mountains infested with brigands. But in the past century and a half, the city has advanced against the mountains themselves and marches down to the sea at Piraeus: modern, hard, concrete, a sprawling whiteness shimmering in the heat of the day, glaring with lights at night. Henry Miller described it as a city which will not ungrasp the light of day. 'The Greek is just as enamoured of electric light as he is of sunlight. No soft shades, but every window ablaze with light, as if the inhabitants had just discovered the marvels of electricity. Athens sparkles like a chandelier; it sparkles like a chandelier in a bare room lined with tiles.'

Athens is one of the major growth points of the Mediterranean: not a pretty town, and historical monuments apart it could almost be described as an architectural disaster area. But the Greeks are not a fastidious people, and the excitement of Athens, like the beauty of Greece, lies in the way its people confront its starkness (and even seem to find such starkness necessary) with an elaborate hodgepodge of fast deals, ornate religion, kamikaze driving, slumbering cafés, flower stalls, markets, exploding tavernas, rudeness, generosity – all of which goes on theatrically, endlessly, a 24-hour non-stop show. Athens, like Paris or New York, has the amphetamine buzz of an insomniac's dreams.

Orientation Athens has two major squares, Syntagma (known also, in English, as Constitution Square) and Omonia, with Stadiou Street running from one to the other. *Syntagma Square* is the international centre of the city, enclosed by luxury hotels like the Grande Bretagne, by airline offices (the airport bus arrives and departs from nearby Leoforos Amalias), a late-night post office and the American Express. On the east side, Syntagma is faced by the Parliament building, while in the centre of the square and on the pavements all around its edge are numerous expensive cafés, crammed with tourists throughout the day and night.

Omonia Square is entirely different. What it lacks in class it makes up for in raw vigour. A fall-out zone for the late-night cinema crowd, it is the sort of place, like Piccadilly or Times Square, which has a fascination for people who like to stand amidst the traffic, noise and neon lights and watch the seamier side of the world go by. It is the Greek centre of the city, surrounded by small shops and open-fronted chicken and kebab joints, less fashionable hotels, hawkers selling lottery tickets, with escalators pouring thousands of workers on to the streets from the Athens–Piraeus underground station down below.

Stadiou Street and the two broad streets running parallel to it, *Venizelou* (popularly called Panepistimiou) and *Akadimias*, are lined with shops, cinemas, more cafés, and halfway down Venizelou the mock-classical facades of Athens University, the Academy and the National Library.

The two high landmarks by which you can never lose your way are Lykavittos hill to the east of Stadiou and the Acropolis to the southwest of Syntagma. *Lykavittos* is the higher of the two, a sudden eruption of ground with a small chapel like a cherry on the top. At night, with the base of the hill in darkness, the upper half is illuminated with floodlights and seems to hover above Athens like a giant dome-topped flying saucer.

On the planed-off top of the *Acropolis* sits the Parthenon, in daylight or floodlight gleaming like a yellow moon over Athens, no more noticed sometimes than the thousands of postcards on which it appears throughout the city. But then you stare at it and seem to see it smile, silent and demure, and 2400 years of time bolt across your imagination. At the base of the Acropolis is *Plaka*, the old quarter of Athens with its steep, stepped and winding streets, quiet by day, frantic with nightclubs, tavernas and discotheques at night.

More or less within the bounds of these four points – Syntagma, Omonia, Lykavittos and the Acropolis – will the visitor find all the sights and activities of greatest interest, as well as scores of places to eat and stay within his price range.

Lykavittós

The best introduction to Athens is from the top of Lykavittos hill from where all of the city, the hills and mountains around it and the Saronic Gulf unroll in a magnificent 360° panorama. The light of Attica favours seeing the city from Lykavittos in the late afternoon, while the early morning is the best time for gazing about from the Acropolis – assuming Athens' modern smog allows you a view at all.

The No. 4 bus takes you to Kleomenous Street from where

you walk up the steps one block for the funicular station at the base of the hill at the corner of Aristipou and Ploutarchou Streets. If you want to walk up, take the path from the corner of Kleomenous and Loukianou Streets.

Atop Lykavittos is the small 19th C Agios Georgios and a restaurant/café where it is worth sitting on the terrace, drink in hand, watching the sun go down. Also there is an observation platform which can get pretty windy. Below you is Athens, a city of white. White marble, white painted houses, and at night white lights, with Syntagma and Omonia picked out in red, blue and green neon. To the left is the Olympic Stadium and beyond that, further to the left, is the airport with its white and green beacon flashing in the evening. To the centre, Syntagma, the National Gardens and the Zappeion, and behind Syntagma is the Acropolis, around its base the close-packed twinkling of Plaka. And beyond that is Piraeus with off-lying ships lit up from bow to stern. To the right of Syntagma you can follow the lights of Stadiou down to Omonia.

Yes, it is best to come as the sun goes down, to catch Athens going from white to gold, and then enveloped by darkness, barely anything discernible but the ribbons of lights in streets and squares. Watch the Acropolis light up (though this is most impressive from the lower elevation of Plaka). The night sky above is only slightly touched by city smoke and haze, the stars and moon shine clearly. Though you have already paid (if you took the funicular) to go both up and down, make your way down Lykavittos by the pathway, Athens' lovers lane. Halfway down is a taverna; the views are not so spectacular as from the top, but then neither are the prices.

The Acropolis

Athens' Golden Age

Athens' Golden Age followed her defeat of Darius' army at Marathon (490 BC) and the defeat by combined Greek forces of the second Persian invasion, under Xerxes, at Salamis (480 BC) and Plataea (479 BC). Her extensive maritime empire made her wealthy and gave her the means to brilliantly celebrate her achievements. And celebrate, rather than commemorate, is the right word. For the victory was not just an isolated military event whose place could be marked by the usual stone pylon. Marathon has been called the birth cry of Europe; and after 479 BC, Athens, full-grown, consciously took upon herself the task of laying the foundations of Western civilisation. 'Men seemed to rise at once to the sense of the high historical importance of their experience. The great poets of the day wrought it into their song; the great plastic artists alluded to it in their sculptures.' And under Pericles the temples on the Acropolis which had been destroyed by the Persians were rebuilt with an historical sense

ATHENS
STREFI
IRAKLIOU
TOSSITSA
STOURNARA
ACHARNON
TO STATION. S.L.
IPIROU
LIOSION
TRITI SEPTEMVRIOU
28 OCTOVRIOU
MARNI
SATOVRIANDOU
AGIOU KONSTANTINOU
OMONIA
THEMISTOKLEOUS
ZOODOCHOU PIGHIS
DIDOTOU
SOLONOS
AKADIMIAS
LYKAVITTOS
VENIZELOU (PANEPISTIMIOU)
LYKOURGOU
PIRAIOS
KRATINOU
SOPHOKLEOS
STADIOU
SINA
KOLONAKI
EVRIPIDOU
ATHINAS
KOLOKOTRONI
VOUKOURESTIOU
VAS. SOPHIAS
PARLIAMENT
PERIKLEOUS
SYNTAGMA
KERAMEIKOS
ERMOU
AMALIAS
NATIONAL GARDENS
MONASTIRAKI STATION
AGORA
PLAKA
LEOFOROS
ZAPPEION
APOSTOLOU PAVLOU
AREOPAGOS
ACROPOLIS
OLYMPEION
TO STADIUM
N
TO PIRAEUS

and as a sacred duty. 'He recognised that the city by ennobling the houses of her gods would ennoble herself.' (Bury and Meiggs, *History of Greece*)

It is best to resist the temptation to climb the Acropolis right away, instead to circle it, view it from many angles and elevations at different times of night and day. View it from the hill of Ardettos, over the columns of the Temple of Zeus against the setting sun; or from Lykavittos, with Phaleron and Salamis as an historical panorama beyond; or from the Pnyx where the Assembly stood in the open air and so often debated Athenian destiny; or from the Kerameikos by the Dipylon Gate, where travellers in ancient times would most likely have entered the city, proceeding towards the Agora and Acropolis along the Panathenaic Way. The rock itself is fascinating, abrupt and ragged, an upraised underworld in whose caves and fissures dwelt the earliest chthonic gods; the sheer masonry walls encircling its heights extending and refining its primitive form; and then the temples, delicate crystal flowers that blossomed in the sunlight of historical consciousness. Walk one night along Odos Thrassilou in Plaka, right under the eastern brow of the Acropolis where the great walls join at an acute angle atop the towering limestone cliffs: the rock rides against the starry sky like some spectral ship ploughing through eternity and engulfs you in its wake.

Early history of the Acropolis

The Acropolis was inhabited at least as far back as 5000 BC. Men were attracted by its natural springs and the defence provided by its precipitous 100-metre height. The Mycenaeans fortified it; later tyrants imposed their rule from here. The Acropolis has these associations of primitive succour and power. But with the fall of the Peisistratid dictatorship in 510 BC the Athenians resigned the Acropolis to the exclusive inhabitation of their gods. It was an act of respect both to the deities and to the rock itself. And perhaps a shrewd political move by a people bent on democracy. Without tyrants over them and with their gods provided for, down below the citizens could say let us, let Man, be the measure of all things. In the century that followed, Athens achieved her apotheosis.

Restoration of the Acropolis

That moment of apotheosis has now in a manner been resurrected atop the Acropolis. When the defeated Turks finally surrendered the rock in 1833, the classical structures, converted and embroidered over the centuries to serve the needs of the day, were obscured in a jumble of dwellings and alleyways, Frankish towers and Turkish minarets, that must have looked like a crowded quarter of Old Stamboul. Demolition of these encrustations began at once, though not without protest. One of the regents of the young Greek King complained that 'the archaeologists would destroy all the picturesque additions of the Middle Ages in their zeal to lay bare and restore the ancient monuments'. Of course it is not the living past the archaeologists have presented to us, but the bleached bones of antiquity. It has been more of an exhumation than a resurrection. A fifth century Athenian, used to seeing his Acropolis crammed with statues, dedications, monuments and sanctuaries; busy with workmen, officials, acolytes and worshippers; used to sniffing the burning incense, hearing the cries of animals slaughtered in sacrifice, seeing the temples luridly painted and indeed, then too, half obscured behind the jumble, might well find this present-day skeleton at least as alien as 'the picturesque additions of the Middle Ages' that the archaeologists have torn down.

Pericles was an unabashed imperialist: 'We have compelled every land and every sea to open a path for our valour, and have everywhere planted eternal memorials of our friendship and of our enmity'; but his imperialism was guided by his sincere belief that Athenian power was Greece's best defence against Persia, its best hope for unification, and that culturally Athens was 'the school of Hellas'. He could be merciless in time of war (see under Aegina), but could also argue at the end of his life that 'no Athenian ever put on black for an act of mine'. It was in this context that the Acropolis temples were raised: 'We shall assuredly not be without witnesses; there are mighty monuments of our power which will make us the wonder of this and of succeeding ages'. And the fact is that our own age has chosen to enshrine both Pericles' rhetoric and his monuments. But this has not always been so through all ages, and something needs briefly to be said about the more than 2000 years of intervening history that has been swept off the face of the Acropolis.

The Romans The Romans were great respecters of the classical achievement and modestly embroidered the Acropolis with a few contributions of their own: the Beulé Gate through which we now first enter the site before making the final sharp ascent towards the Propylaia (the gate takes its name from the 19th C French archaeologist who discovered it embedded in a Turkish wall); a small circular Temple of Rome and Augustus between the modern museum and the Parthenon, now slowly being reconstructed; and the enrichment, under Hadrian in particular, of many of the original shrines. Athens as a whole flourished during this period. But when the

The Byzantines Roman Empire divided in two, the Eastern or Byzantine Empire – resurgently Greek though no longer classical – looked towards its new capital at Constantinople and Athens became increasingly a backwater. The Acropolis, as the home of pagan gods, lost its significance except as a citadel to be fortified as it had been in Archaic times, and the temples were converted to Orthodox Christian churches. The Parthenon became the metropolitan church of Athens; a barrel-vaulted roof replacing the coffered ceiling, frescoes added to the walls, the eastern entrance of classical times turned into an apse to receive the altar, and the inner sanctum of Athena's priestess at the western end opened up to become the narthex or entrance to the Church of the Virgin Mother of God. Even a bell-tower was added to the Parthenon's southwest corner.

The Franks and Turks

After the sack of Constantinople in 1204 by the Fourth Crusade, Greece was divided up in the western European manner amongst feudal barons, and under the Frankish dukes of Athens the Parthenon became a cathedral and followed the Latin rite. It was then predictable, with the coming of the Turks, that it should finally be converted into a mosque, the bell-tower conveniently transformed into a minaret.

Similarly with the Propylaia: the Byzantines used it as an episcopal residence; the dukes transformed it into a Florentine palace; while the Turks employed it as the commandant's headquarters and as a powder magazine.

Even so, right through to the mid-17th C the classical structures remained almost entirely intact beneath their cosmetic overlays. It was the advent of gunpowder that wrought the greatest changes on the Acropolis. Sometime near the middle of that century lightning struck the Propylaia, igniting the powder and blasting away much of the east portico. In 1684, as part of the running conflict between Venetians and Turks, the Turkish defenders demolished the Temple of Athena Nike to better counter improved Venetian gunfire with a battery of their own. And in 1687 a Venetian cannon on Philopappou hill lobbed a ball at the Parthenon, touching off the munitions within, sundering the temple nearly in half and causing a fire which raged for 48 hours. The Venetians also trained their guns on the Propylaia, wrecking the west facade and bringing down the famous ceiling.

The Parthenon explosion

Lord Elgin

In that context, Lord Elgin's removal at the beginning of the 19th C of most of the bas-reliefs from the Parthenon's frieze and its pedimental sculptures (essential viewing at the British Museum before or after visiting the Acropolis) can only be applauded. Whether they should be given back, as the Greeks demand, is another matter – though as recently as the civil war in the 1940s the fighting in Athens again put the temples at risk, while at the outset of their coup in 1967 the Colonels placed guns on Philapappou once more, not ones to miss a lesson in tactics from the Venetians. And now that Athens has attained the distinction of becoming the second most polluted city in the world after Tokyo, with the sulfur dioxide in the atmosphere rotting away the marble stones, there would be a real possibility that the Parthenon would fall down before the sculptures could be put back up (though in admission of this the Greeks would tuck the marbles away in a museum and mount only copies on the Parthenon).

The Propylaia. The zigzag ramp leading up from the *Beulé gate* (1) to the *Propylaia* (2) is similar to the Acropolis approach of Mycenaean and medieval times; in classical times the ramp was straight and extremely steep with an incline of one in four. In either case, one toils towards the Propylaia from below, its elevation and monumentality inducing a sense of humility in the visitor.

The ancients greatly admired the Propylaia and even in its state of partial ruin there are many who think it rivals the Parthenon itself, but the visitor needs time and a reconstructive imagination to appreciate this. The structure, built entirely of Pentelic marble except for a few architectural details in blue Eleusinian stone, comprises a *central hall* with north and south *wings* flanking the approach. At the west (approach) and east ends of the central hall are Doric hexastyle *porticoes*, the sharp-fluted columns spaced to correspond to the five gateways (hence Propylaia, plural of propylon meaning gateway) of the *portal* which transects the hall two-thirds of the way in from the west portico.

The central hall Running through the central hall was a *coffered ceiling* of marble sections, painted blue and gilt with stars, and held aloft by 5.5-metre long, 10,000-kilogram marble *beams*, its effect 'still incomparable', said Pausanias in the 2nd C AD, and indeed probably still so 1500 years later until the Turks and Venetians conspired in its collapse. As marvellous as the ceiling and its beams were, it is the overall harmony of the building, despite the difficult circumstances of its siting, that is most impressive. For not only does the Propylaia rise above the visitor's approach to the Acropolis, but it itself rises up the final scarp of the rock in two stages. This means that the beams supporting the ceiling in the higher east portico can rest upon the architrave, but that some additional lift is required in the lower west portico and the vestibule. This can only be supplied by an *interior colonnade* running through the vestibule, its columns necessarily taller than the columns of either portico. But Mnesikles the architect was working within the Doric order and certain proportions had to be observed: taller Doric columns would mean fatter Doric columns, and the columns of the portico were already massive enough. Instead he took the original step of mixing in the newly-introduced Ionic order, its taller yet more slender columns solving an awkward problem with lightness and grace. It was the central hall which suffered in the 17th C so that only the two outer Doric columns of the west portico rise to their full height of nearly 9 metres and retain their capitals and portions of their architrave. On the left as you near the portal, one of the 10-metre high Ionic columns has been

The south and north wings

restored to position along with a section of the coffered ceiling.

The south wing succeeds in balancing that of the north despite being smaller, as it had to be to avoid trespassing on the Sanctuary of Artemis Vravronia. In the north wing the *Pinakotheke* (picture gallery) displayed the works of Polygnotos, the first great Greek painter (c450 BC), including one, says Pausanias, of 'Odysseus at the river meeting the girls who were washing clothes with Nausikaa, in just the way Homer describes it'. Going round the back, one can see that the outside walls remain unfinished, the rough stone lugs which gave a hold to the ropes still in evidence. The Propylaia was begun immediately upon completion of the Parthenon and cost a fortune; the exigencies of the war with Sparta prevented its completion in detail; and when at length the war was lost the desire or wherewithal to pick up where work had been left off seems to have disappeared.

Nevertheless, Mnesikles succeeded in his essential purpose; the Propylaia in its almost Egyptian monumentality yet its Greek lightness and genius of harmony perfectly humbles and then uplifts – as it must have done those in the Panathenaic Procession as they passed from the profane world below to the sacred precincts atop the Acropolis – preparing the celebrants, as it prepares the visitor now, for that first close and best view of the Parthenon, the whole of its north and west lines of columns sweeping towards the foreground.

Temple of Athena Nike. But instead of making directly for the Parthenon, the visitor should first pause at the Temple of Athena Nike and then, the better to appreciate the plan and historical associations of the Acropolis, make a circuit of the Acropolis walls. There is the advantage, too, of registering the impression the Parthenon makes at every degree.

At the precipitous southwest corner of the rock, to the right of the Propylaia, is the rebuilt *Temple of Athena Nike* (3) – Athena, bringer of victory. From below the Acropolis, the temple blossoms from its bastion; from the height of the rock it lends its charm to the marvellous panorama of the Saronic Gulf. But there is a tragic story associated with this very position, for it was said that from here King Aigeus kept watch for the return of his son Theseus from his expedition against the Cretan Minotaur. If he returned alive, Theseus was to lower his sail of black and raise a sail of white; but he forgot, and Aigeus, thinking his son was dead, threw himself over the edge.

It is striking that the temple specifically dedicated to Athena Victorious should be so unpretentious, even so minor. It stands on a stylobate only 3.7 by 5.5 metres, the nearly square cella graced to east and west by Ionic porticoes, the columns slender monoliths. The *frieze* is badly worn: on

ACROPOLIS

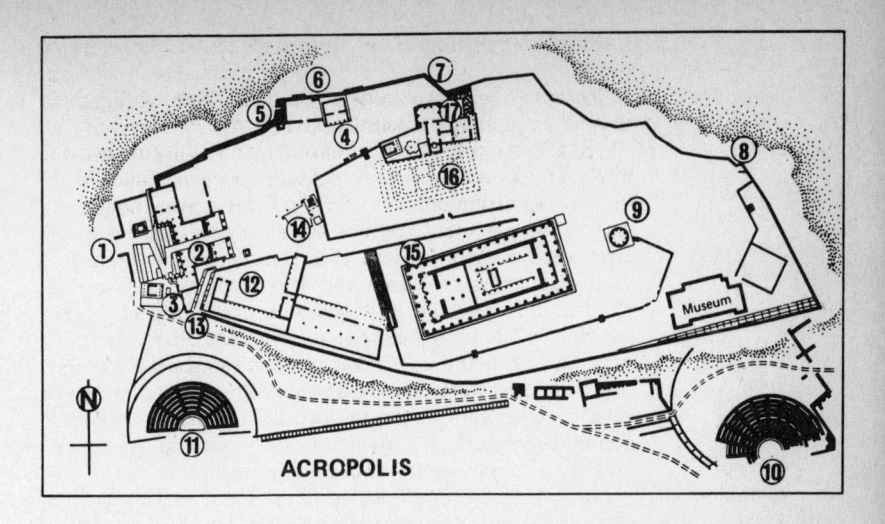

three sides the Athenians struggle against their enemies on the battlefield of Plateia; on the east side 22 (now headless) gods and goddesses seem oblivious to the commotion. The terrace was surrounded by a marble parapet adorned with high reliefs of Winged Victories attendant upon Athena. The lovely *Victory adjusting her sandal* is now in the Acropolis museum – a gesture symbolising the relaxed assurance of Athens at the very moment she plunged into the disastrous war with Sparta. For though the temple was already planned in 449 BC and assigned to the architect Kallikrates, it was only begun in 427 BC, two years after the death of Pericles, four years after the beginning of the war that was to last 26 years in all. There is irony and significance in the dates: Kallikrates was the architect chosen by Pericles' predecessor, Kimon, to build the Parthenon. But Pericles dismissed him after Kimon's death, the dismissal perhaps affecting Kallikrates' opportunity or desire to work on the victory temple too. Then with Pericles dead, Kallikrates got down to work on the Temple of Athena Nike; except that with Pericles dead, Athens substituted arrogance and blunder for a conservative war policy and was forced eventually to bow in surrender. At any rate, as the man who built the leaden 'Theseion' in the Agora and the light-weight Temple of Poseidon at Sounion, Kallikrates here acquitted himself well.

Fertility ritual

Following the walls. Heading past the Propylaia to the *north Acropolis wall* and a little along it to the right you come to the foundations of the *House of the Arrephorai* (4), the residence of the maids in waiting on Athena, noble girls of 7 to 11 years old who once every four years took part in the Panathenaic Procession. Annually, however, two of the girls, each carrying a parcel of unknown contents, would descend a *secret stairway* to the Sanctuary of Aphrodite, there exchange the parcels for others just as carefully wrapped to keep their contents secret, and return with these to the Acropolis surface. The meaning of this mysterious ritual is not clear: it could be that the parcels contained phalluses and loaves of salt, symbolising Aphrodite's birth from the sea, the god of which was Poseidon, worshipped nearby at the Erechtheion – and intended as a rite of fertility and renewal. The likely stairway used in the ritual is the one descending from south to north (5); though a bit to the right is another stairway descending from west to east (6) before turning under the wall: this is Turkish, but leads to a (now covered) Mycenaean stairway descending to a depth of 33.5 metres to a natural spring. From the platform here (the ball court of the Arrephoroi) there is an excellent view west to the Areopagus and below to the 'Theseion' in the Agora.

Reminders of the Persian sack

Further east another platform (7) behind the Erechtheion offers a view along a section of the north wall which was in part built from the *blocks and column drums* from an earlier Parthenon razed by the Persians (480 BC). The *Belvedere* (8) overlooks Plaka, Hadrian's Arch and the Temple of Olympian Zeus and also surveys the mountains enclosing the Attic plain. Once topped by statues of the gods, these mountains now, to the distress of classicists, are topped by 'ugly' radar stations. But when darkness falls these radar peaks are illuminated and they sparkle above the city like jewels suspended from the night. And by day, the bulbous station nesting upon *Hymettos* to the southeast is easily imagined as a giant pterodactyl's egg, as stupefying a sight as any marble-breasted goddess and more likely to keep the Turks away. Since ancient times Hymettos has been famous for its twilight moods, favouring Athens with its violet crown at evening; and famous until recently, too, for its honey. The bees have now retreated to Pentelikon where the aromatic shrubs they love to browse upon still grow in abundance. Hymettos also produced a marble, but inferior to that exploited wholesale from the flanks of *Pentelikon*, to the northeast, from Pericles' day on. All the monuments on the Acropolis are of Pentelic marble, prized for its enduring edge yet, because of its iron oxide content, weathering to a soft golden glow. The coarser grained Parian marble – from Paros in the Cyclades – was still preferred, however, for sculpture. To the north is the *Parnes range*, wild, sparsely populated, crossed by only one paved road, still a barrier, as it always has been between Attica and Boeotia. Finally, to the west running low behind Piraeus towards the Straits of Salamis is *Aigaleos* where Xerxes expectantly perched his throne, only to witness the destruction of his fleet (480 BC).

The mountains around Athens

Between the Belvedere and the museum, directly before

Theatres at the base of the Acropolis

the east portico of the Parthenon, stood the circular *Temple of Rome and Augustus* (9), now being reconstructed. Looking over the south wall of the Acropolis you can see below two ancient theatres. The one on the left is the *Theatre of Dionysos* (10), rebuilt in stone in the 4th C BC to replace the earlier theatre in which the plays of Aeschylus, Sophocles, Euripides and Aristophanes were first performed before audiences on wooden benches; while that on the right is the *Odeon of Herodos Atticus* (11), a Roman construction, where the Festival of Athens is held. Lifting your gaze, the hill opposite is *Philopappou*, named after a Syrian landowner, Roman consul and benefactor of Athens – though the Athenians seem to have lost all sense of proportion in honouring him (AD 115) with the overly-large and now broken-tooth monument dominating the summit. It was from that point in 1687 that the shot which blew up the Parthenon was fired.

Near the southwest corner of the Parthenon are two deep *pits* revealing earlier – at the bottom, Mycenaean – walls. The surface area along this south side of the Acropolis was extended only in the mid-5th C by the construction of Kimon's massive *retaining wall*, providing the space required for the Parthenon foundations. Further on is the *Sanctuary of Artemis Vravronia* (12) where rituals expressing some connection between the Huntress, bears and childbirth were performed, but are not now understood. Between the sanctuary, the Temple of Athena Nike and the Propylaia is a prominent

Mycenaean wall

section of *Mycenaean wall* (13) dating from about 1400 BC; large boulders piled upon one another, the interstices filled with smaller stones. Defences such as these walls and the deep well on the north side saved Athens from being overrun by the Dorian invaders who sacked Mycenae itself at the end of the second millenium. Though the Dark Ages followed, Athens led the reawakening in pottery, sculpture and literature; quite possibly because she had preserved some thread of culture from the previous Mycenaean and Minoan civilisations.

The Parthenon. Back at the Propylaia: the ground rises about 12 metres between here and the Parthenon, so that the ascent towards and through the Propylaia is continued now, though less steeply. As you approach the Parthenon on the crown of the Acropolis, notice that the surface of the rock was cut with *transverse corrugations* in classical times to afford a better foothold; and that along either side of the path *rectangular notches* have been cut into the rock to receive the pedestals of statues. One of the first of these statues to be seen upon entering was of Pericles, erected sometime after his death and certainly still standing when Pausanias visited the

Athena Promachos Acropolis. Much larger was the bronze *Athena Promachos* (14) by Phidias. Standing 9 metres high, the sunlight flashing off her gold-tipped spear and helmet could be seen from ships sailing up the coast from Sounion as soon as they rounded Cape Zoster where Hymettos runs into the sea. At some point this statue, which commemorated the Athenian defeat of the Persians at Marathon, was removed to Constantinople where it survived until 1203 when it was torn down by a mob, drunk, angry and distressed over the imminent sack of their city by the Fourth Crusade, 'unable', wrote one Greek at the time, 'to bear even a symbol of courage and of wisdom'.

But the *Parthenon* (15) was not entered from this west side, although since the explosion the west pediment is more complete than the east and is the more imposing facade. The Sacred Way ran along the north colonnade to the pronaos. The cella at this end exists only in foundation, but at the west end much of its walls still stand. The name Parthenon means virgins' apartment, originally applied to the chamber at the west end of the temple, occupied by the priestesses of Athena whose chryselephantine cult statue towered in the cella. (There is a miniature Roman copy of the statue in the National Archaeological Museum; it looks hideous, but apparently the giant original was awesome and comparable to Phidias' similar cult statue of Zeus at Olympia which was reckoned one of the seven wonders of the ancient world.) The Doric temple was completed in 438 BC, built entirely of Pentelic marble except for a wooden roof, though this too was tiled with marble. Despite its avowed religious purpose, the Parthenon was principally regarded as a work of art and used as the state treasury, the Erechtheion remaining the holy place sanctified by tradition.

The friezes Although Pausanias comments on the pedimental sculptures, he says nothing of the exterior Doric frieze surmounting the peristyle, or the interior Ionic frieze around the outer wall of the cella, both so high off the ground that they could hardly have been appreciated as more than incidental decoration. Indeed the interior frieze, deep within the shadows of the colonnade, would have been yet more difficult to make out; with the roof blown off, this, at least, is no longer the case. Nearly the entire *west interior frieze* is *in situ* and shows Athenian knights preparing for the Panathenaic Procession which, when the frieze was complete, would have paraded off from the southwest corner in opposite directions, meeting at the centre of the east frieze over the main door. A portion of the remaining frieze is in the Acropolis museum; most is in the British Museum. As part of the project to restore the Parthenon and to prevent further damage from pollution there are now plans for the west frieze to be removed to the Acropolis museum. The *exterior frieze*, symbolising struggles against the forces of barbarism – Giants,

Amazons, Centaurs – has either been carted off to various museums (the Lapiths and Centaurs are in the British Museum; fragments in the Acropolis museum) or remains, badly damaged, in place.

The pedimental sculptures

The *east pediment*, being over the entrance, was the most important but is nearly all gone. The sculptural theme was the birth of Athena but all we can see here are the figures (mostly casts of the originals in London) at the furthest angles: on the left, the four horses of Helios' chariot, representing dawn, and the reclining figure of Dionysos; on the right, the horses of Selene sinking out of sight. The *west pediment* pictured the contest between Athena and Poseidon for possession of Athens. What remains is original: Kekrops, the legendary first king of Athens and his daughter on the left; a reclining woman representing the Kallirrhoe spring on the right. It is likely that Phidias himself carved several of the pedimental statues.

The architect of the Parthenon

The Parthenon employs certain optical refinements, like the gentle convexity applied to the stylobate to counter any illusion that it is sagging under its own massiveness; the swelling of the columns (entasis) part way up to correct a trick of the eye by which straight shafts appear pinched; the inclination of the columns inwards lest the burden of their entablature seems to press them outwards. And it is to these refinements, involving high mathematical precision, that credit is often given for the perfection of the Parthenon. Though their use was general in all the better temples of the period, including the 'Theseion' or Hephaisteion in the Agora, and even the much earlier Peisistratid foundations of the Temple of Olympian Zeus display a convexity, the Parthenon remains in a class of its own, at once combining power yet unleashed with buoyant lightness, the optical refinements doing more than correcting illusions, rather creating a tension that makes one believe that the Parthenon might just at any moment levitate if not cut loose from the gravitational bonds of earth entirely.

There is perfection, but it was born of the intuitive genius of the architect rather than in the precision of his mathematical calculations. In fact the Parthenon is Iktinos' brilliant *ad hoc* solution to the problem of having to build a new Parthenon upon the foundations and largely out of the materials of an only slightly older, unfinished Parthenon. The previous architect had been Kallikrates, commissioned by Kimon of the aristocratic party. When the populist Pericles came to power, Kallikrates was dismissed, Iktinos put in his place. The switch might have been political, but that the artistic implications were profound there can be no doubt. Kallikrates had been the architect of the Hephaisteion, still excellently preserved in the Agora. Compare it to the Parthenon. It is on lower ground, admittedly, and though constructed of exactly the same marble has inexplicably weathered badly, turning dull where the Parthenon glows. Even so, a comparison is possible and fair. The Hephaisteion is flat-footed. The Parthenon soars.

The Erechtheion. To the north of the Parthenon are the *foundations of the Old Temple of Athena* (16), thought to have been built in 529 BC (deduced by astronomical calculations from its alignment) during the rule of Peisistratos. It is therefore the only building in Athens whose foundations survive entirely exposed and intact from the years preceding the Persian sack. Immediately adjacent is its successor temple, the *Erechtheion* (17), completed around 394 BC. The particular veneration accorded to both temples was due to their location upon the spot where, it was believed, Poseidon and Athena contested for possession of the Acropolis. The myth probably records a struggle between patrilineal and matrilineal tribes in prehistoric Athens: the city was already Athena's, but Poseidon struck his claim by hurling his trident or a thunderbolt at this spot and causing a gush of sea-water (called Erechtheis); Athena responded by producing an olive tree. By a vote of the gods (in another version, by a plebiscite of the citizens) it was judged that Athena's was the better gift and the city remained hers, though at least one concession was made to the patrilineal claim – from then onwards Athenians took their fathers' not their mothers' names. The crevice caused by Poseidon's blow is exposed through the flooring of the north porch and a section of the coffered ceiling above was left agape in the belief that where once lightning has struck nothing should be built. Pausanias put his ear to the crevice and said that when the south wind blew he could hear the waves of the sea. He also reported seeing Athena's olive tree; and Herodotus, 600 years earlier, tells the story of how Xerxes, punctuating the prophesy that all mainland Greece would be overrun by the Persians, stormed the Acropolis and burnt its temples: 'Now this olive was destroyed by fire together with the rest of the sanctuary; nevertheless on the very next day, when the Athenians, who were ordered by Xerxes to offer the sacrifice, went up to that sacred place, they saw that a new shoot nearly half a metre long had sprung from the stump. They told the king of this'; an omen of Xerxes' defeat at Salamis not long after. The tree now growing against the west wall of the temple was planted in 1917 by an American archaeologist.

The temple's need to house two deities and probably to encompass still older sanctuaries, and the prohibition on levelling the sacred rock on which it stands, accounts for the Erechtheion's unique, highly irregular plan and elevation. This is difficult to appreciate without walking through it (now forbidden), or at least several times around it.

The struggle between Athena and Poseidon

The north porch The shallow *east portico*, with five of its original six columns in place (Lord Elgin made off with the north column), and its cella stand nearly 3 metres higher than the north porch fronted by four columns plus one at either side. It is the *north porch* that is particularly elegant, with its tall columns, coffered ceiling, its doorway decorated with rosettes, and its frieze of blue Eleusinian marble. There is debate as to which cella served Poseidon and which Athena, though it would seem odd if the cella immediately behind the spot where Poseidon's trident or thunderbolt cleft the rock were not Poseidon's own. On the south side is the famous **Porch of the Caryatids** *Porch of the Caryatids*, the entablature here supported by maidens rather than columns, though their long Ionic tunics drape about their legs like flutings. The second from the left is a cast of the original now in the British Museum; the one at the back right is modern, the original having been destroyed in the War of Independence; and the others are now also copies, the originals having been recently removed to an atmospherically controlled chamber in the Acropolis museum. Perhaps it was these maidens that gave the Turks the idea of turning this most harmonious and feminine of temples into a harem.

The Areopagus and the Pnyx

To the northwest, between the Acropolis and the Agora, is the rocky outcrop of the *Areopagus* where cases of murder were heard, the accuser standing on the stone of Insolence, the accused on the stone of Recklessness. It was to this spot that Orestes, after killing his mother Klytemnestra, ran pursued by the Furies, and their chthonic demand of a life for a **Justice and democracy** life was rejected by the new laws of Apollo and Athena. Here also St Paul preached to the sceptical Athenians.

Southwest of the Areopagus is the *Pnyx* (where seating for the *son et lumiere* is placed), a hill on the north side of which a semicircular terrace was cut as the meeting place for the Athenian Assembly. The *bema*, a three-stepped platform from which Themistokles, Pericles and Demosthenes addressed their audiences in the 5th and 4th C BC, projects from a wall of rock about 25 metres from the hilltop. The orators had a marvellous view of the Acropolis off to their right, while at least 5000 citizens (the necessary quorum) gathered before them. Nowadays the assembly area follows the natural slope of the hill down towards the north and your impression is of the speaker talking down to the citizens, but anciently this terrace was tilted upwards by means of a *retaining wall*, about a third of which remains, to a height of 5 metres, at the central part of the arc.

The Agora

The *Agora* may be entered from the southwest off Leoforos Apostolou, on free days from the base of the Acropolis, but is entered more usually from the north over the railway cutting from the flea market west of Monastiraki. At this entry there is a plan of the site from which you can get your bearings.

The broad pathway ahead of you, with the colonnaded Stoa of Attalos on the left, is the *Panathenaic Way* which ran from the Kerameikos, through the Agora, up to the Acropolis. Its gutters are noticeable, and further up some of its paving remains. To the right, the facade marked by sculptures of two Tritons, are the overlapping remains of the *Odeon of Agrippa* (1st C BC) and the *Gymnasium* (5th C AD), the latter the probable centre of the university which when finally closed in 529 by the Byzantine Emperor Justinian marked the eclipse of Athens until modern times.

What now looks like a carefully tended bombsite was once the entertainment, cultural, commercial and legal centre of Athens. Then as now, the Athenians were an open-air people and here life was in full swing: 'You will find everything sold together in the same place at Athens; figs, witnesses to summonses, bunches of grapes, turnips, pears, apples, givers of evidence, roses, medlars, porridge, honey-combs, chick-peas, lawsuits, beestings, beestings-puddings, myrtle, allot-ment-machines, irises, lambs, waterclocks, laws, indictments'. Now it is quiet and fragrant with jasmine.

The Stoa of Attalos

The *Stoa of Attalos* is a faithful reconstruction built on the foundations of the 2nd C BC original. Casting bars of cool shadow across your path, Doric columns which would have been colourfully painted support the ceiling of an open arcade, once lined by shops and a gallery above. The stoa houses a *museum* of finds from all periods made on the Agora site, including Mycenaean artefacts, coins, vases, even a child's chamber pot. Most interesting are the potsherds (ostraka) used in ballots which decided whether a particular citizen should be ostracised. Among the names appearing on the sherds are two of Athens' greatest citizens: Themistokles, victor at Salamis, who was ostracised, and Pericles, who was not. At one end of the building is an interesting set of photographs taken in 1931 and 1959. The earlier shows how even that recently the Agora site was covered by hundreds of little houses and alleys; the latter shows them cleared away, and under as much as 12 metres of soil the ancient masonry laid bare. The upper gallery has plans showing the topography of ancient Athens and stages in the development of the Agora, as well as scale models of the Acropolis and of the Agora at its greatest extent (2nd C AD).

Agora museum

Scale reconstruction of the Agora

Again surveying the Agora, this time from the upper gallery of the stoa, you can see the Byzantine *Church of the Holy Apostles*, stripped of later embellishments to its 10th C form, the narthex decorated with 17th C wall-paintings from another, demolished, church. Just to the northeast of the church and extending westwards were the *Middle* and

Governmental buildings *Second South Stoas* of Hellenistic times, subsequently obliterated by the Roman Gymnasium. Beyond them, below the knoll of Kolonos on which the 'Theseion' or Temple of Hephaistos stands, were the major governmental buildings of 5th C BC Athens. To the left are the circular foundations of the *Tholos* where the Prytaneis, the executive officials, were on duty day and night, easily alerted by a beacon fire or found by a runner and able to respond at once to an emergency. And a bit further left – the foundations are barely traceable – was the *Strategeion*, the headquarters of the ten annually elected generals. (Apart from his prominent role in the Assembly, Pericles was elected strategos – general – each year from 443 to his death in 429, this contributing to his unique authority.) The Prytaneis, who served on the executive by rota, were drawn from the elected tribal deputies who made up the Council of Five Hundred which thrashed out state policy before it was put to the Assembly for approval or rejection. The Council met in the *Bouleuterion*, to the right of the Tholos. Immediately in front of the Bouleuterion was the *Metroon* which contained the state archives.

The Hephaisteion. The *Temple of Hephaistos* (also known as *The Theseion*) owes its renown to being the best-preserved of any Greek temple; only the roof is missing, and the sculptures, of Parian marble (finer but less hard than the Pentelic marble of the blocks and column drums), are badly worn. The interior suffered some damage from the 7th C when it was adapted to Christian worship and an apse, and later a concrete vault, were added. Set into a side wall is the tombstone of George Watson with an epitaph by Byron.

The metopes above the east entrance to the cella depict eight exploits of the legendary hero Theseus to whose worship the temple was wrongly ascribed in the Middle Ages. Indeed, there is a Theseion yet to be unearthed, probably beneath Plaka; for in 475 BC Kimon, discovering some gigantic bones (of a prehistoric animal probably) equal to Theseus' heroic stature, deposited them in a specially-built temple. But the Hephaisteion also bears metopes of Herakles' Labours, was sited appropriately in the metalworkers' quarter, and has been accurately dated to 449 BC.

The Hephaisteion opened Pericles' great building programme; its architect was Kallikrates, who later built the temples at Sounion and Rhamnous, and the Athena Nike. It is Doric hexastyle to the Parthenon's octastyle; its columns are more slender, but the entablature is heavier, while the stylobate seems to impart no vertical thrust. But overlooking the Agora as the ground rises towards the Acropolis, the Hephaisteion does provide welcome shade from where to gaze on greater works.

The Kerameikos

Odos Ermou, running westwards from Syntagma Square, is the fashionable shopping street of Athens, at least until it approaches Monastiraki. The flea market extends along Ifestou and Astingos streets parallel to and south of Ermou. The bargains are often more imaginary than real, though it can be surprising to see what unlikely curiosities have found their way here. Ermou continues past shabby workshops towards the light industrial area along Odos Piraios and just here, between the angle of the two intersecting roads, lies one of the most pleasant, fascinating yet unfrequented archaeological sites in Athens. The part of the Kerameikos within the city walls was the quarter of potters and smiths, while beyond the walls it was the major Athenian cemetery, where beautiful headstones and statues of the worthy dead and monuments to those who fell in battle were placed, the roads from Piraeus, Elefsís and Thebes converging here, the great processions of the Panathenaia and Eleusinian Mystery cult passing by. The site has been excavated to its ancient level. Ermou and Piraios are hot and dusty above, but below along the Sacred Way, along the walls, amongst the marble tombstones, the air is fresh and cooler, grass and flowers grow, and frogs and tortoises move amongst the water plants of the Eridanos stream. The *Sacred Gate* spans both the *Sacred Way* and the stream; a few paces north of it is the larger *Dipylon* (double gateway), most of the city's traffic entering through here and on into the Agora. Between the two are the foundations of the *Pompeion*, a place of preparation for the processions.

Standing back from the walls, on the terrace overlooking the *Street of the Tombs*, you can imagine these roads rising towards the Agora, lined by colonnades, as Pausanias described, 'with bronze statues along the front, of men and women whose stories are glorious', and you can see the Acropolis and its marble monuments as visitors to Athens would first have seen it as they entered here. And from here too, amongst the graves of those who died in the first year of the Peloponnesian War, Pericles asked the mourners to lift their gaze: 'I would have you day by day fix your eyes upon the greatness of Athens, until you become filled with the love of her; and when you are impressed by the spectacle of her glory, reflect that this empire has been acquired by men who knew their duty and had the courage to do it, who in the hour of conflict had the fear of dishonour always present to them, and who, if ever they failed in an enterprise, would not allow their virtues to be lost to their country, but freely gave their lives to her as the fairest offering which they could present at her feast. The sacrifice which they collectively made was individually repaid to them; for they received again and again each one for himself a praise which grows not old and the

ANCIENT ATHENS

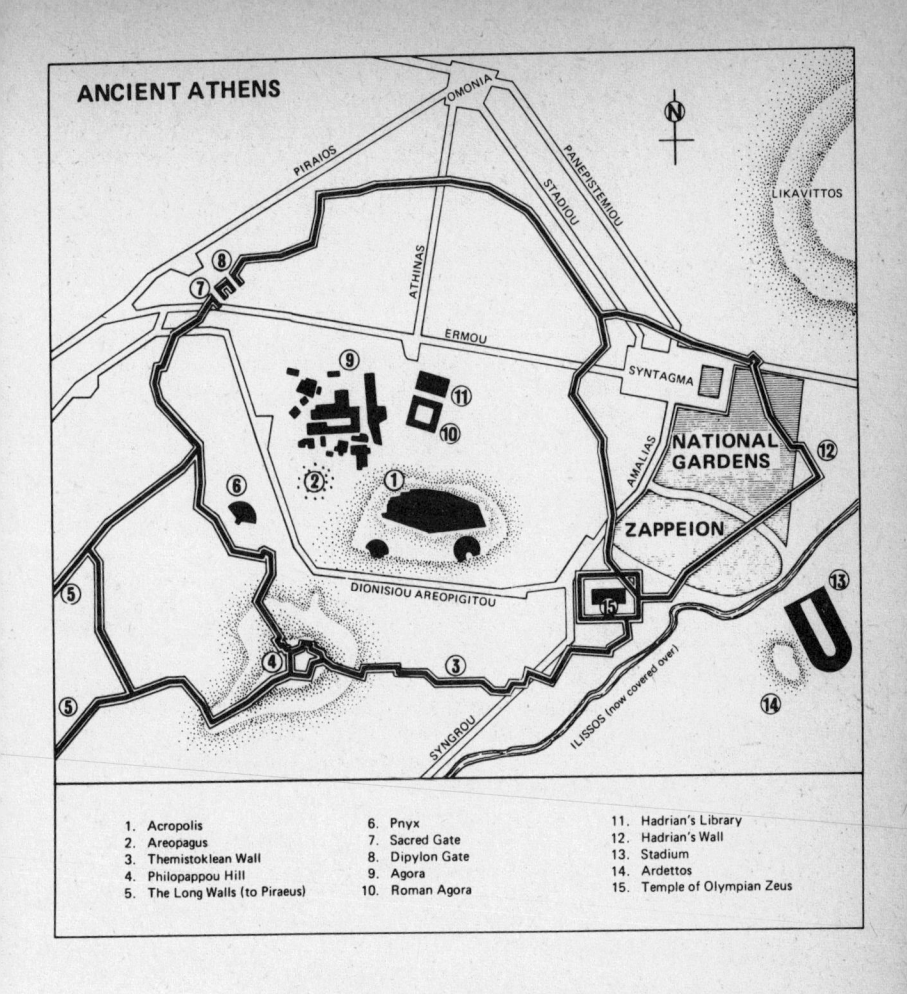

1. Acropolis
2. Areopagus
3. Themistoklean Wall
4. Philopappou Hill
5. The Long Walls (to Piraeus)
6. Pnyx
7. Sacred Gate
8. Dipylon Gate
9. Agora
10. Roman Agora
11. Hadrian's Library
12. Hadrian's Wall
13. Stadium
14. Ardettos
15. Temple of Olympian Zeus

noblest of all sepulchres – I speak not of that in which their remains are laid, but of that in which their glory survives and is proclaimed always and on every fitting occasion both in word and deed. For the whole earth is the sepulchre of famous men; not only are they commemorated by columns and inscriptions in their own country, but in foreign lands there dwells also an unwritten memorial of them, graven not on stone but in the hearts of men. Make them your examples'.

A *museum* exhibits sculpture and vases from the site.

Plaka
Between 8pm and 2am Plaka blazes and blares as the nightlife centre of Athens. During the day it is silent and nearly

dead except for the tourists wending their way up to the Acropolis or an occasional cat slipping along like a shadow against whitewashed walls. Nevertheless, this is the time, during these quiet hours, to walk around and fix the plan of Plaka and its many curious details in your mind.

Plaka gets its name from a white stone slab once at the junction of Adrianou, Tripodon and Kydathenaion Streets near the monument of Lysikrates. About the size of Soho and only one-third the size of Greenwich Village or Montmartre, its maze of narrow streets and steeply climbing steps seem to make it bigger. Plaka is the oldest part of Athens, in plan and architecture little different from how it was before Greek independence except that it has lost what must have been a more Eastern flavour: some of the streets are less narrow than they were, its mosques are gone or in ruins or have been adapted to other purposes, and its bazaars have all but vanished.

Museum of Greek Popular Art

The one vestige of a bazaar is Odos Pandrossou running along the north wall of Hadrian's Library and extending from the Mitropolis (cathedral) to Monastiraki, chockablock with antique dealers and sandal-makers. In the southeast corner of Monastiraki Square (Plateia Monastirakiou) is the 18th C former Mosque of Tzistarakis, its minaret brought down in 1821, now used as part of the *Museum of Greek Popular Art* (this houses the ceramics collection; embroidery, costumes, ikons, the interior of an old village house, etc, are found at 17 Kydathenaion Street in the Plaka). The west and east walls of *Hadrian's Library* still stand on Areos and Aiolou Streets: it takes a moment to realise that all the distance between the two was taken up with a vast building, pool and courtyard in the centre (where the foundations of a 7th C church can be noticed), reading rooms all around, and in nine niches along the east wall bookshelves from floor to high ceiling.

Hadrian's Library

Roman Forum and Tower of the Winds

South along Aiolou is the *Roman Forum*, an eastward extension of the older Agora paid for by Julius Caesar, the graceful octagonal *Tower of the Winds* the most complete and interesting building to be seen here, built in the 1st C BC as a combined weather-vane and clock. Though it had sundials round its walls, it more ingeniously employed an Acropolis spring to fill an upper chamber which then dripped water into a lower chamber in exactly 24 hours, indicating on the outside the level and therefore the time to passers-by. The name and symbol of the cardinal winds adorn each face: Boreas the north wind, bearded and heavily dressed; Zephyros the west wind, young and handsome, scattering flowers; Notos the south wind who brings rain, emptying an urn; Apeliotes the east wind, carrying in his cloak the fullness of the harvest; the themes continued with each of the intermediate winds. In the 18th C it became a tekke, the home of an order of Turkish dervishes, whose strange rhythmic cries and whirling dances convinced the Greeks that both frieze reliefs and inhabitants were the embodiment of evil spirits. Apparently the Turks felt the same way about the Greeks: one 18th C English traveller reported seeing 16 ostrich eggs hung outside to avert the evil eye. In the northwest corner of the forum is the former *Fetichie Mosque*, dedicated to Mehmet II, conqueror of Constantinople, and the only surviving large mosque of the early Turkish occupation (15th C). It is now used as an archaeological laboratory. Just to the north of the Tower of the Winds is the sadly all but destroyed *Mendreses*, an 18th C Islamic seminary, its cells once lining two sides of an enclosed garden, now only the gateway with its Turkish inscription surviving. When in 1821 the Greeks in the Peloponnese rose against Turkish rule, a cadi addressing his people here dissuaded them from massacring the entire male Greek population of Attica.

Fetichie Mosque

Gate of the Mendreses

The Byzantine churches of Athens are modest in comparison to those of Thessaloniki; and certainly modest in size but fascinating in detail is *Agios Eleftherios* in the lee of the ugly 19th C Mitropolis (cathedral) on Odos Mitropoleos which runs west out of Syntagma Square. It dates from the 12th C but is entirely constructed of reliefs from a 6th C church and from blocks and reliefs from earlier pagan buildings. Eagles, angels, Maltese crosses, signs of the zodiac and a calendar of Attic state festivals contribute to the gingerbread effect. That is on the northern 'lowland' fringe of Plaka; climbing higher are numerous little churches and chapels, some passed unnoticed at first and discovered later with surprise and pleasure. *Agios Ioannis Theologos*, halfway up a flight of steps at the corner of Erechtheos and Erotokritou Streets, is a 9th or 10th C church tucked away in the most medieval part of Plaka with its thicket of twisting lanes and sudden flights of steps interspersed with little squares and courtyards. At night the tables of two tavernas spill into the street where Erechtheos and Erotokritou meet and run up the steps like ivy. The sound of bazouki from down the way is not too deafening and the mood is congenial, unlike the cacophony and touting along Odos Mnesikleous, Plaka's taverna strip.

Agios Eleftherios

Off Odos Theorias which runs along the top of Plaka and towards the Acropolis entrance is the *Kanellopoulos Museum*, a diverse family collection of jewellery, church plate, ikons, antiquities and everyday objects. On the northeast slope of the Acropolis and higher still, is what could as well be an island village. It is called *Anafiótika* after Anafi from where its inhabitants came in the late 19th and early 20th C, bringing their traditional Cycladic style of church and house building with them. The islanders came to Athens as building workers, but unable to afford living in the houses they built they took advantage of a Greek law saying if you

Kanellopoulos Museum

An island village

can build your house in the space of the night it is yours, their houses springing up like mushrooms on the Acropolis itself.

Choregic monument

At the southeastern end of Plaka along Odos Tripodon is the *Monument of Lysikrates*, put up in 335 BC after the chorus that gentleman sponsored had won the Dionysos competition. It is preserved because it became part of a Capuchin Convent in which both Byron and Chateaubriand later stayed. Byron wrote home: 'I am living in the Capuchin Convent, Hymettus before me, the Acropolis behind, the Temple of Jove to my right, the Stadium in front, the town to the left; eh, Sir, there's a situation, there's your picturesque! nothing like that, Sir, in Lunnun, no not even the Mansion House. And I feed upon Woodcocks and Red Mullet every day, and I ride to Piraeus, and Phalerum, and Munychia.' Before the monastery burnt down in 1821, the last abbot introduced tomatoes to Athens, the population at first using them as decorative plants.

The market and tradesmen's quarter

Not part of old Plaka proper, but a sociological extension of it, is the area lying to its north (west of Stadiou) running up to Omonia. The reconstructed Stoa of Attalos was meant to give some impression of what the ancient Agora was like but denies the essence of agora life in its own lifelessness. It is better to walk along Athinas, Sofokleous, Praxitelous or any of the smaller streets running between them to feel the pulse of Athens today. Nor along these sometimes sleazy, usually fascinating streets would you get an impression of Athens any worse than you would have got in Periclean days: 'The streets are nothing but miserable old lanes, the houses mean with few better ones among them. On seeing the town for the first time the stranger would hardly believe that this is Athens of which he has heard so much' (the philosopher Dikaiarchos, 3rd C BC). The flower market is in the square of Agia Irini Church along Odos Aiolou; nuts, bolts and whores are for sale down Odos Athinas; the meat and fish market is at the intersection of Athinas and Sofokleous, a series of iron-framed halls covered with glass, live rabbits hopping about, whole animals hanging from giant hooks above, 2-metre long sharks stretched out, their noses lopped off and then their skins ripped right to their tails; and the cornucopian vegetable market is just across the road. A wander here is a marvellous antidote to joining the throngs who perform the Stations of Western Civilisation, kissing cultural ikons like the Parthenon along the way. More important decisions, great and small, were probably made in the fish markets and whorehouses of ancient Athens than were ever made at the shrine of the Wise Virgin atop the Acropolis.

Around the National Gardens and Zappeion

Half surrounding the *Parliament* by Syntagma Square are the *National Gardens*, lush, fragrant and shady with a maze of paths winding through the palms, evergreens and orange trees where people stroll, children play, lovers neck. It is marvellously well-tended, almost continuously irrigated, and sure to be at least ten degrees cooler than anywhere else in the city. It was laid out by Queen Amalia in the 19th C when the Parliament was still the Royal Palace and these were the Royal Gardens. Peacocks and swans make their homes here, and there is also a small zoo. Adjacent is the *Zappeion* with its more formal layout and broad promenades like the Tuilleries, but also a bandstand where an amplified Greek sings popular songs to a café audience (pushing up the price of a coffee five-fold), and there is a free children's playground. The splendid neo-classical rotunda was built towards the end of the last century as a national exhibition hall. Its interior colonnade, encircling an open court, is very fine and the painted walls and ceiling give a good impression of how the classical temples were decorated. At the southern end of the Zappeion where Leoforos Amalias and Leoforos Olgas meet is a *statue of Hellas*, a posturing Byron at her bosom, and behind the two a cringing baldheaded figure who could be a wicked Turk or humble Greek, but looking more like he is about to pick Byron's pocket.

Hadrian's Arch   Across Leoforos Olgas is *Hadrian's Arch* marking the extension of the city in AD 132: on one side it reads 'This is Athens, the ancient city of Theseus'; on the other 'This is the city of Hadrian and not of Theseus'. Towering behind like giant reeds growing along the banks of the Ilissos are the 15 standing Corinthian columns of the *Temple of Olympian Zeus*. A plentifully-shafted octastyle with three rows of eight columns at each end, two rows of 20 along either side, it had 104 columns in all and rose to a height of 27.5 metres, more than half as high again as its columns.

The Olympeion

The foundations of this largest of temples in Greece were laid by Peisistratos and some of the column drums were cut before work stopped with the fall of the Peisistratids and the growing Persian menace. Themistokles incorporated the drums in his wall, now exposed at the north end of the site. The temple was only completed under Hadrian, 700 years later – 'a great victory of time'. In the Middle Ages a stylite considerably increased the distance between himself and this world, and marginally lessened the distance between himself and God, by spending his life atop the architrave of the two westernmost columns of the southeast corner group.

Just south of the Olympeion is the bed of a dried up river, the *Ilissos*, which once flowed down from Hymettos but is now reduced to an underground seasonal trickle and around the bottom of the tennis courts and swimming pool is covered over by a new road. Plato expressed his love for the countryside that was here in his *Phaedrus*. Odos Anapafseos runs up

Athens' principal cemetery
from here to the gate of the *Proto Nekrotafeion Athinon*, Athens' major cemetery, where many famous heroes of the War of Independence, writers, artists, politicians and archaeologists lie buried – the mausoleum of Heinrich Schliemann is here, decorated with Trojan scenes, among many other sumptuous, sometimes outlandish, tombs. It is the modern kitsch counterpart to the Kerameikos and well worth a visit. The Greeks see little in death other than the reminder that life is to be enjoyed, and visitors to the graves and tombs often come in family groups with picnic baskets and bottles of wine, spending many hours talking and laughing, hosing down the sparkling marble and watering the flowers.

The Stadium
The *Stadium* is opposite the eastern side of the Zappeion. 'A thing not so attractive to hear about, but wonderful to see', said Pausanias, though perhaps not so wonderful to see either. It is, after all, just a stadium; impressive in its Pentelic whiteness and symmetry and boring for the same reason. It is an accurate reconstruction of, and built on the same foundations as, the AD 144 stadium of Herodes Atticus – born at Marathon, a Roman senator and benefactor of Athens – who decided to replace the earlier wooden and somewhat dilapidated original. George Averoff, an Alexandrian Greek, decided to do the same thing 1750 years later to provide a venue in 1896 for the revived Olympic Games. Excellent but

Ardettos
entirely ignored is *Ardettos*, the hill in whose slope the Stadium nestles. It is a minor hill; not nearly so high as Lykavittos nor so high as the Acropolis, but the view from the top is one of the best in Athens. The city and the plain climb away towards the mountains; the landscape is gently tipped towards you as a restaurant waiter might slightly tip a bowl of fruit to permit a better view without the apples, peaches and oranges spilling out onto the table.

The royal palace
Odos Herodes Atticus runs up along the eastern side of the National Gardens and passes the newer *royal palace* (the older palace is now the Parliament on Syntagma Square; since the final abolition of the monarchy in 1974 this one has been set aside as a presidential residence). As during the monarchy, huge evzones in their War of Independence uniforms still stand and stamp about outside. This road meets with Leoforos Vasilissis Sofias; turning right leads you to the Byzantine Museum.

The Byzantine Museum. Early Christian, Byzantine and post-Byzantine work, including sculpture, architectural specimens from churches and bits of their decoration, religious vestments, jewellery, manuscripts, mosaics and ikons, are on display in the Florentine-style villa that is now the *Byzantine Museum*. After so much classical art in Athens, it is refreshing here to sense the animism of the natural world, a world in which snakes and eagles, deer, rams, vines and trees entwine to express and enfold God's mysteries. In Byzantine art the ornate and spectacular, even the grotesque, are given full rein.

Church interiors The *ground floor* of the main building chronologically presents sculpture and reproduces a 5th to 6th C basilica (*Room II*), an 11th C Byzantine cruciform church with cupola (*Room IV*), and a flat-ceilinged post-Byzantine church of plain square design like a mosque with 18th C rococo decoration showing a marked Turkish influence (*Room V*), and including a sculptured and gilded ikonostasis from the Ionian islands, a choros, the huge circle of sculptured plaques suspended from the ceiling, and one especially marvellous ikon of St George killing an outrageously spiney dragon.

Ikons *Upstairs* are ikons, frescoes and vestments, *Room II* containing a fine selection of ikons from the 14th and 15th C Byzantine renaissance. The double-sided Crucifixion (169) is particularly noteworthy, as is another Crucifixion (246), showing Venetian or Florentine influence though amply retaining Greek literalness: Mary Magdalen, long hair flowing, reaches her hands up to the nailed feet of Christ; blood squirts from his side as from a garden hose and is caught by an angel in a cup of gold.

To the *right* of the main building a detached wing presents ikons chronologically; while the exhibits in the *left wing* seem always to be changing but usually include some popular ikons, sometimes a whole joyful room of them: amateur and refreshing for their lightness (almost lightheartedness) of touch after the more formal and sombre ikons elsewhere; more idiomatic, often like comic strips, and with a strong Eastern influence. In the Orthodox Church the ikon is an attempt to portray but also to capture Christian truths and so is itself sacred.

The War Museum. Further along Leoforos Vasilissis Sofias, in the direction of the Hilton (east), is the *War Museum*, built during the military dictatorship. Artefacts, graphic battle plans and explanatory maps tell the story of Greek arms from Mycenaenean times through Alexander the Great, the Byzantine wars, the Frankish and Turkish occupations, the Revolution of 1821–32, the Anatolian disaster of 1922, and the Second World War when Greece was occupied by the Italians and Germans, its forces fighting alongside the Allies in the Middle East. Outside are tanks and aircraft, including a Spitfire in Greek Air Force markings.

The Benaki Museum. If instead after leaving the Byzantine Museum you cross over Leoforos Vasilissis Sofias to Odos Koumbari, you will find the *Benaki Museum* on the north-

Jewellery and Greek costumes

west corner. Entry is through the garden by the door facing Vasilissis Sofias. The museum contains the personal and eclectic impedimenta of Antoine Benaki, a man of evident wealth and catholic taste, whose town house this was until he presented it, lock, stock and barrel, to the state in 1931: ancient Greek and Roman art; Byzantine, Moslem, Chinese, Coptic and Western European art; plus jewellery, historical souvenirs, a unique collection of Greek regional costumes, and assorted bric-a-brac. Interesting (*Room K, first floor*) is an ikon of c1560, depicting the adoration of the magi, the earliest known work of the Cretan painter Domenikos Theotokopoulos, better known as El Greco; outstanding (*Room N, first floor*) is the collection of jewellery from the Bronze Age to modern times, and (*basement*) the display of regional costumes.

Kolonaki

Just up Odos Koumbari is Kolonaki Square, the centre of the most fashionable part of Athens with its pavement cafés and tributary streets lined with smart and expensive shops.

The National Archaeological Museum

Every province, or nome, in Greece has its archaeological museum housing local finds. The museum in Athens not only has the city as a prize, but in the past has had the pick of the crop, wherever it may have come from. Though this is no longer the case (the museum has hardly any Cretan antiquities; the Heraklion museum has prior claim), the collection here is superb and includes much of the finest and most famous classical sculpture not already shipped off to London, Paris or Berlin. In particular, its Mycenaean collection is probably the best to be found anywhere in the world. The *National Archaeological Museum* is located north of Omonia on Odos 28th October (invariably known as Patission) at Odos Tositsa. A guide to the sculpture and an illustrated souvenir booklet covering the entire collection are available in the foyer, though a guide book is not necessary at all: the exhibits are labelled, if unimaginatively, in English, French and Greek. Reference is made here only to a selection of the finer or more curious exhibits.

The Mycenaean exhibits

The Mycenaean collection is in the *central salon* on the ground floor and contains gold jewellery, frequent bull images and at the back, frescoes dating from 1550 BC, not unsimilar to those from Thera (upstairs) as the Mycenaeans were the successors to the Minoan empire. The first exhibit to strike you as you enter is the gold '*Mask of Agamemnon*', as Schliemann excitedly and erroneously believed it to be (see under Mycenae). To the left in a case are three *bronze daggers* (394, 395) inlaid in black niello alloy, silver and gold; and further back in separate cases are the gold *Vaphio cups*, one depicting the capture of wild bulls with nets (1758), the other the trapping of bulls with a decoy cow (1759). All of these objects evidence exquisite technique, but the cups in particular, full of movement and drama, are wonderful.

In *Room 6*, off to the right, are objects from the Cycladic islands, many of them having the spare, abstract form of the most modern sculpture, though they are almost all pre-Mycenaean and the statuettes of *male figures playing musical instruments* date from 2400 BC.

Cycladic sculpture

Geometric pottery

With the Dorian invasion and the collapse of Mycenaean civilisation around the 11th C BC, artistic expression in Greece was chiefly limited to abstractly decorated pottery. At first concentric circles – derived from Mycenaean spirals – and then rectangular patterns were employed in this Geometric Period. By the 8th C BC the human form, in the shape of spindly figures, had made a come-back, and an impressive example of this is the *sepulchral amphora* (804) in *Room 7* (to the left of the museum entrance) with its stylised depiction of the laying-out and lamentation over the dead. This vase was found in the Kerameikos cemetery and dates from c760 BC. It is a century later that free-standing sculpture makes its appearance and then in the formalised kouros (nude youth) and kore (draped maiden), both employed as funerary monuments. The arms of each were held stiffly to the sides; the left leg of the kouros was advanced. The restriction was dictated originally by the timber from which they were carved, but carried through, with less reason, to stone. These sculptures of the Archaic Period (*Rooms 7 to 13*) have a zombie lifelessness or at least impassivity. The fine *kouros from Melos* (1558) in *Room 9* seems heir to the Cycladic miniatures of 1500 years before, with a slenderness and delicacy still owing more to the abstract than to reality: if he started moving it would probably take him half an hour to slouch across the room. It was Attica, perhaps because it avoided the brunt of the Dorian dislocation, that first excelled both in pottery and sculpture: in *Room 10A* the *Attic kouros* (1906) from the mid-6th C is also delicate and charming, but has more substance than his island cousin.

Archaic sculpture

The great period of Athenian power and civilisation followed the defeat of the Persians; but the mettle required to beat back the invader had been forged in earlier generations. What was to come was implicit in what had gone before. For that reason, to look upon the *Anavissos Kouros* (540–520 BC) in *Room 13* (3851) is to look upon the awakening youth of the man that was to come. Though the arms are still at the sides, they are no longer at rest; nor is the advanced left leg rooted there by tradition. The beautiful contour between arms and body, the slight leaning forward of the entire statue, impart a tension to the figure – no longer timber or stone, but an aggrandisement of space. When that right leg steps forward, as it must, as it already seems to do, all Greece

The Anavissos Kouros

63

The Poseidon strides forward into greatness. The brilliant *Poseidon* (15161) in *Room 15* is the Anavissos Kouros grown to manhood: tried and tested strength and relaxed mastery of circumstance.

Also in *Room 15* is a *low relief from Elefsis* (126) showing Demeter presenting the seed corn to Triptolemos and behind him Kore (Persephone) crowning him with a garland. It is a famous work, capturing the majesty, one imagines, of the Mysteries. Many of the sculptures in these rooms are funerary monuments and often have the capacity to move us today. In *Room 16* there is a *tombstone* (715) dating from c430 BC showing a dead youth waving farewell while his grieving slave leans sadly on a pillar – and where life goes on, the cat eyeing the bird in its cage.

Continuing clockwise, the rooms progress through the Hellenic, Hellenistic and Roman periods. *Room 20* (leading off from Room 17) should be visited for the copy (129), one-twelfth of original size, of Phidias' chryselephantine *Athena* that stood in the Parthenon. It gives a clear idea of the details of the original, but is uninspiring and fails to convey the essence of Phidias' presumably great statue. *Room 21:* As a technical tour de force, few statues can compare with the *bronze race horse with boy jockey* (15177) found in the sea with the Poseidon statute. The horse leaps forward as though to take a hurdle, nostrils flared, ears bent back, muscles and vessels standing out, adding tension to the vigorous posture. The boy leans forward into the leap, his left hand holding the reins, his right (now empty) probably grasping a whip.

The finest piece in *Room 28* is the bronze *athlete* (13396) – though he is possibly Paris clutching the now missing golden apple – with inlaid eyes, bronze plate lashes and superb musculature, dating from c340 BC. In *Room 30, Aphrodite* threatens to clout Pan in the face with her sandal (3335). But judging by the smile on her face, this is one last formal gesture of resistance before she enthusiastically succumbs to this grinning archetypal sex maniac. Though from Delos, 1st C BC, it is hard to believe that the statue is Greek at all; it looks naughtily French 18th C, an inartistic but entertaining bit of neoclassicism.

Vase rooms The *upstairs gallery* is full of vases, a feast for the aficionado; though even the least interested person must delight in the *white vases* of *Room VII*, where three in particular (17916, 1818, 1935) depict in the most delicate line and colour Hermes conducting a young woman to the banks of the Styx while Charon waits in his boat, and a woman making offerings at a tomb while the dead man stands in a blazing red cloak to one side.

The Thera exhibition Also upstairs is the exhibition of *Minoan findings on Thera* (for over a decade now there have been plans to remove this to Thera, ie Santorini, when a museum to receive it has been built). This is a must. The outstanding features of Minoan art

A dancing bear in the streets of Athens

are the use of brilliant colours and the great freedom of line. There is a fine pagan feeling for nature in the decorations and a frequent recourse to marine motifs. Here there are vases and other pottery with undulating octopus, dolphin and seaweed designs. And wall *frescoes* of monkeys, antelopes, flowers, birds and bare-breasted aristocratic women.

Piraeus

The Long Walls

Piraeus (Piraiévs) is, as it was in ancient times, the port of Athens. The fortunes of the two have been bound together inextricably. When Themistokles determined upon the construction of a great Athenian fleet, he simultaneously chose triple-harboured Piraeus as its base over the nearer but exposed roadstead at Phaleron, and set about constructing the mighty walls that linked the two cities throughout the 5th C. Phaleron lies 6 kms southwest of the Temple of Olympian Zeus, Leoforos Syngrou running between the two and more or less following the course of the *Phaleric Wall*. Odos Piraios covers about 8 kms from the Kerameikos to Piraeus and over most of the distance follows the course of the *North Wall*. Between these two, a *Middle Wall*, often no more than 200 metres from the North Wall, ran from city to port on a line now followed by the electric railway. When Athens declined to barely more than a backwater with the rise of Constantinople, Piraeus lost all importance. At the moment of Greek independence, not a single house was to be found here and it was only the choice of Athens as the capital of Greece that brought Piraeus back into existence. It swelled with refugees in 1922 following the Anatolian disaster, and is now the busiest port in the Eastern Mediterranean, overtaking, some decades ago, Istanbul.

Traces of the past

You will come to Piraeus enroute to the Saronic or Aegean islands, and despite the port's history there is next to nothing in the way of surviving monuments to cause you to linger. (Enthusiasts, however, can see *sections of both the North and Middle Walls* between the Karaiskaki Stadium and Odos Piraios – or Odos Athinon as it there becomes – a short walk from the Nea Phaleron electric train station. Also, it was said by Demosthenes that the *ship-sheds* housing the Athenian fleet were worthy of mention in company with the Parthenon and Propylaia, and the remains of some of these may still be seen in the basement of a block of flats on the east side of Zea harbour. Finally, there is the *Naval Museum of Greece* along Akte Themistokleous to the West of Zea – a part of the Themistoklean wall has been incorporated in a building opposite the main entrance – and the *Archaeological Museum* at 38 Odos Filellinon, on the hill between Zea and Piraeus harbours.)

The pleasure of the port lies not in its past, nor in the imagined *joie de vivre* claimed for it in *Never On Sunday*, but in the routine of its commercial harbour, boats shuttling between the islands, cruise ships awaiting the return of their passengers from day-trips to the Parthenon, and always, beyond the moles, a dozen or more freighters and giant tankers grazing mindlessly like sea-cows. Also a walk around the *Akte peninsula* (Piraeus on its right, the yacht harbours on its left) is recommended for its changing views across the Saronic, especially at sundown when Hymettos fades from honey-gold to violet and the mountains of the Peloponnese stand out in cobalt silhouette.

Yacht harbours

The circular harbour of *Zea*, crammed with yachts, is hemmed by charmless modern apartment blocks; but the smaller yacht basin of *Turkolimano* (*Mikrolimano* to chauvinistic Greeks) lies cosily in the arms of Munychia, terraces of lovely houses falling back upon the hill, café and taverna tables round the quay, and amongst the elegant sailing boats, sturdy fishing craft, large and small, piled with nets, chandeliered with night lamps. It is a good place to come to from summer-sweltering Athens for a cooler, sea-fragrant evening. From the top of *Munychia* there is a marvellous view of all three harbours, the entire Saronic, and Athens spilling down the plain.

PRACTICAL INFORMATION

ACCOMMODATION
For general information on accommodation in Athens and elsewhere see the *Background* chapter.

Amalia (L), 10 Leoforos Amalias. Tel: 323.7301. Overlooking the National Gardens.
Athenee Palace (L), 1 Kolokotroni. Tel: 323.0791. Central; discreetly elegant.
Athens Hilton (L), 46 Vassilissis Sophias. Tel: 72.0201. More than pleasant walking distance from the centre of town.
Athenaeum Inter-Continental (L), 89–93 Syngrou Avenue. Tel: 902.3666. Spectacular (and expensive) view of the Parthenon. Smart shops.
Grande Bretagne (L), Syntagma Square. Tel: 323.0251. What Claridges is to London, the Ritz to Paris.
Saint George Lycabettus (L), 2 Kleomenous, Plateia Dexamenis. Tel: 79.0711. New, tasteful, high up in Kolonaki with wonderful views.
Other luxury hotels: Acropole Palace, Caravel, King George, Ledra-Marriott, Park, Royal Olympic.

Blue House Pension (A), 19 Voukourestiou. Tel: 362.0341. Homey atmosphere, quiet yet close to Syntagma.
Electra (A), 5 Ermou. Tel: 322.3222. Near Plaka.
Electra Palace (A), 18 Nikodimou. Tel: 324.1401. In Plaka.
King Minos (A), 1 Pireos. Tel: 523.1111. Near Omonia; approaching luxury standards.
Olympic Palace (A), 16 Filellinon. Tel: 323.7611. Between Syntagma and Plaka.

Acropolis House Pension (B), 6–8 Kodrou, Plaka. Tel: 322.2344. Old-fashioned charm, yet modern facilities.
Aretoussa (B), 6–8 Mitropoleos. Tel: 322.9431. Off Syntagma.
Athenian Inn Pension (B), 22 Haritos, Kolonaki. Tel: 723.8097. Handy for the smarter discos and restaurants.
Athens Gate (B), 10 Leoforos Syngrou. Tel: 923.8302. Overlooking the Temple of Zeus and Hadrian's Arch.
Lycabette (B), 6 Valaoritou. Tel: 363.3514. In Kolonaki.
Omiros (B), 15 Apollonos. Tel: 323.5486. In Plaka.
Plaka (B), 7 Kapnikareas and Mitropoleos. Tel: 322.2096.
Titania (B), 52–54 Panepistimiou. Tel: 360.9611. Near Omonia.

Achilleus (C), 21 Lekka. Tel: 322.5826. Off Syntagma.
Carolina (C), 55 Kolokotroni. Tel: 322.8148. Between Syntagma and Omonia.
Clare's House (C), 24 Sorvolou, Mets. Tel: 922.2288. In a residential area west of the Stadium, 15 minutes walk from the city centre. Recommended.
Hotel Exarchia (C), 55 Themistokleous, Exarchia Square. Tel: 360.1256. In a relatively quiet residential area.
Hermes (C), 19 Apollonos. Tel: 323.5514. Plaka.
Imperial (C), 46 Mitropoleos. Tel: 322.7617. Near Plaka.
Hotel Museum (C), 16 Bouboulinas at Tossitsa. Tel: 360.5611. Near a small park behind the Polytechnion.
Hotel Phillipos (C), 3 Mitseon, Makriyianni. Tel: 922.3611. Close to the Acropolis.
Phoebus (C), 12 Peta. Tel: 322.0142. Plaka. One of the best of its class.
Royal (C), 44 Mitropoleos. Tel: 323.4220. Near Plaka.

Cecrops (D), 13 Spyrou Tsagari. Tel: 322.3080. Plaka.
Cleo's (D), 3 Patrou. Tel: 322.9053. Plaka.
Kimon (D), 27 Apollonos. Tel: 323.5223. Plaka.
Orion II Pension (D), 105a Emmanuel Benaki, Lofos Strefi. Tel: 362.8441. Close walk to Exarchia or Omonia, yet quiet.
Phaedra (D), 16 Cheraephondos at Adrianou. Tel: 323.8461. Pleasantly situated in Plaka.

Joseph's House (hostel), 13 Markou Moussouri, Mets. Tel: 923.1204. Near Ardettos and the Stadium.
Residence Pagration (hostel), 75 Damareos, Pangrati. Tel: 751.9530.
Student Traveller's Inn (hostel), 16 Kidathenaion, Plaka. Tel: 324.4808.

There are many other dorm-style places, but they come and go. Ask at a student travel office.
YMCA (XAN), 28 Omirou. Tel: 362.6970.
YWCA (XEN), 11 Amerikis. Tel: 362.4291.
There are **youth hostels** at 1 Agios Meletiou/57 Kipselis, open all year; 87 Alexandras; and 20 Kallipoleos. None of these three are very central or attractive. There is reputedly a new (and more convenient) hostel at Karoulou Street. In any event to avoid pointless travelling around, go to the Greek YHA office at 4 Dragatsaniou, Plateia Klafthmonos, off Stadiou (Tel: 3234.107), where they will reserve you a place by phone.

Camping. Sleeping out rough in Athens is unwise (and illegal). The nearest campsite is the large one at Daphni, near the monastery (20-minute bus ride from Plateia Eleftherias at the end of Euripidou). There are also campsites at Varkiza and Voula, on the coast south of Athens.

RESTAURANTS AND TAVERNAS

There are countless restaurants and tavernas in Athens. You should be able to judge for yourself from the menu, the clientele, etc, which you might like. The monthly magazine *The Athenian* has very full listings if you need help, and the following list is of those establishments which can be safely recommended.

The area most tourists head off to is the Plaka, which is full of tavernas. Many are no longer particularly good value. As a guide, avoid those hawking for trade and look where the Greeks are eating. You could try in fact heading away from the principal streets of Adrianou and Kydathenaion, into such streets as Geronda, Iperidou and Nikodimou, or Thrassilou, Vironos and Lissikratous, where you might do better than the more obvious places.

However we can suggest in *Plaka*:
Damigos, at the junction of Kydathenaion and Adrianou. A friendly basement taverna, speciality bakaliaro (fish in batter), barrelled retsina (closed August).
The Cellar, in Kydathenaion at the corner of Moni Asteriou. Choice of island wines. Evenings only.

Hermion, a restaurant in an alley off Kapnikareas near Adrianou. Quality Greek food outside under tents, quieter than most but more expensive.
Piccolino Taverna, Moni Asteriou between Hatzimichali and Kydathenaion, opposite the church. Good pizzas.
Platanos, 4 Diogenous. Tel: 322.0666. One of the oldest tavernas in Plaka.
Psarra, at the junction of Erotokritou and Erechtheos Streets. Tel: 325.0285. Specialty souvlaki. Guitarist.
Thespis, in Thespidos (extension of Kydathenaion beyond Adrianou). Roof garden. Try tiropitta, fried zucchini, bekri meze (beef in sauce).

In and around *central Athens*:
Delfi, 13 Nikis. Tel: 323.4869. Good value, light meals and grills.
Lengo, 29 Nikis. Good Greek cooking, but expensive.
Flvo's Restaurant, Syntagma on corner of Filellinon. The best ice cream in Greece.
Dionissos Restaurant, opposite the Acropolis in Dionysiou Areopagitou. Great view of the rock.
Socrates' Prison, near entrance to the Acropolis at 20 Mitseon. Traditional taverna; nightly, closed Sundays.
Bouillabaise, 28 Zisimopoulou, behind the Planetarium in Syngrou. Tel: 941.9082. Excellent seafood; open nightly.
Akimopapo (Ugly Duckling), 61 Ionon, Ano Petralona. Country cooking, barrelled wine; nightly, closed Sundays.
Salamandra, 3 Montzarou at Solonos Street. A three-level restaurant in a neoclassical mansion; closed evenings and Sundays in summer.
Gerofinikas, 10 Pindarou, Kolonaki. Famous old restaurant taking its name from the palm tree in the dining room. Expensive.
Rouga, 7 Kapsali, Kolonaki Square. Taverna prices; nightly.
Rodia, 44 Aristippou, Kolonaki, near the Lykavittos funicular. Tel: 722.9883. Atmospheric old house; nightly, closed Sundays.
Dionissos, on Mt Lykavittos. Tel: 722.6374. Spectacular view over Athens.
Balthazar, 27 Tsocha at Vournazou, near US Embassy. Tel: 644.1215. Garden dining; nightly.

Costoiannis Taverna, 37 Zaima, close to the National Archaeological Museum.
Eden, 3 Flessa, Plaka. Tel: 324.8858. Vegetarian restaurant.

In the *Piraeus* area:
Vasilena, 72 Etolikou, Akte Kondili, Piraeus. Tel: 461.2457. Old taverna established in a renovated grocery store; nightly, closed Sundays.
Zorbas, 28 Koumoundourou, Turkolimano/Mikrolimano. Tel: 412. 5501. One of several restaurants along the waterfront at this small port between Athens and Piraeus (get the train to Faliro, then five minutes walk), and a good area for sitting out at lunch.

KAFENEIONS AND BARS

Syntagma Square and Kolonaki Square, packed with café tables, are popular places for sitting out at night, the first international, the second stylishly upper class Greek. **Floca's** and **Zonar's**, both at 9 Panepistimiou near Syntagma are famous cafés (writers, artists, composers, etc), though exhaust fumes from passing traffic overwhelm the pavement ambience and it is best to retire indoors.

Some *cafés* with a difference:
Brettania, Omonia Square. For breakfast at all times of the day and part of the night.
Maccheroncino Café Bistro, 9 Anthimio Gazi (off Stadiou). Best at midnight when the youngsters have gone home and the pianist is playing.
Y Orea Ellada (Beautiful Greece), amongst the chaos of an obscure arcade on Pandrossou, Monastiraki, with a view over Plaka to the Acropolis. Daytime only; Saturday and Sunday to 2.30pm.
De Profundis, 1 Angelikis Hatzimihalis, Plaka. Chic French decor and classical music; closed afternoons.
Tourist Pavilion Café, on Philopappou hill, with the smell of fresh pine and deluxe prices; evenings.

Some recommended *bars*:
Dewar's Club, 7 Glykonos, Dexameni Square, Kolonaki. Tel: 721.5412. From 9pm.
Larry's Bar, 20 Lykavitos, Kolonaki. Tel: 3600.100. From 8.30pm.

The monthly magazine *The Athenian*, available from most kiosks, has an excellent list of sweetshops, ouzeries, pubs, etc.

ENTERTAINMENT

For up-to-date entertainment information and listings, visitors should buy *The Athenian*.

There are *tavernas* with Greek music and dancing, laid on mostly for the benefit of tourists (especially in Plaka), and numerous *clubs and discos*.
Jazz Rock, Ragava Square, off Thespidos, Plaka. Live sessions.
Tiffanys, 134 Adrianou.
Disco 14, Kolonaki Square. Drinks only.
Papagayo, 37 Ioakim Patriarchou. Restaurant also.

Boites are more discreet: intimate places where one or a few performers sing traditional or partisan or modern Greek songs. **Skorpios**, **Zygos** and **Zoom**, all on Kydathenaion in Plaka, are examples.

Bouzoukia are places where Greeks go to blow all their money, by buying whisky and smashing plates at astronomical prices – to the accompaniment of ear-splitting amplified music. These are usually outside central Athens, often near the sea, eg **Agios Kosmas**, opposite the West Airport. Tel: 981.0503.

More conventional *nightclubs*, with striptease and international shows, are the **Las Vegas**, 8 Othonos, Syntagma (Tel: 323.4831) and the **Coronet**, 6 Panepistimiou (Tel: 361.7397). Also some of the luxury hotels put on shows.

A clip-joint near Syntagma: **Love Pub**, 2 Navarchou Nikodimou. Amusing maybe.

Cinemas remain very cheap. During the summer most cinemas are outdoors. Check the daily *Athens News* for programmes.

Cultural events, including *plays*, *films*, also *concerts* are put on by the **British Council**, Kolonaki Square (Tel: 363.3211); the **Hellenic American Union**, 22 Massalias (Tel: 362.9886); and also their French, Italian and German counterparts, but mostly not during the summer. The British Council and the Hellenic American Union both have *libraries* with periodicals, etc, which are open all year, weekday mornings.

The **Athens Centre**, 48 Archimidou,

Pangrati (Tel: 701.2268), is a cultural centre which holds exhibitions, provides Greek language lessons and leads field trips to archaeological sites during the summer. The **Athens Exhibition Centre**, 124 Kifissias, holds diverse exhibitions from sailing and surfing to dolls and toys.

The numerous *art galleries* are listed in *The Athenian* with their exhibitions. However there is little activity in July and August.

For the Athens Festival, Dora Stratou Theatre, Sound and Light on the Pnyx, and so on, see the *Background* chapter.

THINGS TO DO

See the *Changing of the Guard* outside the Parliament building, Syntagma Square, Saturdays, 11am.

Visit the *National Gardens* which remain cool even on the hottest day.

Go to the *Karaghiozi Puppet Show*, summer evenings at 8pm, Lysikratous Square, Plaka – one of the few remaining examples of this famous shadow puppetry.

Wander about the *flea markets* Sunday mornings at Monastiraki and, better value, Piraeus on Odos Alipedou near the metro station.

Visit the *Galatsi Plant Market* along Veikou Street from Dryopidos Street, open Friday to Sunday.

See the *Planetarium* in Syngrou Avenue, Monday to Friday, 9.30 to 2.30, all day Sunday. Save it for the rain.

Walk up *Lykavittos* (or take the funicular) and treat yourself to a meal or drink, watching the sun go down.

Take a bus (No. 224 from Akadimias) to Kaisariani suburb and walk 45 minutes (or taxi) to *Kaisariani monastery*, 11th C, with frescoes, on Mount Hymettos. Tavernas and good walks up top.

Go to *Pendeli*, which also has a monastery, 16th C with frescoes; again good walking and many tavernas.

MUSEUMS AND SITES

Note: The times given below, which anyway are subject to change, are so far as the sites are concerned the summer hours; the hours are shorter in winter.

Acropolis. Daily 8am to 7pm. 250 drachmas.

Agora. Entrance from Thission Square and 24 Adrianou. Daily 9am to 3pm. Sundays and holidays 9.30am to 2.30pm. 150 drachmas includes entrance to museum.

National Archaeological Museum, Patission and Tossitsa Streets. Tel: 821.7717 for up-to-date information on hours. Daily 8am to 7pm. 200 drachmas includes Thera exhibition. Closed Mondays.

Benaki Museum, 1 Koumbari (corner of Vas. Sophias). Tel: 361.1617. Daily 8.30am to 2pm. Closed Tuesdays. 100 drachmas.

Byzantine Museum, 22 Vasillisis Sophias. Tel: 721.1027. Daily 9am to 3pm. Closed Mondays. Sundays and holidays 9.30am to 2.30pm. 150 drachmas.

Museum of Greek Popular Art, 17 Kydathenaion, Plaka. Daily 10am to 2pm. Closed Mondays. Entrance free.

Kanellopoulous Museum, Theorias and Panos Streets, Plaka. Daily 9am to 3pm. Closed Mondays.

Kerameikos, Ermou and Pireos Streets. Daily 9am to 3pm. Price includes entrance to museum (148 Ermou), which is closed Tuesdays.

National Gallery of Art, 46 Vasillisis Sophias. Daily 9am to 3.30pm. Sundays and holidays 10am to 3pm. Closed Mondays. Admission free.

History and Ethnological Museum, Stadiou at Kolokotroni Square. Daily 9am to 2pm. Saturdays and Sundays 9am to 1pm. Closed Mondays and August. Free.

Museum of the City of Athens, Klafthmonos Square, Plaka. 9am to 1.30pm Mondays, Wednesdays and Fridays.

War Museum, Vasillisis Sophias, next to the Byzantine Museum. Tel: 729.0543. Daily 9am to 2pm, free. Closed Mondays.

Goulandris Natural History Museum, 13 Levidou, Kifissia. Daily 9am to 1pm, and 5 to 8pm, 1 to 4pm Sundays and holidays, closed Fridays.

Piraeus Archaeological Museum, 31 Charilaou Trikoupi. Tel: 542.1598. Daily 9am to 3pm, Sundays and holidays 9am to 2pm, closed Tuesdays.

Naval Museum of Greece, Akte Themistokleous, near Zea, Piraeus. Tel: 451.6822. Daily 9am to 12pm, Sundays and holidays 10am to 12pm. Closed Mondays.

SWIMMING POOLS AND BEACHES

Swimming can be an expensive activity in Athens. You can swim at the Athens Hilton if you are not staying there, but it will cost you around 3500 drachmas. Either go to the pool at the Apollon Palace, Kavouri, or use the beach at the Astir Palace, Vouliagmeni, both at a fraction of the price, although a good bus ride away (No. 89 from Leoforos Olgas).

TOURIST INFORMATION

The most obvious source of information is the **National Tourist Office of Greece (NTOG)** which has a desk inside the National Bank of Greece, 2 Karageorgias Servias, Syntagma Square; there is also an office at 4 Stadiou as well as at the airport. The NTOG has brochures, maps (including a useful map of Athens showing banks, post offices, museums, etc) and much travel information.

Really to know what is going on in Athens, buy a copy of *The Athenian* from a kiosk. It contains an excellent guide to the month's events, together with lists of hotels, restaurants, nightspots, shops, markets, and so on. There are two other monthly publications, *Greek Travel Pages* and *Key Travel Pages*, which have detailed travel information. Any travel agent in Athens should have a counter copy for you to look at. The daily newspaper *Athens News*, printed in English like the monthlies, contains world and Greek news chiefly, but also lists of useful information.

In addition there are of course **travel agencies**, and not least **hotels** which will probably have brochures for tours, car hire, etc.

TRAVEL WITHIN ATHENS

There are the usual alternatives: buses, the metro (or electric train), taxis and walking (sometimes the quickest).

Yellow trolley-buses serve the city centre and **blue buses** serve the suburbs. They operate from early in the morning to about 1am and are cheap. You can only get on or off at a bus stop which tells you the number of the service and the destination. Piraeus is reached from Athens by the 70 (blue) bus from Omonia and the very frequent 165 (green) bus from Filellinon (Syntagma). Buses for beaches such as Glyfada and Vouliagmeni leave from Leoforos Olgas at the Zappeion and buses to Sounion and other points in eastern Attica leave from Mavromateon Street (at the southwest corner of Areos Park). See the *Practical Information* section at the end of the next chapter.

The **electric train** runs in a direct line between Kifissia and Piraeus (40 minutes) with stops at Omonia, Monastiraki and other intermediate stations. Again very cheap.

Taxis are also a very inexpensive way to travel around Athens. However the rate per kilometre doubles once you are outside the city limits.

TRAVEL BEYOND ATHENS

Air. The **Athens airport**, known as Elleniko, which is about 10 kms from Syntagma, has two terminals. The West Terminal is exclusively used by Olympic Airways for international and domestic flights. The East Terminal is for foreign airlines. Olympic Airways are the exclusive operator within Greece, and therefore for any internal flight you will be using the West Terminal.

During the summer, domestic flights, particularly those to the islands, can be booked up days and even weeks in advance. It is strongly recommended that you make your bookings as early as possible, eg before getting to Greece. You can collect and pay for your domestic tickets on arrival.

There are flights at least once daily to Alexandroupolis, Heraklion, Thessaloniki, Ioannina, Kavala, Kalamata, Corfu, Kefallonia, Kos, Lemnos, Mykonos, Mitilini, Rhodes, Samos, Santorini (Thera), Skiathos, Chania, Chios, Kithera, Milos and Paros.

There are several flights per week to Larissa, Preveza, Kastoria, Kozani and Zakinthos.

The flights (which are never more than an hour long) are relatively inexpensive. Flying may be the most sensible way to reach some of the further islands, particularly if you do not want to spend a day (or night) at sea. For example the flight to Samos costs only about double the cheapest boat ticket and saves you a 12-hour sea journey. On the other hand, what price the wine-dark sea?

71

The head office of **Olympic Airways** is at 96 Syngrou Avenue (from Syntagma, beyond the Temple of Zeus). Booking offices are at 96 Syngrou (Tel: 9756.811); 6 Othonos, on Syntagma (Tel: 9292.555 for international, 9292.444 for domestic flights); and at the Athens Hilton (Tel: 9292.445).

Other airlines (all on or near Syntagma): British Airways, 10 Othonos (Tel: 3222.521); Pan Am, 4 Othonos (Tel: 3235.242); TWA, 8 Xenofondos (Tel: 3236.831); Air France, 4 Karageorgi Servias (Tel: 3230.501); Lufthansa, 4 Karageorgi Servias (Tel: 3294.1); Qantas, Filellinon and Nikis Streets, on the corner (Tel: 3232.792).

For airport information:
West Terminal (Olympic), telephone: 981.1201.
East Terminal (other airlines), telephone 979.9466.

To and from the airport. West Terminal: Olympic Airways runs its own bus service from 96 Syngrou, leaving every half hour from 6am to midnight; also there is the 133 bus from Othonos. East Terminal: There are two urban bus lines connecting with the city centre; one is the 121 bus from the Olgas Avenue side of the Zappeion between 6.40am and 10.40pm, and the other is the special yellow airport bus from 4 Amalias Avenue (near Syntagma) every 20 minutes from 6am to midnight, after which from May through October there are hourly buses. From Piraeus to the East Terminal there is the 19 bus hourly from Akte Tzelepi, 8am to 8pm, and the 101 from Klissovis Street every 20 minutes, 5am to 10.45pm; to the West Terminal there are buses 107 and 109 from Klissovis also. Allow 30 minutes from Athens or Piraeus. There is a free but infrequent bus between the two terminals.

Taking a taxi can be easiest and should not cost more than 700–800 drachmas between the airport and Athens or Piraeus, and much less between the East and West Terminals.

Train. The Hellenic Railway Organisation (OSE) operates the railway network. The head office is at 1 Karolou Street. Tel: 5222.491. The central ticket office is at 6 Sina (off Akadimias). Tel: 3624.402. Information can also be obtained at the stations or you can dial 145 or 147.

Eurail and Interail passes are valid within Greece. You can also obtain a 20% reduction on return fares within one month, and there are touring cards allowing unlimited travel. Trains within Greece are in any event relatively cheap.

There are two principal stations in Athens: **Stathmos Larissis** for trains to central and northern Greece, and **Stathmos Peloponnisou** for trains to the Peloponnese. The two stations are next to each other in the northwest part of Athens, about 10 minutes walk from Omonia. Trolley-buses 1 and 5 both go there from Syntagma. From Larissis there are for example some 7 or 8 trains a day to Thessaloniki (about 1100 drachmas; 8 hours), 10 or 11 trains to Levadia and Thebes; from Peloponnisou, on the slower narrow gauge railway, there are about 6 trains a day to Patras (about 475 drachmas; 3½ hours), and 5 to such places as Mycenae, Olympia and (in 10 hours) Kalamata.

Bus. There is a much wider bus network than train system. The majority of long-distance buses are operated by private companies (KTEL). In addition there are buses operated by the OSE from the stations of Larissis and Peloponnisou.

The two principal long-distance **KTEL** bus terminals are at:
100 Kifissou Street for buses to the Peloponnese, Epiros, the Ionian islands and Macedonia; this is reached by the 51 bus from the corner of Vilara and Menandrou Streets, near Omonia.
260 Liossion Street for buses to Euboea, central Greece and Thessaly; this is reached by the 24 bus from the Amalias Avenue entrance of the National Gardens, by Syntagma, a half-hour journey.

Information on times and routes can be obtained from the NTOG desk inside the National Bank of Greece, Syntagma Square. Tel: 3222.545.

The **OSE** buses to the Isthmus and the Peloponnese depart from **Stathmos Peloponnisou**; those for the north from **Stathmos Larissis**. Information and booking as for trains. The prices are the same as on KTEL buses.

It is important to arrive early for buses, particularly if you have not yet bought a ticket. They are usually full and can leave early.

Information on buses within Attica will be found at the end of the next chapter.

Boat. The simplest way to obtain information on sailings from Piraeus is from the NTOG desk inside the National Bank of Greece, Syntagma (Tel: 3222.545). Or you can contact Piraeus Port Authority (Tel: 4511.311). Make sure your information is up to date, as times of departure may vary from week to week. Shipping agencies can help, but they tend only to tell you about their own boats. Fares are standard to particular destinations, irrespective of the boat (except for the hydrofoils), although the routes and duration of journey will vary. The cheapest way to travel is deck class (adequate, except possibly at night), and this will cost for example about 1800 drachmas to Crete and 1150 to Paros. It is not necessary to buy a ticket in advance unless you want a cabin (or you are travelling by hydrofoil) – you buy it at the harbourside. However to keep you on your toes (or to blow last night's retsina away) many boats depart quite early, about 7am or 8am.

Many of the boats carry cars.

The easiest way to reach Piraeus is by the electric railway from Omonia or Monastiraki stations. The trains run from 5.30am to midnight, it takes under half an hour and the Piraeus station is a short walk away from the boats. Otherwise take the green bus from the Syntagma end of Filellinon Street or a taxi (no more than 600 drachmas) – but the traffic is at times very heavy.

From Piraeus there are boats daily to Heraklion, Chania, Patmos, Leros, Kalymnos, Kos, Rhodes, Tinos, Mykonos, Paros, Naxos, Sifnos, Serifos, Syros and Thera (Santorini), and several a day to Aegina, Poros, Hydra and Spetses. There are less frequent boats to Chios, Mitilini, Ikaria, Samos, Amorgos, Sikinos, Folegandros, Anafi, Milos, Monemvasia, Karpathos, Kassos, Astipaleia, Nisiros, Simi, Kithnos and Kithera. These boats all depart from the main harbour of Piraeus.

In addition there are departures each day **from Rafina** (opposite Euboea) for Andros, Tinos and Karystos and Marmari on Euboea, also once weekly to Syros. Buses for Rafina leave from Green Park Terminal, Vasilissis Alexandras and Patission Streets, every 20 minutes. For information telephone 0294.2330.

The faster and more expensive **hydrofoil** service leaves from Zea marina at Piraeus (about a 10-minute walk from the railway station), except for the service to Aegina which leaves from the main harbour. Tickets can be bought in Piraeus (at the main harbour for Aegina departures, near Zea for the others: 8 Akte Themistokleous), or in Athens at 2 Karageorgis Servias, by Syntagma. For information call 4527.107. Hydrofoils run daily in summer (weather permitting) to Aegina, Poros, Hydra, Hermioni, Spetses, Porto Heli (all frequently), and to Nafplion, Leonidion, Monemvasia and Kithera (less so). Winter services are reduced. It is sensible to buy tickets in advance, since every passenger has a seat and seating is limited.

Car hire. Agencies include **Avis**, 48 Amalias (Tel: 3224.951–5); **Hertz**, 12 Syngrou (9220.102–4); **Hellascars**, 7 Stadiou (9235.353–9); **Athena**, 32 Amalias (3243.900). There are many other car hire firms in Syngrou and Amalias.

An **international driving licence** is required except for those with a British, Austrian or West German licence.

The **Automobile and Touring Club of Greece (ELPA)**, 2–4 Messogion Avenue (Tel: 7791.615), provides motorists with assistance and information, including free legal advice, international driving licence, insurance, and details on camping and road conditions. Ring 104 for roadside assistance which is free for members of automobile clubs in your own country (otherwise you will have to join ELPA on the spot, at a cost of some 5500 drachmas – and a garage might be cheaper). Ring 174 for ELPA's tourist information (24 hours).

Tours and cruises. There are many companies offering guided bus tours, both to the sites in Athens and to those elsewhere. The leading tour operator is **CHAT**, 4 Stadiou. Others, usually less expensive, include **ABC**, 47 Stadiou; **Hellenic Express**, 17 Filellinon; and **Key Tours**, 2

Ermou.

A half-day tour of Athens, including a guided tour of the Acropolis, will cost up to 1300 drachmas. A one-day visit to Delphi, with lunch, up to 3250 drachmas. And a two-day tour (including accommodation and meals) to Corinth, Mycenae and Epidavros, up to 6500 drachmas. There are also longer tours taking in as much of the country as you like.

The choice is almost unlimited. There are air tours of Crete, Rhodes and Corfu from Athens. A 4-day air tour of Crete and Rhodes might cost about 40,000 drachmas. Then there are sea cruises from Piraeus to Hydra, Poros and Aegina (in a day), Mykonos and Delos in 2 days (around 15,500 drachmas), as well as longer trips through the Aegean to Turkey or Egypt or even the Black Sea. Travel agents will have full details.

TRAVEL AGENTS

There are hundreds of travel agents in Athens; many are situated around Filellinon and Nikis Streets, off Syntagma Square. The big guns however are **American Express**, 2 Ermou Street (Tel: 3244.975); **CHAT Tours**, 4 Stadiou (3222.886); and **Wagons Lits/Thomas Cook**, 2 Karageorgis Servias (3242.281–8).

For youth/student discounts, try along Filellinon Street. **Transalpino**, which offers discount rail fares for those under 26 is at 28 Nikis Street (Tel: 3230.503).

OTHER THINGS

Aliens Bureau (work/residence permits), 9 Halkokondili, Plateia Kaningos. Monday to Friday, 8am to 1pm. Tel: 362.8301.
Athos permits. Ministry of Foreign Affairs, 2 Zalakosta. Monday to Friday, 8am to 1pm.
Banking. National Bank, Syntagma Square; open 7 days a week, 8am to 9pm Monday to Friday, 8am to 8pm Saturday and Sunday.
Bookshops. Compendium Bookshop, 33 Nikis; Eleftheroudakis, 4 Nikis; for second-hand books try Vassiotis, 24 Ifestiou, Monastiraki.
British Council, 17 Kolonaki Square. Tel: 363.3211.
Car repair. For emergency roadside service ring 104 (ELPA).
Health food stores. Propolis, 3 Fidiou Street (between Akadimias and Panepistimiou). Centre for Physical and Spiritual Renewal, 168 Kifissias Avenue.
Laundromats. In Plaka there are two, in Kydathenaion (normal shop hours) and Angelou Yeronda Street near Daedalou (stays open all day and evening).
Lost property, 14 Messogion. Tel: 770.5711.
Mail drop, c/o American Express.
Medical emergency. Dial 166 (First Aid Centre) which will direct you to a hospital, or ring the Tourist Police on 171.
Pharmacies. If closed, they should have a notice in English stating where to find one open. Homoeopathic remedies from the Marinopoulous branches in Patission and Panepistimiou. Herbalist at 19 Pindarou at Skoufa Street.
Police. Dial 100.
Post office. Central Post Office, 100 Eolou, open 8am to 8pm, Monday to Friday; also in Syntagma Square.
Shopping. The main shopping area is around Ermou Street, particularly for shoes and clothing. The Syntagma–Kolonaki area is smarter but more expensive: jewellery, leather goods, imported clothes, etc. Mitropoleos Street has good quality flokatis and woven goods. Monastiraki is a huge bazaar area, with handicrafts, etc, while Omonia is the down-market end of town with shops selling just about everything.
Sport. There is usually a very full list carried in *The Athenian*. Golf course at Glyfada (18 holes, A class). Tel: 894.6820. You can play tennis at the Panellinios Athletic Club, Evelpidon and Mavromateon Streets.
Telegraph office. Athinas Street; open 24 hours.
Telephone (OTE). Offices at 65 Stadiou and Patission/28 Oktovriou; open 24 hours.
Tourist Police, 7 Leoforos Syngrou. Open 24 hours, or dial 171.

EMBASSIES AND CONSULATES

Embassies are indicated by E, consulates by C.
British (E,C), 1 Ploutarchou. Tel: 723.6211.

United States (E,C), 91 Vasilissis Sofias. Tel: 7212.951.
Australia (E,C), 15 Messogion. Tel: 360.4611.
Canada (E,C), 4 Ioannou Gennadiou. Tel: 7239.511.
France (C), 7 Vasilissis Sofias. Tel: 361.1664.
German Federal Republic (E,C), 3 Karaoli and Demetriou. Tel: 722.4801.
Ireland (E,C), 7 Vasileos Konstantinou. Tel: 723.2771.
Italy (E), 2 Sekeri. Tel: 361.1722.
Netherlands (E,C), 5–7 Vasileos Konstantinou. Tel: 723.9701.
New Zealand (E,C), 15–17 An. Tsoha, Ambelokipi. Tel: 641.0311.
Sweden (E), 7 Vasileos Konstantinou. Tel: 722.4501.
Switzerland (E,C), 2 Iassiou. Tel: 723.0364.
Turkey (E), 8 King George B. Tel: 724.5915.
Yugoslavia (E), 106 Vasilissis Sophias. Tel: 777.4344.

AROUND ATTICA

Monasteries at Kaisarianí and Dáphni

Only about 5 kms from the centre of Athens, up the slopes of Hymettos and near the source of the Ilissos, the 11th C monastery of **Kaisarianí** sits tucked away amidst the shade of plane and cypress trees at the head of a ravine. A fountain just above was reputed in classical times to cure sterility, and the spot was made famous by Ovid in his *Ars Amatoria*. The Germans favoured the ravine during the Second World War for executing hostages; Athenians favour the fountain today for washing their cars. The well-restored convent buildings and the church with its 17th and 18th C frescoes are now a national monument.

The more famous monastery near Athens is **Dáphni**, 10 kms west on the way to Elefsis, following the route of the ancient Sacred Way and passing the litter of 20th C life: motels, snack bars, gas stations; also, more endurably, a leper colony. The surprise is that in its leafy gardens behind battlemented walls the monastery entirely eludes the encroaching present. Founded in the 5th or 6th C, it stands on the site of a sanctuary of Apollo (deriving its name from the laurels – *daphnai* – sacred to the god). The very pleasant flagged courtyard is lined by low cloisters dating from the 13th to 15th C; the entrance to the excellent 11th C Byzantine church is just beyond, its exonarthex especially satisfying for its uncommon incorporation not just of ancient fragments but of entire architectural features such as Ionic columns into the overall design of pointed arches and crenellations.

The mosaics   The mosaics within, jewels of this supreme art of Byzantium, are rivalled in Greece only by those at Osios Loukas and Thessaloniki. In the dome the *Pantokrator*, Christ Almighty, glares to the right and a great gap yawns between his fore and middle fingers as though with mind and body he is struggling to keep the cosmos from cracking apart. The *Baptism* is delicately worked to show Christ's body shimmering through the translucent waters of the Jordan; and Mary, in the *Annunciation* and in the *Nativity*, is at once graceful and resplendent in her night-blue robe illuminated in gold. The four mosaics on the pendentives show Christ as meek and mild; as an infant, as a young man – as incomplete. The Pantokrator, then, comes as a great whack: Christ with the gloves off; terrible and awesome in his revelation and power.

Apart from these, the finest mosaics are in the choirs: the *Entry into Jerusalem*, the *Crucifixion*, the *Resurrection*, and *Thomas*.

DAPHNI CHURCH

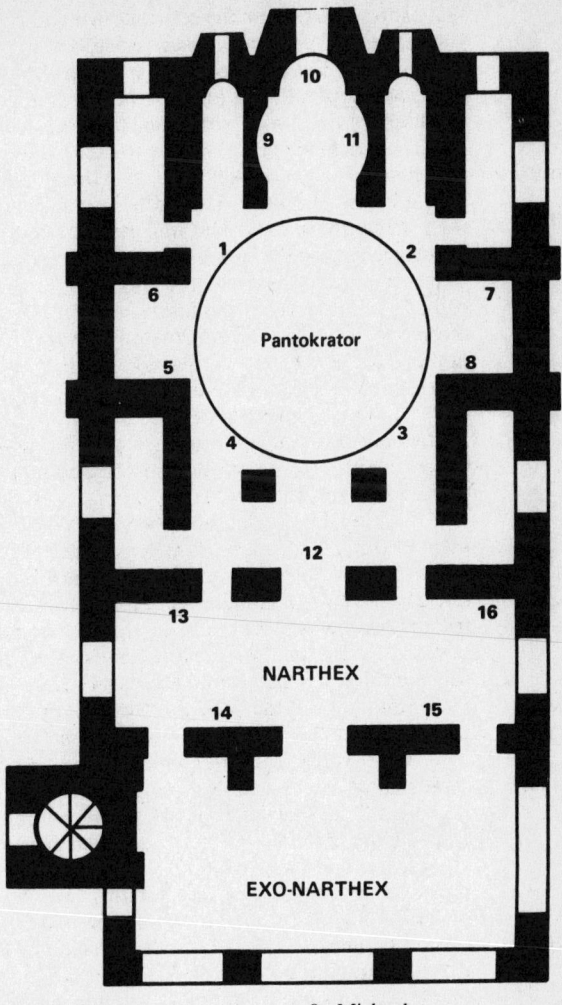

1. Annunciation
2. Nativity
3. Baptism
4. Transfiguration
5. Entry into Jerusalem
6. Crucifixion
7. Resurrection
8. Thomas
9. Michael
10. Virgin with Child
11. Gabriel
12. Assumption of the Virgin
13. Last Supper
14. Judas' betrayal
15. Prayer of Joachim and Anna
16. Presentation of the Virgin

Eléfsis

From Mycenaean through Roman times Elefsis (Eleusis) was the goal of millions of pilgrims who came here to be initiated into the Mysteries. Today the mystery is gone. The town, 22 kms from Athens, anciently the birthplace of Aeschylus, is now a centre of heavy industry, occasionally dramatic when blazing gas erupts from tall pipes into the night sky. The site, on a low rocky hill, is a jumble of excavations of interest to the archaeologist but baffling and without charm for the layman – and in any case, badly affected by pollution.

The Mysteries

A lesser Eleusinia took place in Athens, on the banks of the Ilissos, in late February and early March, the celebrants then being accepted as initiates, or Mystai, to the Greater Eleusinia held in September. In the course of the nine days' proceedings of the Greater Eleusinia, the Mystai walked from Athens to Elefsis the first day, returning to Athens on the last. This part of the ceremony was public and full of pomp. But at Elefsis, in the high-walled and windowless Telesterion within Demeter's sanctuary, 'the holy things' were shown and 'the unutterable words' were enacted, and the Mystai were pledged to a secrecy so faithfully kept that in the course of 1700 years nothing of the culminating revelation found its way into record.

Yet it is possible to guess at the form of the ceremony and to appreciate its import. It was probably like a medieval Passion play but performed mute and therefore all the more engaging to the imagination. The level at which it was taken, and the precise interpretation put upon it, would have been a matter of individual response. Certainly the response could be profound. Pindar wrote that 'he who has seen the holy things and goes in death beneath the earth is happy: for he knows life's end and he knows too the new divine beginning'; while Cicero, 400 years later, said 'the greatest gift of Athens to mankind and the holiest is the Eleusinian Mysteries'. Peisistratos, Kimon, Pericles, Hadrian and Marcus Aurelius all contributed to the magnificence of the sanctuary with new and greater walls and buildings.

Legend of Demeter and Persephone

It was anciently accepted that the cult was founded by Demeter (literally Earth Mother), goddess of agriculture in the Olympian scheme. While searching for her abducted daughter Kore (Persephone), she paused at Elefsis and was told by the king's son Triptolemos that Kore had been carried off to the underworld by Hades. Demeter at once put a curse upon the land, forbidding trees to bear fruit, crops to grow, until mankind was extinguished. Zeus intervened with his brother, commanding Hades to return Kore. But she had eaten a pomegranate beneath the earth; she had tasted the food of the dead, Hades said, and must stay. A compromise was reached: Kore would live nine months in the world with her mother, three months underground with Hades as his queen, and life would flourish, then wither, and then be born again in turn. To Triptolemos, Demeter gave wheat seeds, a wooden plough and a winged chariot to travel about the earth teaching mankind the blessings of agriculture.

In Homer both Persephone and Demeter are mentioned but not linked. That the queen of the underworld should be brought back to the land of the living by a grieving mother was a later invention, answering a growing need amongst Greeks for a doctrine of the soul otherwise lacking in the Olympian religion. The late Egyptian myth of Isis and Osiris grappled with the same question, and finally when a young man was crucified outside Jerusalem's walls, a doctrine incorporating and satisfying this Eastern Mediterranean quest was launched with considerable success upon the world.

Attica's Southern Coast

Beaches

The coast road from Athens to Sounion passes the airport and just beyond comes to **Glyfáda** (17 kms) with numerous hotels and sandy beaches crammed with Athenians escaping the stifling city heat. At 20 kms is **Voúla**, also a seaside resort, though smaller. **Vouliagméni**, at 25 kms, has the finest beaches, well-developed by the NTOG with all facilities. It is a fashionable place for wealthier Athenians to summer with many luxury flats to rent. There are no hotels under B class. All of these beaches can be reached from Leoforos Olgas at the Zappeion by bus.

The road winds along the rocky and beautiful coastline, passing the bay and (2 kms inland) village of Anavissos where the marvellous kouros now in the National Archaeological Museum was found. At 70 kms at the southeastern extremity of Attica the Temple of Poseidon perches high on its cliff and outstares the sea.

Temple of Poseidon

Soúnion was a lookout post for the Athenian navy; the temple dedicated to the god of the sea. For sailors running wheat down from the Black Sea or from Egypt across the open Mediterranean, Poseidon's gleaming columns were the final landfall with a last tack along the sheltered Attic coast to home. The temple was built by Kallikrates in 444 BC, immediately after the Hephaistion. Twelve Doric columns still stand: back in the days when a man could carve his name where he damn well pleased, these columns were a favourite target; they are wormed with lettering, including BYRON by that arch-graffiti artist of the Mediterranean.

Apart from graffiti, Byron also wrote poetry:
Place me on Sunium's marbled steep,
    Where nothing, save the waves and I,
May hear our mutual murmurs sweep;
    There, swan-like, let me sing and die:
A land of slaves shall ne'er be mine –
Dash down yon cup of Samian wine!

Attica's Eastern Coast

Silver Mines The land, however, or rather the mines beneath it, toiled with slaves throughout the 5th C BC: just up the coast is **Lavrion** whose silver mines earned Athens the surplus that financed the construction of its fleet in time to counter the Persian attack; the fleet that then ensured Athens' imperial grandeur. During the period of their greatest output, the mines are estimated to have employed the labour of 30,000 slaves.

Sanctuary of Artemis The road north from Sounion and Lavrion passes through Markopoulou, a market town with vineyards surrounding and a reputation for good retsina. The Sanctuary of Artemis Vravrona on the Athenian acropolis has its origins 5 kms towards the coast from here, at **Vravrón**. Iphigeneia and Orestes were said to have fled from Tauris in the Crimea with a primitive wooden statue of Artemis, and founded her cult here. It seems that an earlier bear-goddess cult was incorporated; at any rate, every four years girls of Attica between five and ten years old came here dressed in saffron robes and impersonated bears. The foundations of the sanctuary of Artemis and near it a cave venerated as the tomb of Iphigeneia are evident, and below them several columns of a Doric temple.

At dawn on 12 September 490 BC, 9000 Athenians and 1000 Plataians attacked 30,000 Persian soldiers on the plain of **Marathón**. Within a few hours 6400 Persians lay dead at the loss of only 192 Athenians. Athenian courage gave the lie to Persian invincibility and decided the fate of Europe for the next 2400 years. **Athenian burial mound** The mound under which the Athenian dead were buried is scratchily covered with grass in spring; by summer it is a bare brown pile of dirt worn by tourists. But from the top there is a fine view over the plain, green and cultivated with olives and probably not so different now than it was. Behind are the mountains.

The battle The Athenians showed daring from the start. They had left their fortified Acropolis to fight on the beaches, though they now waited four days on the mountain slopes for Spartan reinforcements. The Persian cavalry and archers, combining with their larger infantry, would have proved fatal to an Athenian attack across level ground. Thinking the issue would not be resolved here, on the fifth day the Persians embarked their cavalry to advance on Athens by sea, sending their infantry forward to cover the operation. At that moment Miltiades, Spartan help or no, sent his men racing down the slopes and quickly under the Persian arrows to engage in close combat. The Athenian centre was kept purposely weak while the wings were reinforced. The Persians resisted the Athenian centre but the momentum of the wings soon engulfed them on either side and to the rear. The Persians panicked, scattered, and were beaten into the marshes and the sea.

The remainder of the Persian force now sailed round Sounion to land at Phaleron, but Miltiades had brought his army back to Athens by forced march and stood ready to meet the enemy again for the second time. Instead the Persians fled. Courage, intelligence, and that astonishing burst of energy – 10,000 men marching 37 kms in full armour after fighting one battle to fight, if need be, another – overwhelmed Persian morale and announced the spirit of the civilisation that entered into manhood that day. Aeschylus was one of the soldiers at Marathon; it was the moment in his life of which he was most proud.

Temples of Themis and Nemesis

Difficult of access and unviolated, **Rhamnous** is the most delightful of the minor archaeological sites in Attica. It lies 26 kms further up the coast from Marathon, the ruins of its two temples romantically lost upon an overgrown plateau above the sea, with good swimming below the site. The smaller temple was dedicated to Themis, goddess of law, custom and equity. The larger temple, built by Kallikrates in 436 BC, was dedicated to Nemesis, the goddess who doled out happiness to the miserable and misery to the happy. Part of the entablature of the Temple of Nemesis has been reconstructed on the site.

PRACTICAL INFORMATION

Some additional sites worth visiting are also mentioned here. Roads go to or close to all the sites listed, but buses sometimes stop short of them and you may have to walk the last part. It is worth checking beforehand either with the NTOG, the bus station, or the information telephone numbers given.

KAISARIANI
Travel
Bus from Kaningos Square (information: 321.3571), or bus 224 from Akadamias.

Activities
There are several good tavernas in the suburb of Kaisariani, then by foot (45 minutes) or taxi to the monastery, excellent for picnics and walks.

MONI PENDELI
A similar excursion to Kaisariani is to a monastery on the side of Mt Pentelikon called Moni Pendeli. Founded in 1578, the chapel has 17th C paintings.

Travel
Bus from Kaningos Square (information 804.1765).

Activities
At the bus terminus near the monastery there are tavernas, also a hotel, Achillion (C). Good walking. You can see the ancient quarries, and also reach one of the summits.

PHYLE
4th C BC Athenian fortress which guarded the routes from Thebes to Athens.

Travel
Bus from Plateia Vathis to the village of Fili (several good tavernas). The fortress is 2 hours away on foot. The road continues to Moni Kliston, a picturesque monastery founded in the 14th C.

DAPHNI
Travel
Frequent buses from Eleftherias Square.

Activities
Tourist pavilion for refreshments; also a camping-ground. The Wine Festival takes place in the evenings from mid-July to early September, with tastings, folk dancing, etc (tickets at the entrance).

ELEFSIS
Travel
Same as for Daphni (about a 45-minute journey).

Site/Museum
9am to 3pm daily; Sundays 10am to 4pm; closed Tuesdays. The museum has helpful models of the ancient buildings.

Accommodation
Melissa (C), Stegi (D).

SOUTH COAST BEACHES
Travel
Buses to Glyfada, Voula, Vouliagmeni and Varkiza leave from Leoforos Olgas.

GLYFADA
Accommodation
Numerous hotels, including Astir (L); Atrium, Palace (opposite beach) (A); Emmantina (opposite beach), Miranda, Florida, Delfini (B); Beau Rivage (opposite beach), Themis (C); Evriali (D).

Food
Many good fish restaurants on the harbour, especially Psaropoulos; otherwise try Andonis, 22 Armenidos; Kyra Antigoni, 54 Pandoras; or, more expensive and in an old mansion by the water, Glafkos, for its seafood.

Activities
Glyfada possesses an 18-hole golf course. Tel: 894.6820 (open to visitors; club hire).

VOULA
Accommodation
Hotels include Voula Beach (A); Atlantis, Plaza (B); Rondo (opposite beach) (C); Miramare (D). There is a campsite.

Food
For fish, Smaragdi on the seafront.

VOULIAGMENI
Accommodation
Astir Palace (opposite beach) (L); Greek

Coast (opposite beach) (A); Strand, Hera (B). There are no cheaper hotels than B.

Food
For expensive international cuisine, Moorings (by the marina); then for seafood To Liminaki, Vakhou Street, and Lambros (opposite the harbour).

VARKIZA
Accommodation
Hotels include Glaros (opposite beach) (A); Stefanakis (C). There is a campsite.

SOUNION
Travel
There are two routes: 1. by the coast road (1½ hours), buses from Plateia Egyptou (approximately hourly); 2. by the inland route (the Mesogeia), buses from Odos Mavromateion (also approximately hourly, but the journey takes longer). Information: 821.3203.

Site
9am to sunset daily; Sundays from 10am. There is a Tourist Pavilion for refreshments, swimming on the beach below.

Accommodation
Cape Sounion Beach, Egeon (A); Surf Beach Club (B); Saron (C). There is a camping-ground.

VRAVRON
Travel
Bus from Plateia Egyptou to Markopoulo (frequent, in about one hour), and then local bus or walk (6 kms) to site, or take local bus to Porto Rafti on the coast and walk by track (8 kms).

Site museum
Helpful models of the ancient site. Closed Tuesdays.

Accommodation
Vraona Bay (A), on the shore. Also, at Porto Rafti (beautiful bay, good swimming), several tavernas and hotels, Artemis (A); Korali (C).

RAFINA
For connections to Euboea, Andros and Tinos.

Travel
Frequent buses from Odos Mavromateion.

Accommodation and Food
Avra (C); Akti (D). Good fish restaurants.

MARATHON
Travel
Frequent buses from Odos Mavromateion to near the Sorós, the Athenian burial mound.

Museum
About 3 kms from the mound, at Vrana, contains neolithic and later finds from the area including pottery from the Sorós and the tomb of the Plataeans (near Vrana).

Accommodation and Food
Near Soros on the coast, Marathon (C); further south, Golden Coast (B). Hotels also at the resorts of Agios Andreas and Mati. Campsites at Skinias and Nea Makri. There are tavernas on the coast near the Soros.

Swimming
Magnificent beach at Skinias, but crowded at weekends.

RHAMNOUS
Travel
Bus from Plateia Egyptou for Agia Marina, then about a 2-km walk to the site.

Site
Daily 8.30am to 12.30pm, 4pm to 6pm; Sundays and holidays 9am to 3pm.

Swimming
Good swimming in secluded coves below the site.

AMPHIARAION
North of Rhamnous, the sanctuary of Amphiaraos, an oracle and spa, in an attractive wooded site, with a small museum.

Travel
Infrequent buses from Plateia Egyptou in about an hour. Or half-hour walk from Kalamos (more frequent buses). Information: 821.3203. (Agioi Apostoli, on the coast 5 kms from Kalamos, is also reachable by frequent buses from Egyptou, and has hotels and tavernas.)

THE ISLANDS OF THE ARGO-SARONIC

As well as visiting some of the places easily reached by land from Athens, consider the islands which lie, at most, just a few hours' sailing time south of Piraeus: Aegina, Poros, Hydra and Spetsai. Any of them are suitable for day-trips or longer stays and just the voyage itself, through the narrow blue waters separating the islands from the stark mountains of the Argolid, is an eye-filling experience.

Aegina

An unpretentious island and the nearest of the four to Athens, Aegina (Aígina) is on the tourist route for its Temple of Aphaia but is otherwise commonly underrated. Shaped on the map like an upside down triangle, its southern point is marked by the magnificent cone of Mt Oros, the highest peak in these islands and of volcanic origin, visible on a clear day from the Athenian acropolis. The centre and eastern side of the island is mountainous; a gently-sloping fertile plain runs down to the western extremity where Aegina town overlays in part the ancient capital of the island. Pericles, brooding out across the Saronic Gulf, called Aegina 'the eyesore of Piraeus', a purely political rather than aesthetic judgement, for in contour and variety the island is well-endowed, and plentiful today in pines, pistachios, olives and citrus fruits. Pindar celebrated this 'beloved city', this 'city thronged with strangers, the Dorian island, Aegina', which kept 'glory perfect from the beginning and is sung of many for her shaping of heroes'.

A Mediterranean power

When the world was small and a city or an island could aspire to be a Great Power, Aegina, strategically situated between the Peloponnese and Attica, looking out upon the Aegean and all the Mediterranean beyond, became a great and wealthy trading state, with shipyards, fleets and a sophisticated banking system, outstanding athletes, sculptors and temple-builders. In the 7th C BC Aegina was the first place in Europe to use coinage, and such was the prestige of its currency that its silver coins stamped with a tortoise were readily accepted throughout the known world. Its merchants set up a temple on the Nile and sailed as far west as Spain. The island was a centre of Greek art and was renowned for its pottery and bronze-founding. At Salamis in 480 BC it was the Aeginetan fleet that was awarded the laurels after the Persian rout.

But Pericles saw Aegina, her fleet and her Dorian ties with Sparta, as a threat to Athens' burgeoning maritime empire. In 457 BC and again at the beginning of the Peloponnesian War the Athenians defeated the Aeginetans at sea, on the second occasion ruthlessly expelling the island's entire population after first hacking off their thumbs lest even from exile the Aeginetans might return upon their enemies with spears and bows.

Just as little remains of ancient Aegina, so it is difficult on this pleasant island to imagine the air once filled with the clamour of battle and the screams and weeping of defeat. But in the most silent hour of Aegina's scented nights you may hear those sounds echoing between the harbour and the mountains, incongruous, sad and startling, a civilisation ripped from the pages of history.

The voyage from Piraeus

Frequent ferries pass through Piraeus harbour and clear the Akte peninsula to port with the Bay of Phaleron – where the Persian fleet was beached the evening before the Battle of Salamis – sweeping away to the airport beyond. To starboard extends the long, scrubby island of **Salamis** itself and between it and the belching smokestacks of Elefsis is the narrow dog's leg channel where the Greek fleets lured and broke the pursuing Persians that August morning nearly 2500 years ago. Out in the open water, small silvery fish leap high in the air from the ferry's churning wake, some to be caught in the smiling beaks of seagulls wheeling, plunging and dancing behind.

Aegina's acropolis

Just before the port, atop a promontory which served as the acropolis of Aegina from Mycenaean through classical times, stands a single snapped-off Doric column, all that remains above foundation level of the *Temple of Apollo*. From the sea the position is not impressive, but to stand on the very point of that promontory, especially as the sun is setting over the Peloponnese, is to enjoy one of the grandest views in Greece, Mt Oros behind you, the great mountains of the Argolid lying off to the left, and before them **Anghístri**, an island inhabited by Albanians which can be reached from Aegina port by motor launch. The sugarloaf of the Acrocorinth is just discernable ahead, while sweeping off to the right are the Megarid, the island of Salamis and the ring of mountains round Athens.

The harbour

There are harbours more pretty in Greece, but the port here is delightful for its busyness, its sailing boats in summer, brightly painted caiques, and on the quayside the tiny chapel of St Nicholas, beaming white in the sunshine. To the left as you sail in is the *ancient military port*, now a bathing area, dredged and protected by a breakwater built during the Greek War of Independence by the American Philhellene, Samuel Gridley Howe (later married to Julia Ward Howe, authoress of *The Battle Hymn of the Republic*), in part to provide work for the starving Greek refugees from Egypt, Asia Minor and Turkish-occupied Greece who were pouring into the little town which briefly in the late 1820s was the capital of the new nation.

Aegina town possesses a few undistinguished churches, lacking in rich Orthodox ornament and musty atmosphere (though left off the Aphaia road, 15 minutes out of town, is the 13th C *Omorfi Ekklesia* with well-preserved frescoes), and a new *museum* on the acropolis site containing some broken and badly worn sculptures from the pediments of the Temple of Aphaia (the best were taken to Munich) and much smashed pottery – a collection which emphasises by its skimpiness what is evident elsewhere around the island: Athenian destruction, Venetian neglect, the butchery in 1537 by an Ottoman landing party under Barbarossa of the entire male population, the women and children carried off to slavery, and finally the depredations of 19th C culture vultures.

But though largely shorn of visible evidence of its history, there is the island itself, its rich cultivation, varied topography, and a hardworking, prosperous population of fishermen, farmers and merchants who feel near enough to the bright lights of Athens not to want to abandon their homes as has happened on so many other islands. And in the security of their well-being they are not obliged to fawn upon the tourist trade for their living, though in summertime Aegina is a favourite day-trip for Athenians wanting an afternoon swim and an evening meal on the harbour front before catching the last crowded ferry home. Aegina is a workaday place with fishermen back from a night at their nets selling their catches at the covered fish market, caiques over from the Peloponnese loaded with melons and courgettes for sale, bed and furniture makers, grocers and butchers in the backstreets, and bored guards puffing cigarettes outside the prison, formerly a museum, and originally an orphanage built by Capodistria, the first president of Greece, which stands hot and white beyond the town.

Visitors to the island intent on improving themselves make for either the *Monastery of Agios Nectarios* or the Temple of Aphaia. It is Greeks who make for the former, some of them while still on the boat already thumbing through their Bibles and mumbling prayers, leaving it to foreigners to consult mere guide books for revelations on the pagan temple.

Agios Nectarios Nectarios is the most recent of Orthodox saints, though how he became one is unclear as the Orthodox church had not canonised anyone for hundreds of years and the procedure for doing so was forgotten. Still, just one look at old Nectarios (he only died in the 1920s) on any local postcard or lapel button, his stern features and magnificent white beard, is enough to convince anyone that this was a man to be reckoned with, as now some reckon with God through him. Following the Aphaia road out of town you slowly climb into the mountains and halfway across the island alight by a taverna and a souvenir shop, and a large hotel and yet larger church. The Nectarios business is booming. The saint himself has been embalmed and is well concealed within a stone sarcophagus. An old woman takes you round his rooms, left as they were when he passed on to better things, leaving his collection of seashells behind.

The monastery stands on a hill across from another littered with the remains of more than 20 churches and monasteries. These once dotted the precipitous streets of the old chora, the capital of the island from the 9th C to 1826, built high and inland as a fruitless defence against attack, for it was twice destroyed by Barbarossa and once by the Venetians. When the Turks were thrown off the island in the 1820s the inhabitants of **Palaiochora** came down to the port, lugging the stones of their houses with them but leaving their churches behind.

Every year the islanders celebrate the Assumption of the Virgin (15 August) by climbing, either from here or further back from Agioi Asomatoi, the mountain (on the right-hand side of the road as you come from town) rising above Palaiochora. On its peak is a small white chapel. Beyond, set in a bowl green or gold with wheat and ringed by peaks, is the *Monastery of Panagia Chrysoleontissa*. Goats, chickens and peacocks wander peacefully in its grounds; a Shangri-La entirely removed from sight and everyday contact with the world around. The church should be visited for its remarkable ikonostasis. The monastery once owned a third of the island; since 1935 it has been inhabited by no more than 14 nuns who on any day of the year will offer you accommodation for the night.

Temple of Aphaia

Further along the road, amidst fragrant pinewoods at the northeast point of the island high above the Saronic is the *Temple of Aphaia*, superior to Sounion and Lindos for its magnificent panorama. Built in celebration of the victory at Salamis, the temple was dedicated to the protector of women who presumably realised that need after narrowly escaping the clutches of lustful Minos, fleeing Crete, and reasserting herself as a local goddess on Aegina. She seems to have been a version of the goddess Artemis and was worshipped in Sparta under that name, elsewhere as Dictynna or Britomart, figuring in Edmund Spenser's *The Faerie Queene* as 'Britomartis a Lady knight, in whome I picture Chastity'. Her nine-month pursuit by Minos, says Robert Graves in *The White Goddess*, is 'the basis of the Coventry legend of Lady Godiva. The clue is provided by a miserere-seat in Coventry Cathedral, paralleled elsewhere in Early English grotesque woodcarving which shows what the guide-books call "a figure emblematic of lechery": a long-haired woman wrapped in a net,' – Dictynna means a net – 'riding sideways on a goat and preceded by a hare'. For all that, the feeling of the temple is masculine, with the heaviness and power of late archaic

Lady Godiva

architecture and unusual for its two storeys. The pedimental sculptures depicting combats before the walls of Troy are now in Munich's Glyptothek, while an earlier group discovered buried are in the National Archaeological Museum in Athens (though they may soon be in Aegina's own new museum).

The road twists down to what was once the little village of **Agia Marina** on a beautiful bay, now fast becoming a German package holiday centre, a thick film of Ambre Solaire upon the water.

More secluded swimming is to be had at Marathon, on the road between Aegina town and the fishing village of **Perdika**, or off the rocks of the islet of **Moní** reached from Perdika by launch. Also from Marathon, or from Agioi Asomatoi (on the Aphaia road), the three-hour ascent of *Mt Oros* (531 metres) can be made; or more directly from Perdika, in half that time reaching the summit from where there is a commanding view of the island seemingly rising from a vast lake almost entirely encircled by coastline.

Highest lookout in the Argo-Saronic

The Méthana Peninsula and Póros

The next port of call is at **Méthana**, frequented (if at all) for its sulphur springs, huddled beneath the terraced hillsides of a bulbous extension of the Peloponnese. From here, or further on from Galata, opposite Poros, you can backtrack along the north coast of the Argolid to Epidavros (though with some difficulty if journeying by bus as the schedules are not always convenient), or more easily you can visit the traces of ancient **Troezen**, birthplace of Theseus, whose wife Phaedra fell in love with his bastard son Hippolytos as told in the tragedies of Euripides and Racine.

The boat now threads its way through a hairpin strait and puts in at the island of **Póros**, linked by proximity but often contrasted to the island of Hydra, like unidentical twins. Poros is less commercialised than Hydra, less trendy, more visited by vacationing Greeks. Less commercialised it may be, but as you step off the boat a bustle of waiters pounce upon you (the waiters on Hydra have enough business already!), and the presence of motor cars comes as a mild shock after days of seeing only donkeys clambering up the steep stepped streets of Hydra. The internal combustion engine and **Galata** only a stone's throw away on the Poloponnese shoreline create also the impression that Poros is not quite an island.

On the other hand you can climb to the *Monastery of Zoodochos Pigi* which lies on a hillside among pine trees to the east of the town. There is a beach below which can be reached by boat from Poros town. From the monastery the vestigial ruins of the *Temple of Poseidon* situated on a saddle between two hilltops can be reached by foot in about 1½ hours. Galata is opposite, olive trees cover the mainland hills, dark mountains rise behind them.

Hydra

If Hydra (Ídra) is to be faulted, it can only be for the large number of tourists who show up over Easter and during the summer. The town itself and the landscape all around it is strikingly beautiful. One of the peculiarities of tourists is that they charge about en masse like lemmings, and here they are very trendy lemmings indeed: elegant French boys reeking of eau de Cologne; English yacht-owners who never go to sea, conspicuously drinking Martinis on their poops; sunburnt Swedish girls painfully ensconced at café tables; Adonis-like artists displaying themselves before wretched canvases; armies of Americans disembarking from cruise ships; all of them compacted along the harbour front lined with commercial gyp-joints, catered to by humourless waiters. Not as bad as St Tropez, but going that way.

But the higher reaches of the town and the hills beyond remain surprisingly untouched, charming and full of colour. Walking up through the maze of steep lanes, the clean air is filled with the varying scents of flowers, dung, the sea and cooking. Donkeys' hooves grip the cobbled streets; vistas of harbour, town and surrounding hillsides change at every pause. Doorways of mahogany or brilliant blue, marble architraves, brass hand-shape knockers, and in springtime flowers everywhere, sometimes growing right out of the walls and rock.

The harbour The Hydra you see today was settled by Greeks escaping from the Turkish occupation of the Peloponnese. Her maritime power guaranteed her wealth and independence: Little England she was called, and flourished into the 19th C with a population of 16,000. Approaching from Poros through the narrow stretch of water dividing the island from the Peloponnese, the town is invisible until the last moment when a break in the coastline reveals her horseshoe harbour between two headlands mounted with gun emplacements. Climbing sharply back against the hillsides are the glistening houses, the occasional windmill, cubes of white, but also dashes of red, ochre, pale blue, green and turquoise. Now with a population of only 3000, many of them foreign writers and artists, you notice old abandoned houses crumbling in the vegetation above the town.

The island of Hydra is quite large, but as it is mountainous and without roads, the only settlement is the small port of Hydra. So it is very easy to get away from it all just by turning your back on the harbour and walking uphill. It is typical of the Greek mania for putting a church on every likely spot of land that on this depopulated island there are 366 churches

Easter on Hydra

and monasteries. Easter is a marvellous time to be here, when the island takes on the sombre mood of the Passion and then explodes with joy and festivity at the Resurrection.

Walking up the hillside directly away from the town along a steep and rocky path you come to a grey-walled, red-tiled church atop the hillcrest; a strenuous walk in the heat of the day: do it in the morning or late afternoon, but not so late that you are forced to inch your way uncertainly down in the darkness. Climbing these hills you are surrounded by the sound of a thousand ringing bells attached to unseen donkeys, lambs, horses and goats, loudest in the evening as the flocks are brought in, an ancient music as though the hillsides themselves are singing in the still air. From the church you can see the open sea across the far side of the island, and to the left on a low hill sits the *Monastery of Agia Tria*, its white walls surrounded by huddled stables in which the musical flocks spend the night. A sign on the door reads: 'Women and improperly dressed men are utterly refused admission to the monastery'. On this Saturday before Easter Sunday the monastery hums with chanting. Dry with thirst, you knock and are greeted silently by a startled monk who disappears and returns with a cold glass of water and a Turkish delight handed to you on a silver tray. You drink, watch the sun set over the black mountains of the Peloponnese, listen to the last tinkling of the goats and stumble in darkness down the thorny hillsides back into Hydra where the smell of roast lamb and a sense of expectancy announce the imminent celebration of a miracle.

On Good Friday the church bells had tolled and all of Hydra settled into quiet mourning. The atmosphere went deeper than convention. The pain of thorns, the sour taste of vinegar, the slow heaving death upon the Cross were worn into people's countenances. Now on Saturday a subtle shift in mood and mounting activity as red Easter eggs and long white candles disappear from shops and stalls while tavernas prepare lambs over bright wood fires. Black-robed priests come down from hilltop monasteries carrying bundles of palm fronds which are arched across the streets and interwoven with coloured lights. Mourning has been supplanted by tense expectation, crowds gather around the churches, and you make your way into the stark white courtyard of *Panagia Faneromeni*, the church that stands right on the harbour front.

The night is black and still but here warm chants roll along the dark-timbered nave, richly carved and bossed with gold, a final midwifery of Easter. As midnight chimes from the tall clocktower the bishop emerges into the courtyard and from a bower of palms calls out 'Christ is risen!' and every face in the gathering flushes with joy at the miracle renewed. A single candle brought from the altar lights another and each in turn carries the message of rebirth from candle to candle in outstretched hands until throughout the courtyard and its stairs and balconies and out into the harbour front itself thousands of candles flicker and reflect in shining eyes.

Fireworks explode above the waters, ships' sirens blast through the starry night, people cry and kiss each other and laugh – and some just stare into their candle flames, at the birth of life, for the three-day ritual has impressed its meaning deeply on people's minds.

Spétsai

Spetsai (scene of John Fowles' *The Magus*) is the furthest and smallest island of the group. Covered with pine-woods it is distinctly cooler than elsewhere in the Argo-Saronic. For this reason it is a favoured retreat of wealthy Athenian families who in summertime occupy spacious mansions in the pretty town. Recently it has become a popular holiday resort for the English, with a modest but lively nightlife.

The island was originally colonised by Albanians, probably after the fall to the Turks in 1460, and they settled in the area known as *Kastelli* at the top of the present town. Some walls remain from Kastelli in the northeast of the area and four churches still survive. Kastelli was burnt after the Orlov rising in the late 18th C and the town then developed along the shore. The Spetsiots built a merchant fleet which later played an important part in the War of Independence. The island is distinguished for being the first in the archipelago to revolt against the Turks in April 1821 and the fortified point, still bristling with cannon, now forms the town's plateia. The many handsome houses in the town recall the island's wealth at this period. After the War of Independence the fleet declined, although the tradition of shipbuilding continued. Caiques are still built in the Old Harbour.

The small *museum*, open in the mornings, in the imposing 18th C house of Hadziyannis Mexis, contains memorabilia of the War of Independence including the relics of the famous woman rebel Bouboulina.

Beaches The town's beaches are skimpy, but there are good sandy beaches at Agioi Anargyroi and Zogeiria and elsewhere around this attractive, green island.

PRACTICAL INFORMATION

TRAVEL TO THE ISLANDS
There are several **boats** a day in summer from the main harbour of Piraeus to Aegina, Poros, Hydra and Spetsai, usually with stops at Methana and Ermioni in the Peloponnese enroute.

There is an excellent **hydrofoil** service during the summer to all these destinations (and on to Porto Heli in the Peloponnese, whence you can reach Nafplion, Monemvasia and Kithera). The hydrofoil reduces travelling time by half or more but it costs half as much again (or more) than the boat. The service stops during rough weather. You should book tickets in advance if possible, at 2 Karageorgis Servias, off Syntagma Square, Athens or at 8 Akte Themistokleous, at Zea, Piraeus. Tel: 452.7107.

The hydrofoils for Aegina depart from the main harbour in Piraeus. The other services depart from Zea Marina.

AEGINA
Travel
Buses (from the bus station near the ferries) travel throughout the island from Aegina town. You can rent bicycles or mopeds.

Aegina town
Hotels: Nausica (B); Avra, Brown (C); Miranda (D).
Tavernas: Numerous along the waterfront. Try Maridaki or To Spiti tou Psara there, or Michalatzikos in the street behind the port and sample its barrelled retsina. Also *disco*.

Souvala
Regular *ferries* to/from Piraeus, mostly at weekends.
Hotel: Ephi (C).
Tavernas along the harbour.

Agia Marina
Ferries to Piraeus also. Several *discos*.
Numerous *hotels*: Apollo (B); Ammoudia, Galini (C); and *restaurants*.

Perdika
Hotels: Aegina Maris (B); Hippocambus (D).
Seafood *tavernas* along the front; sandy beach.

Boats to *Moni island*: swimming, tavernas and camping-ground.

Island of Anghistri
Motor launch from Aegina town; the island is a dull place, favoured by Germans.
Numerous *hotels*: Kekryfalia (C); Dina, Galini (D); Anagennisis (E) on the beach.
Taverna: Skala Beach, a few minutes walk from Skala.
Disco at Anghistri Club by the sea.

POROS
Travel
Frequent bus service along the island's only road to the Monastery of Zoodochos Pigi and then past the Temple of Poseidon. You can hire bicycles and mopeds.

Accommodation
Latsi (near waterfront), Neon Aegli (near Askeli beach), Sirene (below monastery) (B); Aktaeon, Manessi (C). Takis Travel Office near the ferry landing can arrange *rooms*.

Eating, entertainment and shopping
Many good-value *tavernas* along the seafront. Try Caravella. Also Zorba's Taverna on Canal Beach. *Discos* include Kavos and Corali. There is an excellent *street market* with handicrafts, leather, pottery, etc.

Activities
Beyond the canal bridge the road divides left for the *beaches* of Neorion (waterskiing and windsurfing schools), Agapi (quieter) and Russian Bay; and right for Askeli beach (watersports school) and Monastery beach (seafood tavernas).

Water-taxis also travel to most of these beaches as well as to the beaches of Aliki and Plaka on the *Peloponnesian coast* opposite. From Plaka you can walk through the lemon groves up to the Kardasi Taverna for lunch.

There are frequent boats to Galata from where you can take a bus to Damala (8 kms) near ancient *Troezen*, see the scattered remains including a large tower, and walk to the picturesque Devil's Bridge in the gorge of Yefiraion.

From Poros there are *tours* in the summer to Epidavros, Mycenae and Corinth; also day-trips to Aegina, Hydra and Spetsai.

HYDRA
Travel
There are no roads and no motor vehicles. You travel by foot or mule or by boat.

Accommodation
Difficult to find at Easter and in summer, and more expensive than most places. For *rooms* try the Tourist Police situated near the church with the clock tower.
Hotels: Miranda (A); Delfini, Hydroussa (B); Leto (C); Sophia (D).

Eating and Entertainment
Tavernas: Plentiful, with a wide range of prices (and quality). Up-market there is Bajazza for international nouvelle cuisine or La Grenouille; less expensive is The Garden, among the lemon and orange trees, also Theodori's (10 minutes' walk from the port) and Pierophani in Kaminia. Cheap and cheerful is the Three Brothers behind the clock tower or the Café Laikon by the port.
Bar: Hydronetta for drinks at sunset.
Discos: Cavos or Lagoudera, at the two corners of the harbour.

Activities
There are no very good *beaches*; usually overcrowded stretches of coast reached by walking or by boat. The best is Mandraki. Or use the rocks at the harbour entrance.
Walks: 1. to Episkopi, west of the town, reached via the monastery of Elias above the town (one hour), then about 1½ hours further; return along the coast by Vlikhos (swimming, taverna); 2. to the monasteries of Agia Triada and Zourvas (3 hours) in the east of the island.

If you want a picnic, go early to the central market behind the port: Hydra imports all its food and it soon goes.
Festival: 20 June, Miaoulia (named after the hero of the war against the Turks Miaoulis) culminating in fireworks and a boat-burning.

ERMIONI
On the Peloponnesian coast opposite Hydra, Ermioni is a pleasant fishing village now surrounded with several holiday hotel complexes. It has become one of the major *windsurfing* centres of Greece. Near the school some fine *mosaic floors* remain from an early Christian basilica.
Hotel: Nandia (D).

SPETSAI
Travel
Not as restricted as Hydra; there is a road and a bus, and you can hire bicycles and mopeds to go about the island. In the town you can travel in style in a carriage. There are few motor vehicles apart from taxis.

Accommodation
Hotels: Kasteli (A); Roumanis (near beach) (B); Faros (C); Acropolis (D).

Takis Travel Office (to the left of the ferry landing) can arrange *rooms*, or seek out the Tourist Police.

Eating and Entertainment
Tavernas: Try Stelios on the front near Takis, Lazarus up the hill from the main town, Ta Tzakia by the town's main beach for grills, and on the Old Harbour Charalambos and Paleo Limani. There are many pleasant kafeneions overlooking the Dapia, the modern harbour.
Discos: Several, but try the Delfinia.

Activities
The best *beaches* are at Agioi Anargyroi and Zogeiria. Also at Agia Paraskevi (festival on 26 July) and Agia Marina (several tavernas and a disco). Boats for most of these leave the town in the morning and return in the mid-afternoon. The bus travels across the island to Agioi Anargyroi and back. Or you can make a pleasant *walk* to Anargyroi in about 1½ hours: you pick up the path above the church of Agios Vasilis at the top of Kastelli, and you follow it through the pine trees and across the central ridge. Tassos' Taverna gives you lunch by the beach.

PORTO HELI
Travel
Daily boats in summer from Spetsai; also from nearby Kosta.

Accommodation
Like Ermioni, Porto Heli has several large

holiday hotel complexes nearby. Otherwise there is Flisvos (D); also a campsite at Kosta.

Activities
Dimitris Kourounis runs a well-known *waterski school*.

THE ARGOLID

The Peloponnese, a giant hand of which the Argolid is the thumb, is rich in ancient associations, and for the Greeks at the time of the Persian invasions it was the heartland to which they would have withdrawn and made their stand had not Themistokles just barely convinced them that Athens could not be sacrificed. Today some parts of the Peloponnese are among the least developed in Greece, with formidable mountains, magnificent scenery, untouched traditional villages and friendly people.

Some of the ancient sites, like Mycenae and Olympia, are on the tourist circuit, and certain coastal towns, like Nafplion and Kalamata, are established resorts. But the beauty and interest of the Peloponnese is not confined to beaches and antiquities, even though the tourists are. A meander through the interior or to the further extremities is highly recommended for the more adventurous.

The Road to the Peloponnese

Approaching the Peloponnese from Athens you follow in reverse the route that Theseus took when he left Troezen. **Theseus' route** Past Elefsis and Megara (mother-city of Byzantium) the road mounts a corniche above the waters of the Argo-Saronic. It was here that Theseus vanquished Skiron who, demanding that passers-by should wash his feet, would kick them over the precipice into the waiting jaws of a huge tortoise. In ancient times this path was known as the Kaki Skala, or Bad Stairway; now there are two roads, one slow and toll-free, the other a motorway: both are cut into the sheer rock face and present no danger, but the way (particularly on the more winding toll-free road) remains awesome, with stunning views of the gulf below from all along its 215-metre high, 10-km stretch.

The isthmus The route descends to the isthmus, the narrow hinge connecting the Peloponnese to the rest of Greece, cut by the **Corinth Canal**. The first attempts to cut a canal were made by the Romans, with even Nero delivering an imperial blow with a golden pickaxe. But it took the technology of the Industrial Age to do the job, and the canal only became a reality in 1893. The achievement is most impressive when you glide through aboard a ship; from the wobbling roadway that crosses over it you have no perspective and therefore no sense of scale. Even if a ship passes through far below you, it is not until you notice how incredibly small the passengers are and how very large the ship must be that you become amazed.

But before crossing over the canal you might turn right

and, running north along the Gulf of Corinth, come to **Loutráki** (80 kms from Athens), an old watering place into which new life has been breathed by recent development and prosperity. It is a pleasant place to idle, for its hot springs, its good swimming, its sunsets over the gulf, and the charm of its pre-war hotels with balconies, elaborate entrances and staircases, and occasional circular rooms, although much damage was done in the earthquake of February 1981. Thirteen kilometres north of Loutraki (and 25 kms from Corinth) is the village of **Perachóra**. There are fine views all along the route. With the rise in the price of resin, the village, set on a small plateau about half a kilometre from the sea, is emerging from its historical poverty. Between the village and the sea is a lake, a few tavernas on its north shore. The road continues towards the western tip of the pine-covered peninsula where, amidst jagged tumbling rocks, the site of ancient Perachora commands a magnificent view down the entire length of the Corinthian Gulf. An *agora* and *stoa* surround the modest harbour (strong currents and the occasional shark make it unwise to swim beyond it), while a *sanctuary of Hera* and the remains of an *8th C temple* lie on higher ground. The museum in the village was very badly damaged in the 1981 earthquake, and the exhibits have been transferred to the Perachora Room in the National Archaeological Museum in Athens. Barely more than a stone's throw from the crossroads of Greece and beautifully described by Dilys Powell in *An Affair of the Heart*, Perachora is rarely visited.

An Affair of the Heart

Corinth

Modern Corinth (Kórinthos), 81 kms from Athens and just across the isthmus, is in that category of towns which includes Troy in New York State and Athens, Georgia: the place bears no relation to the original. It is lifeless, unattractive, with wide empty streets and box-like houses. This is at least partly because the modern town, which was built at a distance from the classical site to avoid earthquakes, was itself flattened by an earthquake in 1928.

Ancient Corinth

Those living in ancient Corinth inhabit a small village which occupies part of the site upon a rocky plateau 6 kms southwest of the modern town. A coffee in its little plateia with plane-tree and fountain is the only self-indulgence available. The classical city of at least 300,000 owed its wealth and power to its strategic position at the isthmus, but owed its fame to its life of indolent luxury. St Paul ranted against Corinthian whores and was answered with a riot. The Roman ruins of the city Paul visited – refounded by Julius Caesar one hundred years after the Greek city had been razed to the ground for participating in a revolt against Roman rule – are extensive. But of Greek Corinth almost nothing remains except the seven columns of the *Temple of Apollo*, one of the oldest in Greece (c550 BC), with monolithic Doric archaic columns and a squatness about it that reflects the uncertainty of early architects when building with heavy stone instead of wood. However below the northeast corner of the Roman forum the starting lines of a 5th C BC racecourse have been found; there are 17 starting positions, and the curve in the line makes it unique in Greece.

Philosopher in a barrel

It was at Corinth that Alexander the Great encountered Diogenes, the Cynic philosopher who, shunning worldly pleasures, chose to live inside a barrel. Taking pity on this abject figure, Alexander asked if there was anything he wanted. 'Yes', replied Diogenes, 'stand aside a little, for you are blocking the sun'. 'If I had not been Alexander, I would have wanted to be Diogenes,' came the reply.

The fantastic **Acro-corinth** which looms on the sunset horizon like an Aztec mesa red with sacrifice was originally topped with a temple to Aphrodite and serviced by a thousand sacred prostitutes. It rises precipitously 575 metres above the ruins of the classical city, a 1½ hour walk to the top or a drive along the road from the museum. From a distance there is a hint of fortifications along the top, and now as you climb closer the enormous crenellated walls and towers of the medieval fortress loom sombrely above you. Corinth was so often sacked that successive Byzantine, Frankish, Venetian and Turkish rulers retired to the Acro-corinth and built up one of the most imposing medieval monuments in Greece.

One set of gargantuan walls sits within another, seemingly impregnable, with commanding, magnificent views of Corinth on the plain below, the isthmus and the two gulfs it divides and the far shores of the Megarid and Attica. Yet the fortress was several times taken in desperate battles by lunatic warriors who heaved up the steep hill and battered against its stones, their blood and screams still lingering, tangible, in the atmosphere. Here myth prefigures history: Zeus ravished Aegina, daughter of the river-god Asophus, and Sisyphos, for exposing Zeus to her father, was condemned by the gods ceaselessly to roll a rock to the top of the Acro-corinth, whence the stone would fall back of its own weight. The gods had thought with some reason that there was no more dreadful punishment than futile and hopeless labour.

Myth of Sisyphos

Mycenae

The road and railway weave across one another all the way to Argos; the railway narrow gauge, single track, the trains themselves like trolleys, wobbling with suburban complacency through the fierce landscape as if conveying you for an afternoon's picnic to the Vienna Woods. To the west are the ruins of **Nemea** where Herakles slew the Nemean lion.

The *Temple of Nemean Zeus* is being restored by the University of California, Berkeley, and the *stadium* has been almost completely unearthed.

Not far off the Corinth-Argos road or railway line (from Corinth 42 kms), almost lost in a fold between the twin hills of Zara and Agios Elias, is the low mound on which **Mycenae** (Mikínai) stands. Drawing closer, the mound rises steeply and spread upon it like broken shingles are the grey, brooding ruins of Agamemnon's citadel. On the bare curtain of mountains behind it, a watchman sighted the beacon signalling his lord's return from Troy and cried, 'All hail, bright father of joy and dance in Argos', while bitter Klytemnestra and her lover Aegisthes set the stage among these stones for murder.

From this ground and in this light grew the civilisation which followed upon the collapse of Minoan Crete. In all such places, primordial in aspect and associations, there is a sense of timelessness, of dream-history. Once in through the Lion Gate and standing on the Cyclopean walls overlooking the richly-patterned Argive Plain fanning out below, you feel funnelling in upon you shards of time and legend, of warriors, kings and gods, of tourist buses, cold orange drinks and finely-beaten masks of gold.

Origins of Mycenaean civilisation

From 1600 to 1200 BC, Mycenae was the leading city in Greece, its highly hierarchical society dominating the Argolid and exercising some kind of feudal control or influence over other Mycenaean kingdoms such as Iolkos in Thessaly, Thebes and Orchomenos in Boeotia, Athens in Attica, Pylos in Messenia and perhaps a kingdom (though a Mycenaean settlement has yet to be found there) in Lakonia. The origins of Mycenaean civilisation are obscure: for some decades it was thought to have derived from the Minoan, though now Crete is thought only to have moderated and refined an independent and already vigorous culture; the prevalent theory is that Mycenaean civilisation was introduced by invaders coming from the East, across Anatolia and to Greece via Troy around 1900–1800 BC.

Homer's world

The world that Homer describes in his epics is the Mycenaean world, the tales and oral history of an expansive 400 years dramatically focused on the Trojan expedition and encapsulated within the 10-year span of the *Iliad* and the following 10-year span of the *Odyssey*. Many of the great figures of Greek literature – Theseus, Jason, Kadmos, as well as Agamemnon – were born of this period, as was the Greek language itself and the elements of later Greek religion. To the extent that Western civilisation has developed from that of Greece, it is to Mycenae, if no further, that we must look for the foundations of 3500 years of culture.

From the village you can walk the final kilometre up a gradual hill to the citadel. You enter the citadel by passing

Touring the citadel and nearby tombs

through the *Lion Gate* (1), so named for the massive triangular relief over the lintel of two rampant lions on either side of a downward tapering column probably once surmounted by a double-headed axe, reminiscent of Knossos. The Cyclopean unmortared stones making up the adjoining walls are cleanly cut and well fitted into place, and the execution of the relief above all adds up to the intended impression of architectural mastery and cultural achievement.

Twelve metres in from the Lion Gate is the *grave circle* (2) originally excavated by Schliemann. In the last shaft he excavated, he found the well-preserved body of a high-ranking man who appeared to have died in his thirties. He wore a gold mask. Schliemann removed it, found the eyes, the mouth, the flesh still intact, and sent a telegram to the King of the Hellenes: 'I have gazed upon the face of Agamemnon'.

In fact, the actual burial spot of Agamemnon is not known and the mask, now dated with some accuracy, must have belonged to a still more ancient personage. Apart from the shaft Schliemann excavated, there is the beehive-shaped *Tomb of Agamemnon*, also known as the Treasury of Atreus, and while the possibility is open that it could be the former, it is certainly not the latter. It was Pausanias who passed on the misinformation that the tholos was Atreus' treasury, for by his time (2nd C AD) such tombs had been plundered; only in the late 19th C was a tholos tomb found near Athens containing remains of the dead and so confirming their use. At the burial ceremony, the mourners laid the body – if he were a king – on a carpet of gold, with vessels of food and flagons of wine around him. Weapons of war were added too. Rams and other animals were slain within the tholos itself, while outside, beyond the great bronze doors, the horses that had drawn the funeral chariot were slaughtered within the dromos – the cut leading to the tomb – before this was filled in with stones and earth. The Tomb of Agamemnon is on your left as you come up the road out of the village and are approaching the citadel. Passing along the *dromos* running into the side of a hill, you enter an enormous, cool, dark interior where all echoes converge with great force at the centre. Looking back at the doorway (the bronze doors long since plundered), notice the curved *lintel* above it. It is about 9 metres long, 5 metres wide and a metre high, weighs 10,900 kilos and is made from a single piece of limestone. The Mycenaeans put this in place around 1300 BC, without aid of jacks, pulleys or other mechanical inventions. All the stones making up the curved interior surface are beautifully fitted and smooth. Closer to the citadel and to the right of the road are the so-called tombs of Klytemnestra and Aegisthes, both smaller than the tomb of Agamemnon, though the *Tomb of Klytemnestra* is of superior workmanship and so probably of later date, while the poorly constructed *Tomb of Aegisthes* is earlier (c1470 BC).

Mycenae 'rich in gold' was Homer's phrase, and he need not have been referring only to the panoply of dead kings: near the tombs of Klytemnestra and Aegisthes are the *remains of merchants' houses*, the House of the Oil Merchant with a dozen rooms on its lowest floor alone, the House of the Sphinxes and that of the Shields (the names derive from the objects discovered within) found with carved ivory inlays for furniture, fragments of frescoes, fine pottery, vases of serpentine, Linear B tablets recording a variety of spices for scenting the oils and, architecturally, staircases evidencing upper storeys – all suggesting a town of considerable wealth and elegance beneath the royal citadel.

Back atop the citadel at its centre is the *Palace* (3). To the west of the open *Great Court* (4) is the *Throne Room* (5); to the east, passing through a porch and anteroom, is the *Megaron* (6) with its sacred hearth. The small rooms to its north are thought to have been the *private apartments* and in one of them, rather fancifully, a red-stuccoed bathtub is said to be the very place of Agamemnon's murder. But all of this is in broad daylight as much of the palace is levelled to its foundations. The panorama from the palace or the *House of Columns* (7) – a smaller palace complex – provides a complementary sense of grandeur, and there is a touch of evil too in the associations, the giant stones, as the citadel crouches beneath the nearby mountains. But to feel the intensity of menace you should cross the citadel to its western point where, by the narrow *sally port* (8), a twisting, falling passageway leads to the *secret cistern* (9).

For finding your way about inside, matches will not do; their feeble illumination is swallowed by the darkness. Bring a flashlight. Where daylight ends, just a stone's throw from the entrance, you turn left and descend the stairs into time-erasing blackness. There are no initial pitfalls and you can guide yourself by running your hands along the damp stone walls pressing in from either side. Only claustrophobia and the growing conviction that this will be the moment, after thousands of years, that this ancient engineering marvel will collapse and entomb you as surely as Agamemnon need deter you. The vaulted passageway turns right (it is dangerous to go further) for a last long descent to a high-roofed cistern deep underground, well beyond the citadel walls, the guarantee of a water supply at times of siege.

A walk to the Argive Heraion

A path runs 3 kms south along the mountainside and then east from Mycenae to the **Argive Heraion**, or Sanctuary of Hera, queen of the Olympian gods, which stands upon a promontory by the village of Konika with a fine view down to the Argolikos Gulf. The extensive ruins date from archaic and classical times, though the site had been in use much

CITADEL OF MYCENAE

AGAMEMNON'S TOMB

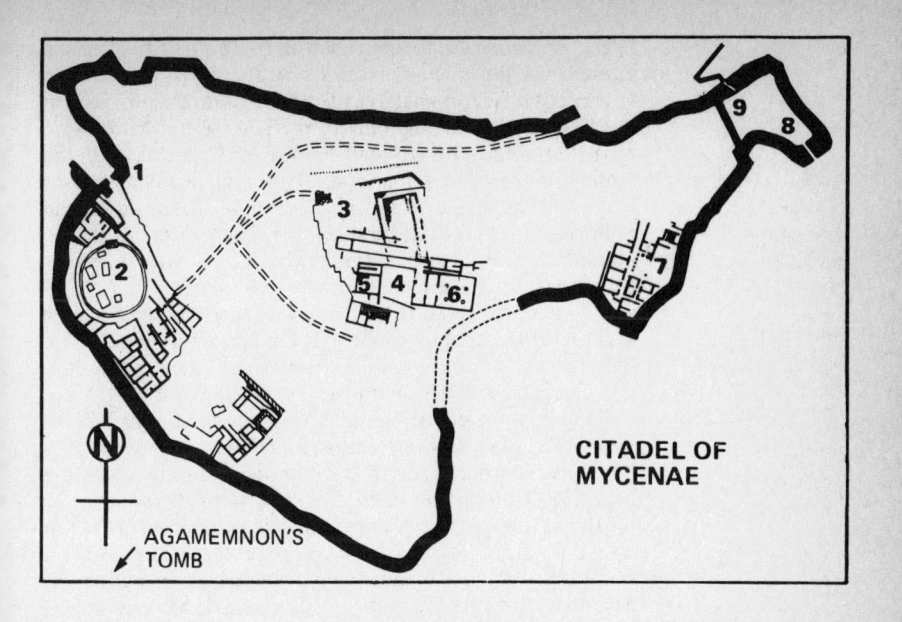

earlier than that. It was here that the Greek chiefs gathered to pledge loyalty to Agamemnon in the great expedition against Troy. Pausanias describes the chryselephantine cult statue of Hera, famous for its grandeur and beauty, which stood (but no more) in the *New Temple* in his day. He also mentions a gold peacock dedicated by Hadrian and Nero's golden crown and purple robe, testimony to the longevity of the cult. The New Temple is at the centre of the site, the *Old Temple*, believed to be the first example in the Peloponnese of a temple built of stone as well as wood, to the north east. The Heraion is rarely visited today and so can be unusually enjoyed in some solitude.

The Way to Náfplion

The prosperous but otherwise unexciting town of **Árgos** (from Corinth 48 kms) occupies the site of the ancient city and is possibly the oldest continuously inhabited town in Europe. Argos' past from Middle Helladic through Roman times is represented by the exhibits at its *museum*, opposite the church of Agios Petros in the main plateia; in the vicinity is a lively market. Leaving the plateia by Odos Sokri you climb towards the two hills dominating the town and offering fine views of the Argolid and the Gulf of Nafplion. The lower, rounder hill to the east is the *Aspis*, the original Argive acropolis built over the remains of a Bronze Age settlement of c2000 BC. The higher, steeper peak to the west

Oldest town in Europe

is the *Larissa*, which superseded the Aspis as the principal citadel of Argos in ancient times; here there is a fine medieval *kastro* cobbled together by Byzantines, Franks, Venetians and Turks on earlier foundations. Walking down from the Larissa, or following the Tripolis road southwestwards to the edge of modern Argos, you come to the still largely built-over *agora* to the east of the road, and, opposite, extensive *Roman baths* and above these, hewn out of the hillside, a 4th C BC *theatre* which could accommodate 20,000 spectators, making it the largest in Greece after Dodona.

At Argos the road forks, the left fork leading to Nafplion (12 kms) and, 4 kms before Nafplion, **Tiryns**, a considerable Mycenaean citadel though always subject either to Mycenae itself or to Argos. This is one of the two reputed birthplaces (Thebes the other) of Herakles and served as the base of operations for many of his labours. The citadel surmounts a hill which rises like an island from the surrounding plain, the sea only a kilometre or two distant. Though lacking the imposing position and atmospherics of Mycenae, Tiryns offers a better preserved and more extensive *palace complex*, surrounded by *walls* famous as the finest specimens of Mycenaean military architecture.

With Mycenae, Tiryns and Epidavros all within easy reach, **Náfplion** (Nauplia) makes a good centre for travelling around this part of the Peloponnese. It is a lovely and stylish resort, hugging the base of a steep headland atop which the great Venetian *fortress of Palamidi* gazes out across the Argolikos Gulf. This was the residence of the new King of the Hellenes during the first few years of independence, and so the better hotels have an old European elegance while the placid harbour front is set with tables for afternoon teas and views of the diminutive kastro on the close-by island of *Bourdzi*. The climbing streets are overhung with iron balconies overgrown with flowers, with always a delicate combination of salt and scent in the air. There is good swimming off the West Mole towards the point of the peninsula.

Mycenaean collection

The *museum*, on the upper floors of an early 18th C Venetian building, is one of three in Greece (Athens and Heraklion are the others) with an important Mycenaean collection. On the first floor are stelai from Grave Circle B at Mycenae (a grave circle found outside the citadel), one with what is possibly the oldest bas-relief in Greece; pottery from sites around the Argolid, showing marked Minoan influences; and most remarkable (also unique), a complete suit of bronze Mycenaean armour. On the second floor there is a Mycenaean helmet from Tiryns.

On a beautiful bay is **Tolón**, an overblown resort 10 kms behind Nafplion. On the rocky headland above are the remains of prehistoric Asine, with Helladic houses, Hellenistic ramparts, Roman baths and Venetian fortifications.

Epídavros

Forty-one kms north of either Nafplion or Tolon, on the north coast of the Argolid, is the Sanctuary of Epidauros. A new highway now runs from the Isthmus of Corinth permitting direct and speedy access from Athens and also the possibility of touring right round the Argolid without retracing your route. The site is most famous for its *theatre*, the best preserved and most beautiful in Greece. During the last two weekends of June and the first three weekends of July the celebrated festival of drama at the theatre ensures that Epídavros (Epidaurus) is still more easily reached by the special boats that are laid on from Piraeus.

Annual drama festival

The sanctuary was once a religious centre and fashionable spa associated with the cult of Asklepios. Set in a broad and (tourists permitting) lonely valley, it rivals in extent the sanctuaries of Olympia and Delphi, though its interest for the layman lies entirely in its theatre. To Henry Miller, 'Mycenae, like Epidaurus, swims in light. But Epidaurus is all open, exposed, irrevocably devoted to the spirit. Mycenae folds in upon itself, like a fresh-cut navel, dragging its glory down into the bowels of the earth where the bats and lizards feed upon it gloatingly. Epidaurus is a bowl from which to drink the pure spirit; the blue of the sky is in it and the stars and the winged creatures who fly between, scattering song and melody'.

Agamemnon's Tomb, Mycenae

PRACTICAL INFORMATION

TRAVEL TO AND AROUND THE ARGOLID
Refer also to the *Practical Information* section under Athens.

Buses leave from 100 Kifissou Street for Argos, Corinth, Mycenae and Nafplion (all frequently, approximately hourly); also for Loutraki and Nemea (5 or 6 a day); and for Ligouri to reach Epidavros (about 2 a day).

Trains depart from Stathmos Peloponnisou for Corinth, Mycenae and Argos (about 5 a day).

The **hydrofoil** service reaches Nafplion and Tolon daily in summer from Zea Marina.

LOUTRAKI
Apart from the Athens *bus* there is a service from Corinth.
Among over 50 *hotels*: Park, Paolo (A); Pappos (B); Mitzithra (C).
Taverna: Horiatiki, 70 El. Venizelou.

PERACHORA
Bus from Loutraki, or you can *walk* along the coast from Loutraki in about 3 hours.
Hotel: Anessis (D).

CORINTH
Accommodation
Hotels: Kypselos (B); Ephira (C); Apollo (D). At the village of old Corinth there is a Xenia (A), otherwise *rooms*.
Camping: Blue Dolphin at Lechion, and Corinth Beach at Diavatika.

Eating and Activities
Anaxagora and Ippopotamos, both along the waterfront, and Fotis, 2 kms along the Patras road. There is swimming on beaches to the west of town.

Sites
Buses go hourly from the centre of town to *ancient Corinth*, about 5 kms to the southwest. The site and museum are open 8am to 7pm weekdays and Saturdays; on Sundays and holidays 9am to 7pm; the museum is closed on Tuesdays.

The *Acro-corinth* is a hot 1½ hours' walk from the museum; or get a lift along the road. There is a Tourist Pavilion at the first of the gates of the fortress.

ISTHMIA
About 2 kms from the bridge over the Corinth Canal, the ancient site has scant remains of the *Sanctuary of Poseidon*, once famous for its games; also nearby are the walls of a *Byzantine fortress*. The *museum* houses local finds, and mosaic panels from Kenchreai.

MYCENAE
Travel
The site is about a 15-minute walk from the village. The fencing in of the citadel has spoilt an immediate appreciation of its situation; nevertheless it is best to approach on foot, preferably out of tourist hours. The village itself has become lamentably commercialised.

The *train station* is about 4 kms from the site, a 45-minute walk. In summer there is a *tour bus* from the Argos museum; also *local buses* from Nafplion via Argos, apart from Athens buses. There is a *car park* below the citadel.

Accommodation
Hotels: Xenia (A); and in the village La Petite Planete, Agamemnon (C); Orea Helene tou Menelaou (E).

There is a *youth hostel* at the restaurant Iphegeneia, and there are 2 *campgrounds*.

Site
Open 8am to 7pm daily; Sundays and holidays 9am to 7pm.

ARGOS
Local *bus* service Nafplion-Argos-Mycenae.
Hotel: Mycenae (C).

The *ancient site* (along the Tripolis road) and the *museum* (on the central square) are open 9am to 1pm and 4 to 6pm weekdays and Saturdays, and 10.30am to 2.30pm Sundays and holidays, but the museum is closed Tuesdays.

TIRYNS
Open 9am to 6pm daily, Sundays and holidays from 10am. Take a flashlight.

NAFPLION
Travel
Frequent *buses* to Tiryns, Argos,

Mycenae and Corinth; less frequent to Ligouri (for Epidavros site): all from Syngrou Square.

Caiques visit the fortress on Bourtzi island, where there is a Tourist Pavilion.

Accommodation and Eating
Hotels: Numerous, including the brand-new Xenia (A); Agamemnon (B); Park (C); Leto (D) for best views.

There is a *youth hostel* on Neon Vyzantion Street; also a *campsite*.

There are many good fish *tavernas* along the waterfront; try Hundalas, 63 Bubulinas, and Savouras, Akte Miaouli.

Museums
Archaeological Museum, open 9am to 1pm and 4 to 6pm; Sundays and holidays 10am to 2pm; closed Tuesdays.
Popular Art Museum, with traditional costumes, etc; similar hours.
Palamidi fortress, 9am to 6pm; Sundays and holidays 10am to 4pm.

TOLON
Travel
Frequent *bus* service to Nafplion; *excursions* to Corinth, Mycenae, Epidavros, Olympia, etc; *cruises* to Hydra and Spetsai, as well as trips to islands in the bay.

Accommodation
Numerous *hotels*, including Sophia, Dolphin (B); Romvi, Koronis (C); Kali Kardia (D). *Campgrounds* at Tolon and Drepano.

Activities
Good, safe sandy *beach* with tavernas, bars, discos. Various *watersports* facilities, including a waterski school in front of the Hotel Dolphin. Also *tennis courts*.

EPIDAVROS
Travel
The ancient site is not at either Nea (new) or Palaia (old) Epidavros but inland of them, near *Ligourio*. Be sure to get the right *bus*. In summer *boats* from Piraeus come into Palaia Epidavros.

Accommodation
There are *hotels* at Ligourio: Alkion, Asklipios (D); at Nea Epidavros: Epidavros (C); and at Palaia Epidavros: Stratos (B); Koronis (C). Near the ancient site there is a Xenia (B); also a Tourist Pavilion. Also *campgrounds* at Palaia Epidavros.

Site
Ancient site and museum: open 8am to 7pm daily; Sundays and holidays 9am to 7pm; the museum is closed Tuesdays.

Drama festival
The festival runs from mid-June to mid-September, Saturday and Sunday evenings at 9pm. Buses arrive back in Athens in the early hours. Tickets can be bought at the theatre before performances, or (safer) at 4 Stadiou Street, Athens (Tel: 322.3111).

THE CENTRAL PELOPONNESE

South of Argos, **Lerna** (10 kms) is one of the oldest (4th millenium BC) sites in Greece, with an Early Helladic *palace* and *fortifications*. **Paralia Astros** (31 kms further) has tiers of houses rising up from its small harbour, a medieval castle and a long sandy beach. But if after Lerna you follow the signs for Tripolis you are carried aloft over the Ktenias range, the Argolikos Gulf a sheet of brilliant blue below, and down into Arcadia.

To Trípolis and Megalópolis

But the flat, monotonous, treeless plain on which Tripolis squats, wracked by the extremes of punishing heat and violent hail and thunderstorms in summer, enclosed within an amphitheatre of barren mountains, is anything but Arcadian. A modern manufacturing town, noted for its tanneries and carpet factories, **Trípolis** (60 kms from Argos) is the communications centre of the Peloponnese. Three attractive plateias enlivened by cafés belie the atrocities that were committed here in 1821 by the besieging Greeks during the first months of their revolt against Ottoman rule. Previous failed revolts led to barbarous retaliation by the Turks; this time the Greeks determined to kill every Turk in the Peloponnese, and here within the now vanished walls of this fortified capital of the Pasha of the Morea the Turks made their final stand when all of the remaining Peloponnese had been ripped from their grasp. While supposedly negotiating with the inhabitants for their safety, the Greek brigand-general Kolokotronis suddenly led his men in a storm of the town: in two terrible days they put 10,000 Turks to death, often cutting off their arms and legs and roasting their living bodies over fires.

Ottoman capital of the Peloponnese

Eight kms southeast of Tripolis at the village of Alea are the scattered remains of ancient **Tegea**, once the largest city in the plain and an early enemy of Sparta. There is a small but well-arranged museum, and not far from it the ruins of the *Temple of Athena Alea*, one of the most famous sanctuaries in ancient Greece. Here the east pediment was decorated with sculpture (fragments in the local museum and the National Museum, Athens) representing the hunt of the Kalydonian boar in which Atalanta, born in Tegea and fleetest runner of her age, was the heroine. Nine kms north of Tripolis are the ruins of **Mantinea,** age-long rival of Tegea. During the Peloponnesian War, Tegea, which had been subjected to Sparta nearly two centuries before, fought on the side of its masters against Athenian-allied Mantinea. Mantinea was again to become a front-line state when the Theban general Epaminondas built the walls (the ones now visible) as part of his Arcadian strategy against a Spartan revival following Sparta's defeat at his hands at Leuktra in 371 BC. Epaminondas was in fact killed here at the moment of triumph in his last battle against Sparta in 362 BC.

The perfection of the theatre at Epidavros rightly attracts the many, but for the few there is the theatre and buried city of **Megalópolis**, 34 kms southwest of Tripolis. The site is barely excavated and infrequently visited and looks like a painting of an idealised Arcadia hung in a Paris salon. This was in fact a planned city, built in 371 BC by Epaminondas as a buffer between recently defeated but always threatening Sparta to the southeast and the Arcadian states, of which it was meant to be the federal capital. But the city never took root and by 194 BC it was destroyed and left to be covered by earth, grass and trees.

Ancient theatre and buried city

When you arrive you see an attendant sitting on a chair in a field in the sun; you can see nothing of the city. He smiles, pulls out his one and only plan of the site, and in Greek, or broken English, French or German, takes you on a private guided tour, leading you first around a hill and, *voila*, set into the side of it is one of the largest *amphitheatres* in Greece, built to hold 20,000. Only the first half-dozen rows have been excavated. The rest of the theatre climbs the hillside as a series of ridges under the grass, with a crescent of tall pines occupying the upper circle seats. The acoustics are still marvellous. When you take your seat with the trees at the top you can hear very clearly the normal conversation of people on the stage below.

And spread out before is the rest of the city. Immediately behind the stage is the *Thersilion* or federal assembly hall which had a capacity of 16,000. The attendant points to a row of cypresses, an electricity pylon, leading your eye to ridges and mounds of earth across the river where stoas and temples once stood, where indeed their foundations, perhaps more, are still in place below the cloak of a few feet of earth. It is a lovely and relaxing place; birds chirp, pines creak in the breeze, otherwise not a sound and it may be an hour before another visitor comes.

Following the Alpheios

Medieval Greece

Some of the loveliest countryside in the Peloponnese lies southwest of Megalopolis: rich, grassy valleys, dark pine-clad hills, cypress groves and irregular mountain outlines. About 16 kms along the road there is a steep hill with a village wrapped round like a shawl beneath the Frankish kastro at the peak. This is **Karítaina**, a part of medieval Greece, looking like a hill village in the South of France, or even like a Tibetan lamasery. It is reached by a switchback road which finally brings you amidst houses attached to the hillside like clams, where old men with enormous waxed moustachios puff along the alleyways to meet at one of the two kafeneions by the statue in the village centre, where the view of the surrounding plain is magnificent and the feeling is one of being cut off totally from the 20th C.

Coming away from Karitaina you now start along a mountain road with a deep gorge to the right, the crystal-green Alpheios splashing along its rocky bed. The river is the longest in the Peloponnese, rising in southeastern Arcadia and flowing westwards past Olympia and out into the Ionian Sea. It was the favourite river of Zeus, and on its banks first grew the wild olive, the reward of victors at the Olympic Games. You pass through a succession of beautiful villages, like **Andrítsaina** for instance, where more moustachioed old men sit about in chairs watching the younger rakes drinking ouzo, playing backgammon. A still more mountainous road cuts off after the church in Andritsaina and bounces you upwards to the wild spot where incredibly the Greeks built a temple to Apollo. This is **Vássai** (Bassae), and like Delphi it soars above a primitive landscape; a temple of sombre grey stone upon a mountain surrounded by mountains, small goatherding villages in the distance, the sound of bells and whistling and dogs barking their flocks in, a blast of wind against your eardrums.

Temple of Apollo Epikourios

Over 1200 metres above sea level on a mountain scored by ravines (*vássai* in Greek, hence the modern name), the *Temple of Apollo Epikourios* is missing its roof, while its superb frieze is now in the British Museum, but the general structure is well preserved due to the temple's inaccessibility. Built by Iktinos, architect of the Parthenon and almost certainly at a later date (probably 420 BC), the unusually aligned temple, facing north, with its outer Doric columns is particularly interesting for its use of three-face Ionic columns within and, making its first appearance in architectural history, at least one Corinthian column (the capital no longer extant) at the sanctuary end of the cella.

Olympia

History of the Olympic Games

Starting in 776 BC, five midsummer days were set aside every four years for the Games at **Olympia** (Olimbía) (101 kms from Megalopolis). Contestants came from all over Greece, and eventually from throughout the Mediterranean; hostilities ceased, arms were forbidden and athletes competed peacefully for the highest honour, the olive wreath from the banks of the Alpheios. Social and even diplomatic intercourse were also features of the gathering, with the evenings taken up in philosophical debate, music and song, feasting and the signing of treaties. Initially the Games had a religious content, but increasingly they became more secular and open to commercialism and corruption, especially under Roman influence. The absurd Nero once came and entered the lists, the judges prudently declaring him the victor in every competition, even when, as in the case of the chariot race, the Emperor was thrown and failed to finish. Nero also imposed upon the Games contests in singing and playing on the lyre. During his interminable performances he would permit no one to leave, so that men feigned death in order to escape. Those Games contaminated by Nero, however, were struck off the sacred register after the Emperor's death.

The Games continued here for 1000 years in all and were only wound up at the command of the Roman Emperor Theodosios I, whose new-found Christian sensibility objected to these 'pagan rites'. The site itself was then brought to ruin by succeeding emperors, barbarian invasion, earthquake and the rising of the river. Excavations were undertaken in the 19th C by the French and Germans, and it was Baron de Coubertin who initiated the modern Olympic Games in 1896.

Legendary origins

The athletic contests probably developed from the funeral games of a local hero, Pelops (whence Peloponnese). It was prophesied that King Oinomaos would be killed by the man who married his daughter. So the King challenged each suitor to a chariot race and stabbed his rival in the back before reaching the finishing line. Thirteen suitors were killed in this way and Oinomaos was already talking of building a temple of skulls by the time Pelops came along. Pelops' lover, Poseidon, gave him a team of fast horses, but not satisfied with that, Pelops also replaced the lynchpin from the King's chariot with one of wax. Needless to say, the King took a fall and was killed while Pelops got the girl. It is not how you play the game that counts, but whether you win or lose.

The site

The pleasure of the site is in its leafy and cool pastoral setting, but if you come in the summer heat you will probably get only dust (though the Games were indeed held in August). And even in springtime when the pines are smelling fresh the number of visitors disturbs the tranquillity of the spot. As recently as the late 1950s only 500 tourists came here each year; now the figure is well over a million. The crowds come but the Games have gone and the temples and treasuries have a hollowness about them; Olympia seems to have lost its spirit of place.

But there is a partial remedy, and that is to walk straight down the avenue leading from the entrance, and ignoring the ruins of the temples of Hera and Zeus to turn left between them. Some distance behind the Temple of Hera there is a tunnel and it leads to the *Stadium*. Now this seems real. The starting and finishing lines, the judges' stand and the dedication to Demeter are still evident. You can make out the spectators' terraces under their covering of earth and grass. You can run back and forth along the length of the track, cheer from the sidelines, wait for the judge to clear his throat. Here you can relive the ancient Games (though purists

Stadium

should do so stark naked) and put some spirit back into Olympia.

Temple of Zeus

Returning through the tunnel you enter the *Altis*, the irregular quandrangle that was the sacred precinct of Zeus. Across it to the south are the remains of the massive *Temple of Zeus*, built some time between 470 and 456 BC. It was completely shattered by earthquakes 900 years later. Access was by a ramp at the east end; now there is only the level stylobate to see (lacking, incidentally, that optical curvature which so enhances the Parthenon) and a column drum or two in their original positions – on the south side they lie as they were thrown by the 6th C AD earthquakes. The east pediment was filled with sculptures depicting preparations for the chariot race between Pelops and Oinomaos; the west pediment sculptures representing the battle between Lapiths and Centaurs at the wedding of Perithoos. The surviving sculptures are now in the Olympia museum. At the west end of the cella was an enthroned chryselephantine *statue of Zeus* by Pheidias. Though one of the Seven Wonders of the ancient world, no certain copy of its exists nor any detailed description except by Pausanias who noted that no list of its measurements (it was seven times life-size) could do justice to the impression it made on the spectator. Caligula wished to move it to Rome and replace the head of Zeus with his own, but every time his agents came near the statue it burst into a loud peal of laughter. Finally it was taken to Constantinople by Theodosios II where it was destroyed in a fire in AD 475.

Temple of Hera

To the north was a small grove, the *Pelopion*, with an altar to Pelops, and somewhere near it an *altar to Zeus* where daily blood sacrifices were made. And beyond these is the *Temple of Hera*, the oldest but best preserved building at Olympia. Begun early in the 7th C, it was first made of wood and even in Pausanias' time (2nd C AD) some of its columns were still the wooden originals. But the worship of Hera played little part in the history of Olympia (the temple was initially for Hera and Zeus jointly and was left to the goddess' sole use when the grander Temple of Zeus was built), and characteristically Pausanias finds a peculiar anecdote the most interesting thing about it. The roof had recently been repaired and the body of a hoplite was found between it and the ceiling. The soldier had apparently fought in the 401–399 BC war between Sparta and Elis, during which a battle had swept across the Altis. Wounded, the hoplite had dragged himself up into this shelter, but died there and remained undiscovered for 500 years.

Atop a flight of steps between the Temple of Hera and the Stadium are the foundation ruins of the *Treasuries* of various Greek states where sacrificial vessels may have been stored, and gear used in the Games. Below these is the *Metroon*, a small temple dedicated to the Mother of the Gods. To the

OLYMPIA

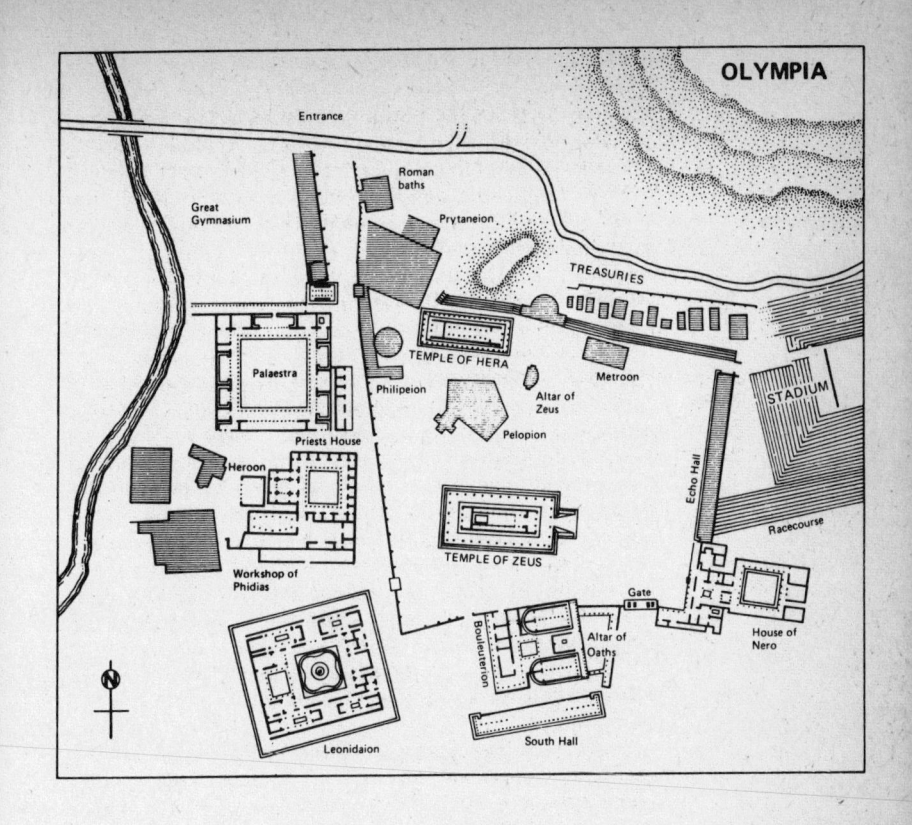

west of Hera's temple are the foundations of the *Philipeion*, a circular monument begun by Philip of Macedon after his victory at Chaironeia and completed by his son Alexander the Great. The *Prytaneion* to the north of this is where the Olympic victors were feasted; its remains are scanty.

On the south side of the Altis, the *Boulouterion* was the seat of the Olympic Senate; on the *altar of oaths* competitors swore they would not use foul play in the Games. Across the avenue, the *Leonidaion* served as a hostel for distinguished visitors and was later the residence of the Roman governor of Achaia. The *workshop of Pheidias* is not a fanciful attribution; Pausaunias described it and in modern times a cup bearing the master sculptor's name was found there, as well as tools and moulds used in the manufacture of his great statue of Zeus. North of this was the *Palaestra*, the wrestling school.

The museum   Opposite the site entrance and back behind the car park and the trees is the new museum. In its *entrance hall* is a model of the Altis; you should follow the galleries clockwise, their most outstanding items mentioned here. *Gallery 4*: the

111

helmet of Miltiades, victor at Marathon. *Gallery 5*: The *Victory* or *Nike of Paionios*. *Gallery 6*: The Hermes of Praxiteles, one of the best-preserved of classical statues, it was found in the Temple of Hera in 1877 in the place where Pausanias described it. The *Central Hall* contains the *pedimental sculpture* from the Temple of Zeus together with those *metopes* depicting the Labours of Herakles that were not taken off to the Louvre.

Into the Mountains to Kalávrita

Mountain villages

Driving out of Olympia on the road to Lalas you climb into the mountains and get a good view of the ancient site below. Beyond this you are wandering about in a Peloponnese which could have been like this one hundred years ago. The villages are isolated; some of them are plain and rough, like Foloi and Koumanis on the edges of a great forest with a fern-covered floor. Here it comes almost as a shock to see men working with timber instead of herding goats. Other villages are like flowers on the mountainsides. **Lábia** is such a village, in a niche between two mountains with a view over valleys and mountains beyond. Whitewashed stone houses, blue doors, wooden balconies, red-tiled roofs, the houses climbing up gentle slopes with terraces above and below thick with figs and grapes, flowers, fruit trees and shrubs. In 1948 this was the headquarters of the Communist forces in the Peloponnese.

From mountain villages like Labia or from coastal Patras, the roads towards **Kalávrita** (95 kms from Patras), wind higher, the mountains now capped with snow even early in June. This is a resort town, summer and especially winter, and though not very pretty itself its situation is marvellous. (In 1943 the Germans here massacred 1436 males over the age of 15 and burnt the town. The schools have since been endowed by the government of the German Federal Republic). It lies in a valley which when approached from the south is broad, well-cultivated, with waves of wheat along its floor and brilliant spots of poppies and jonquils.

The gorge and the rack-and-pinion railway

When Kalavrita is approached from the north, the road slips through a powerful gorge which cuts directly through the mountains, massive outcrops of worn, rounded, oddly-shaped rock shoved to either side like unwanted dough. But rather than take the road, treat yourself to a ride on the Kalavrita Railway, engineered in 1885–95, which creeps up the gorge, sometimes pushed, sometimes pulled by little 75 cm gauge diesels, along gradients as much as 1 in 7 from **Diakoftó** on the Corinthian Gulf.

The **Monastery of Megaspeleion** is 10 kms north on the road out of Kalavrita, or a long donkey ride out of the gorge at Zaklorou, one of the railway stops. The old monastery was destroyed by fire in the 1930s and the new one, built into the cliff face, looks like a cross between a hotel and a prison. Nevertheless, it is worth trudging up here for the view over the gorge and the valley beyond. Inside is the Treasury containing sacred relics, including a miraculous ikon, 9th to 11th C Gospels, the heads of the monks Theodore and Symeon, founders of the monastery, and assorted hands of the martyrs and saints, while hanging out the windows monks in their underwear call to one another or brush their beards into the wind.

Revolt against the Turks

Seven kms south of Kalavrita is **Agia Lavra,** the monastery where Bishop Germanos was first to raise the standard of revolt on 21 March 1821.

To the Coast and Patras

Had you instead followed the main road west from Olympia you would find yourself in **Pírgos** (22 kms), a dull market town. Travelling north from here you would pass at 15 kms the Frankish castle of **Chlemoútsi** on a high cape with fine views in one direction across the channel to the island of Zakynthos, in the other across the entire plain of Elis.

Frankish castle

The road carries on to **Patras** (Pátrai) (96 kms from Pirgos, 135 kms from Corinth), the largest city of the Peloponnese and western gateway to Greece. You may leave Greece from here in sadness, or arrive here full of anticipation; but with the possible exception of the Byzantine kastro (though containing many later features) built on the site and incorporating fragments of the ancient acropolis and offering a fine view along the coast, and the gold-encased head of St Andrew in the church of the same name on Odos Trion Navarkon, there is little here of particular interest. The church, which is modern and reputedly the largest in Greece, is said to have been built on the site of Andrew's martyrdom and the head was returned here by Pope Paul VI from Rome as an ecumenical gesture towards the Orthodox Church after 900 years of schism. It is the civility and generosity of the inhabitants that is most appealing, as when you have bought food for the voyage home and then have been presented with more as a gift: the heart is touched, the separation so much harder, the need to return and somehow to repay so much stronger. Patras, characteristically, is the one city in Greece which still enjoys its pre-Lenten carnival in the traditional, colourful manner, unlike Athens, for example, where the season has become no more than an excuse for knocking strangers over the head with plastic hammers.

Head of St Andrew

Carnival

Along the Gulf of Corinth

The National Highway from Athens runs along the littoral of the northern Peloponnese from Corinth to Patras, a good fast road for those in a hurry, but the older road meandering along the coastline from village to village past vineyards and

113

olive groves, cypresses and willows, is more pleasant. Coming from Patras, or after the descent from Kalavrita to the coast near Diakofto, you can cross the Gulf of Corinth at **Ríon** by car ferry, landing at Andirrion on the other side (see *Road to Delphi* and *Northwest Greece* chapters).

From Diakofto, 41 kms east is **Xilókastro**, a major resort with a sandy beach and camping site, the mountains behind almost tumbling into the gulf. Another 13 kms towards Corinth is Kiato, the name derived from **Sikyon**, one of the most ancient of Greek cities famous for its cultivation of the arts and extolled by Homer as 'a lovely and fruitful city, adapted to every recreation'. The original settlement was on the shore, but following its destruction by the Macedonians in 303 BC it was rebuilt on an acropolis 3 kms inland from which there are fine views. There is a two-level gymnasium with fountain and, the most obvious feature of the site, a large 3rd C BC theatre cut into the hillside.

PRACTICAL INFORMATION

TRAVEL TO THE CENTRAL PELOPONNESE
Refer also to the *Practical Information* section under Athens.

Buses leave from 100 Kifissou Street, Athens, for Tripolis (about 10 a day), Megalopolis (5–6 a day), Andritsaina (1), Olympia (3), Pirgos (9), Patras (17–22), and Xilokastro and Kiato (14–15).

Trains depart from the Stathmos Peloponnisou for Tripolis and Megalopolis (about 5 a day), and for Xilokastro, Diakofto (connection to Kalavrita), Aigion, Patras and Pirgos (6 a day). From Pirgos twice a day there is a connecting train to Olympia.

By way of comparison, the bus to Patras takes about $3\frac{1}{2}$ hours whereas most of the trains take well over 4 hours; however the bus costs half as much again as the train. To Tripolis the difference is less marked, but most of the trains take longer than the bus (4 hours) and they cost about 75 drachmas less.

TRIPOLIS
Accommodation and Eating
Hotels: Menalon (A); Arkadia (B); Galaxy (C); Acropole (D).
Tavernas: Kipos tou Sosoli, 40 John Kennedy; To Kanake, Petrapoulou Street.

Travel
Local *buses* run to and from Megalopolis. There is a regular mid-morning bus to Andritsaina (for Vassai).

TEGEA
Hourly *buses* from Tripolis.

MEGALOPOLIS
Hotels: Achillion, Paris (D).
Site: 8am to 6pm daily, 9am to 3.30pm Sundays and holidays.

You can visit the site of *Lykosoura*, 14 kms to the west via Apiditsa: remains of a temple among olive trees and a small museum (keys from nearby village).

ANDRITSAINA
Accommodation and Eating
Theoxenia (B); Pan (D); Vassae (E) opposite a reasonable restaurant.

Travel
Two *buses* travel to and from Pirgos, early morning and early afternoon. There is also the local bus from Tripolis apart from the daily bus from Athens.

To reach *Vassai* (14 kms) you must take a *taxi* (unless you hitch or walk) as there are no buses up to the site; the taxi will cost about 500 drachmas and will wait while you visit the site. To *walk* takes about 3 hours. It might also be interesting to walk from Vassai to the sea, but we have not done it.

OLYMPIA
Accommodation
Hotels: SPAP (A); Xenia, Neon Olympia, Apollon (B); Ilis, Achilles (C); Pelops (D).

There is a *youth hostel* in the main street; *camping* at Diana Camping and (better) Olympia Camping; and many *rooms* to rent, especially in the street parallel to the main street up the hill.

Eating
Karachaliou, opposite the turning to the station; Thraka, on the Pirgos road; O Manos, inexpensive, near the Hereon Hotel.

Travel
Local *buses* to Pirgos (5 a day) and Tripolis (2); also 2 *trains* daily to Pirgos and onwards.

Site and Museums
Open 8am to 7pm daily (best to be there early to avoid the coaches), 9am to 7pm Sundays and holidays. The site museum is closed Tuesdays.

There is also an *Historical Museum of the Olympic Games* 3 kms along the road to Tripolis.

KALAVRITA
Accommodation
Chelmos (B); Maria (C); Paradissos (D).

Zaklorou (whence *Megaspeleion Monastery* may be reached in one hour by foot) has a hotel, Romantso (D), and tavernas. The monastery provides beds for men only (arrive before 8pm).

115

Travel
The spectacular *train* journey from Diakofto takes about an hour; the train runs 4 to 5 times a day. Also there is a daily *bus* from Tripolis to Patras via Kalavrita.

To reach *Agia Lavra* from Kalavrita (7 kms) either walk or take a taxi.

PIRGOS
The Orpheus theatre sometimes puts on shadow plays.

KILLINI (near Chlemoutsi)
Daily *ferries* to Zakinthos and Kefallinia. Good *swimming*. *Camping*.

PATRAS
Accommodation and Eating
Numerous *hotels*, e.g Acropole, Moreas (A); Galaxy, Majestic (B); El Greco (C); Anglias, Delphi (D); Parthenon (E). There is a *youth hostel* at 68 Odos Heroon Polytechnic. Many *tavernas* along the waterfront: try Evangelatos, 9 Agiou Nikolaou.

Travel
There are frequent *local buses* to Rion (whence the ferry to Andirrion, every 15 minutes during the day, every 30 minutes between 11pm and 7am), Aigion and Diakofto, as well as a regular service to Pirgos. Apart from Athens, the *longer-distance buses* serve towns across the Gulf such as Messalongi and Navpaktos, also Agrinion, Levkas, Arta and Ioannina. Buses leave from the area to the east of the railway station.

Boats leave Patras for the Ionian islands regularly.

Information and Activities
Tourist Police, 14 Othonos Amalias.

The *museum* is in the Plateia Olgas. In summer plays, etc, are staged at the *Roman Odeion* during the evenings. Visits can be made to the *Achaia-Klauss winery* in the hills behind Patras (closed 2 to 4pm). There is good *swimming* at Ities, 4 kms west of Patras, where there is also a camping site; other camping sites are to the east at Agia and at Rion.

XILOKASTRO
Hotels: Apollon, Miramare (B); Hermes (D); Kentrikon (E).

There is now a *museum* commemorating the poet Angelos Sikelianos in his former villa.

SIKYON (Kiato)
Hotels: Triton (B); Galini, Sicyon (C).

To reach the *ancient site* on the plateau behind the modern town take the bus or walk the few kms to the village of Vasiliko, which lies close to the acropolis of the original ancient city. There is now a *museum* in the former Roman baths.

From Kiato you may take a *boat* to Perachora (see *The Argolid* chapter).

THE SOUTHERN PELOPONNESE

Into the Lakonian Plain
Unlike Athens, **Sparta** (Spárti) made little effort to glorify itself with monuments, and Thucydides said, 'Posterity will find it difficult to believe its power corresponded to its fame'. So it is that the traveller approaches the Lakonian plain in a suitably dismissive mood.

Defended by a great wedge of mountains, the Parnon range to the east, the Taigetos to the west, the Lakonian plain narrows to a spear point at its northern end. The 63-kilometre road from Tripolis runs through a long defile through Parnon and hesitates along a ridge with spectacular views of mountains all around. At this moment, as the road begins to twist down into the plain, you realise that Thucydides was not a man for describing superlative scenery, nor did he care to suggest the mystery of penetrating these mountain walls as though entering a secret garden, this extensive and bountiful Lakonian plain shimmering with olive groves and thick with the scent of oranges, watered by the Evrotas, and cooled by late afternoon breezes as the sun sets early beyond the high Taigetos. At few places in Greece can you so suddenly and completely appreciate the strategic location and hence the power of an ancient city.

Homeric Sparta
In Homeric legend, this was the home of Menelaos, husband of Helen, brother of Agamemnon of Mycenae. According to the *Iliad* Menelaos exercised control or influence over most of the Greek principalities, though archaeologists – perhaps only through oversight – have failed to turn up evidence of a settlement here comparable to Mycenae at the same period. In any case, Menelaos is likely to have been based at Amyklai, 8 kms south of Sparta, where the not very illuminating remains of a Sanctuary of Hyakinthos (accidentally killed by his friend Apollo – a flower grew on the spot) have been discovered. But as with classical Sparta, the true fortifications of the Mycenaean settlement here were probably the mountains themselves.

Spartan character and history
The latter-day Spartans, however, did not look back upon the Mycenaean inhabitants of the Lakonian plain as their ancestors. The Dorians, a tribe which had previously lived in northern Greece on the edge of the civilised world, overran the Mycenaean cities of the Peloponnese in two waves, the first about 1200 BC, the second about 200 years later. Whether the Spartans were pure Dorians or some mixture of conquered and conquerors cannot be ascertained, but the Spartans themselves claimed a pure descent from the rugged newcomers, spoke their dialect and lived by their austere traditions. Good conversation, particularly the sharply witty though not ungraceful retort, leavened their hard lives.

Plutarch records that one Spartan, being asked to go hear a man who exactly counterfeited the voice of a nightingale, answered, 'Sir, I have heard the nightingale itself'. Nor, despite their restraint, were they without fine poetry and sculpture or mastery in the art of pottery. Sparta was even infamous for the freedom of its women and did not acquire its reputation for philistinism and repression until the 6th C when state anxiety strangled culture at home as surely as its military juggernaut crushed the real or imaginary threats of external rivals.

Sparta's problem was that as a land-based power locked away in the Peloponnese she failed to take advantage of the expanding commercial horizons which were being exploited by 6th and 5th C maritime states like Athens. Agriculture was the basis of her conservative economy. The use of a freely-exchangeable currency was forbidden. Territory was the measure of wealth and power. The inner core of Spartan villages came to an accommodation with the peripheral villages of the Lakonian plain, the perioikoi ('dwellers around'), whom they dominated but declined to conquer. This master-client relationship was later extended where convenient to other states in the Peloponnese. The Spartans kept to the duties of their estates and of government, leaving commerce and crafts to the perioikoi, who lived as freemen (though without voting rights in the mother city).

Perioikoi

As Sparta's needs and ambitions grew, so necessarily did her hunger for land. Towards the end of the 8th C BC Sparta attacked the fertile plain of Messenia across the Taigetos to the west, then moved north against Tegea (c600 BC), and finally defeated Argos (494 BC), her only serious rival in the Peloponnese. The peoples she defeated and did not supervise as client states she reduced to the condition of helots, enslaved populations whose only function was to cultivate the Spartan estates now too extensive for personal attention.

Helots

But Sparta was caught up in a vicious circle. With a population jealous of its own privileges and never exceeding 10,000, instead of extending rights, sharing prosperity and evolving towards a more liberal society as were many other Greek states, the fear that one of her 'allies' might prefer greater independence, or that the vastly outnumbering helot masses might revolt – as did the Messenians in the 7th and again in the 5th C – led her into oppressive reaction on the one hand and on the other still further aggression abroad to acquire the resources needed to hold down what she already brutally possessed.

The Messenian revolt

The 'reforms' of Lykourgos which put power in the hands of a gerontocracy may have come either immediately before or immediately after the Messenian revolt early in the 7th C BC, that is, either in anticipation of efficiently governing an extending land empire or in fear of losing it. Their effect

Political reaction

was to repress individual initiative and vagaries. Weak and deformed children were left to die on Taigetos; the stronger surviving males being taken from their mothers at seven to be educated in camps where privacy was denied, flogging employed to develop fortitude, and stealing encouraged towards the attainment of self-reliance. At the age of 20 these young men joined the army or perhaps the Krypteia, the secret police who from time to time were let loose on the helots. From these few thousand highly disciplined Spartans was forged the most powerful army of pre-Hellenistic Greece.

The mountains magnificently impose and provide the reminder of Spartan power even if their own lack of monuments, as Thucydides said, do not. But the harsh reality of that power is lost amidst the luxuriance of this peaceful plain and it is with some satisfaction that one scuffles through this banal, provincial modern town and thinks how nicely it commemorates the anonymity Spartans strove for.

The modern town, in fact, occupies only the southern third of the full extent of the ancient city. A short walk northwards through olive groves brings you to the low mound that served as Sparta's *acropolis* surrounded by the remains of Byzantine walls. Just to the west, built into the side of a hill, is a 2nd or 1st C BC *theatre*, nearly as large as the one at Megalopolis, but unimpressive as most of its masonry was put to use in the building of Mistra. Leaving the acropolis by the north gate and turning right along this side of the Evrotas brings you to some remains of the *city walls*, a feature of Sparta's decline, as in her heyday she claimed that her fighting men were her best defence. About a kilometre further along this course (not far east of the Tripolis road, between the road and the Evrotas; a battered blue sign points the way) is the *sanctuary of Artemis Orthia*, where Spartan boys were flogged. The Romans, perverse where the Spartans were merely brutal, built a theatre here for spectators to witness what had by then become a folk entertainment. Back in town, the *museum* contains most notably a marble bust of Leonidas, commander of the Spartan troops at Thermopylae (*Room 3*), archaic bronze figurines (*Room 4*), and some mosaics from Roman villas in the town (*Room 5*).

Six kms to the west of Sparta and hard beside the flank of Taigetos, the ruined Byzantine city of **Mistrá** ascends a steep hill crowned at the summit by a Frankish fortress. Fascinating in itself, Mistra is not least worth visiting for its enchanting position overlooking the Lakonian plain. The fortress was built by William de Villehardouin in 1249 to protect medieval Sparta from marauding Slavs coming down from Taigetos and after several alternations in ownership became firmly Byzantine in the early 14th C. By this time the plain had been deserted by its inhabitants who clustered beneath the citadel

Sparta's acropolis

Museum

for security, and for the next hundred years and more the city flourished as the seat of the Despotate of the Morea – governed by either sons or brothers of the emperor in Constantinople – and nurtured the last Byzantine renaissance. The philosopher Plethon, rediscoverer of Plato, lived here during the first half of the 15th C. Constantine XI Paleologos was Despot of Mistra from 1443 to 1448 before succeeding to the Imperial throne at Constantinople.

The Lower Town

Entering the gate to the Lower Town and turning right, the *Metropolis*, built in 1309, stands in a spacious court from which there is an agreeable view across the valley of the Evrotas. Along with the paintings and intricately carved marble ikonostasis inside, also interesting is the double-headed eagle in the floor, possibly commemorating the coronation of the last emperor, Constantine XI. The *museum*, containing decorative fragments from the churches, is next door. A bit further uphill is the *Vrontikion*, monastery and cultural centre, and burial place of the Despots. Of the two churches within this complex, the *Aphentiko*, furthest on, is outstanding for its interior proportions and boldly coloured frescoes depicting the Miracles of Christ. Had you turned left at the entrance gate you would after some distance along the path have come to the *Monastery of the Perivleptos* and its 14th C church with excellent frescoes and a Pantokrator glowering down from the dome. But it is most convenient to stop here on the return journey down.

The Upper Town

Passing through the *Monemvasia Gate* into the Upper Town you come upon the *Palace of the Despots*, a rare and impressive example of a Byzantine civic building. Though roofless and crumbling, its facade now spare of ornamentation, its vast hall and gaping windows convey a grandeur appropriate to the surrounding landscape. Left from the gate is the *Pantanassa*, in plan similar to the Aphentiko but more slender in its proportions and containing some of the finest examples of late Byzantine fresco. The church belongs to a convent, the nuns now the only inhabitants and guardians of a city which once had a population of 40,000. A breathtaking view of Mistra spilling back down the mountainside is the reward of those who sweat their way up to the fortified summit.

The last Emperor of Byzantium

Often the humblest village in Greece will erect a proud statue to the local boy who went away and made good, and in the same way, a short walk down the road at the top end of the present village of Mistra, a statue has been put up to Constantine XI Paleologos. On a May night in 1453 a crescent of fire embraced the Land Walls of Constantinople as the overwhelming army of Sultan Mehmet prepared for the morning kill. This last emperor, named Constantine like the first, gathered his followers in Agia Sophia, the most magnificent church in Christendom, to celebrate a final mass amidst sobs and wailings and cries of *Kyrie eleison*. Calling 'God forbid that I should live an Emperor without an Empire! As my city falls, I will fall with it!' he rode out against the Turks and was immediately cut down. Around the plateia, its plane tree and spring, are several small tavernas and kafeneions where you can refresh yourself after a hot day's climbing with a meal and some wine, Byzantium lingering in the evening light.

Over the Taigetos and into the Messenian Plain

The Langada Pass

The steep and twisting road from Sparta to Kalamata (63 kms) cuts by way of the 1525-metre high Langada Pass through the Taigetos range, providing some of the most spectacular mountain views in Greece. Goat-footed nymphs and the goddess Artemis were said to frequent this high-alpine country.

Kalamáta (officially Kalámi) is best known for its olives and among Greeks is favoured as a resort, though atmosphere is entirely lacking in the recent sprawl towards the sea and the beaches are dull. In 1829 the French landed 14,000 troops here to encourage the army of Ibrahim Pasha, which was assisting Turkish efforts at crushing the Greek revolt, to return to Egypt. It is from this period that the old part of town dates, and this lies about 2 kms inland from the Messenian Gulf and centres round Plateia Martiou, an area of interest and some charm. The *market* is here; also the *museum*, in two fine old houses, and contains relics of the War of Independence along with a good Roman mosaic and Byzantine ikons. A few streets north is the *citadel*, built in 1208 by the nephew of that Geoffrey de Villehardouin who chronicled the Venetian betrayal and sack of Constantinople four years earlier.

The Messenian plain extends northwards, but the modern town of Messeni just to the west of Kalamata is in no way related to the ancient object of Spartan rapaciousness. That site, now partly occupied by the attractive village of Mavromati, lies 20 kms to the north. The colossal walls of **Messene**, once encompassing the city's farmlands within their 10-kilometre length, are the most complete extant from the Hellenic period. They too owe their construction in 369 BC to Epaminondas and his anti-Spartan strategy (see Megalopolis and Mantinea). The foundations of a fine temple have very recently been excavated on the site which wraps about the southwest slope of Mt Ithome, 792 metres high, where from its summit Messenian helots, during their final rebellion against Spartan humiliation, held their besieging oppressors at bay for five years, from 464 to 459 BC. The view from here takes in most of the Messenian plain, rich in cotton, wheat, dates and bananas.

The Western Finger of the Peloponnese

Battle of Navarino

Fifty-one kms west of Kalamata is **Pýlos**, doubly famous for the Palace of Nestor and, under the more familiar name of *Navarino*, for the spectacular destruction of the Turkish and Egyptian fleets at the hands of the combined British, French and Russian squadrons under the command of Admiral Codrington. Without the loss of a single one of their own 26 ships, the European allies on 20 October, 1827 sailed into the bay and sank 53 enemy ships, killed 16,000 men and, by breaking the Ottoman Empire's control of the seas around Greece, ensured Greek independence. The magnificent natural harbour closed to the Ionian Sea by the long and undulating island of Sphakteria, the surrounding pine woods, a Turkish and a Venetian castle and good swimming, make Pylos the most pleasant place to stay when exploring this area.

Palace of Nestor

Nestor's Palace is in fact 17 kms up the coast from modern Pylos which sits at the southern end of the bay. The panorama befits a great king, and Nestor, according to Homer, provided the Greeks with their second largest fleet in their expedition against Troy. In searching for his father Odysseus, Telemachos, in company with Athena (disguised as Mentor), was received here with generous hospitality. 'The travellers now came to Pylos, where they found the people on the sea-beach sacrificing jet-black bulls to Poseidon, Lord of the Earthquake, god of the sable locks. There sat Nestor with his sons, while their followers around them were piercing meat with skewers or roasting it in preparation for the banquet. But as soon as they caught sight of the strangers they all made a move in their direction waving their hands in welcome, and beckoning the newcomers to join them. Nestor's son, Peisistratos, who was the first to reach them, took them both by the hand and gave them places at the banquet on downy fleeces spread over the sandy beach.'

The best preserved of all Mycenaean palaces, and now largely under a protective roof, the walls of Pylos still stand a metre high over a considerable area. Excavations under the direction of the American Carl Blegen took place in 1939 and from 1952 to 1965, revealing vast rooms with lofty, probably 3.5-metre high ceilings, brilliant frescoes (now in the museum 4 kms away in Chora), and numerous Linear B tablets, the first to be found on the Greek mainland.

Venetian outposts

Worth the journey 12 kms south from modern Pylos is the great Venetian castle at **Methóni**, its vast walls mingling with the sea, a way-station for pilgrims to the Holy Land and merchants engaged in the Levantine trade, towers and crenellations wavering in the heat, a dream-image of the East. **Koróni**, 32 kms southeast of Methoni (29 kms from Kalamata), is a small and picturesque medieval town on a promontory fortified by the Venetians which surveys the Messenian Gulf and the mountains of the Mani beyond.

Mani

The road south from Kalamata to Areopolis winds along the ruggedly beautiful western coast of Mani, the central peninsula of the Peloponnese formed by the arching backbone of the Taigetos which plunges finally into the sea at Cape Matapan, famous for wrecks and known to the ancients as Tainaron, the gateway to Hades.

The peninsula is traditionally divided into Outer Mani where the bleak mountains are relieved by plains of olives, figs and grain running down from Kalamata to Kardamyli and beyond, and Inner Mani which begins just above Areopolis, rocky and treeless, where stone towerhouses, built in defence against vendettas, accentuate the forbidding landscape. The Maniots claim direct descent from the ancient Spartans and are a stern though hospitable people.

Its history Certainly, with the decline of Sparta the Maniots organised themselves into the Confederation of Free-Lakonians, whose independence was recognised even by Augustus after he had subjected the rest of the Peloponnese to Rome. The great Byzantine general Belisarius reported only pagans when he landed in Mani in AD 333, and the Maniots as a whole probably only converted to Christianity during the reign of the Emperor Basil I (867–886), though four churches dating back to the 6th, possibly to the 5th C have been identified. The Slavs made only minor inroads and the Turks had to content themselves with the nominal allegiance of the principal clan chieftain, the Bey of the Mani. Petrobey Mavromichalis, the last such titleholder, ensured his place in the pantheon of Greek heroes by leading his people in rebellion against the Turks in 1821, his home town of Tzimova being renamed Areopolis, city of the war-god Ares, at the outset of the revolt. The scarce soil of Mani never afforded much livelihood; the attraction of Mani was as a last rugged sanctuary from where Greeks could resist foreign invasion. With that purpose gone after independence the region suffered from depopulation and impoverishment which is only now being reversed as the Greek government is encouraging the first trickle of tourism into the area. Anyone wishing to familiarise himself with this least explored part of Greece should read Patrick Leigh Fermor's classic *Mani*.

Along the coast of Outer Mani Leaving Kalamata the road first follows the Messenian Gulf but then twists and rises inland. **Kámbos** (20 kms), though not interesting close at hand, sits prettily in a broad basin filled with olives and oranges and dominated by the *Castle of Zarnata* with its Frankish enceinte and Turkish keep. About 9 kms further a side road leads to **Tséria** (signposted), a beautiful village on a mountain ledge with a dramatic view from its southern extremity over the great Taigetos gorge that spills down from Profitas Ilias, the highest mountain in the Peloponnese. The main road returns to the coast and turns a high flank from where a magnificent panorama of the coastline bursts upon you, **Kardamýli** (36 kms) far below amid its plain of olives.

In the 1950s the road used to end at Kardamyli; from here you went by donkey over stony tracks or, far easier, called along the coast in a caique. Now the village can claim to have a strip, with a few general shops and tavernas catering to the pausing or passing trade, and a few more tavernas by the sea where there is swimming off the jetty and the beach. This is what Fermor described as the lower village of fishermen's houses; these are whitewashed and would not be out of place anywhere else in Greece. But if you follow the dry streambed (the last gasp of the great Taigetos gorge) or wander up through lanes that pass between the roadside houses, you come eventually to the *upper town* of solid well-cut stone, deserted now but even in its neglect displaying a finesse, a small grandeur, that is pocket-sized Venetian. Here a church and a prison form two sides of a plateia where Kolokotronis joined with Mavromichalis before they stormed Kalamata and on these flagstones played human chess to pass the time – a third side bounded by a shattered tower-palace is your first introduction to the many towerhouses bristling like prickly-pears from the hard landscape of the Inner Mani further south. This pattern of a well-built older town at some distance from the sea and a lesser settlement on the littoral is common throughout Greece as a defence against pirates; and now in peaceful times the old strongholds are abandoned and the population gathers round the harbours.

Apart from some rock-cuttings of Mycenaean date, Kardamyli reveals nothing of its ancient past, though it was once of sufficient significance to form part of an offer by Agamemnon to Achilles to appease his wrath. About 8 kms south a sudden *acropolis* rises from the sloping coastland, the site of ancient Leuktra which the indefatigable Pausanias visited. He reported a sanctuary of Athena on the table-top hill, and below, where the stream still flows by what is now called **Lévktron**, a sacred grove of Love. Castle Beaufort occupied the acropolis during the Middle Ages. As at Kardamyli, Levktron describes the abandoned inland village; a small population now lives round the tiny and beautiful port of **Stoúpa**, which together with Kalogria cove immediately north has the finest sand beach in the Mani. The small road connecting Stoupa and Kalogria is Odos Nikos Kazantzakis for it was here that he lived and met the man who became Zorba the Greek – not in real life a Cretan but a mad Maniot who worked a lignite mine in the cliff-face to the northeast of Kalogria. A road from Stoupa runs inland to Neachorion and further up to **Pírgos** on a mountain ledge, a delightful village where at evening you can pull up a kafeneion chair, order an ouzo and enjoy the most romantic sunset view of the Mani coast.

About 6 kms south of Stoupa the mountains again fall directly into the sea and the road must climb over their flanks, passing through a succession of villages – Pigi, Platsa, Nomitsi, Thalamae and Langada – with small Byzantine churches, and sometimes more ancient fragments incorporated into the walls of a schoolhouse or well; at **Langáda** (56 kms from Kalamata) a crop of towerhouses rises in terraces. You are now nearing the border between Messenia and Lakonia, between Outer and Inner Mani, and the landscape becomes harder, rock-strewn and tortured. It is the gorge at **Oítilon** that traditionally marks the divide; on the southern side, opposite the village, you can make out the sprawling enceinte of *Kelefá*, the Turkish fortress on the edge of the land they could not enter. In those times Oitilo was a slave market, where Moslems sold Christians and Christians sold Moslems, though each were not above selling their coreligionists too. Napoleon put in here on his way to Egypt. **Limeníon**, the tiny port of Areopolis, lies just further on, a silent, barely inhabited place of charm and superb views, fine for a swim and a simple meal at the waterfront taverna.

On a headland high above is **Areópolis** (76 kms from Kalamata), 700 inhabitants strong, the chief centre of Mani. Its towerhouses, twisting narrow lanes suddenly blooded by a flow of bougainvillea and its stark churches, especially the *Taxiarchis* with a primitive panel of martial saints over its door, compete with a creeping ordinariness, the usual concrete tattiness that in Greece announces concourse with the wider world. It is best to press on into the unclad land.

Avoiding perhaps the *caves of Diros*, 10 kms south, where luridly illuminated stalactites and stalagmites are viewed by boat on an underground lake, you should follow the Gerolimin road to **Koíta** (21 kms from Areopolis), a good example of a towerhouse village. Until the end of the last century Maniots so jealously guarded their honour and their poor stony ground that most often it was watered by their blood. A vendetta could work its way through generations, though the warring families might live cheek by jowl, allowing free passage to their women to work the fields while the men built their stone houses higher and higher, to dominate the enemy neighbour, to throw rocks upon his house or blast it with muskets or cannons. Walk up beyond the village and then turn to survey the amazing view. There are towerhouses everywhere, Koita in the foreground, then across the valley **Nómia** sitting on the edge of a plateau, and **Stavrí** further on – the entire landscape is fortified, every

Inner Mani

Towerhouses and vendettas

house a fortress, the houses clustered into villages which themselves become fortresses, while between them are the brown bare fields and stone walls. It is an early medieval landscape, Tuscany without the green and gentle roll of the land, the spare, slightly mad feeling of a pre-Renaissance painting.

From Stavri you can walk down to the promontory of Tigani, though you need stout boots to cross the fractured rocks and dry crackling spiney plants (globe thistle, euphorbia, etc) to the *Castle of Maina* built by William II de Villehardouin in 1248. Its huge ramp and walls are ruinous, its graves once beneath the chapel floor torn open, some still containing a scattering of Frankish bones.

Gerolimín (27 kms from Areopolis), is a small port built only in the 1870s and despite its stone houses on the stony shore is without feeling for the intense mood of the hinterland. The road runs southeast along the coast to **Vátheia**, the classic Maniot village where towerhouses seem to climb over one another to erupt from the hilltop like a natural extension of the rocky landscape. A dirt road continues with spectacular views towards **Cape Matapan**, but a new paved road swings north again from near Vatheia and along the east coast of Mani – Sunny Mani as it is called locally to distinguish it from the sombre Shadow Mani just departed. This eastern coast is pleasant but uneventful; the road loops back towards Areopolis from where a road follows a low pass through the Taigetos to Gytheion.

Once the ancient port of Sparta and now the capital of the Mani, **Gýtheion** is hardly like the settlements of the interior. It lies on the edge of the Lakonian plain where it spreads out before the gulf, and so the mountains are at some distance, the immediate landscape not at all rugged, the town itself a placid, wash-coloured place, agreeable rather than fiercely austere. The ancient city was on the low hills about a kilometre back from the present shoreline where a small theatre has been excavated; the new town is built on reclaimed land and has a pleasant promenade with many tavernas. The very earliest settlement was on the islet of Marathonisi, now reached by a causeway, and it was here

Helen of Troy that Helen and Paris were said to have spent their first night together before leaving Menalaos' kingdom and setting course for Troy.

To Monemvasia

Around Sparta the Laconian plain is flat and luxuriously cultivated, but heading seawards there is a ridge of low rock-strewn hills assiduously deforested of their pine cover and

The approach by land planted with olives. The ridge marks the earliest limit of the Spartan villages and subordinate perioikoi. Perhaps the first drums were heard in Sparta's aggressive expansion when her

The authors' traverse of the Taigetos from Sparta into Mani

army topped that ridge and bore down on the fan of land below. Making for Monemvasia along the main road from either Gytheion or Sparta (about 90 kms by either route) takes you through the market town of **Skála** after passing over the Evrotas on its way to the sea. The coastal plain is flat and green, thickly cultivated with cotton and rice. There is an uneasy sense of exposure, of vulnerability, the security of the mountains being so far off on either side, yet with the knowledge that well-girded at the point where the mountains join to the north, but also girding itself for war, lies Sparta. For it is here, just below Skala, that ancient **Helos** stood, the first to be enslaved as 'helots', and you feel its doom, as though yet impending, as though the landscape is what it was 2700 years ago and the marsh-cultivating folk of Helos realise with terror their imminent subjection as the steady, growing sound of Spartan drums advances down the plain as certainly as the Evrotas itself.

An alternative and seldom followed route from Sparta to Monemvasia (also about 90 kms) is along the rugged road which skirts the flanks of Parnon and passes through Geraki, a large village on the site of ancient **Geronthrai**, its towering 427-metre acropolis still guarded by imposing Cyclopean walls, possibly pre-Mycenaean, in which case they have survived on a scale unique in Greece. Nearby, on a detached mountain rib, stands a Frankish kastro surrounded by several beautiful Byzantine churches with frescoes and mosaics dating from the 12th to the 16th C.

Across the top of the Malea peninsula, the burning rocks

and dry scrub of diminishing Parnon give way to an assuaging vista of blue Aegean. Except that almost at once your eye is caught by the sight of a giant rock rising forbiddingly from the sea. 'At night it seemed to me a terrible beast lying in wait; today in the light of dawn it gleamed above the water like a monstrous anvil', as Kazantzakis records his first impressions of **Monemvasía** in *Travels in Greece*. Yet as your eyes search the wading hulk you can see nothing of the expected medieval town which flourished there as the commercial counterpart to Mistra, political capital of Byzantine Morea. Arriving at **Géfira**, the modern nondescript sprawl at the mainland end of the causeway linking rock with shore, it seems depressingly certain that you have been misinformed.

The approach by sea

The bus arrives at that blank and shadowless time of day when the sun is fiercest and the inhabitants of Gefira are sleeping off their noon-day meals in the cool of their shuttered homes. The streets are dead. The rock simmers uninvitingly through the heat haze. Nor does the sea approach from Piraeus reveal anything more of the 'Venice of the Peloponnese', as this invisible city on the rock has been called in comparison with that great enchantress, that magician of the seas, though after the six to eight hour voyage the sun is sinking, the great anvil glows red against the darkening mainland mountains and the atmosphere is wildly romantic.

The Byzantine town

Crossing the causeway, the sole landward access to Monemvasia (*moní émvasis*, single entrance), a road along the gentle shelving at the base of the rock runs round towards its far side but is suddenly halted by a great towered and crenellated wall reaching right down to the sea. Once through the crooked portal, broad enough for entry by foot or donkey only, the enchantment begins, though tantalisingly piecemeal as narrow stone-paved streets and still narrower alleyways diverge and twist in several directions, offering momentary perspectives of this beautiful and melancholy town.

Much of the *Lower Town* has fallen into decay and is permanently inhabited by only a few dozen people, though recently – like Hydra, but on a far lesser scale – it has attracted Athenians and foreigners, particularly writers and artists, who have bought and are repairing old houses, whitewashing their steps and tiling their roofs, bringing some vitality and bold colour back to the town and modestly enlivening the main street which runs into the Cathedral square with some late night dining and laughter. During the day there is a pleasurable routine of descending via steps and paths through tunnels and under arches to the narrow ledge of rocks under the seawall and diving into the fresh deep sea.

Its history

Like Mistra, the rock began as a refuge against the Slav invasion and thereafter was nearly always the last outpost of the Morea to fall to the succeeding waves of conquerors.

Until 1464, Monemvasia was Byzantine and it is the Byzantine atmosphere that pervades it today. Subsequently it several times changed hands between the Venetians, the Pope and the Turks; the last, after four months of siege and hunger – alleviated by a diet of oats and mice, asses' ears and, occasionally, Greek children – surrendering it in 1821 to Maniots under the command of Mavromichalis. Malmsey, a corruption of the Greek Monemvasia, was how the English knew the rock in medieval times and was the name of the sweet wine imported from here. There is an apocryphal story that the Duke of Clarence, sentenced to death by Edward IV, asked to be drowned in a cask of it.

Churches

At the height of its prosperity when the rock sheltered 30,000 people, the Lower Town alone had as many as 40 churches (though it defies the imagination that such a number could have been crammed within the fortifications along with so many houses which even now seem piled upon one another for want of space). Now only five remain, though another nine are said to be discernable, either as ruins or walled up in gardens. The *Cathedral* dedicated to Elkomenos Christos (Christ in chains) forms one side of a charming central square where a cannon points out to sea. It dates from the 13th C, though the portal was rebuilt by the Venetians in 1697 and a typically Venetian bell tower added. Services are still held here. Next door a marble relief of the Lion of St Mark decorates the doorway of the priest's house. Across the square under a low dome that is visible only from higher in the town is *Agios Pavlos*, built in 956, transformed by the Turks into a mosque, by the Greeks into a kafeneion after independence, and now a locked sometime-museum. Through an archway at the north end of the square is the *Myrtidiotissa* with a fine drum and dome, and inside a 13th C ikonostasis taken from the Cathedral. East out of the square along the main street, the gaunt 18th C *Agios Nikolaos*, now used as a schoolhouse, is an example of the Greek cruciform reduced to its bare essentials, a remarkable expression of structural form without the distraction of a decorated facade. Beyond this and towards the parapet overlooking the sea is the whitewashed *Panagia Chrysaphitissa* from the 16th C.

As can only really be appreciated once you get here, the Lower Town is a complete though miniature medieval city, rewarding your exploration of its churches and houses, and delightful as you wander its intricacy of streets and alleyways, passing from patches of broiling sun into deep sharp shadows along your way, and at night, in a pitch blackness only here and there illuminated by paraffin lamps hung from walls in glass boxes, ghostly and evocative. From higher in the town you can look down upon roofs of Moorish tile, sensitive to contrasts of light and shade, and peer into walled gardens of figs, pomegranates and oranges, and blazing bougainvilleas.

Fortress in the clouds Climbing up the steep lane past the Myrtidiotissa towards the seemingly sheer wall of rock you fall in with a path which switches upwards through an iron-clad gate and tunnel (conveniently open here and there at the roof to permit boiling oil or molten lead to be poured upon the heads of attackers) to the *Upper Town*, levelled and formless, with occasional gaping holes and underground cisterns for the careless tourist to fall into – the visit is certainly not recommended at night. The one exception to the desolation upon this 'fortress in the clouds' is *Agia Sophia*, a superb 13th C church with a plan similar to that at Daphni, sculptured marble lintels above the doorways, frescoes adorning the squinches and a 16-sided drum supporting the considerable dome. Where it is comfortable and enclosing down below, up here it is eerie, with 250-metre vertiginous drops most of the way round, but also breathtaking views of the wrinkled sea and at sunset the outlines of mountains receding further into the violet spectrum under a brilliant pink and orange sky.

Kíthera

Though Kithera is geographically an extension of the Peloponnese, it has shared the fortunes of the Ionian islands since becoming a Venetian possession in 1717 and part of Britain's Ionian Protectorate from 1815 to 1864. Its position on the sealanes round Greece and between the mainland and Crete made it attractive to the reigning seapower of the day. The Phoenicians came for the abundant murex from which they extracted precious purple dye, and the Minoans made the island a colony. The Athenians seized it from the Spartans during the Peloponnesian War, and the British evacuated nearly 1000 troops from here when the Germans overran Greece in 1941. Even now Kithera is administered from Piraeus – and is economically dependent on remittances from Australia where most of the islanders have emigrated, fondly calling their old home a Kangaroo colony.

Only 8 kms off Cape Malea, the island is large (30 kms long by 18 kms across), a rolling table-land, its coasts high and scarped. There is an atmosphere of soft neglect, a combination of past prosperity and heavy emigration. Few visitors come to Kithera, and these along with summering emigrants speaking a painfully whining pidgin seem to congregate chiefly at the northern port of **Agia Pelagía**, a nasty concrete blot with beach. Otherwise the island holds a rare beauty for those who enjoy quietude and lonely rambles.

Island walks A path from Agia Pelagia leads south along the coast to **Paleochóra**, an abandoned Byzantine town built high on the rocks and hidden from the sea in Monemvasia style. Between here and Potamos are numerous tracks with many monasteries and chapels along the way. There is also a good road directly from the port to Potamos. Once you climb up onto the table-land the way becomes Italianate, a countryside of olives and figs, cypresses and terraces of vines, the houses cream not white, two storeys not one, everything a bit more abundant than one associates with a Greek backwater – but much of it lying in desuetude. Which is why **Potamós** makes an agreeable impression, a busy market town with plenty of shops selling fresh vegetables, a bakery and a butcher, tractors rumbling in from the fields at evening, some good kafeneions and doorway trellises laden with grapes; and a good local retsina.

Milopotámos, about 15 kms south, is built by the edge of a ravine, fresh with the rush of water (if it is not too late in summer). This is the Nairiada (Nymph), approached down an old stone path through a jungle of palms, figs and banana trees, with a taverna on terraces below where there is music and dancing at night. There are some ruinous Venetian houses in the village and a plateia with a kafeneion shaded by planes alongside what once must have been a watermill. From here you can walk to *Kato Chora* within the walls of a 16th C Venetian kastro and to the cave of *Agia Sofia* (3 kms) by the sea, with stalagmites and stalactites, small lakes, and even frescoes and mosaics inside from a time when the cave served as a church.

A very lonely station

The gentleness of the landscape only changes as you reach the southern extremity of the island at **Chóra** (called also Kithera), with 700 inhabitants the largest settlement. Suddenly crags and bare rock and deep clefts. White chapels painted onto granite verticals. And the close white and pale blue cluster of Chora itself; this is Cycladic. There are some Venetian houses, and a medieval *kastro* on a high promontory overhanging the double bays of **Kapsáli**, a yacht station where the Piraeus boat also calls; also modern concrete white houses and only a shingle beach, but the backdrop of cliffs rising to the kastro and Chora is too striking to be put out by dull buildings. Back in Chora there is a *museum*, two large rooms, the first containing amphora, coins, bits of marble statuary, Venetian crests from houses, an undistinguished collection, most of it broken, nothing Minoan. The second serves as a storeroom, things lying on the floor or in boxes. But a surprise here – several English gravestones, some for soldiers, more for their infant children, who died here in the early 19th C. The garrison was relieved every six months; it was 'a very lonely station'.

PRACTICAL INFORMATION

TRAVEL TO THE SOUTHERN PELOPONNESE

Refer also to the *Practical Information* section under Athens.

Buses leave from 100 Kifissou Street in Athens for Sparta (about 7 a day, 5½ hours), Kalamata (10 a day), Pylos (2), Gytheion (4), and Monemvasia (1 a day, 8 hours).

Trains depart from Stathmos Peloponnisou for Kiparissia (4 a day, 8 hours) and Kalamata (3, in about 10 hours – almost twice as long as the bus). At Kiparissia there are connecting buses to Pylos and Methoni.

Boats leave Piraeus twice a week for Monemvasia, Neapolis, Kithera and Gytheion. There is a daily hydrofoil from Zea to Monemvasia, and a regular service to Neapolis and Kithera.

There are **flights** from Athens to Kalamata and Kithera.

SPARTA
Accommodation and Eating
Hotels: Xenia (A); Leda (B); Dioscouri (C); Cecil (D); Sparti (E).
Camping on the road to Mistra.
Tavernas: Kali Kardia, 39 Agesilaou; also *psistaries* along the Tripolis road.

Travel
There are local *buses* to Monemvasia (about 2 a day), Kalamata (2), Areopolis (2), and Gytheion (2). Buses travel to Mistra about every hour. You can also travel to Geraki (for Geronthrai) and other Lakonian villages. Buses depart from various stations near the central square.

Site and Museum
The site of ancient Sparta is not enclosed. The museum, near the central square, is open 8.30am to 12.30pm and from 4pm to 6pm daily; from 9am to 3pm Sundays and holidays; closed Tuesdays.

MISTRA
Accommodation and Eating
There is a *hotel*, Byzantion (B), and a *campsite* on the road from Sparta.
Tavernas in the village and a Xenia just below the ruins.

Site and Museum
If taking the bus from Sparta, get off at the very last stop (past Mistra village) for the site, which is open 8am to 7pm daily, 9am to 7pm Sundays and holidays. The museum is closed on Tuesdays.

TAIGETOS
It is fairly easy to climb *Profitas Ilias*, the highest peak of the Taigetos range and highest mountain in the Peloponnese (2407 metres), from the east side. The best detailed description of the ascent (it does not cover a possible descent down the other side) is *Greece on Foot* by Marc Dubin.

The setting off point is Nikos' kafeneion near Poliana hamlet, which is about 9 kms to the west of Paleopanagia. You can get a bus to Paleopanagia which is about 15 kms south of Sparta off the Gytheion road; there are about 6 buses a day from Sparta. But from Paleopanagia you must walk or if very lucky hitch the 9 kms west to the kafeneion. A taxi would be quite expensive and the road is very poor. From the kafeneion it is about 2 hours walk to the refuge operated by the Hellenic Alpine Club which provides shelter at 1690 metres (keys from Vasili in Sparta; Tel: 24898). The way to the refuge and the further 2½ hours ascent to the summit is posted (not always clearly).

The authors of this guide, having descended the western side with great difficulty to Exochorio near Kardamyli, strongly recommend returning instead to Niko's kafeneion. If foolhardy enough to attempt the traverse, note that there is no water along the way (about 9 hours), and no human life; there would be no help if you injured a leg for example. Wear stout walking boots, take a strong walking stick, carry 3 litres of water per person, and travel at least as a pair. For bearings, obtain a Lakonia nome map (see *Background* chapter). *Kálo taxídi.*

KALAMATA
Accommodation and Eating
Hotels: Numerous, including Elite (by the shore), Rex (B); Achillion, America (by

the shore) (C); Vasilikon, Acropolis (D); Nevada (near the shore) (E).
Camping: 2 kms east along the water (bus No. 1) and further along.
Tavernas: Acroyali, near the America hotel; Taigetos, 42 Athinon; Gallia, Skadios Avenue.

Travel
There are regular local *buses* to Koroni, Pylos and Kiparissia; about 3 buses a day run to Kardamyli and Areopolis and twice daily to Nestor's Palace (Chora) and the ruins of Messene at Mavromati. The main bus station is in the west of the town, across the river from Plateia 23 Martiou. To reach the waterfront (about 3 kms away) take bus No. 1 from Plateia Martiou.

For a *taxi* anywhere in the area (Messenia, Lakonia) at reasonable rates try our good friend Konstantine ('Con') Stathopoulos. Tel: 0722.23.111. Con speaks English and is good company.

The *airport* is at Triodhos, 16 kms northwest; buses and taxis available.

Other Things
Tourist Police, 46 Aristomenous Street (the main street).

The *Archaeological Museum* is just north of Plateia Martiou next to a busy market.

Festival: In the early part of July there is a three-day festival of traditional dance held in the Frankish castle.

MESSENE
The ruins at the village of Mavromati can be reached by *bus* from Kalamata twice a day, early in the morning and again in the afternoon.

PYLOS
Accommodation and Eating
Hotels: Kastro, Nestor (B); Galaxy (C); Astir, Navarino (D). Also *rooms* for rent. If in the summer you cannot find anywhere to stay or not at the right price (the town is crowded in high season) you could try Methoni down the coast.
Tavernas: Several on the main square, also good fish restaurants on the harbour.

Travel
There are frequent *buses* to Kalamata, and about 4 a day to Kiparissia (via Nestor's Palace and Chora), and to Methoni and Finikous.

Activities
Swimming: There is a small town beach, but it is better to swim either off the rocks across the road from the Kastro hotel or off the dock in front of the Nestor. Also there is good swimming in a small bay north of Navarino Bay, below the Venetian castle (Paleocastro); this can be reached by boat from the harbour. On the slope of the hill below Paleocastro you can visit 'Nestor's Cave', with animal-shaped stalactites.

The *museum* in the town has relics from the famous battle.

NESTOR'S PALACE
Take the *bus* from Pylos for Gargaliani and Kiparissia.

The *site* is open 8.30am to 12.30pm and 4pm to 6pm daily, 9am to 3pm Sundays and holidays. Some finds from the palace, including frescoes and various gold objects, are displayed at the *museum* (same hours, closed Tuesdays) at Chora, 4 kms further along the road.

Chora has a couple of *hotels*: Nestor (B); Galini (E).

METHONI
Buses from Pylos.
Hotels: Methoni Beach (B); Alex (C); Iliodyssion (D). Many *rent-rooms*.
Castle: Open 8.30am to 7pm daily, 10am to 4.30pm Sundays and holidays.

Large, sandy *beach*.

KORONI
Buses from Kalamata.
Hotels: Flisvos (D), Diana (E). Also *rooms*, including at the Parthenon taverna.

The Venetian *castle* is open during the day. There is a sandy *beach*.

KARDAMYLI
Buses from Kalamata (for Areopolis).
Hotel: Dioscouri (D). Also *rooms*.

STOUPA
There is a new *hotel* here, a *campsite*, several *tavernas* and a fine sandy *beach*.

The Kalamata-Areopolis *bus* stops if asked.

AREOPOLIS
Accommodation
Hotels: Pyrgos Kapetanakou (converted towerhouse) (A); Mani (C). Also *rooms*.

Travel and Diros Caves
Buses serve Kalamata, also Gerolimin (about twice daily) and Gytheion (3 daily).

You can visit the *caves* on the bay of Diros, south of Areopolis. They are open 8.30am to 7.30pm in summer, but as they are best explored by boat and the boats are small and the number of visitors is large you must get there by early afternoon to be sure of having your turn. (You buy a numbered ticket on arrival and must then wait until your number is called; you can swim on the beach nearby and there is a taverna). To reach the caves you can travel by road via the village of Pirgos Dirou (limited bus service; rooms at Ta Spilia in the village) or you can walk about 5 kms along the coast from Areopolis.

GEROLIMIN
Buses about twice a day to and from Areopolis.
Hotel: Akroyali (E).

VATHEIA
There is an NTOG scheme to convert a number of towerhouses in this almost deserted village into *tourist accommodation*. Enquire through the NTOG.

GYTHEION
Accommodation and Eating
Hotels: Lakonis (A); Laryssion (C); Actaeon (D). Many *rent-rooms*.
Tavernas: Cork House, and Kali Kardia (for good souvlakis), both near the plateia.

Travel
Buses from Areopolis, also from Sparta. There is also a bus to the caves at Diros and to Gerolimin, and you can reach Monemvasia via Tarapsa and Molai.

Boats leave Piraeus twice a week for Monemvasia, Neapolis, Agia Pelagia (Kithera) and Gytheion, continuing via Kapsali (Kithera) to Kasteli in Crete. On one of the return trips from Crete the boat does not call at Gytheion, so there is only one boat a week back to Agia Pelagia, Neapolis, Monemvasia, etc, which is on Fridays.

Activities
The town has a small beach, but there is a bigger, *sandy beach* to the north of Gytheion off the road to Skala.

On the hillside behind the modern town near an army barracks there is a small *ancient theatre*.

GERONTHRAI (Geraki)
Bus from Sparta.

MONEMVASIA
Accommodation
Hotels on the mainland (Gefira): Monemvasia (B); Minoa (C); Akroyali (E). There are *rent-rooms* along the waterfront in Gefira and also in Monemvasia itself but these are expensive if available at all.

Activities
There is a sandy beach 4 kms north of Gefira.

KITHERA
Travel to the Island
Daily *boat* from Neapolis. The steamer from Piraeus via Monemvasia and Neapolis comes to Agia Pelagia twice a week before going to Gytheion. Kapsali is served twice weekly from Gytheion by the same boat which goes on to Crete. Twice weekly the boat returns from Crete calling at Kithera enroute for Piraeus. The *hydrofoil* from Zea arrives at Agia Pelagia several times weekly via Monemvasia.

There is a daily (sometimes twice daily) *flight* to and from Athens to the airport near Potamos. Olympic Airways has an office at Potamos. The plane is a flying bucket which rarely manages to climb over 400 metres throughout the flight.

Internal Travel
Daily *bus* between Agia Pelagia (meeting the hydrofoil) and Kapsali. Other intermittent services around the island. Every Sunday a bus leaves Kapsali early in the morning for the market at Potamos, returning midday. There is no *car hire* on the island; there are *taxis* and you can hire *mopeds* in Chora.

Accommodation and Eating
No *hotels* except the Kytheria (B) at Agia

Pelagia. There are *rooms* in Agia Pelagia, Kapsali, Chora, Milopotamos and Livadi. You may be able to stay at one of the *monasteries* on the island, like the Panagia Myrtidon on the southwest coast. You should experience no trouble *camping* anywhere.

There are several *tavernas* at Agia Pelagia, Kapsali (try Kapsi Kamales) and Chora.

Activities and Other Things
There are **beaches** at Agia Pelagia, Kapsali, Vroulaia (taverna) and Avlemonas.

There is a *bank* at Potamos.

THE ROAD TO DELPHI

Into Boeotia

Beyond the mountains of Kithairon and Parnes which form the northern boundary of Attica, the plains of Boeotia (Viotía) extend between Mt Helikon in the west and Klomon in the north to the feet of Parnassos. This is one of the most fertile areas in Greece. Enclosed by the distant hills, the pale fields of cotton and wheat appear to stretch endlessly ahead as you travel for 80 kms with hardly a gradient. In fact until the end of the last century there was a large marshy lake fed by the river Kephissos in the middle of the area directly east of Levadia, which was then drained and later cultivated by a British company. Boeotia is no stranger to foreigners: as the only land approach to Attica and the Isthmus of Corinth it has long known the march of armies through its fields, from the Persians in the 5th C BC down to the Germans a generation ago. Its fertile land has supported the early civilisations at Orchomenos and Thebes, the numerous city-states of the classical period, the Frankish dukes of Athens and Turkish pashas at Levadia. Now the Boeotian towns and villages enjoy a quiet prosperity, but their fortunes in the past illustrate the history of foreign interference in Greece and also the destructive rivalries amongs the Greeks themselves.

The Way to Thebes

There are two main ways into Boeotia from Attica. The first is by the National Highway to the east, which is dull, although it offers fine views across to Euboea (Évvia); the railway goes this way also. The alternative is to take the old road over the mountains from Elefsis: at the entrance to the pass over Kithairon you can still see on a hillock on the right the fortress of **Eleutherai** which guarded the approach to Attica for the Athenians. Fine though its 4th C BC walls remain in parts, they do not compare with the contemporary fortress of **Aigosthena** on the coast of the Corinthian Gulf, reached (in 20 kms) by a turning to the left about 2 kms before Eleutherai. Aigosthena is almost complete, with several huge towers still standing, although the upper part of the southeast tower fell during the earthquake of February 1981. In the afternoon shadows, amidst the greenness of the holm-oak and olive trees, the place seems Wagnerian. The nearby village of **Porto Germano** has good swimming, with several tavernas.

Athenian fortresses

Oedipus exposed

It was on *Kithairon* that Oedipus was said to have been exposed at birth: Pausanias the traveller of the 2nd C AD naively writes, 'no-one knows where this occurred in the way that we know the Schist Road to Phocis, where Oedipus killed his father', (more of which later). From the top of the pass, with Kithairon on the left, Boeotia spreads out below and Parnassos is visible beyond Helikon. From Erythrai it is

5 kms westwards to the ruins of **Plataea,** near where the famous battle took place in 479 BC when the Greeks defeated the Persians commanded by Mardonius.

The ruined city is on a low triangular plateau above the plain, which is often muddy from the numerous watercourses. Its walls are in places well preserved but represent several different periods as the town was often destroyed and rebuilt. Probably the *classical city* was in the southern part of the site while in the north there are ruins of various *Byzantine churches*, and also the foundations of a *temple* (perhaps that of Hera which stood outside the city in 479), and of a building called the *Katagogion*, an inn for visitors, built in the late 5th C by the Thebans.

The battle of Plataea

The importance of Plataea lies chiefly in the battle which finally decided the fate of the Persian invasion of 480 BC. It is still not agreed where exactly the battle took place (whatever the locals say) despite the almost contemporary account in Herodotus. There is something in the descriptions of topography both by the ancient and modern Greeks which often leads to uncertainty, a vagueness at odds which the hardness of the landscape's features in the bright light. The battle was fought in September when the fields must have been dry and stubbly: the Persians were camped near the river Asopos with their Boeotian allies (who had 'medised') and the eventual battle, which was fought in two separate areas, can generally be placed to the north and east of the city, between it and the river. The Spartans defeated the Persians and killed Mardonius, while the Athenians and Plataeans defeated the Boeotians and Thebans; the majority of the Greek allies took no part until the end when victory was clear. The treacherous Thebans had their revenge in 427 when, this time allied with the Spartans against the Athenians, they took the city of Plataea after a long siege, killed the gallant defenders and destroyed it for the first but not the last time. The modern village of Plataia was virtually destroyed in the 1981 earthquake.

Legendary associations

Thebes (Thívai), 73 kms from Athens and about 14 kms from Erythrai across the small Asopos stream, is a dull modern town belying its former importance. The town centre occupies a steep plateau, formerly the ancient acropolis known as the *Kadmeia*. The very name of Thebes conjures up many of the legendary figures of Greece. It was the birthplace of Dionysos (whose Bacchantes ran wild on the slopes of Kithairon) and, some say, of Herakles. Traditionally founded by Kadmos, who here sowed the dragon's teeth, Thebes was the city of Laius and Oedipus, Kreon and Antigone. The walls and towers of the 'seven-gated' city were said to have been built to the music of Amphion's harp. But the curse on Oedipus lived on long after the quarrels of his sons Polyneikes and Eteokles and there were repeated destructions of the city, of which the most notorious was that by Alexander the Great in 336 BC. Two years after the battle of Chaironeia he killed or enslaved all the inhabitants of Thebes, destroyed all the buildings save the house of the poet Pindar, and completed Thebes' humiliation by restoring its old rival, Plataea.

Consequently as the traveller William Mure said, having visited Thebes in 1838 and seen a jumble of ruined buildings after the fresh destruction of the War of Independence against the Turks, 'there is no Greek city whose site and aspect are so little in unison with the associations either of poetical or historical celebrity that attach to them'. Even after Mure's visit the town was twice damaged by earthquakes in the 19th C.

Its history

At several periods Thebes was of major consequence. Excavations below the regular modern streets in the centre of the acropolis have revealed two Mycenaean palaces, destroyed by fire. The stories of the descendants of Kadmos plainly recall this era, but little tangible remains to be seen. After the Trojan War Thebes was said to have taken from Orchomenos the leadership of the cities of the Boeotian League, which she retained – except for a period after the battle of Plataea – until the war between Athens and Sparta at the end of the 5th C: by allying with Sparta she helped in breaking the power of Athens. Then in 371 BC after a change of alliance, at the battle of Leuktra – 'the most famous battle ever won by Greeks over Greeks' (Pausanias) – the Theban army led by Epaminondas defeated the Spartans and through the subsqent foundation of Megalopolis and Messene in the Peloponnese the Thebans achieved the permanent loss of authority by Sparta. For a few years until Epaminondas' death Thebes led the whole of Greece.

If Thebes contributed to the division and decline of the Greek city states, in 338 BC the Thebans redeemed their reputation from Plataea by allying with the Greek forces who faced the common enemy, Philip of Macedon, at Chaironeia: the Theban Sacred Band was annihilated. After the destruction by Alexander the city was restored in 316 by its allies, and despite the depredations of the Romans, Mummius (146) and Sulla (86 BC), Pausanias found its temples and sanctuaries intact. But it was taken by the Goths a century later, and in the Middle Ages was prey to the Bulgarians in 1040 and the Normans of Sicily in 1146, by which time the city was a centre of silk manufacture. In the 13th C the Frankish dukes of Athens made Thebes their capital – their only monument is now a solitary *tower* in the courtyard of the museum. In the mid-15 C the town, with most of Greece, fell under the torpid rule of the Turks and became little more than a village.

The museum

It is the *museum* alone, at the north end of Odos Pindarou (on the acropolis) which justifies a visit to the town. It is approached through a charming courtyard and is one of the best small museums in Greece. The collection includes 14th C BC *cylinder seals* from Anatolia, *Linear B tablets* found in the Mycenaean palaces, 6th C *statues from Ptoion*, painted and incised *gravestones* of Boeotian soldiers probably killed at Delion in 425 BC, and many *Tanagran-type clay statuettes* of the 5th C. Above all there is a unique collection of painted Mycenaean *sarcophagi* from Tanagra: some show women mourning, others have bulls and some form of tree or double axe worship, reminiscent of objects from Minoan Crete.

Levádia

The road from Thebes to Levadia (46 kms) passes a turning on the left to Thespiai, from where via Palaiopanagia you can walk in about 1½ hours to the attractive *Valley of the Muses* which has scant remains of an altar and a theatre. (Recently a surface study in the valley provisionally identified the site of Hesiod's town, Askra.) On the right of the road after Aliartos commences the area which was formerly *Lake Kopais*. Nearing Levadia you can see to the northeast the long finger of Akontion, 'the javelin', reaching into the plain, with the small acropolis fortress of Orchomenos just visible on the southern end.

Levádia is by contrast with Thebes a town whose past is not oppressive: it rises on a slope up against a northern spur of Helikon and although it does not impress much if you are merely passing through on the way to Delphi or Lamia, it is worth a visit. The town is a local centre of some importance, and the capital of the nome or county of Boeotia. If you go straight on at the traffic island rather than turn right for Delphi, you pass along a busy street leading to the main plateia: beyond this the road narrows, and a right turn (Odos Lappa) leads you over unexpected water rushing between crumbling stone buildings. The street which you then meet at right-angles, Odos Strategou Ioannou, has the atmosphere of another age: there are cobblers and cavernous grocers' shops, a coffee store, dark tavernas that back onto the stream, and at the bottom of the street a small shady square where old gentlemen in dark clothes pass their time over empty coffee cups; in the opposite direction (which you take) is another small plateia, at one time the centre of the old Turkish town, where on one side the bridge used to be draped with colourful blankets from the nearby fulling-mill, now derelict. The water becomes more insistent as you go on past the old milling factories and under a large tower which descends from the Catalan Castle above, and there amongst huge plane-trees are the *springs of the Herkyna*. The springs issue from the rocks to left and right, one source now channelled below the incongruously placed Xenia restaurant and another emerging beyond the more congruous *Turkish bridge*.

A feeling of the past

It is in this area that they direct you, incorrectly, to the *oracle of Trophonios*. On the right hand side there are holes in the rocks for votive offerings (in the largest of them the Turkish governor used to retire for a cool smoke of his pipe) but the oracle itself was elsewhere, although no one knows exactly where, despite Pausanias' personal visit to it. If you walk on from there, the cleft between the rocks opens out into an immense gorge with high cliffs on one side, and a rocky hill on the other crowned by the castle. It is a wild place only a few minutes from the town centre. High on the left hand side is a small *Chapel of Jerusalem* on the site of a spring, to which you can climb by seemingly endless steps and obtain a good view of the countryside to Parnassos. It is also possible to scramble up to the castle from the gorge, but easier to walk up from the town side.

The hole-in-the-ground oracle

Levadia was a prosperous classical city, largely owing to its oracle. Trophonios, by tradition the son of the King of Orchomenos and an architect, was according to Robert Graves lucky enough to be chosen as a sacrifice for the dedication of the very first stone temple of Apollo at Delphi, which he had helped to build; he was then rewarded with his own oracle at Levadia. The oracle was sufficiently important to be consulted by King Croesus and Mardonius, as well as Pausanias, who described the terrible experience: after drinking the waters of Forgetfulness and Memory, the first to forget what he had been thinking previously, and the second to remember his later adventures (probably these were the two springs of the Herkyna), the inquirer would descend into a hole, from which he would be shot out again, if fortunate, that day or several days later. When he had been debriefed by the priests as to what he had seen or learnt of the future, his relatives carried him off 'paralysed with fear and unconscious of himself and everything around him'.

The oracle was, it seems, somewhere on the hill between the sacred grove and sanctuary of Trophonios, and the unfinished Temple of Zeus. The sanctuary was probably on the site of the church of the Panagia in the town, where ancient inscriptions have been found. The unfinished *Temple of Zeus* can still be seen on the hill of Agios Ilias, some distance to the southwest of the town in a marvellous position surrounded by mountains. One possible site for the oracle is under the chapel at the top of the castle, but Frazer dismissed this as only a cistern. So the hole-in-the-ground oracle keeps its secret.

The *castle* was built by the Catalans during their brief rule, following victory over the Frankish knights in the marshes of Lake Kopais in 1311. Later under the Turks the town became the second city of Greece, and boasted 'a gay assemblage of mosques, minarets, houses and gardens'. Yet the Turks have left little other than the attractive bridge over the Herkyna:

when Mure made his visit here, Levadia too was a mass of recent ruins, but somehow it still retains in its narrow streets an atmosphere quite missing at Thebes. (Mure stayed in the Turkish *khan* or inn, a square two-storeyed building around a central courtyard; this structure, he observes, was very similar both to buildings described by Homer and to the 5th C BC Katagogion or inn at Plataea.)

Ancient sites around Levádia

From Levadia the modern route to Delphi goes westwards along a much improved road (50 kms). The ancient route went northwards via Chaironeia and Panopeos (above Agios Vlasios) and through a valley now called Tseresi, before arriving at the Schist Road. In this direction are several interesting places.

About 6 kms out of Levadia on the Lamia road is a turning across the plain to **Orchomenós** (about as far again), a dull town full of shops looking like warehouses, lying at the bottom of a bare sloping hillside. But at one time Orchomenos was one of the richest cities in Greece and the slope above the modern town has yielded evidence of almost continuous occupation from the Neolithic to the Hellenistic periods. Its fame dates from the Mycenaean period when the Minyans (after a King Minyas) achieved great wealth and importance: they succeeded in draining Lake Kopais through canals and dikes, and may have placed the fortress at Gla to guard one of the lake's natural outlets. With the decline of the Minyans the area became a lake again – the story of the Theban Herakles blocking up the outlets suggests their deliberate obstruction by the Thebans – and remained so for two millenia. Their civilisation is comparable to that of Mycenae owing to the similarity of the so-called Treasuries, and also of the pottery (although at Orchomenos there is a distinctive wheelmade 'Minyan Ware', as the excavator Schliemann termed it).

The *Treasury of Minyas* is at the bottom of the hillside, down a short lane across the road from the Church of the Koimisis, near the remains of a 4th C BC *theatre*. Like the 'Treasury' of Atreus at Mycenae, the Treasury of Minyas is a **Beehive tomb** beehive tomb but its roof has fallen in. There is a massive lintel of dark-grey marble and, inside, a long marble pedestal (for statues) which is a much later Macedonian intrusion. To the right is a doorway leading to a small chamber which was hewn out of the rock from above: the ceiling has slabs of greenish schist decorated with spirals and rosettes (take a flashlight with you).

You can walk up the slope to the *acropolis* fortress above by a path opposite the church: this was the acropolis of the Hellenic city which was enclosed by a triangular wall, remains of which can be seen on the north and south. The fortress, approached by about 90 steps in the cliff-face, has magnificent 4th C *walls* on the south and west designed to combine with the natural defences of the cliffs to north and east. The Orchomenians needed their defences: Thebes which had anciently robbed Orchomenos of its preeminence destroyed the city twice in the 4th C.

First cross-in-square church

The Byzantine *Church of the Koimisis* or Assumption of the Virgin Mary is another remarkable building. (If it is closed – and Greek churches often are, owing to the valuable objects inside – the priest who lives in the old monastic buildings to one side has the keys.) The church was built in 872 and incorporates a lot of material from a Temple of the Graces previously on its site: circular column drums are clearly visible in the outside walls. The structure of the church is interesting: it was the first cross-in-square church built in Greece, although it retains basilical-style side aisles which are, however, blocked off from the central nave. The dome rests directly on the walls without the device of squinches such as at Osios Loukas. The frescoes are badly damaged.

Giant fortress

The fortress of **Gla** can be approached by the road which runs eastwards from Orchomenos along the northern edge of the Kopais basin to Kastron (19 kms) – or of course via the National Highway. The fortress occupies a low triangular rock, a short walk to the east side of the Highway (or it can be reached by car). It is surrounded by a wall almost 3 kms long, and so is far bigger than Mycenae or Tiryns. Yet its precise role and even its date remain uncertain, although broadly speaking it is contemporary with Orchomenos and Mycenae. There are four gates of which the main gate is in the south: from there a street led to a 'market-place' in the middle of the fortress, which was linked in turn to a palace at the highest point towards the north. The palace had two wings and a courtyard within an enclosing wall. The whole place seems too large and important to have been only a fortress of Orchomenos – guarding an outlet of Lake Kopais.

Sarakatsani shepherds

Returning to the main road to Lamia it is not far to **Chaironeia** (14 kms from Levadia). On the left of the road before the village you can still see in places on the hillside crude huts made from pine branches and reeds which are used by the Sarakatsani shepherds for their animals. The Sarakatsani, formerly nomads, used once to live in such shelters themselves but now they have built only slightly less crude houses from brick as permanent homes, particularly around the nearby village of Thourion.

Chaironeia battlefield

'As you approach the city, there is a common grave of the Thebans who were killed in the struggle against Philip. It has no inscription but there is a lion on top, which probably refers to the spirit of the men' – that is Pausanias' succinct description of the lion of Chaironeia. The battle took place in the plain between the road and the river Kephissos, on the bank of which the young Alexander led the cavalry charge which destroyed the Theban Sacred Band. (The Sacred Band was a small force, some 300 strong, comprised of pairs of homosexual lovers – an older and a younger man, fighting side by side; their loyalty to each other ensured they would fight to the finish). Philip of Macedon had been able to use the pretext of the perennial squabbles over the plain of Krisa to invade Greece: the Macedonian victory over the Athenians and their allies including the Phocians and Thebans marked the end of the significant period of the Greek city-states, whose competitive ethos had contributed both to their previous importance and to their ultimate downfall.

The *marble lion*, 5.5 metres high, now sits bolt upright over the Theban grave but it had disappeared from view under the earth until discovered in 1818: shortly afterwards the ignorant Odysseus Androutsos, a bandit-general in the War of Independence, smashed it to pieces to see if it contained treasure. It is easy to forget that the statute was erected by the defeated, for in its face and through the tension in its body it expresses a quiet pride. The eyes look out towards the scene of the battle and the one token of defeat is its tail tucked between its legs.

Next to the lion is a small *museum*.

Plutarch festival

The *acropolis* of the old city of Chaironeia is on a rocky hill above the *theatre*: in the theatre once a year at the beginning of June there is a short festival in honour of its most famous citizen, Plutarch, the historian of the 1st C AD, who taught there and became a priest of Delphi; for a couple of evenings the almost invisible grey stone seats are filled with colour as the spectators, after the conventional eulogistic addresses from local and national officials, watch traditional dancing and ancient tragedy, looking out over the innocent cornfields in the fading light.

Phocian city-states

Chaironeia which owed its wealth to the manufacture of ointments from flowers was only one of a number of city-states hereabouts. As you go on to the northwest you pass into the old region of Phocis. Today Phocis (Fókis) has mysteriously shifted to the west and is the name of the nome or county west of Parnassos, but it once extended in a large semi-circle to the north, east and south of the mountain. Of Phocis' many cities, none was of first importance (except Delphi, and that was only because of the oracle) but collectively they assumed importance, particularly in the 4th C BC.

There was **Panopeos**, for example, the ruins of which lie above Agios Vlasios, a small farming village of brown tiled roofs and whitewashed stone farmhouses, a short way on and to the left of the main road. Panopeos guarded the passes through the hills towards Delphi: on the hill above the village are well-preserved 4th C walls, where you can wander alone amongst the tortoises and look across to Davlia and the nearer peaks of Parnassos. In the 2nd C AD Pausanias was unimpressed by the city on his visit – he asks if one can call Panopeos a city when it possesses no government office, no gymnasium, no theatre and no market-place – but by then the city like the other Phocian towns had fallen low: both Daulis and Panopeos were destroyed by Xerxes in 480 and Philip in 348. In the small village plateia the farmers now sit and complain of the extortions of the middlemen, the merchants; perhaps near here laughter once came from the Thyiads, the Attic girls who, on their way to celebrate the Dionysian orgies at Delphi, paused at Panopeos to dance.

From Agios Vlasios it is possible to walk beside the Platania river through the beautiful, quiet valley of Tseresi to the main Levadia-Delphi road: this was the old route to Delphi and in the middle of the valley in a field on the left can be seen a few marble blocks which are all that remain from the *Phocicon*, the old meeting place of the Phocians.

Dávlia is a walk of 1½ hours away across the plain (like Agios Vlasios, and Tithorea, below, it is off to the left of the Lamia road). The village is strung out on a hill at the feet of the steep, fir-dark slopes of Parnassos: half-way up the village is the plateia, where there is cold mountain water and the men sit outside under the shade of the planes. The old houses of stone or mud brick under clay tiles are two-storeyed, the living-rooms reached by an outside staircase and balcony over the store-rooms and animal quarters. Here and there a new concrete taratsa intrudes; it is hard to blame the villagers for building their flat-roofed villas, because the old houses do not even have a tap inside and are infested with rats. But it is encouraging that a growing number are building with pitched roofs: concrete may not become universal after all.

View of the plain

If you travel up the vertiginous street above the plateia, you emerge at the top of the village. The view is spectacular back across the plain, towards the mountains near Thebes. To the south is *Helikon* and, under it, across a valley of olive trees, where water falls past old stone mills, is the ancient acropolis of **Daulis**, the city of Tereus. Only a few courses of wall ring the hill, and there is little there except wild flowers and a restless spirit.

Above the village high up in a cleft in the mountains can be seen the **Monastery of Jerusalem**, reached by a turning off the new road which now runs through Parnassos from Davlia to join the road from Levadia to Delphi. The monastery has become a summer resort, apart from being a place of pilgrimage for the Orthodox: you can camp outside amongst the firs. The monastery has been renovated in recent years by the handful of nuns who live there and who have given charm to the monastic buildings by an abundance of flowers in the courtyard around the church. The buildings themselves have little interest.

It is possible to walk in about three hours along the lower slopes of the mountain from Davlia to another ancient Phocian town, **Tithorea**: you pass through the small village of Agia Marina, in a tobacco-growing region, which has a small frescoed chapel dedicated to the saint. Tithorea is in an even more spectacular position than Davlia, since the village lies beneath a huge cliff towering over a deep ravine which runs back into the heart of Parnassos. Firs reach high up the cliff, and a solitary ancient tower stands amongst them; below in the village itself are the remains of another tower and some walling from the 4th C Greek city. You reach the famous *cave*, once used by the klepht Odysseus Androutsos, by walking along the side of the ravine from the top of the village, and continuing some way beyond an oak grove near a spring: the cave is high up on the right. It is a grandly romantic setting for a story of bravery and treachery, for in 1825 during the War of Independence Androutsos, at one time a hero of resistance against the Turks, was captured (and later killed) after fighting against his own countrymen.

The new road through Parnassos from Davlia joins the direct Levadia-Delphi route, near the turning for Distomo (3 kms), in a valley enclosed by mountains. The Davlia road emerges from the north into the valley at '*the cross-roads of Megas*', so called after one Johannes Megas, a local police officer who lost his life in 1856 after surrounding a band of brigands on the rocky hillock nearby; they had just robbed the Jerusalem Monastery. The 'cross-roads' is at the base of the Zimeno, a deep cleft between Parnassos and Mt Kirphis (along the side of which the main road now climbs), and here the ancient track from Delphi met those from Davlia and Thebes. This was the great *Schist Road*, and it was hereabouts that Oedipus was said to have killed his father Laius as they encountered each other travelling in opposite directions. Pausanias speaks of seeing Laius' tomb in the middle of the 'cross-roads', and he was probably only referring to the hillock itself, now (inevitably) topped by a Christian monument in memory of Megas.

Where Oedipus killed his father

Ósios Loukás
It is necessary to drive through Distomo on the way to the Byzantine monastery of Osios Loukas. **Dístomo** which has the memory of a particularly awful massacre of its inhabitants during the German occupation is now an unattractive small town dependent on the local bauxite industry. The reddish earth so noticeable in this area contains bauxite from which aluminium is made, and on the coast at Aspra Spitia is one of the biggest bauxite factories in Europe, near the uninspiring village of Andikyra.

The monastery of **Ósios Loukás** is 8 kms to the east of Distomo, on the side of a hill which looks over the valley towards Helikon. It is said that monks take all the best sites for their monasteries: that is certainly true here. On the terrace of the monastery a huge plane-tree gives shade as you sit and look at the rich earth and listen to the echo of the bells from the flocks in the valley below.

Beyond the handsome tower is a courtyard with monastic buildings lining two sides, while the refectory occupies another, and *two churches* together the fourth side. The churches are built adjacently, in such a way that a passage runs from the monastic buildings through the loggia of the church on the left to the gallery of the north transept in the larger church. A good idea of the relationship between these two buildings can be gained by walking around to the back of them, under the buttresses on the south of the larger church (and past the entrance to its crypt), so you can see the external façades of the apses. The smaller church is that of the *Theotokos* or Mother of God; the larger is the church of *St Luke*.

History of the monastery

St Luke of Stiris (the village between the monastery and Distomo) was a local hermit who probably died in 953. His disciples built a chapel over his tomb and the monastery was founded in about 955. However the precise dates of the two existing churches remain uncertain. The church of St Luke was probably commissioned by the Byzantine Emperor Basil II after his victory over the Bulgars in 1014. The mosaic decoration dates from the first part of the 11th C. The church of the Theotokos which at least in part predates the larger church may represent the original oratory over the tomb of the saint as later altered or rebuilt to allow for a better architectural relationship with the newer church.

The church of St Luke

It is the church of St Luke which has earned for the monastery its fame as one of the most important Byzantine buildings in Greece. The rough external walls of stone and brick conceal a startling richness inside: the church, which is in the conventional cross-in-square form with a narthex, at one time had all its flat surfaces covered with marble of different colours while all the curved surfaces were decorated with mosaics against a gold background. A lot of the marble still survives and a good many of the mosaics, though they are gone from the central dome where they have been replaced by paintings. The light is subdued and the corners between the arms of the cross remain dark owing to the windows being partly filled with sculptured marble, but that only increases the mystery.

The mosaics

The mosaics in the *narthex* are the most easily seen. Of these the *washing of the Apostles' feet* and the *Resurrection* are particularly fine, and they well illustrate the combination of grave majesty and lifelike expressions and gestures characteristic of the mosaics as a whole. In the first, as Christ washes their feet, the Apostles share an uncertainty, even diffidence, expressive of their lack of understanding and the general frailty of mankind compared to the certainty of Christ or God. Christ's quiet confidence in the mosaic becomes in the Resurrection a strident triumph expressed by the cloak flowing behind the figure as His strong left arm firmly holds the limp hand of Adam who is being pulled, again uncertainly, to his salvation: here the contrast is at its greatest between the autocratic Byzantine God and the paltry human being.

In the *nave*, the squinches supporting the dome have fine mosaics of the *Nativity, Presentation* and *Baptism*. The hands of the Virgin Mary in the Nativity seem almost to caress the cradle as the Child looks wide-eyed at the animals. A graver *Mother and Child*, of conventional form, is to be seen in the *apse*.

The mosaics, while they follow a strict decorative system and sufficiently emphasise the various important Biblical events, are dominated by portraits of saints of every description. *St Luke* himself amongst an important group of mosaics in the *north transept* is represented as a stern ascetic: the strength of the dark figure comes partly from the contrast with the smallness of his hands, but the mosaic is characteristic of the spirituality of the portraits as a whole.

On the marble *ikonostasis* there are four beautiful 16th C ikons. Neither the saints nor the scenes from the Bible depicted on the walls are of consequence to the Orthodox as pieces of art history but are there like the ikons to instruct us in the Orthodox faith. John of Damascus said, 'if a pagan asks you to show him your faith, take him into church and place him before the ikons'. The saints themselves are examples of faith for the rest of us, and form a backcloth which is both historical and contemporary since the saints are with us, watching us, as indeed is Christ from the dome and elsewhere. Their ikons, like those of Christ and the Virgin Mary or Panagia, are symbols, idealised symbols of ideal figures, and form a route by which we can more easily approach the subjects of the images. As the bus or taxi drives away from the monastery, the colourful cardboard ikons in front of the driver perhaps have slightly more significance.

Parnassós

From the Distomo cross-roads the road climbs up the side of Mt Kirphis past low animal shelters. Beyond the Khan of Zimeno, at the point where the ravine of the Pleistos opens out to the left, travellers formerly had the choice of descending into the valley, where a path led up again to Delphi, or of ascending to Arachova: Gell, for example, in the early 19th C preferred the first route, and it is probable that the same choice existed in the time of the oracle at Delphi. The road now passes through Arachova, while the valley of the Pleistos has recently been affected by the aqueduct carrying water to Athens from the Mornos dam project.

The town of **Aráchova** (38 kms from Levadia) hangs on the side of the mountain, 942 metres high. Even in the summer it is cool, particularly in the evenings (and hence the object of much local praise) and in winter the road is sometimes blocked with snow. Many of the fine-looking inhabitants are shepherds who in summer graze their flocks on Parnassos but in the hard winters are forced to quarter their animals away, in the plain of Kephissos or as far afield as Athens. They produce the best cheese in the area.

Apart from cheese Arachova has two other well-known products: they make an unresinated 'black' wine which is free of the chemicals often added to Greek wines, and is usually very good; and from the plentiful wool they handweave colourful rugs or blankets, good examples of which can be found amongst the other bric-a-brac in the tourist shops. But there are other simpler pleasures in Arachova, like sitting in the small plateia by the fountain and listening to the rumble of men's voices under the Judas trees, or walking into the small streets away from the road, past stone houses where rugs hang over iron balconies and chopped wood is neatly piled beside elegant arched doorways, and where the red roofs hide secret gardens.

A long flight of steps leads from the plateia up to the *church of St George*: around St George's Day at Eastertime the old men race each other up the slope above the church – one year two of them found it so easy they even stopped midway and performed a dance before resuming. In this way they recall the charge by Greek forces in a famous victory over the Turks in 1826.

Climbing Parnassos

On leaving Arachova you see a road to the right signposted to the ski club. When it reaches the top of the ridge the road passes over a large plateau, called Livadi, which in late spring is carpeted with wild flowers; at its far end, you can turn off the road (which otherwise continues to the old Phocian towns of Lilaia and Amphiklia), to the left to reach the Corycian Cave (see below), or to the right to drive up to the ski stations. The *Athens Ski Club* is about 2½ hour's walk from the main summit of Parnassos, *Liakoura* (2457 metres); the summer is the only practical time to attempt it. Above the club near the ski lift there are red markers to show you the way, but it is better to take a guide because only with a guide can you travel in the very early hours and thus reach the summit at dawn and obtain the fabled view over much of Greece, before it recedes in the mist. A guide can be found in Arachova, and you then stay the night at the refuge not far from the ski club. If however you insist on doing it by yourself, take plenty of warm clothes and, if you intend to sleep out, a warm sleeping bag and enough food – it gets very cold indeed at night.

Arrival at Delphi

Delphi is situated 10 kms from Arachova, below a huge crack in the wall of Parnassos. Vultures and eagles wheel around the crags of the cliffs above, a pattern of terraced olive-green land slopes sharply away to the gorge of the Pleistos below. Rugged, savage, lonely Delphi where the shrine of Apollo camouflages the earlier appeasement of the Earth Goddess. Here there is no chance of disappointment: this is one of the most magnificent sites in Greece.

Approaches

As the road descends from Arachova, around a corner you see first the museum and then the sanctuary itself, identified by the columns in brownish-pink tufa of the Temple of Apollo, which lies at the bottom of the more western of the two Phraedriades, the Shining Rocks. The modern town of Delphi is around the next corner, beyond the museum. Another dramatic approach is to walk up through the olive trees from Kirrha, the old port of Delphi, alone the banks of the Pleistos stream and under the rock which holds the modern town of Delphi: you then look up at the sanctuary as many a visitor did in the past and realise how ideal is its position not only in relation to the cliffs above but in its height above the valley – it is at the meeting point between the two. (This walk takes about three hours.)

Both of these approaches draw you towards the sanctuary, but it is from the sanctuary that the true magnificence of Delphi's position is appreciated for it faces out not only over the olive-filled valley but across the gorge to the blank walls of Mt Kirphis. The sanctuary, within the bowl formed by the twin cliffs above, relates also to the hills opposite, so that the whole forms a huge amphitheatre.

It is a very beautiful place, but no enumeration of the physical characteristics of Delphi can ever completely describe its beauty, because this lies as much in a mystery or atmosphere beyond the power of words. The place is numinous – it has a presence and it feels very old. Perhaps centuries of worship have caused that: more likely Delphi always possessed this feeling, and was thus an obvious place for an oracle. Certain it is that the first oracle was that of Ge or Earth, the chthonic goddess worshipped by the pre-Hellenes in the second millenium BC. Delphi was well suited to be considered the centre of the Earth in view of its natural position, and the springs and fumes which came from its rocks. Above the sanctuary, the twin cliffs of the Phraedriades echo the two (invisible) peaks of Parnassos, and possibly recalled the breasts of the Earth Mother. More concretely, Delphi was and still is in an earthquake region, and the worship of the Earth Goddess here was probably an

The oracle

attempt to mitigate these forces: Poseidon, the 'Earth-shaker', was also associated with the cult at this early stage. According to tradition, the early oracle known as Pytho was situated at a cave or fissure in the ground, guarded by the serpent Python: the Pythia, who was the priestess of the goddess, was the oracle's mouthpiece and delivered prophesies after breathing vapours from the fissure.

Mythological origins

Later, Apollo took over the oracular shrine of Mother Earth after killing the Python. According to Robert Graves, certain northern Hellenes invaded central Greece and the Peloponnese where they were opposed by the pre-Hellenic worshippers of the Earth Goddess, but they captured her chief oracular shrines: at Delphi they killed the sacred oracular snake, and to placate local opinion regular funeral games were instituted in honour of the dead hero Python, and the priestess was retained in office. In some legendary accounts Apollo had to obtain purification from the river Pineios in the Vale of Tempe, and from there brought back the bay-tree, the leaves of which were perhaps chewed by the priestess before giving the prophesies. The god's coming to Delphi is also associated with Crete: in one version he came ashore in the form of a dolphin, *delphis*, hence possibly the name Delphi. In any event Apollo, a male Hellenic god, displaced the Earth Goddess before the end of the Mycenaean period.

Its history

The oracle's subsequent history was bedevilled by natural disasters, periodic warfare between Greek rivals for its control (the so-called Sacred Wars), and foreign intervention and plundering. The calm, serene sanctuary was not always so: after all, it contained immensely rich offerings to the god. At the beginning of the 6th C BC the Amphictyonic League – a 'united nations' of Greek tribes and states, of which Delphi was the centre – declared war on neighbouring Krisa because it was taxing the oracle's visitors who landed at the port of Kirrha: both Krisa and Kirrha were destroyed, and their territories – the plain below Delphi – confiscated and dedicated to the god. No cultivation was allowed there, and it is extraordinary to think that during the ancient period one's eyes could not have feasted on the sight of the silvery olive-trees stretching down to the bay of Itea.

The 6th C became a period of prosperity, amidst comparative calm: the Pythian games were properly organised, and were now held once every four years in late summer: several treasuries were added which held rich offerings from various cities. Gifts were received from the kings of Lydia and Egypt. In 548 BC the temple built by Trophonios was burnt down, and a new temple built, munificently faced with Parian marble by the Alkmaeonid family from Athens. Following the Persian Wars at the beginning of the 5th C – when the oracle's reputation for impartiality suffered owing to its favourable attitude towards the invaders (in advocating the Athenians to flee, thus protecting its own position, although this became unnecessary in fact when divine intervention or human hands sent large rocks crashing down on Xerxes' approaching force, destroying both the force and the Temple of Athena in the process) – Delphi lost further prestige as it became involved in the rivalries between the Greek city-states. The Athenians, who after Marathon had dedicated a treasury with spoils from the battle, in the Second Sacred War in the mid 5th C attempted to place the control of Delphi in the hands of its allies the Phocians, but the Delphians aided by Sparta managed to retain their autonomy.

In 373 BC the temple was destroyed by earthquake, and it is the new temple built later in the 4th C that we see partly restored today. The first large-scale pillage of the sanctuary treasures occurred in about 356 BC when the Phocians, who had been fined for cultivating the Krisaean plain, seized the sanctuary and then used some of the treasures – chiefly the gold – to finance the war which developed: the Phocian general Philomelos built a fortification on the spur west of the stadium which can still be seen. Philip of Macedon intervened and destroyed the Phocian cities, and the Macedonians took the place of the Phocians on the Amphictyonic Council: the Phocians were then fined a large amount, which was used towards the rebuilding of the temple. Delphi was now central to the entire fortunes of Greece: in 339 the city of Amphissa was accused of cultivating the sacred plain and in the Fourth Sacred War the appeal by the council to Philip resulted in his large-scale invasion of Greece, the battle of Chaironeia and the effective loss of autonomy of the Greek city-states, including Delphi itself, to the power of the Macedonians.

Following the Macedonians Delphi was subject first to the Aetolians and then the Romans. In 86 BC Sulla plundered the sanctuary, and later Nero took away some 500 statues, but Pausanias found the sanctuary still rich and substantially intact in the 2nd C AD. It was the Christian emperors Constantine and Theodosios who dealt the finishing blows to the sanctuary and oracle: Constantine took many of the treasures to Constantinople, and Theodosios abolished the oracle towards the end of the 4th C AD. The priestess had uttered her last oracle to the Emperor Julian:

Tell ye the King: the carven hall is fallen in decay;
Apollo hath no chapel left, no prophesying bay,
No talking spring. The stream is dry that has so much to say.

The continuing mystery   By the 19th C there was little visible except the stadium, and the village of Kastri occupied the site. Since 1892 French archaeologists have revealed the sanctuary and theatre, but they have not lessened the mystery and the questions remain. Where for example was the oracle? What was the nature of the Pythia's inspiration? Where lay the power of Delphi in its great days? No sign of any cave or chasm has been found beneath the temple, and no vapours which might induce a trance (chewing bay leaves does not do so). As to the influence of Delphi, many of its better known prophecies (even if apocryphal) were vague, or even misleading. Oedipus was told he would murder his father and marry his mother; after deciding not to return to Corinth, the home of his imagined parents, he unknowingly killed his real father Laius only a few miles away. The historical figure Croesus, King of Lydia, was told that his projected expedition would destroy a great empire, which turned out to be his own. Although in many instances the prophesies must have amounted to practical advice both in large affairs of state and in more personal matters like a possible marriage, Delphi's influence may not have lain chiefly through the mouth of its oracle. As much through its position at the centre of the Amphictyonic League and through its network of informants in the Greek cities, which were necessary to give the oracle any degree of credibility in its oracular responses, above all as a Panhellenic sanctuary it operated as a centre of political and commercial dealings of every kind. The treasuries and offerings of the cities are rather the expression of their prosperity, and political or military fortunes, than of religious zeal. But all this is not to deny its sacred nature, especially for the ordinary worshippers.

Exploring Delphi

Pausanias is the best guide to the site as a whole, and many of the objects have only been identified through his help. This guide will be more selective.

The Marmaria are to the left of the road as you arrive, a group of buildings significantly placed at the approach to the sanctuary of Apollo and so called because their marbles were later quarried. There are the ruins of five building side by side forming a sanctuary of Athena. The first building (from the east, or Arachova) was the *Temple of Athena Pronaia* – Pronaia meaning fore-temple (to the larger Temple of Apollo). This temple was damaged by the falling rocks in 480 as the Persians approached (the rocks now lying about the ruins came from a similar accident in 1905) and finally destroyed by the earthquake of 373. Next to the temple were two treasuries and the round building further again to the west is the famous *Tholos*, a rotunda of the early 4th C BC: three of its Doric columns from the peristyle have been re-erected, the two metopes being copies of originals in the museum. Finally there are the foundations of the *new Temple of Athena* built in the 4th C to replace the older one.

If you walk out of the western end of the Marmaria the path leads to the area of the **gymnasium**. The existing remains are from the 4th C, as rebuilt by the Romans. On the upper level were two *tracks* for training purposes, one covered, one open, and both the length of a Pythian stade, 178 metres. Below was the *palaestra*, a square building for the wrestlers, and a cold *bath* with a round pool.

The **Castalian spring** is at the point where the two Phraedriades form an angle or cleft between them. Here has been found the base of a statue dedicated to the Earth, and here it was said the Python lived and Apollo brought back the bay-tree from Tempe. It is possible that this was indeed the site of the oracle itself, but its subsequent function was as the place where all the visitors to Delphi purified themselves in the pure waters of the Castalia. The water was collected in a large basin from a trough-like reservoir behind, above which was once an elaborate facade: steps enabled visitors to wash in the basin.

Site of the original oracle?

The **sanctuary** is reached by a path, bordered by bay and oleander shrubs; unfortunately, it is now fenced – and the entrance from the road is the only official way in, since the other entrance near the stadium, reached from above the town, seems permanently closed.

The ancient town spread up the hillside to the sanctuary, and it is not difficult to imagine visitors being persuaded to buy small offerings as they passed through the streets and arrived at the *paved square* immediately outside the walled enclosure. The village of Kastri or Delphi was moved in the 1890s by the French to its present position further west, but the rows of tourist shops are in a good tradition.

The sanctuary is contained within four great *walls* dating from the 6th C (the north and west), the 5th C (the south) and the 4th C (the east). Inside we have to imagine it was crammed with countless offerings of every description, literally thousands of statues and scores of treasuries. There were tripods and weapons dedicated to the god. There were statues of gods, men and beasts – some of gold, others gilt, yet others bronze or a mixture of each. Statues of marble and clay were brightly painted, as were the friezes and decorations on the buildings. Rising above the cluttered terraces was the large Temple of Apollo, resplendent white but with coloured sculptures and gold armour below its red-tiled roof. The total effect would have seemed extraordinary to our eyes.

Following the Sacred Way

The way through the sanctuary is by the Sacred Way. Immediately you pass inside the wall you see the bases of various statues, and the near ones provide a good example of the rivalries of the city-states and the spirit in which their dedications were often made. On the left is a long base for 16 statues, an *offering of the Athenians* erected some years after the battle of Marathon of 490 BC; directly opposite is a large rectangular or recessed structure, once containing 37 bronze statues of gods and generals, an *offering of the Spartans* made after their victory over the Athenians at Aigospotami 80 years later. However, immediately in front of the Spartan monument was placed the *offering of the Arcadians*, nine bronze statues to commemorate their recent successes against the Spartans. Moreover next door to the Spartan monument along the Sacred Way is a semi-circular exedra known as the *monument of the Kings of Argos*, put up to commemorate the foundation of Messene under the Theban Epaminondas in about 370 BC – another slight to the Spartans.

Further up the path on the left were two treasuries, first the Sikyonian and then the Siphnian. The *Sikyonian Treasury* was built about the beginning of the 5th C with material from previous buildings: from one of these survive some metopes now in the museum. The *Siphnian Treasury* built in about 525 BC had two caryatids as its west entrance, parts of which are in the museum, and a frieze of Parian marble also in the museum. Turning the corner on the path you see in front the reconstructed *Treasury of the Athenians* – inscriptions on the walls enabled the reconstruction to be made. This elegant little building of Parian marble was built from the spoils of Marathon, trophies from which were displayed on the triangular terrace. Parts of the frieze of metopes are in the museum, those on the building being copies. The inscriptions on the walls include decrees in honour of Athenians, lists of Athenians sent in official capacities to the Pythian festival, a hymn to Apollo with musical notations, and on the supporting wall at the back of the Treasury records of the liberation of slaves. After the humiliation of the Athenian expedition to Sicily in 415 BC, it seems the Syracusans could not resist putting up a treasury almost opposite.

Ascending the Sacred Way and past the *Council House* of the Delphians, where day to day administration of the sanctuary would have been looked after, you arrive at a circular area or *Threshing Floor*; here every eight years the story of the killing of the Python by Apollo was re-enacted. North of this, under the *south retaining wall of the temple* (of fine polygonal masonry of the 6th C BC and covered with decrees of a much later date granting freedom to particular slaves), is the *Stoa of the Athenians*: on the top step is an inscription which reads, 'The Athenians dedicated the colonnade and the arms and the figure-heads which they took from their enemies'. It is unclear from which naval victories the Athenians took the ships' figure-heads, possibly from those both over the Persians (notably at Salamis) and over her later Greek rivals.

To the left of the stoa is a rock which formed the base of the *Naxian column* supporting a large sphinx of about 560 BC, now in the museum. Further to the left it seems was the old

ANCIENT DELPHI

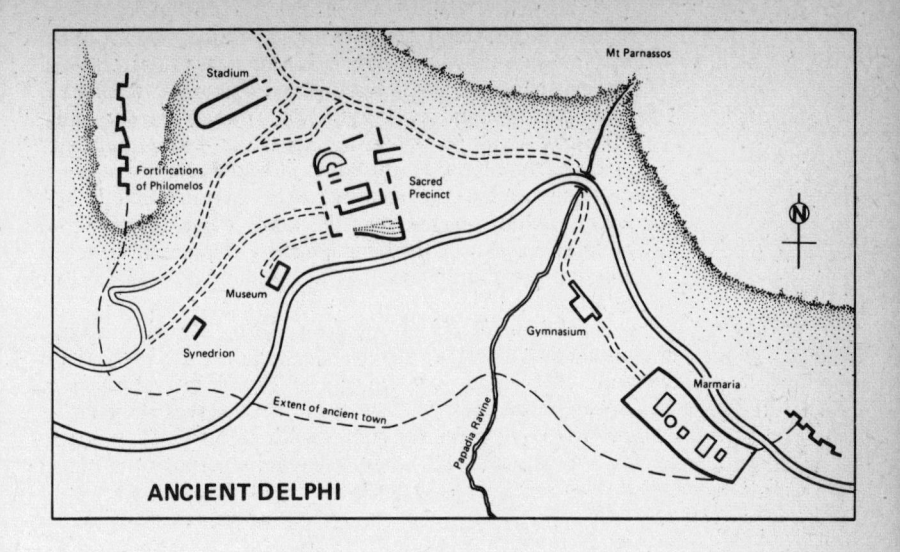

sanctuary of the Earth near a spring: between this and the Sacred Way can be seen a large rock with a fissure, known as the *rock of the sibyl*, since it may have been here that the early priestess or sibyl chanted the oracles.

The path now passes in front of the temple: on the right were several offerings, amongst which is a circular base which supported the common Greek *monument of Plataea*, a gold tripod and basin set on three large bronze serpents, dedicated from the spoils of the battle of 479 BC. The bodies of the serpents even without their heads were over five metres high, and on them was engraved the list of the Greek cities who had taken part in the battle, to whatever slight extent. The Phocians took the gold parts of the monument in the Third Sacred War in the mid 4th C: the Emperor Constantine took the bronze serpents, which were later used as fountains and can still be seen without their heads and tails in Istanbul. It is possible too that the gilt horses now outside St Mark's Cathedral in Venice were originally taken by Constantine from the *Chariot of the Sun*, the base of which is behind the Plataean monument.

At the top of the Sacred Way, where it turns left to the temple terrace, is the base of the *monument of Gelon*, the tyrant of Syracuse: he and his brothers erected four tripods and Victories of gold, weighing in all some 600 or more kilos, to commemorate their victory over the Carthaginians at Himera in 481 BC. To the left was the *Acanthus column*, now in the museum: behind was the *Thessalian monument* erected in honour of the tyrant Daochos, several statues from which are in the museum.

Monuments taken to Istanbul and Venice

Outside the Temple of Apollo is a terrace with a large restored *altar* erected by the inhabitants of Chios. On this terrace, to judge from Pausanias, were a great number of statues, many of them of Apollo. The remains of the **Temple of Apollo** are of the 4th C and clearly it was designed to dominate the sanctuary: the bare tufa of the columns re-erected by the excavators is misleading, as originally they were covered with a lime and marble stucco. The columns are of the Doric order, and the temple had six columns at the front and rear, and a single row of columns along the sides. Inside, in the pronaos were the famous inscriptions 'Know Yourself' and 'Nothing in Excess', maxims which the god Apollo himself only learnt late in life after a tempestuous and violent youth. The pronaos also held a statue of Homer. Within the cella there was an altar of Poseidon, plus statues of the Fates and of Apollo and Zeus, and the hearth of Apollo where a fire was kept perpetually burning. Pausanias also speaks of a gold Apollo in the innermost part of the temple, or adyton. Nearby was the famous *Omphalos*, the circular 'navel of the Earth', which some took to mark the grave of the Python or of Dionysos. And what then of the oracle? We do not know exactly, but the answer is perhaps simpler than is often thought. The adyton was probably at a slightly lower level than the rest of the temple and here the priestess of Apollo sat on a tripod, possibly over a small artificial opening in the ground, holding a branch of bay in one hand. She was neither frenzied nor in a trance, and her *enthusiasmos* was the inspiration of her faith in Apollo. The enquirer would address his question to the priestess, usually a simple question on a religious matter, and he would receive a simple answer which he would believe to be that of Apollo. There then lies the mystery of the oracle; not in its magic, but in the faith that sustained it for so long a time.

Final site of the oracle

The pediments on the outside of the temple (completely gone) included the figures of both Apollo and Dionysos with his Thyiad women (or Maenads). Why Dionysos? This is another of the surprises at Delphi: apart from Apollo, the god of the intellect, they worshipped Dionysos, the god of the senses and of wine. For the winter months Apollo was absent and his oracle was silent; in his place reigned Dionysos. Plutarch, who was himself a priest here, says that Delphi belonged as much to Dionysos as to Apollo. Behind the cool facades were deeper passions which sometimes ran free in the orgiastic rites on Parnassos, itself sacred to Dionysos and his Maenads.

Above the temple, in the northwest corner of the enclosure is the **Theatre**. Nearby was a statue of Dionysos, and the god also had a small sanctuary directly to the east of the theatre. (Further to the east still was the *Cnidian Club*, a meeting place built in about 450 BC and decorated by the painter

Origins of drama

Polygnotos with scenes of the capture of Troy and the Underworld – none surviving.) Dionysos was closely connected with the ancient theatre: at the festivals in praise of the wine god, the songs and dances slowly developed into the recognisable forms of drama of the 5th C. The theatre at Delphi dates from the 4th C and contains 35 tiers of seats which could hold about 5000 people.

The Pythian Festival consisted initially of music competitions and hymns in honour of Apollo, held in the theatre, and athletic competitions in the stadium: later, performances of drama were added, and chariot-racing in the Krisaean plain. The prizes were merely crowns of bay.

The **Stadium** is a short climb through the pines above the theatre. (Between the theatre and stadium is the *Kerna spring*; this fed the Kassotis fountain somewhere to the east of the theatre, from the waters of which the priestess probably drank before prophesying.) It is on a high piece of ground which was artificially levelled in the 5th C: you can see the supporting wall on the south side. The stone seats, probably built at the expense of the benefactor Herodes Atticus, could contain 7000 spectators. Half-way along the seats on the north side can be seen the place for the officials. Lines are also visible at the start and finish of the Pythian stade (178 metres). At the eastern end are remains of a Roman triumphal arch.

Picnic views

From the stadium you can see across to the uplands on Kirphis: the dark sides of the hill look uninviting enough, but there is a spectacular zigzag path up its side to the village of Desfina (hidden from view). A good place to picnic is above the stadium in the pines, or best of all on the *fortress of Philomelos* to the west (it is outside the fence and so requires a little enterprise although it can also be reached from the town): from there, you can look in every direction from Kirphis to the peaks of Mt Giona, and sometimes see Egyptian vultures wheeling below.

The **museum** has many good exhibits, which are all well labelled. The following therefore includes only some of the more important items. (As the museum at Delphi is the one major museum in Greece in which the rooms are not numbered, a plan with rooms numbered in relation to the text is here provided.) On the *landing*, the Omphalos. This is a marble version which although found in the area of the temple is not thought to be from the adyton. *Room 1* has vases and cult-objects. *Room 2* includes an exquisite bronze figurine of a young man c650 BC. *Room 3* has the famous statues of Kleobis and Biton, two large kouroi of the early 6th C, very strong figures and illustrative of the monumental style briefly borrowed from Egypt. There are also five metopes from the Sikyonian treasury c560 BC, the best of which contains Kastor and Pollux and Idas bringing home cattle stolen in Arcadia. *Room 4*: archaic silver bull (reconstructed) of the 6th C BC and other objects from the deposit recently discovered in front of the Stoa of the Athenians. *Room 5*: most of the frieze of the Siphnian Treasury, the best preserved being the north side (battle of gods and giants) and east side (gods watching the Trojans fight the Greeks): surprisingly naturalistic for the date (c525 BC) – especially the fallen figures. Also in this room is a graceful Caryatid from the Treasury, and the Naxian sphinx. *Room 6*: metopes from the Athenian treasury, probably after 490: they show the exploits of Herakles and Theseus, and the battle of the Amazons – there is now far more movement if you compare, for example, Herakles and the Arcadian stag with the earlier Sikyonian or even Siphnian sculptures. *Rooms 7 and 8* have statues from the pediments of the old Temple of Apollo (destroyed in 548). *Room 9* includes a round altar from the Sanctuary of Athena Pronaia with a frieze of young girls (1st C BC). *Room 10* has part of the restored entablature of the 4th C Tholos in the Sanctuary of Athena. *Room 11* has 4th C sculpture: there is the Acanthus column (which once supported a tripod) with three women, probably Thyiads, dancing around it; of the five statues from the Thessalian monument the most notable is that of the Olympic victor Agias, one of Daochos' ancestors.

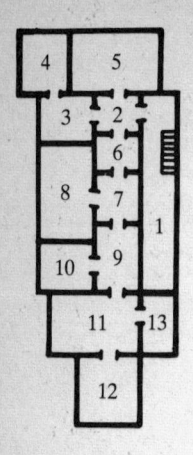

Room 12 has the Charioteer which would probably be less admired if it were not one of the very few surviving 5th C Bronzes. The figure has been crowned and commemorates a victory at the Pythian games: the self-confidence and steady gaze from the beautiful onyx eyes seem to say 'I won, but it really was not that important'. Through all the human statuary runs one unifying theme, a brave assertion of Man's importance, from Kleobis and Biton to the Charioteer – there may be gods, but Man is still expressed confidently as an end in himself. *Room 13*: miscellaneous items include a fine, effeminate Antinous (Emperor Hadrian's boyfriend) and objects from the Corycian Cave.

Excursions from Delphi

In the town of **Delphi** itself there are several adequate restaurants which overlook the valley of the Pleistos and give wistful views of the sea on a hot day.

The **Corycian Cave** takes about three hours to reach, so take food. Get to the fortress of Philomelos from the town by following signs for the stadium and ascending the hill to the left of the (closed) entrance, and you then take the winding track up the cliff. After an hour you reach the top of the *Phaedriades* – near here those whom the Delphians judged guilty of sacrilege, like poor Aesop, were thrown over the edge. You turn to the north along a fold in the land to some watering-troughs (1½ hours), and then turn east, when it is easiest to follow the dirt road which skirts the

Aesop's sacrilege

Shepherd on Parnassos

valley. The cave is high up on the side of the leftward hill at the valley mouth: this hill is about half a mile beyond a new chapel beside the road, and takes about an hour to reach from the troughs. You then trust there is a cave up there and scramble up the hill, following goat tracks, when you are amazed to see first the low dark mouth of the cave and then a road which the Greeks have thought to bulldoze right up to it – this goes down the other side of the hill, joining the Arachova road, and would take much longer from Delphi.

Pan's sacred cave   The large cave was sacred to Pan and Nymphs, as inscriptions testify: Pan was an old shepherd-god from whom Apollo learnt the art of prophesy, but he was also a consort of the Maenads, who celebrated the Dionysian orgies in the plain below. The high, dripping cave with its large stalagmites and stalacites and greenish light is impressive. As impressive are the bare slopes of Parnassos across the plateau of Livadi. Descending the road, then across Livadi and down to Arachova takes three hours.

Mt Kirphis and Desfina by the zigzag path on the hill opposite Delphi also takes about three hours. You get down to the Pleistos by descending the terraces to the left of the town of Delphi, and then turn towards the sea, underneath the cliffs on the right which hold the town. About one hour from Delphi, beyond a large bluff on the left, you trace the path from Chriso to Desfina, and you shortly get on to the zigzag, which takes only about an hour to the top: Delphi looks very small. It is a further hour across the red earth (and in June wild delphiniums) to **Desfína**, a poor but picturesque village: much of the population works at the factory at Aspra Spitia. The plateia has one or two tavernas. The new road from Distomo to Itea which passes near Desfina carries buses down to Itea and beyond.

North shore of the Gulf of Corinth
The road down to the Krisaean plain bypasses the village of **Chrisó**, anciently Krisa: the only ancient remains are traces of an enclosed wall of the Mycenaean period near the chapel of Agios Georgios. The village has a plateia with fountains and plane-trees and several tavernas nearby, and makes a good stop. When the road hits the plain, it divides, straight on to Amfissa (20 kms from Delphi) or left to Itea (16 kms).

Ámfissa is at the head of the Krisaean plain, an old Locrian city destroyed by Philip of Macedon, and now a substantial market town. The Franks here built a *castle* on the walls of the ancient acropolis above the town; it is pleasant to walk up to it.

Itéa is an expanding town which now embraces at its eastern end the village of **Kirrha**, once the port of Delphi.

You pass through Kirrha to the campsites further round on the coast. Apart from the cafés on the sea-front the best feature of Itea is its demotic song of the same name. The ferry to Aigion has stopped, and the harbour is chiefly used by cruise ships for Delphi.

From Itea the road runs along the north coast of the Corinthian Gulf to Navpaktos (70 kms) and the Andirrion-Rion ferry to the Peloponnese. This stretch of coast is very beautiful, apart from the impact of the road itself, and has **Good swimming** several small villages and bays where you can swim: on clear days there are dramatic views across the water to the Peloponnese. After you pass some large-scale bauxite operations the first village is **Galaxídi**, 17 kms from Itea, which sits on a small promontory with an attractive harbour. In the 19th C it became an important shipbuilding and ship-owning community – the small *museum* in the town hall has pictures of old sailing vessels and of the busy port: now many of its handsome houses are empty, and idly reflect the bright light from their gaily painted doors and windows. The 4th C *walls* of the old Hellenic city (probably Oeanthia) are visible in places, and the large *church of St Nicolas* has a fine early 19th C wooden screen, but the chief pleasure is to sit at one of the several kafeneions or tavernas on the harbour and look past the pine forest, across the bay to Delphi and Parnassos. From this point the mountain appears exactly like a reclining woman.

On the hills behind Galaxidi, about an hour's walk away, is the small monastic *church of St Saviour*. It is in a wonderful position, looking down over almond trees at the village, which in the Middle Ages and before was often forced to take refuge on the hills, owing to the frequent raids by pirates and other adventurers on this coast.

Návpaktos, formerly Lepanto, about an hour's drive from Itea along the coast, is a beautiful small town, with a 15th C *Venetian castle*, the walls of which run down to the sea and form a very picturesque harbour: you can walk through a gateway onto the beach, and the Peloponnese seems so close you could swim to it. Navpaktos, an old Locrian city, long had importance being at the mouth of the Corinthian Gulf. The Athenians kept it under control, through a colony of Messenians, for half a century until the end of the war with the Peloponnesians. The town often changed hands between **Battle of** Venetians and Turks, and in the famous sea battle of Lepanto **Lepanto** in 1571 the Christian fleet of the Holy League destroyed a large Turkish fleet – although in the end the Turks outlasted the Venetians, and ended their oppressive rule in proud idleness inside the walls.

Andírrion to **Andírrion** is 10 kms to the west: the ferries to Rion are **Rion ferry** frequent, each quarter to half-an-hour in the day, slightly less often at night, and relatively cheap.

PRACTICAL INFORMATION

TRAVEL ALONG THE ROAD TO DELPHI
Refer also to the *Practical Information* section under Athens.

Buses leave 260 Liossion Street, Athens, for Thebes (hourly), Levadia (hourly, takes 2 hours), Arachova, Delphi, Itea, Amphissa (all about 5 a day), Osios Loukas (one a day in the morning, about 4 hours), and Galaxidi and Navpaktos (both twice a day).

Trains leave Stathmos Larissis for the north, stopping at Thebes, Levadia (frequently), Davlia, Tithorea and Amphiklia (infrequently). All these stations are a little distance from the centre of the place concerned; sometimes a bus connects, otherwise you may have to take a taxi or walk.

Ferries cross the entrance of the Corinthian Gulf between Rion and Andirrion every quarter of an hour, day and night.

PORTO GERMANO (for Aigosthena)
Hotel: Egosthenion (C).

THEBES
Hotel: Niove (C).
Bus: from Thebes about every 2 hours to Chalkis in Evvia.
Museum: 9am to 3pm daily, 9am to 2pm Sundays and holidays, closed Tuesdays.
Festival: on Shrove Monday at the end of Carnival there is a mock wedding, the *Vlachikos Gamos*, famous in the region; its origin is obscure but it may recall a springtime Dionysian festival.

LEVADIA
Hotel: Levadia (B); Helikon (C).

Levadia is the centre of *buses* for the nome of Boeotia; the bus station is at Odos Kaliankaki just below the central plateia. There are additional local buses on the Levadia-Delphi-Amfissa route; there are also buses to Distomo and Andikyra, to Orchomenos and (less frequently) to Chaironeia, Agios Vlasios, Davlia, Tithorea and Amphiklea.

ORCHOMENOS
Frequent *buses* from Levadia.

The *Treasury of Minyas* is closed between 1 and 3pm.

CHAIRONEIA
The *museum* is open 9am to 1pm, 4pm to 6pm, closed Tuesdays.

DAVLIA
Rooms and *tavernas* in or near the central plateia.

TITHOREA AND KATO TITHOREA
Rooms in Tithorea; Kato Tithorea which is near the railway station has a *hotel*, Ziakas (C).

AMPHIKLIA
Hotel: Leonidas (D).

DISTOMO
Hotel: America (D).

There are fairly frequent *buses* from Levadia.

Swimming in the bay of Andikyra is not advised owing to the nearby aluminium factory.

OSIOS LOUKAS
There is a *Xenia* at the monastery which at one time had rooms for visitors and would allow a more leisurely visit, but they appear no longer to be available.

Apart from the daily *bus* from Athens (which allows only 1½ hours before returning) there are 2 buses a day from Distomo (early morning and early afternoon) so that by staying a night at Levadia or Distomo (unexciting) you could spend longer at the monastery. Some *tours* include Osios Loukas on the way to Delphi. The monastery is open 8am to 7pm daily, 9am to 7pm Sundays and holidays.

ARACHOVA
Hotels: Xenia (B); Apollon, Parnassos (D).

There are several *tavernas* along the main road.

The Festival of St George is on 23 April, but the race is held on the first Monday after Easter.

PARNASSOS
You can contact the Greek Alpine Association which manages the *refuge*, at 68 Aeolou, Athens; Tel: 321 2429.

The *guide* in Arachova was last known to be N Georgakos, Tel: 31391.

Apart from the route indicated for climbing Parnassos, an alternative would be to go up to the NTOG Ski Centre at Phterolacca (by turning off the road to the Ski Club) where a dirt road continues to just below the summit. From there it is only about a ½-hour climb to the top. Private transport is necessary both to the Ski Centre and the Athens Ski Club.

You can usually *ski* at both stations from December through April. The NTOG centre has much the better facilities now: for information, Tel: 0234 22694/5.

DELPHI
Accommodation
Hotels: Amalia (view), Xenia (A); Vouzas (view), King Iniohos, Kastalia (B); Hermes (view), Parnassos (view), Stadion, Odysseus (C); Sivylla, Lefas (D).

There is a *youth hostel* at 29 Apollonos. The Apollon and Delphi *campsites* are both out on the road to Itea.

Eating and Entertainment
Apart from the many quite expensive *restaurants* along Pavlou and Frederikis Street with views, you can get cheaper meals at the Vachos (near the youth hostel) and the Taverna Asteras (near the petrol station). There is a *disco* at the Maniatis Restaurant, just on the road to Itea.

Information and Travel
Tourist Police: 25 Pavlou and Frederikis Street.

The *bus station* is in the west of the town just beyond the junction of the two principal parallel streets. *Buses to Athens* get full, so buy your ticket well in advance. Apart from the through buses there are additional *local buses* between Itea, Delphi, Arachova and Levadia. It is possible with some inconvenience at Levadia to catch a *train* back to Athens (or do it the other way round).

Site and Museum
The *site* is open from 8am to 7pm daily, 10am to 4.30pm Sundays and holidays. The *museum* is the same, but closed Tuesdays.

CHRISO
Campground (6 kms from Delphi).

AMFISSA
Hotel: Stallion (C).

Frequent *buses* between Kirrha/Itea and Amfissa.

ITEA AND KIRRHA
Hotels: Panorama (B); Parnassos (D). Also *camping* at Beach Camp, Kirrha, and the Kaparelis on the Desfina road.

There are 2 to 3 *buses* a day to Galaxidi and to Desfina.

Swimming at Itea and Kirrha.

GALAXIDI
Hotels: Gannymede (C); Possidon (D). There is also a *campground*.

Tavernas: several along the harbour.

Good *swimming* across from the harbour.

There are 2 to 3 *buses* a day to Itea; the through buses from Athens go on to Navpaktos.

ERATINI
Hotel: Delphi Beach Club (B). Also a *campground*.

NAVPAKTOS
Hotels: Amaryllis (B); Aegli (D).

You can here connect with *buses* for Patras.

EUBOEA AND THE NORTHERN SPORADES

From Thebes a road goes northeast across wooded hills towards Chalkis, the capital of Euboea. Before crossing the narrow channel between the mainland and the island, you can turn right along a bad road, past the cement works, to the ruins of ancient **Aulis**, which has the remains of the *Temple of Artemis* (10 kms). Here it is said Iphigeneia was sacrificed to the goddess by her father Agamemnon, the leader of the Greek expedition against Troy which was held up at Aulis by adverse winds. The sacrifice was used as a pretext by Klytemnestra for killing Agamemnon on his return years later.

The sacrifice of Iphigeneia

Euboea

The enticing island of **Euboea** (Évvia) is about 170 kms long, lying roughly parallel with Boeotia and Attica, and there are ferries to the island from several places on the mainland, including Rafina and Skala Oropou in Attica and Arkitsa in Phthiotis (north of Boeotia). Second in size only to Crete, Euboea is heavily wooded and wonderfully green, with mountains rising to nearly 1800 metres but also several fertile plains. Roads are few and often poor, and the east coast, where the mountains drop suddenly into the sea, is particularly undeveloped. The island is only just beginning to attract visitors, and the west coast near Eretria is being developed for tourism.

History of the island

Anciently, the two main cities were Chalkis and Eretria on the west coast, both being on the important north–south trade route through the Evripos channel and both prolific founders of colonies elsewhere. Athens took Chalkis in 506 BC and divided its land amongst settlers. After the Persian Wars, during which Eretria was destroyed by the Persians as punishment for assisting the Ionian revolt, Athens established control over the whole island to ensure her corn supply. In the Middle Ages Euboea was fought over by the Byzantines, Franks and Venetians, and nowhere in Greece is there such a concentration of medieval towers and fortresses to be seen. The Venetians, who lost the island to the Turks in 1470, regarded Negropont, as they called it, as one of their most prized possessions.

Mystery of the Evripos

The *Evripos* is the dangerous, fast-flowing channel of only about 40 metres across between the island and the mainland. Inexplicably it changes direction six or more times a day, and it is said that Aristotle was so baffled by this that he drowned himself in its waters. A modern retractable bridge crosses to **Chalkís**, an unattractive, large industrial town. The name probably derives from the Greek word meaning bronze (*chalkos*), for the manufacture of which Chalkis was famous; its name was then given to the Chalcidici in northern Greece through the number of colonies sent there by the mother city. The former Venetian walls have been demolished, but there is one unique monument in the older part of town, namely the *church of Agia Paraskevi*, near the plateia. This is a basilica which the Crusaders converted into a Gothic cathedral with pointed arches. Also in this quarter, known as Kastro, a former *mosque* has been restored as a museum with remains from the Middle Ages; nearby is a fine *Turkish fountain*. Across the Evripos, on the mainland, the Turks have left the *fortress of Karababa* which once guarded the strait. The *archaeological museum* in Leoforos Venizelou has several interesting pieces of classical statuary, in particular the group of Theseus carrying off Antiope, from the west pediment of the Temple of Apollo at Eretria.

Northern Euboea

The north of the island has particularly fine scenery, and a good journey to make is between Chalkis and Loutra Aidipsou (153 kms). The road first climbs over the ridge between Mt Kandilion and (on the right) Mt Dirphys; the slow winding descent from 610 metres presents a grand panorama across forests and ravines to the sea and the Sporades beyond. Below, in a broad and beautiful valley is Prokopion, also known as **Akmetaga**, at the centre of a large estate formerly in the possession of a Turkish pasha and until recently run as a model farm by a British family, the Noel-Bakers. The village contains a *chapel* with the relics of St John the Russian, brought from Turkey by refugees in 1923. Proceeding, you will see a fork left to the picturesque fishing village of **Limni**, with good swimming off a sandy beach nearby.

At the northern tip of Euboea is **Cape Artemision**, reached by a track shortly before Agriovotanon. Here there are the ruins of a temple of Artemis, but more famous are the straits below, where the Greek and Persian fleets fought inconclusively before the battle of Thermopylae. To the west of the modern town of Istaia, which looks over the plain in the north of the island, is **Oreoí**, the site of ancient Histaia. It has a Venetian fortress on Hellenic foundations. At the end of the road is **Loutrá Aidipsoú**, an important spa, used by ancients and moderns alike.

From Chalkis across the exuberantly fertile Lelantine Plain dotted with medieval towers lies **Erétria** where surprisingly there are extensive ancient remains, whereas Chalkis has none. For although Eretria made some recovery after destruction by the Persians, it was destroyed again during the Mithridatic Wars (87 BC) and then abandoned. Above the modern town are the remains of a 4th C *palace*, a *theatre* and, higher up, an acropolis with *Hellenic towers* from where there is a magnificent view all around: the shores of Attica to the left, Pentelikon and Parnes in front, Kithairon a little to the right and further right still Parnassos. In front, near and below lies the Lelantine Plain, latticed with vineyards. In the middle of the town are the foundations of the *Temple of Apollo* (c510 BC). The city produced some good pottery, examples of which are in the local *museum* at the northwest of the town, but most of the finds are in the Archaeological Museum in Athens. The modern town has become a popular seaside resort.

Southern Euboea

East of Eretria there is also a beach at **Amárinthos**, and at 57 kms from Chalkis the road divides, going left to Kimi on the east coast (a further 36 kms) and right to Karystos on the south coast (a further 69 kms). **Kími**, a cheerful town embraced by vineyards and orchards, stands on a 262-metre ridge overlooking the sea and the island of Skyros. It is reached by an attractive route through a valley mutely guarded by Frankish towers and across hills covered with olive trees. Its port, 4 kms distant, is the only harbour along the mountain-walled east coast of the island.

Off the road to Karystos is a marshy lake, on the east side of which are the ruins of ancient **Dystos**. It is reached in about half an hour by a path south from Krieza or more directly by a track leading to the ruins which are visible at this point from the Karystos road. Within the walls the ground plans of houses of the 5th C BC can be made out. Part of the acropolis was made into a Venetian fortress. There is another Venetian castle at **Stíra**, further on the road to Karystos, while **Néa Stíra** is a coastal resort. **Kárystos**, an attractive town and resort, also has a Venetian fortress of reddish stone on the site of an ancient acropolis a little distance inland, near the small village of Mili. The Hellenic city was famous for a white and green marble (cipollino) popular at Rome, which is still visible in the old quarries nearby.

The Northern Sporades

To the north and east of Euboea are the nine islands of the Northern Sporades, though only the four largest – Skyros, Skiathos, Skopelos and Alonissos – are dealt with here. Skyros, the most southerly, is usually reached from Kimi, on Euboea; the others are reached either from Volos or, if coming direct from Athens, via Agios Konstantinos in Phthiotis, north of Boeotia. The islands are varied and attractive, with picturesque villages of the Cycladic type.

Skýros

The largest of the islands is Skyros, rugged and mountainous. Its southern face is barren and forbidding, and the southerly port of **Trís Boúkes** is often swept by gusts of wind down from the mountains. Near Tris Boukes there is the grave, set in a

Grave of Rupert Brooke

peaceful olive grove, of *Rupert Brooke* who died on a hospital ship off the shore of Skyros in 1915. The boat arrives at **Lineriá**, further up the southwest coast, and it is usual immediately to take the bus the 12 kms across to the capital, **Skýros**, on the green and fertile northeast side of the island. Here, beneath a dramatically abrupt rock crowned by a medieval citadel, the streets are narrow and winding, the white cubic houses topped by flat grey roofs. An invitation to someone's house should be eagerly accepted; the interiors are famous for their Byzantine-style carved furniture and tapestries. Also you should visit the *museum*, housed in the town hall, for its collection of medieval church furniture. There is a beach nearby – the island has several good beaches.

Theseus and Achilles

Skyros was anciently a dependency of Athens. Kimon found here the giant bones he imagined were those of Theseus and carried them back to Athens to be housed in the Theseion. In legend, Thetis sent young Achilles here disguised as a maiden to keep him out of the Trojan War, but Odysseus lured him away and he died by Paris' arrow.

Skiáthos

The gentle slopes of Skiathos are green and wooded, its landscape sharing the softness of Pelion on the nearby mainland. For those who do not miss sharp Cycladic outline, it is the most beautiful of the Northern Sporades. A community of English have built villas here, and in the summer the island now becomes very crowded. **Skiathos** town drapes attractively over two low hills above the harbour on the southeast coast, and a few kilometres westwards is **Koukounariés**, one

A fine beach

of the Aegean's finest beaches, sandy and fringed with pines, though with the building of a Xenia, less tranquil than it once was. Two hours' walk to the north is the deserted medieval town of **Kástro**, perched upon a rocky outcrop, abandoned early in the last century when piracy was finally eradicated. There is a derelict *Church of Christ* (with frescoes) and the remains of two *monasteries* – that of the Annunciation has a fine Byzantine church.

Skópelos

Skopelos, like Skiathos, is green and even more intensely cultivated, though it is also more rugged, its landscape and architecture having more character. There are vineyards and groves of olive and fruit trees, and it is most enjoyable to come in August when prunes, the island's speciality, are being home-dried in slow ovens, and removed now and again for tasting. Pottery and weaving also flourish. **Skópelos** town, towards the northeast of the island, rises like an amphitheatre round its bay, the whitewashed houses and churches splashed lightly with the red and blue colours of the doors and shutters and the ridges of alternating slate and tiled roofs picked out in strokes of white, boldly emphasising their irregular geometry. But the town is exposed to the intermittent blasts of the summer meltemi, and **Glóssa**, on the northwest coast, is the first – and in strong winds the only – port of call.

A walk up from this pleasant hamlet into the especially lush hills on this side of the island is rewarding for its views across to Skiathos and distant Euboea.

Barbarossa In 1538, having performed the same service for Aegina the year before, Barbarossa paused at Skopelos to slaughter the entire population.

Alónissos

Eastwards lies Alonissos, a hilly and wooded idyll only sparsely populated and not much visited by tourists. The beautiful village of **Chóra**, 300 metres high and looking down over the harbour, was largely abandoned following a severe earthquake in 1965 and the islanders now live in the modern port of **Patatíri** where the boats arrive. There are many sandy beaches and the clear waters are excellent for underwater fishing. For seekers of tranquillity the walks and waters of Alonissos are superb.

Underwater fishing

PRACTICAL INFORMATION

TRAVEL TO EUBOEA
From *Athens* there are **buses** to Chalkis from 260 Liossion Street (see *Practical Information*, Athens), leaving every half-hour during the day, hourly in late evenings; the journey takes about 1½ hours. From the same bus station 3 buses a day go to Arkitsa for the ferry to Loutra Aidipsou, in all 3½ hours, a useful route if you want to go to the north end of the island and to avoid possibly a long wait for a bus in Chalkis. There are frequent buses to Rafina from Mavromateon Street (about every half-hour; journey one hour) and also to Skala Oropou from Plateia Egyptou.

There is also a **bus** from *Thebes* about every 2 hours to Chalkis.

From Stathmos Larissis in Athens (see *Practical Information*, Athens) a **train** goes to Chalkis about every hour (journey about 1½ hours).

Numerous **ferries**: Rafina-Karystos (2 hours), about 3 daily; Rafina-Marmari (1¼ hours), 3 daily, 4–5 weekends; Skala Oropou-Eretria (½ hour), every half-hour until 9pm, then 10 and 11pm; Agia Marina-Stira (50 minutes), 6 daily, more at weekends; Arkitsa-Loutra Aidipsou (one hour), about every 1½ hours, last at 10pm; Glyfa-Agiokambos (½ hour), every 2 hours from 6am to 8pm.

TRAVEL WITHIN EUBOEA
From the **bus** station in the centre of Chalkis there is a good service throughout the island although it is better to the south than to the north. There is a frequent service to Eretria (about 16 daily), about 3 buses a day to Karystos (journey 3 hours), and 7 to Kimi (where you must change buses or take a taxi down to the port of Paralia for the ferries – see below).

CHALKIS
Hotels: Paralia (on waterfront) (B); Hara (C); Iris (E) – or stay at Artaki, 9 kms north, at the Telemachos (C), where you can swim.
Tourist Police: 32 Venizelou.

There are excellent *restaurants* along the waterfront.

AKMETAGA (Prokopion)
Hotel: Anessis (E).

LIMNI
Hotel: Plaza (C). To the north there is a long stretch of pebbly beach where there is unofficial *camping*.
Daily *bus* from Chalkis.

LOUTRA AIDIPSOU
There are 100 or more *hotels* for the hypochondriacs and others who come here. You could try the Kentrikon (B); Capri, Knossos (both near beach) (C).
Tavernas along the waterfront.
Many small *beaches* in the bay to the northwest where the crowds thin out.

PEFKI
This makes a pleasant place to stay on the north coast, with a quiet *beach*. *Rent-rooms*.

ERETRIA
Hotel: Delphis (C).
The *archaeological site* is open 8.30am to 12.30pm, 4 to 6pm, Sundays and holidays 9am to 3pm. The *museum* has the same hours but is closed Tuesdays.

LEFKANDI (between Eretria and Chalkis)
Hotel: Lefkandi (C).
Here the site of *one of the earliest temples* yet discovered, from the 9th C BC, has been excavated; also a number of *rich burials* from the 10th C.

KIMI
Hotel: Krinon (E). At Paralia, the Aktaeon (D).
Buses go every 2 hours down to the port of Paralia, whence *ferries* go to the Northern Sporades (further details below), and also about once a week to Limnos. From Kimi you can travel by *bus* to Karystos (below).

There is a *museum* on the road for Paralia devoted to Euboean craftwork, open on weekdays during the mornings and evenings.

169

KARYSTOS
Hotels: Apollon Resort (B); Galaxy (C) – both by good beaches; and Louloudi (C).

Taverna: Melissa, Theochari Kotsika Street.

You can *bus* to Kimi by changing at Lepoura.

TRAVEL TO THE NORTHERN SPORADES
Flights from Athens to Skiathos several times a day.

Boats from *Kimi* (Euboea) 2–3 daily to Skyros (1¾ hours), and 2–4 weekly to Alonissos, Skopelos and Skiathos (5½ hours); from *Agios Konstantinos* (near Kammena Vourla and served by hourly buses from 260 Liossion Street, Athens) daily boats to Skiathos (3¼ hours) and Skopelos (5½ hours), about 3 weekly to Alonissos (6 hours); from *Volos* several daily to Skiathos (3 hours) and Skopelos (4½ hours), and every day except Monday to Alonissos (5 hours). From Volos during the summer there is also a **hydrofoil** service to Skiathos and Skopelos (more expensive).

Combination bus and boat tickets to Skiathos via Agios Konstantinos can be arranged through Alkyon, 98 Akadimias, Athens.

There are frequent boats between Skiathos, Skopelos and Alonissos, both ferries and local excursions. But boats between Skyros and the other islands are infrequent and you may have to travel via Kimi.

SKYROS
Accommodation
Skyros town: for a *hotel*, Xenia (B), and many *rooms* both in town and near **Magazia beach**, large and sandy, an easy walk from town.

Linaria: for a *hotel*, Aegeon (E), and many *rooms* for rent.

Eating and Entertainment
Skyros town: Moraiti *taverna* on the main street; Kabanera (cheaper). There are *discos*.

Travel
There is an infrequent *bus* service between Linaria and Skyros town connecting with the ferries. You can hire *mopeds* and *ponies* for getting around the island, or simply *walk*. Boats to beaches (below).

Other Things
Boats serve *beaches* around the island: there are pleasant beaches at Kalamitsa (which you can also reach by track south of Linaria; it has a taverna), Atsitsa and Tris Boukes.

The pre-Lenten *carnival* here is famous for the cavorting of the young men dressed in goatskins or in drag.

The *archaeological museum* is closed Tuesdays.

SKIATHOS
Accommodation
Skiathos town (Chora): *hotels* (many): Esperides (Achladia beach) (A); Alkyon (Ammoudia beach), Meltemi (by the harbour) (B); Christina, Akti, Koukounaries, Pothos (C). There are many *pensions*, *villas*, *rent-rooms*; if you have any difficulty with accommodation (Skiathos is very full in high season), the Skiathos Tourist Organisation may be able to help (by the harbour). There are *campgrounds* at Kolpos and Megalos Aselimos (but no public transport).

Koukounaries: *hotels:* Skiathos Palace (L); Xenia (B).

Eating and Entertainment
Skiathos town: many kafeneions and tavernas along the harbour-front; several good fish restaurants in the street that leads up from the harbour. Try Kanapitsa or Marimari (cheaper) on the waterfront, or again for good cheap fare, Elias Taverna, Papiamondi Street.

There are several *discos*; try the one on Bourtsi islet or the Scuna Club.

Travel
Buses between Skiathos town (Chora) and Koukounaries every half-hour to hour serving the many beaches on the way. In summer these buses get very crowded, and an alternative is to take one of the many *boats* from the harbour.

You can also hire *mopeds* and open *jeeps*.

Activities
There is a *golf course* on the island.

Antiques can be purchased at Galerie Vorsakis, Plateia Trion Ierarchon, Skiathos town.

The *festival* of Agia Paraskevi is on 26 July.

Boats from Skiathos town harbour serve the many superb sandy *beaches* along the south coast; you can also visit Lalaria on the north side, with *caves* nearby, and you can take *boat trips round the island*.

At Koukounaries there is *windsurfing*. If the beach is too crowded you can walk to the more *isolated beach* of Agia Eleni (taverna) facing Pelion, or if you prefer there is Banana Beach for nature-lovers.

From Chora you can also walk in about one hour to the *monastery of Evangelistria*, though you must go either in the morning or in the early evening as it closes at midday.

SKOPELOS
Accommodation
Skopelos town (Chora): *hotels:* Amalia, Xenia (B); Aeolos (C); Amerika (D). Also *pensions*, *rooms*, etc. If you have problems with accommodation, Skopelos Tours may be able to help (at the harbour).
Loutraki has a couple of *hotels* including Avra (C), also *rooms*.
Staphilos: *hotel:* Rigas (B).
Glossa: 2 *inns* and a taverna; a better place to stay than Loutraki.

Eating and Entertainment
Chora: Many *tavernas*, *cafes*, etc, along the harbour-front. A good fish restaurant is Angilos, or try Ta Kymata (along the harbour).

A couple of *discos*, a *bouzouki club* at the end of the bay, and a *jazz club* – O Platanos.

Travel
Bus about 4 times daily between Glossa/Loutraki and Skopelos town (Chora), and more frequent buses between Skopelos and Agnontas.

There are also *boats* from the harbour at Chora to beaches around the island (mostly shingle). You can hire *bikes*, *mopeds* and (perhaps) a *car* in Chora.

Activities
There is a sandy *beach* near Chora. Otherwise there are beaches all round the coast from Skopelos to Loutraki. Staphilos is perhaps the principal one. There are good beaches at Agnondas, Panormas and Milia (all with tavernas). There is *nude swimming* at Velanio, around the headland from Staphilos.

Boat trips round the island from Chora.

From Glossa you can walk in 45 minutes to Perivoliou, the only good beach on the north side of the island, or to the monastery of Agios Ioannis in about 1½ hours. From Chora you can walk or hire mules to go to the monasteries of Evangelismos (one hour) and Prodromos (1½ hours) – both close for a few hours at midday.

Festival on 6 August.

ALONISSOS
Accommodation
Patitiri: *hotels:* Alkyon (B); Galaxy, Marpounta (20 minutes out of town, holiday chalets) (C); Alonissos (E). Also *rooms*. Ikos Travel Agency by the harbour can help with accommodation.
Steni Vala beach: *campground* at Ikaros Camping.

Travel and Activities
There is no bus. You can hire *mopeds*, or use the *boats* from the main town of Patitiri to the various beaches along the east coast; the boats also go to a number of the surrounding small islands.

Patitiri has a small stony *beach*. Most of the beaches on the island are of fine shingle. There are good beaches at Kokkinokastro and Krisamilia. Some places served by the boats have nowhere to eat, so enquire and if necessary take your lunch. There are also *tours by boat* around the island.

In the old Chora (Alonissos) you can eat well at the Paraport Taverna and enjoy the view.

CENTRAL GREECE

Thessaly: the Southern Gates

Across the centre of Greece there is a great mountain barrier, which stretches from the Euboean Gulf in the east to Levkas on the western coast. The two modern highways which go northwards to Epirus and Thessaly skirt these mountains to left and right, and there is only one road through the middle, where the roads from Amfissa and Levadia join together and traverse the Bralos pass, between Mt Oeti and Kallidromon. This road, after a steep descent, emerges onto the Maliac plain slightly to the east of the gorge of the river Asopos; anciently, the city of Trachis (later called Herakleia – it was the last home of Herakles before his death on Mt Oeti) guarded a track over these mountains to the cities of Doris, and ruins of the acropolis of Trachis have been identified on the top of high cliffs at the mouth of the gorge. But the track guarded by Trachis was not suitable for a large force of men: as the Roman historian Livy tells us, the only military road which afforded the means of transit to any army was by the seashore through the pass of **Thermopylae**, 'when it meets with no impediment from an opponent'.

Xerxes' invasion

In 480 BC when the Persians invaded Greece in enormous numbers, the Greeks sent a force of some 7000 men under the Spartan general Leonidas to defend the pass. At that time Thermopylae was a narrow defile of about 6 kms long between the steep wooded slopes of Kallidromon and the sea; the pass was only a few paces wide at either end, although it widened somewhat in the middle, near the hot springs. Thermopylae, which means hot gates, still has these mineral waters and is a spa with a big hotel visible on the landward side of the National Highway; this road roughly follows the line of the ancient track, although it tends to the north of it. But the gates have gone, no longer is there a pass between mountains and sea, because mineral deposits from the springs, and the silt carried down by the river Spercheios, have created a large expanse of land on the seaward side. As Robert Liddell observes, Thermopylae originally would have looked more like Kammena Vourla, a pleasant seaside resort (also a spa) used mostly by Greeks, further to the east. Moreover, the ugly *monument of Leonidas*, erected in 1955, would have found itself in the sea.

It was almost opposite this monument that the Greeks under Leonidas restored an old wall across the pass, the 'wall of the Phocians', and for several days, advancing in front of it into the wider part of the pass, fought off Xerxes' army of over a quarter of a million men based at Trachis. Xerxes might have been forced to abandon his expedition at this point, had not a Greek, Ephialtes, shown a Persian force the way through Kallidromon to take the Greeks in the rear: the *path*, still traceable, comes out about 1½ kms to the east of the monument. Leonidas had stationed 1000 Phocians to guard the path, but they ran away: hearing of the Persian move, he then sent away all his force except 300 Spartans, 700 Thespians and 400 Thebans. Surrounded on both sides, Leonidas' men retired first to the wall, then to a small *hillock* nearby, at which point the Thebans deserted, and almost all the remaining Greeks were killed. On the hillock, which is across the road from the monument, there is a new *plaque* with the old, poignant inscription:

The Spartan stand

'O stranger, go and tell the Lacedaimonians, we lie here obedient to their commands.'

Why did the Spartans, and the Thespians, stay behind? Perhaps it was just obedience, perhaps a gesture had to be made, as at Borodino. In any event, the Persians swept on and only at Plataea a year later were they finally defeated on land.

There was an odd sequel. Brennus leading the Gauls in 279 BC turned the Greek position at Thermopylae in the same way. When he later arrived at Delphi, like Xerxes' force his army was also panicked by rocks crashing down from Parnassos.

The area of the Maliac plain has other historical associations. At the Alamana bridge over the Spercheios a small Greek force under Diakos heroically fought a Turkish army in 1821. Across the plain at **Lamía**, now the capital of the nome of Phthiotis, the Athenians, after Alexander the Great's death in 323, almost put an end to Macedonian dominion when they blockaded the Macedonian general, Antipater, in the town. However, the siege was lifted, and the Greeks were later defeated at the battle of Krannon in Thessaly. In the Middle Ages the town belonged first to the Frankish dukes of Athens (like Thebes) and then to the Catalan Duchy of Neo-Patras – on the hill above the town are the ruins of the Frankish and Catalan *castle* built on the ancient acropolis, from which there is a fine view of Oeti and the valley of the Spercheios. West of Lamia along the valley, beyond the spa of Ipati, is the charming village of **Ipáti** (24 kms); this is the site of the ruined *castle of Neo-Patras*, possessed in turn by the Franks, the Greek Angeli of Epirus, the Catalans (their second capital) and the Turks (the seat of a pasha). Much further up the valley, and below Mt Timfristos is **Karpenísi**, a small country town (78 kms from Lamia); from there it is 109 kms by a spectacular road to Agrinion, which is on the route to Epirus.

Medieval castles

Routes through Thessaly

Lamia's former importance owed a lot to its position commanding the Furka pass into central Thessaly over Mt Othrys; the road went (and still goes) via Thaumakoi (now Domokos), so called because of the wonder – *thauma* –

caused by the sudden view of the apparently unending plain of Thessaly. Once over the pass into the plain, the road divides after 53 kms, left to Karditsa (91 kms from Lamia), Trikala (118 kms) and Kalambaka-Meteora (141 kms) and right to Farsala (67 kms) and Larissa (113 kms). Alternatively, the National Highway, which goes round Othrys to the east and passes a little to the west of Volos (111 kms from Lamia) then continues to Larissa (146 kms) and, after the Vale of Tempe, along the east coast to Thessaloniki.

Vólos and Pelion

The town of **Vólos** is situated at the base of Mt Pelion, which then extends to the southeast and hooks round to form the Pagasitikos Gulf, so that the town stands at the head of a large enclosed bay. The capital of the nome of Magnesia and an important outlet for Thessalian produce, Volos is a prosperous town with several good hotels and restaurants, but with little charm: it was badly damaged by earthquake in the 1950s, and is largely rebuilt, although the old district of Ano Volos remains above the town. There is an attractive fishing harbour at the western end of the long quay. On the large square behind, a bazaar is held in early August, of the kind that travels around central Greece in the summer selling everything from clothes and rugs to frying pans and walking-sticks – and, of course, souvlakia; villagers come from miles around for their one big shopping expedition of the year.

The *museum*, which is at the other end of town, about 2 kms from the centre, is quite exceptional, and illustrates the long occupation of the area around Volos. A visit to the museum should be made before going to any of the sites of Iolkos, Sesklo, Dimini and Pagasae-Demetrias which are rather specialist tastes.

The unique collection of *painted stelai* of the Hellenistic period, found at Demetrias, is the principal attraction, more perhaps for their survival in their present state than for their subject matter – several are clearly copies of the same theme, probably from the same workshop, although others have the poignancy of the best *relief stelai* (of which there are also examples in the museum, notably from Phalana and Pherae) and their faded earthy colours have a delightful, soft effect. There is a very well laid out room of *exhibits from Sesklo* – fine Neolithic pottery with striking abstract patterns, well worked stone daggers and knives with bone handles, and household goods including pottery sieves. There are also *Neolithic objects from Dimini*, and *Mycenaean finds from Iolkos*. At the other end of the museum are two rooms, showing Thessalian graves and grave goods over the ancient period: finest of all is the *gold jewellery* of the 4th and 3rd C BC which alone justifies a visit to the museum.

Ancient sites round Volos

Sesklo is, like **Dimini**, to the south of the road from Volos to Larissa. Both these sites are Neolithic, Dimini dating back to the 4th millenium BC and Sesklo is even earlier, indeed one of the earliest sites found in Greece. (Buses go to both places from Volos and it is possible to walk between the two in about 1½ hours.) Dimini is just outside Volos near the village of the same name; the prehistoric remains spread over a low hill. To reach Sesklo: turn off the Larissa road after 12 kms across the railway, continue towards the village, and just before it turn left for the site (one km further on). The site (fenced but with an attendant about) is on a hillock, which backs onto a small ravine issuing out of higher hills, and has something of the look of Mycenae on a far smaller scale; there are low walls, the ruins of a large palace, and small pieces of pottery littered everywhere. **Iolkos**, the home of Jason and the leading city of Thessaly in the Mycenaean period, was situated within present day Volos; a mound (Agioi Theodori) showing traces of two Mycenaean palaces has been found on the northwest side of the town, near the railway, on the right of the Larissa road.

Jason and the Argonauts

The site of **Pagasae-Demetrias** spreads on either side of the Lamia road, beginning 4 kms south of Volos. (There is a bus stop nearby, or you can walk to it in about 45 minutes.) By tradition it was at Pagasae, the port of Iolkos, that Jason's ship the Argo was built which brought back the Golden Fleece from Colchis with the help of Medea; later it was the port of Pherae (modern Velestinon) in the 5th and 4th C BC. When Demetrias was founded adjacently in the early 3rd C it depopulated Iolkos (long since shrunk in importance anyway) and succeeded Pagasae. The ruins extend over a wide area, the principal remains being the walls of Demetrias, best preserved on the west of the road.

Less ancient and only just excavated is the *early Christian township* near the village of Néa Anchíalos, a few kilometres further south. Among other buildings, five Christian basilicas have been uncovered together with mosaics. There is a small museum on the site.

An unusual corner of Greece

Pelion (Pílion) is the name not only of the mountain, but of the whole peninsula area which forms one of the strangest regions of Greece. It has few classical or historical associations, although it was the legendary home of the Centaur Chiron, who here taught Jason and Achilles. It is remarkable rather for its climate and vegetation, and the different style of its villages and churches. The climate is comparatively cool in summer and often damp, and in winter there are large snow falls: consequently, the vegetation is exceptionally rich from the plentiful water, particularly on the east coast where the beech-woods and sweet chestnuts, and the oaks, planes and walnut trees reach down to the olives near sea level. Most of the villages are high up on the leafy slopes, with distant views of the sea. The attractive houses, usually of whitewashed stone under slate roofs, lie spread over the valleys on the east coast, amongst fruit trees and gardens of hydrangeas and chrysanthemums; only the small plateias with a church and perhaps one or two shops and a kafeneion attract any concentration of buildings. The churches too are different in Pelion: built in the style of the old aisled basilicas they have a refreshing, almost Renaissance look in contrast to the conventional Byzantine cross-in-square, frozen in tradition. Their interiors are usually uncluttered except for elaborate candelabras and heavy screens, while outside the distinctive feature is a cloister of wood or stone running along part of the building. The churches spread low over the ground, rather than reach up, as if pressed by the too-close sky.

Swimming

There are plenty of hotels and rooms in the area, and buses serve all the larger villages from Volos (see the *Practical Information* section). For a short expedition (although longer than it looks on the map, as the roads are narrow and winding, like Devon lanes) you can drive in a circle round the central part of Pelion, via Portaria and the Chania pass over Pelion itself (with marvellous views over the gulf), Kissos, Tsangarada, Milies and Kala Nera. There is good swimming on sandy beaches on the east coast at Chorevto (below Zagora), Agios Ioannis (below Kissos) and Milopotamos (below Tsangarada), and at several places on the west coast. Walking is a little difficult, at least in central Pelion: you find yourself either forced onto the road or through almost impenetrable woods, for example between Milies and Tsangarada.

Villages on the slopes of Pelion

There are some 30 villages on the slopes of Pelion: the following three may serve as examples for the others. **Makrinítsa** (from Volos 16 kms) is a beautiful little village reached by turning left at Portaria: it hangs on the southern slopes of Pelion, a greener and smaller Arachova. The plateia looks directly over Volos and the gulf (you can see particularly well the area of Pagasae-Demetrias) and, apart from the standard plane tree, has a sculptured fountain (maybe it will be decorated with a watermelon cooling under its water) and a small church (*Agios Ioannis*) with a stone-pillared cloister along two sides, and a sculptured exterior to the apse. Above the plateia, inside a courtyard reached by a stone track past handsome white houses is the large 18th C *church of the Panagia* (it was formerly a monastery): a wooden cloister runs around three sides of the building.

Tsangaráda (55 kms) is typical of the Pelion villages on the east coast, being spread out over a long distance, mostly off the road. Stone tracks run beside banks of rigani between the four plateias, which form separate local centres within the village. The principal plateia of *Agia Paraskevi* (near the post office) has some attractive old buildings, a monstrous plane tree with the church bell hanging from it – unfortunately the church itself is modern and ugly – and a good taverna. From here it is a ½ hour walk to the next plateia to the south, that of the *Holy Taxiarchs*, which is exquisite, with a whitewashed church, cloistered on north and south, a shop and kafeneion: this plateia is only a short step from the road (where it curves, by a restaurant) and yet is hidden from sight. (Between these two plateias a road descends in 8 kms to Milopotamos which has two tavernas and some excellent swimming.) Further on, actually on the road, is the *church of Agios Ioannis*, rather similar to the Panagia in Makrinitsa: outside there is a wooden cloister on three sides; inside it has elegant aisles behind high arches, and local people say that the wooden slats above the windows were used to store arms, under both the Turks and the Germans.

Miliés (27 kms) is in the middle of the peninsula. At one time a railway ran from Volos through the olives, but no more: it must have been one of the prettiest stretches of line in Greece. The principal plateia, some way above the desolate area around the old railway station, has several cafés, a cloistered church (*church of the Taxiarchs*, with frescoes) and the *library of Agios Athanasios* – at one time the village was a centre of Hellenic culture under the Turks. It is possible to walk from here, southeast, to the *chapel of Agia Triada* (one hour) and then south to the modest remains of the ancient town of *Korope*. But if you really want to get to grips with the countryside you can walk up through the village, then past the planes and the water and the patches of fruit trees, into the woods on top of the hills, then go northeast through the chestnut groves to a small village on the road near Tsangarada: it takes 4½ hours, but in the past there was a good path between the villages and it would have taken half that time. All over Greece the new roads are ruining the old paths, by their disuse. An encounter that day was with an old man with a bad eye, who was strapping firewood onto his mule; he was using just his arms, as years ago some dynamite had blown off his hands. '*Ti na kanome*' – 'What can one do', he said with a sad smile.

Walking

Across the Plain of Thessaly

After bypassing Volos, the National Highway on its way north crosses the eastern side of Thessaly via **Lárissa** (58 kms from Volos), an important town and capital of the province of Thessaly. It has little to show for its long history. You can see the ruins of a Byzantine *fortress* in the north of the town. From the Turkish occupation of almost 500 years up to 1881, there remains in the centre of the city near the market a mosque with a minaret, which now contains the *Archaeological Museum* with a large collection of Palaeolithic and Neolithic objects found in Thessaly, amongst other exhibits. Otherwise you can sit in the large central square, Plateia Stratou, under the orange trees and sip an ouzo or eat some halva (a sweet made of honey and sesame), for both of which products Larissa is well known, or stroll across the Pineios river to the Alkazar park (on the right of the Kozani road) where there are some cafés in the shade. Twenty-four kms southwest of Larissa is **Krannon**, near the site of the battle in 323 BC when the Macedonians re-established control over the Greeks: earlier it was an important city, and remains have been found of a temple of Asklepios and also two 5th C beehive tombs.

Vale of Tempe

At the northeast corner of the plain of Thessaly the Pineios finds an outlet to the sea through the *Vale of Tempe*, between the slopes of Lower Olympos to the north and those of cone-shaped Ossa on the south. The valley, along which the Pineios flows past plane trees and willows, is a narrow defile about 10 kms long, under high cliffs. Anciently it contained a sanctuary of Apollo, who was said to have purified himself in the waters of the Pineios after killing the Python at Delphi; later at intervals a procession of young men came from Delphi to gather the bay which still grows here. Tempe was also one of the main routes into Greece, and at first sight a good position for defence: in 480 the Greeks took up position here until Xerxes found a way round to the north via Gonnos, and then the Greek force retired to Thermopylae. Whatever beauty and tranquillity Tempe formerly possessed have been destroyed by the modern road and the railway which both go through its middle.

Climbing Mt Olympos

The road emerges onto the coastal strip to the east of Olympos, and after several depressing-looking camping and swimming places passes on the right of the road at 52 kms from Larissa, the *castle of Platamon* built by the Crusaders in the early 13th C. It is worth visiting, as it is well preserved and has good views towards Olympos and the coastal area to the north, known anciently as Pieria. At 58 kms there is a turning left at Leptokaria and a poor road runs through Olympos to Elasson via Karia and Kriovrisi, beyond which a road to the right leads up to the Army Ski Centre. This is one way to approach the ascent of **Olympos** (Ólimbos), but **Litóchoron**, a small town on the east slopes of the mountain, is the usual starting point for climbing up to the legendary home of the gods. The mountain has seven peaks of 2750 metres or over, the highest of which is *Mytikas*, 2917 metres: it is, like Parnassos, only practical to climb it in the summer owing to the presence of snow for most of the year. From Litochoron it is about 10 hours to the summit, and a night should be spent at Refuge A at 2100 metres, 2½ hours from the summit. There are red markers to Mytikas from the town, but it is advisable to engage a guide: information, etc, from the Greek Alpine Club in Litochoron. A minimum of two days is necessary.

The summit can also be reached by driving via Elasson (southwest of Olympos and 61 kms from Larissa), Elevtherochorio, Kallithea and Olympiada, and then taking the military road on the left up to the Army Ski Centre (the approach to this from the east has been described above); nearby is Refuge B, and from there Refuge A can be reached, but get good directions or preferably a guide first – it can be a dangerous mountain. Always carry plenty of water with you and some spare food.

Coast route The National Highway continues past Katerini, a market town (85 kms from Larissa), from which there are good views of Olympos to the south; it then passes between the village of Kitros and the site of ancient *Pydna* on the coast (this was a Macedonian city, near which in 168 BC the Romans inflicted a decisive defeat on the Macedonians), and crosses the wide Aliakmon river and finally a large area of reclaimed land to Thessaloniki (153 kms).

Inland route More interesting than the coastal route to Thessaloniki via Larissa is the longer inland route via Trikala and Kalambaka-Meteora. (The obvious solution is to do one route going north, and another on the way south, if you can). Trikala is 118 kms from Lamia (and 63 kms from Larissa by a good road across the plain). If you come from the direction of Lamia, at 53 kms there is the fork right to **Fársala**, to the west **Julius Caesar** of which at the battle of Pharsalus in 48 BC Caesar defeated **versus Pompey** Pompey and so won control of the whole Roman world. You take the Karditsa road to the left; the huge wall of the Pindos mountains draws closer on the west as you drive past agricultural villages rich in cows and tractors beyond the dreams of most Greek farmers. Sometimes, near the villages, you see groups of the distinctive circular tents of the gypsies. **Karditsa** itself is an uninteresting market town – apart from the storks' nests, which are on almost every roof in late spring. Forty-one kms to its south in the Pindos foothills is the pleasant spa of **Smokovo**.

Trikala, 27 kms further on across the river Pineios, has more interest. As ancient Trikka it had the oldest sanctuary in Greece of Asklepios, the god of medicine, and attracted many visitors: from the pastures around the city came the best of the famous Thessalian horses. Now the capital of its nome, it is a pleasant town making the most of its position on either side of the river Lethaios: in the town centre, two plateias face each other across the river, while in the northwest of the town is a *Byzantine fort*, below which is the former *Turkish bazaar* with old houses and many churches amongst the narrow streets. Like Karditsa, Trikala is the winter quarters of a good many Vlachs who come down from the summer pastures in the Pindos. Southwest of Trikala there is an attractive way into the mountains: you take the road to **Pili** (19 kms), a village at the entry of a defile which carries water down from the Pindos and was formerly a route through to Arta. At 1½ kms above the village in a beautiful position by the side of the stream is the *Porta Panagia*, a basilical church founded in 1283 by the Greek rulers of Neo-Patras: it has some 13th C mosaics and early 15th C frescoes. Further upstream is a narrow 16th C *bridge* built by St Bessarion, the abbot of Dousiko, a monastery which he founded visible to the north of Pili. It is possible to drive on up to the mountain village of Pertouli and beyond.

Kalambáka, 23 kms from Trikala, is the usual place to stay when seeing the Meteora, as it lies below one of the largest of the blue-grey rocks, which rise dramatically and inexplicably from the plain: as at Delphi, Egyptian Vultures fly overhead, and the small town seems dwarfed by the massive pedestals

'Silent troops of mammoth'

'gathering like silent troops of mammoth halted in meditation on the tundra's edge' (Patrick Leigh Fermor). Across the wide, sandy bed of the Pineios is the facade of the Pindos mountains. Kalambaka itself is a modern town and not particularly attractive: it was burnt by the Germans in 1943. If you wish to spend a night nearby, Trikala might be preferable, but Kalambaka does retain undamaged the extraordinary, former *cathedral church of the Koimisis*: you find it towards the top of the town, not far from the station. The existing church, an aisled basilica, was founded in the mid-12th C, but it incorporates features and materials from several earlier buildings: in its middle is an ambo, a canopied pulpit made from marble, said to be unique in present day Byzantine churches; in the apse behind the ciborium, an elaborate canopied altar, is a three-stepped synthronon, where the priests used to stand. According to the caretaker, who is probably as reliable as anyone else, these features belonged to a previous church of the 7th C or earlier: the mosaics visible under the floor near the screen belonged to the earliest church built about the 5th C. Whatever the exact history, the continuity of worship is obvious: the church was already very old when most of the frescoes were done in the 16th C. The pillars in fact derive from a pagan temple, and you can see Ionic capitals on the two nearest the door; outside, on the south wall there are clear traces of classical or Hellenistic masonry, with one piece of ancient statuary actually built into the wall – a man or god with a child.

The Metéora

Mid-air monasteries

The Meteora are the monasteries built on the huge rocks behind Kalambaka, so called because they are 'suspended in mid air'. The rocks and monasteries form an extraordinary congregation, which are deeply impressive at any time, whether in the rain when the rocks menace you with their blackened walls, or in the sunshine when they gleam like

One of the monasteries of the Meteora

metal and the red-roofed monasteries look peacefully over the green valleys.

Their history   The precise history of the monasteries is not entirely clear. At first hermits and ascetics came to live in the caves amongst the rocks, and by the late 13th or early 14th C, and possibly before, a group of hermits had their centre at the skete of Doupiani. Then during the 14th C the hermitages began to be developed as monasteries on top of the rocks, where they would be immune to the troubled times beneath them. The largest monastery on the largest rock, the Great Meteoron, was founded by St Athanasios in the mid 14th C: this monastery and the others were totally inaccessible until recently – except by way of retractable ladder or rope and windlass. How then did Athanasios (and others like him) get up there in the first place? The story goes that *he* at any rate got there on the back of an eagle.

At one time there were over 20 monastic communities on these precipitous rocks. They continued to flourish even under the Turks – as often happens with the church, under oppression the monasteries were both a refuge and a symbol – and their decline has only been in the last century or so. At the end of the 19th C the Bishop of Trikala was given control over the monasteries, and in the 1920s he ordered steps to be cut up to them. Their properties have since been confiscated or looted, and they have become almost emptied of monks. The four major remaining monasteries of Great Meteoron, Barlaam, Agi Triada and Agios Stephanos are with the exception of the last (which is a nunnery) little more than museums.

The Meteora are reached by a road to the west of Kalambaka, which goes past the village of Kastraki into a valley between the elephantine rocks. It is about 21 kms by road to visit the furthest monasteries and to return, so transport of some kind is necessary unless you slog it out on foot, either on the road or by the shorter paths. If you are pressed for time, visits to Agios Nikolaos, the Great Meteoron and either Agia Triada or Agios Stephanos should be on your shortlist.

Touring the Meteora

After 2½ kms on the left is the *chapel of Doupiani*, probably built on the foundations of the first communal church of the then hermitages: the skete of Doupiani was on the rock above. Shortly after, again on the left, is the **monastery of Agios Nikolaos**, founded in the 14th C and recently restored. Although it is almost an anti-climax to see the small building perched amongst other far higher rocks, it is worth the climb: tucked away in the attractive monastic buildings is a tiny church with magnificent frescoes by the Cretan Theophanes (1527), which for once are easy to see owing to the church's scale. Further on the right is the *monastery of Roussanou*, founded in about 1380 and now being restored.

After 6 kms the road forks left to Barlaam and the Great Meteoron, and right to Agia Triada and Agios Stephanos. If you go left, after ½ km a road on the left goes to the **monastery of Barlaam**, founded in the early 16th C by two members of a Ioannina family on the site of an earlier hermitage. It is reached by an iron bridge across a great cleft, and then by steps in the rock. The *Church of All Saints*, with a narthex, has frescoes painted in the mid 16th C by Frangos Kastellanos of Thebes, who like Theophanes also worked on Athonite churches: the frescoes, now restored, are somewhat fussy compared to those at the Great Meteoron. The refectory houses a *museum* for the monastery's treasures.

The **Great Meteoron** is, as it always was, the most important of the monasteries. Founded by the athletic Athanasios in the 14th C it enjoyed the protection and support of the Serbian rulers of Thessaly, one of whom under the name of Ioasaph lived here as a monk. It is approched across a bridge, and through a tunnel cut in the rock, under the old tower which retains the original wooden windlass (now aided by an electric motor): a retractable ladder still hangs against the wall.

This monastery, like Barlaam, has much the same form as the monasteries on Athos: Athanasios had in fact first become a monk on the Holy Mountain. The monastic buildings surround the Katholicon, the main church, giving a courtyard effect. The *Church of the Transfiguration* built in the mid 16th C but retaining the 14th C apse of Ioasaph's church, is very like the Katholicon of an Athonite monastery: it is a domed, cross-in-square church with a square narthex, apsidal ends to the transepts which are lined with wooden stalls, and every inch covered with fine frescoes; there is a carved, gilded ikonostasis (as at Barlaam), and overall the interior has something of the warm, golden light of an Athonite church. Outside, in the cloistered gallery to the north hang the *simantra*, huge wooden beams the shape of a waisted ice cream stick which a monk would beat with a mallet, in groups of three sharp notes commemorating the Trinity, to bring his fellows to worship.

Treasures of the Great Meteoron

The monastery's *refectory*, a barrel-vaulted room of the 16th C, has the monastic treasures, which are comparable to those on display to the average visitor on Athos. It has early illuminated manuscripts, 14th C crysobuls, and many 16th C ikons; there are old vestments and intricately carved wooden crosses. A good 18th C engraving shows all the monasteries at that time – and the Great Meteoron towering over them all.

Nearby is a *cloister* with the monks cells, and an *ossuary*, if you like skulls.

You can escape the crowds (which are a problem) by walking for half an hour to the north of the Meteoron to the ruined 14th C *monastery of Hipapanti*: there is a church in a cave, with frescoes.

Agia Triada (Holy Trinity) is $2\frac{1}{2}$ kms in the other direction from the junction. It is across a deep ravine from the road and the rock must have been one of the most difficult to ascend: there are now steps. The monastery's foundation and its church are ascribed to the 15th C, and there is a later *chapel of St John The Baptist* hewn out of the rock. It has attractive monastic buildings, with arches and columns, under a solitary cypress tree.

Shortly after is **Agios Stephanos**, founded in the 14th C. This is the one monastery which can just be seen from Kalambaka, and from it you get a good view over the town and the Pineios to the Pindos wall: it is also the easiest to reach, across a small bridge. The building is now a thriving nunnery,

A feminine touch

and their feminine touch is evident in the neat balconied courtyard. The only charge you pay is for visiting the modest treasures in the refectory, as if a reminder that everything else is definitely not a museum. The late 18th C *Church of Agios Charalambos* without any frescoes is strangely bare, except for its carved screen; a silver reliquary contains the saint's head. The earlier *church of St Stephen* is apparently closed at present: its 14th C frescoes were damaged by German gunfire in the last war. The monastery was also looted by the Italians. In the civil war the Greek Communists committed several atrocities here, apart from desecrating a portrait of the founder. Until those years, this monastery, and the others, had remained inviolate on their great rocks.

PRACTICAL INFORMATION

TRAVEL TO CENTRAL GREECE
From Athens **buses** depart from 260 Liossion Street (see *Practical Information*, Athens) for Kammena Vourla (about 15 daily, in 3 hours), Lamia (15), Larissa (7, in 5 hours), Litohoro near Mt Olympos (3 daily, in 6 hours), Trikala (7 daily), and Volos (9, in about 5 hours).

Trains depart from Stathmos Larissis, Athens, 8 times a day for Lianokladi (Lamia), Larissa (about 5 hours) and other intermediate stations to Thessaloniki. At Paleopharsala, a junction in Thessaly, there are connecting trains to Trikala (4 daily) and to Kalambaka/Meteora (3 daily, in about 2 hours; however the only really practical train is at midday from Paleopharsala, which involves a 7am train from Athens; alternatively catch a train at 11.30am in Athens arriving Trikala 5.30pm and stay in Trikala the night or maybe catch a late bus on to Kalambaka). From Paleopharsala there are also connecting trains to Volos. At Larissa too there are connecting trains to Volos (7 a day, in about 1 hour).

THERMOPYLAE
This is on the *bus* route to Lamia and the north, so you could descend one bus and catch the next, it does not merit longer. For the truly romantic there is the *hotel* Aegli (C).

KAMMENA VOURLA
This large resort down the coast from Thermopylae has well over 100 *hotels*; recommended is the Acropole (C), near the beach; and the Delfini (C). There are at least 3 *campgrounds*.

If you are taking the *ferry* to the Northern Sporades or Euboea, **Agios Konstantinos** has several C and D class hotels and also a campground, and there are about half a dozen hotels at **Arkitsa** – try Panorama (C).

LAMIA
Hotels: several in and around the area of the central Plateia Eleftherias, also a number of D class hotels in Rozali Angeli Street. A *campground* east of Lamia, 3 kms from Stylis.

There is a good *taverna* in the square from where most of the buses leave (Plateia Laou). *Buses* go to Volos, Larissa, Trikala, Amfissa, Karpenisi, etc.

GLYFA (ferry to Euboea)
Rooms to rent and several small hotels – try Acroyali (C).

VOLOS
Accommodation and Eating
Hotels: many, including Xenia (beach), Alexandros, Aigli (B); Kypseli, Avra (C) – all these are on or near the waterfront; Thessaloniki (D).

There are many good *restaurants* along the waterfront: try Socrates, 33 Argonafton, or Metaftis, 23 Argonafton.

Travel
Long-distance buses leave from 2 Metamorphoseos, more *local buses* from the bus station by the main square at one end of the waterfront, Plateia Riga Feraiou. There is a good service to the villages of Pelion: to Portaria and Makrinitsa (about 10 a day), Zagora and Chorefto via Hania (4), Agios Ioannis (3), Tsangarada (4; the early morning bus goes on to Milopotamos), Milies and Visitsa (6), Afissos via Agria, Gatsea and Kala Nera (7), Platania (3).

Ferries leave Volos for the Northern Sporades (*qv*). About once a week a boat calls at the harbour of Trikeri, at the very end of Pelion.

Other Things
Tourist Police: 87 Hatziargyri.
Tourist Office: Plateia Riga Feraiou. Maps of Pelion, travel details, etc.
Festivals: at the end of Nautical Week in early July there is a re-enactment of the sailing of the Argonauts; during July and August there is a municipal festival, with concerts, dances, etc.
Museum: at east end of waterfront (15 minutes walk), open 9am to 1pm, 3 to 6pm daily, Sundays and holidays 10am to 2.30pm. Closed Tuesdays.

Buses go up to **Ano Volos**, the former town a few kilometres above, with many attractive old houses; at nearby **Anakassia** one mansion has become a museum for the wall-paintings of a modern primitive painter from Lesvos, Theophilos Hatzimihail (died 1934).

MAKRINITSA
Three mansions have been converted into *hotels* by the NTOG (expensive). Also pensions and rooms.

TSANGARADA
Hotels: Xenia, Kentavros (B); Agios Stephanos (C). Also *rooms*.

Buses to *beach* at Milopotamos in the summer.

MILIES
Rooms for rent.

LARISSA
Accommodation
Divani Palace (A); El Greco (near Volos/Trikala buses), Doma, Olympion (close to Plateia Stratou), Esperia (near museum) (C).

Eating
Dionysos in Roosevelt Street; Xabah, Kouma Street. Other places at Alkazar park.

Travel
Buses hourly to Volos and Trikala from near the junction of Patroklou and Megalou Alexandrou Streets, south of Plateia Stratou. About 8 buses a day go to Kalambaka (1¾ hours).

MT OLYMPOS AND LITOCHORON
Accommodation
Litochoron: Myrto (D) is the best of the *hotels*. Also a *youth hostel*.
Nearby: there are several *campgrounds* along the coast here and many *hotels* in the resorts of Paralia Katerinis, Leptokaria and Platomonas.

Travel
Bus services between Larissa and Katerini pass close to Litochoron on the main highway, but you may have to walk the last few kilometres.

There is a *train station* on the coast, with the same problem.

Climbing Mt Olympos
There is a *Greek Alpine Club* information booth in the plateia; their official *guide* was last known to be Kostas Zolotas from Litochoron (Tel: 0352.81329) who however spends much of the summer up at the Club refuge A. The Club's Athens address is 68 Aeolou (Tel: 321.2429) for information before you depart.

Refuge A is open from May to October (when the mountain is clear of snow); it has beds and adequate food.

For a detailed description of the climb(s) see *Greece on Foot* by Marc Dubin.

TRIKALA
Hotels: Achillion, with a good restaurant (B); Rex, Dina (C); Panhellinon (D). All these hotels are near King George Square.

Frequent *buses* to Kalambaka (in about ½ hour) every ½ to one hour until midevening.

PILI
Hotel: Babanara (D).

Frequent *buses* from Trikala.

If the *Porta Panagia* is closed you can get the key from a woman who lives nearby; ask around.

KALAMBAKA
Accommodation
Hotels: Divani Motel, Xenia (A); Aeolikos Astir (on the main square), Odyssion, Helvetia (C); Rex (D); Meteora (E). Also *rooms* for rent.

At **Kastraki** there is *camping* and the *hotel* Kastraki (E); also *rooms*, *taverna* and *disco*.

Eating and Information
Meteora *taverna*, on the main plateia.

The *Tourist Police* are at the police station, 33 Rammidi Street.

Travel
Frequent *bus* service from Trikala; some buses may continue to Kastraki, nearer Meteora. In summer there is a bus service to the Meteora 4 times a day. From Kalambaka there are 4 buses daily westwards to Metsovo and Ioannina (2¾ hours).

For *trains* see the general travel information at the beginning of this *Practical Information* section.

METEORA
Travel
Bus service from Kalambaka 4 times daily in summer, less out of season.

Taxis (from the main square) would cost 750–1000 drachmas for a round trip visiting perhaps three of the rocks in a couple of hours. For a longer visit, take a picnic.

Remember that if you set off *walking* you can always ask one of the buses to stop.

Visiting the Monasteries
The monasteries all close over midday; the hours vary from place to place, but as a rule of thumb they are open 9am to 1pm and 3pm to 6pm, although to complicate things the Great Meteoron is closed on Tuesdays, Barlaam on Fridays, and Agios Stephanos on Mondays.

To visit the monasteries men should wear trousers, not shorts; women should wear neither, instead skirts, and arms should be covered.

NORTHERN GREECE AND THE ISLANDS OF THE NORTH AEGEAN

Leaving Kalambaka, after 10 kms there is a fork in the road: you turn left onto a spectacular road (which requires some care from the driver) over the Katara pass (1707 metres) to reach Metsovo (67 kms), an attractive Vlach town, and eventually Ioannina (126 kms). The right fork leads north via Grevena (70 kms); 28 kms north of Grevena beyond the Aliakmon river, which here has carved out from the red stone limbs of land like mini Meteora, the road again divides, going right to Kozani and ultimately Edessa (173 kms from Grevena) and left to Kastoria (93 kms).

Western Macedonia

Land of lakes

Kastoría, a centre of the fur trade, is pleasantly situated on a lake: it has a number of wooden houses from the 17th and 18th C and countless churches, which are almost all of basilical form and many are frescoed. This is the Lake District of Greece: northwest of Kastoria are the two Prespa Lakes, the larger of which lies between the three countries of Albania, Yugoslavia and Greece. Both lakes are important ornithological areas (permit needed). The road north of Kastoria goes within a few kilometres of the Lakes, then turns east via Florina to join the road from Kozani. Then the road to Edessa (which is 139 kms from Kastoria) passes through beautiful, rolling country between the mountains on the Yugoslav border, and the misty lakes below Mt Vermion.

Édessa, the capital of the nome of Pella, is situated on a plateau above the plain which stretches to Thessaloniki in the east, and beyond the border with Yugoslavia to the north. With its abundant streams, which fall in great waterfalls over the cliffs below the town, and its commanding position both above the fields of Macedon and astride the *Via Egnatia* (the road to Byzantium from the west), Edessa has always been of some significance. It was long thought to have been the capital of the Macedonian kings (Aigai) before it was transferred to Pella at the end of the 5th C, but Aigai has now been almost certainly identified with Vergina (below). With that romantic association gone there is little to justify stopping in the modern town, now a centre of the carpet industry, except to look at the falls and perhaps to see the very old bridge on the north side of the town which once carried the Via Egnatia.

The road descends into the fruit trees, and follows the old Via Egnatia eastwards, past the site of Pella to Thessaloniki (95 kms). But first, some 14 kms from Edessa is a right turn for Verria and Vergina: taking that road, you will see not far

Temple tombs and hidden churches

before the turning to Naoussa (a town with an exaggerated reputation for its red wine) a small road on the left, across the railway, to a large temple tomb, the *Tomb of Levkadia*. This is one of several similar Macedonian tombs in the area (the most famous of which is the tomb recently excavated at Vergina, below): its facade, part Doric order, part Ionic, has well-preserved paintings. The distinction of **Vérria** is the number of small churches built behind houses to deceive the Turks: some have frescoes. Many of the churches are now signposted, although they are often locked.

Vergína is 16 kms southeast of Verria. Here in 1977 Professor Manolis Andronikos of Thessaloniki University made one of the great archaeological discoveries of the century when having moved nearly 30,000 metric tons of earth from a large tumulus which had only previously yielded fragments of Macedonian funeral stelai he finally discovered two tombs. One was a *barrel-vaulted temple tomb* with a painted facade and was undisturbed; the other smaller tomb had been pillaged but had important wall paintings. The larger tomb had two rooms, each containing a marble sarcophagus containing a gold casket for the ashes of the dead; in addition there were many rich objects of gold, silver, bronze and ivory. The larger of the two caskets weighed 11 kilos of solid gold and contained the bones of a man between 40 and 50 together with a gold wreath; the other had the relics of a young woman. Both caskets had the stylised stars of the Macedonian royal house.

Tomb of Philip of Macedon

Professor Andronikos also found five tiny portrait heads in ivory, one of which has a striking resemblance to a medallion bearing what is thought to be the profile of Philip II of Macedon. The evidence including the dating all points to the conclusion that this is the tomb of Philip, the father of Alexander the Great, and also his last wife, Cleopatra, and that Vergina is to be identified with the ancient Macedonian capital of Aigai where the kings continued to be buried even after Pella became the new capital.

In 1982 an ancient *theatre* was discovered close to the palace, and this is probably where Philip was assassinated in 336 BC.

Owing to further excavation work it is unclear when the new tombs will be open to visitors and you should check first before setting out. The objects found are now on display in Thessaloniki's Archaeological Museum. What you can do at Vergina is to visit the original *Tomb of Vergina* discovered last century, another temple tomb containing a fine marble throne, and also the ruins of the *Palace of Palatitsa*, a large building dating from the 3rd C BC.

The main excavated area of **Pella** lies just to the left of the road some 40 kms from Thessaloniki in the middle of a dull, empty expanse. Formerly there was a marshy lake to the south, navigable from the sea, and the city lay between the lake and its acropolis, which was on a hill to the west of the present village of Palea Pella, north of the main road. The few buildings excavated so far were probably somewhere in the city centre. As the eventual capital of the Macedonian kings, Pella was thus a large, important city. The court of King Archelaos (413–399) attracted painters and writers – Euripides for example died here – but the later kings, in particular Philip and Alexander, sought to assert their Hellenism more by leadership and conquest than by the civilised cultivation of the arts. Macedon's major legacy still remains the memory of the militarist ambitions and exploits of Alexander the Great, whose birthplace it was. Following Alexander's death, the whole Greek world was subjected to the rivalries of the successor kings. Finally in 168 BC, Pella and Macedonia fell to the Romans, after the battle of Pydna.

Birthplace of Alexander the Great

At Pella the principal legacy is the group of *mosaics* found amongst the three excavated buildings. The building to the east, the foundations of which have been completely exposed, was a large important structure, perhaps a government office, built in about 300 BC and containing several open courtyards with porticoes: it was surrounded on three sides by streets complete with sewers and waterpipes. In the rooms on the west were found the best of the mosaics now in the new museum across the road, including the famous Lion Hunt, and the mosaic of Dionysos riding a panther. Other mosaics still remain in situ.

These pavement mosaics are very different from the later religious examples which were primarily used in decorating walls: they are made from pebbles and not from cubes of stone and glass paste; parts of the pictures are also outlined with strips of metal. Partly as a result of the differences in technique they are more fluid, less stiff than most of the religious mosaics – note the movement in the hunting scenes and the grace in the Dionysos, two qualities largely absent in the Byzantine mosaics. They are worth going out of your way to see. In the attractively laid out *museum*, amongst other exhibits is a romantic head of Alexander, and a fine round table inlaid with ivory.

Thessaloníki

Thessaloniki (often called Salonika), situated on the lower slopes of Mt Chortiatis at the head of the Thermaic Gulf and historically at the crossroads of international trade, has long been an important centre of commerce. Now the second largest city in the country and the seat of the Ministry of Northern Greece, it spreads far beyond the confines of the old Byzantine city walls. The walls still dominate the upper part of the town and define, even where they are missing, the central area of the modern city which rises in layers from the seafront esplanade to the old Turkish quarter huddled under the remaining ramparts. You can walk across this central area inside half-an-hour, and unlike Athens there is a reasonable modus vivendi between traffic and pedestrians. In fact, Thessaloniki has several good points over Athens: the atmosphere is metropolitan without being that of a bazaar (despite the long occupation of the Turks who only left in 1912) and there is some degree of style in the planning of the modern city, albeit the result of the disastrous fire in 1917 which destroyed part of the town. Without having a supreme monument such as Athens possesses in the Acropolis, Thessaloniki has a number of exceptional Byzantine churches, many of them with important mosaics, although the feast is less full than one is sometimes led to expect. The churches reflect the long history of the city as an important Byzantine centre.

Its history   Although founded in the 4th C BC, Thessaloniki only achieved real importance after 146 BC when it became the capital of the Roman province of Macedonia. It was of increasing importance under the later Roman Empire, as the balance shifted to the east, and it became the second city of the Byzantine Empire. It managed to withstand the constant attacks by Goths and Slavs, but was sacked by the Saracens in 904 and the Normans of Sicily in 1185. After the Fourth Crusade, Thessaloniki became the capital of a Latin kingdom for a few years until taken by the Greek rulers of Epirus, but in 1246 reverted to the Byzantine Empire of Nicaea. Despite the destructive rivalries of different religious factions within the city in the mid-14th C, and temporary occupation by the Turks in 1387 and 1394, Thessaloniki did not finally fall to the Ottoman Empire until 1430.

Under the Turks the city was comparatively prosperous, particularly after the influx of a large number of Jewish refugees from Spain at the end of the 15th C. There developed a very mixed population of Greeks, Slavs, Albanians, Vlachs and Armenians – apart from the Jews, and of course the Turks. In 1912 the Greeks retook the city, and in 1923 under the exchange of populations the majority of the Turks were replaced by Greeks from Asia Minor. In the last war the city lost almost the entire Jewish population of over 60,000 people.

Orientation. Owing to the grid-like layout of the streets, Thessaloniki is an easy town to get about in. The sea front is called *Leoforos Vasileos Konstantinou*: several streets run parallel with it to the north, *Megalou Alexandrou* (Tsimiski), *Ermou, Egnatias, Filippou* and *Agiou Dimitriou*. In the middle of the seafront, an avenue leads at right angles from the *Plateia Aristotelous* to a huge, rather empty area in the city centre called *Plateia Dikastirion*, in the upper part of which was recently found the old Roman Forum when they were about to build new law courts. Beyond Agiou Dimitriou, the streets of *Olympiados* and *Athinas*, meeting at the *Church of Profitis Ilias* (1) in the form of a crescent, contain the old *Turkish quarter*.

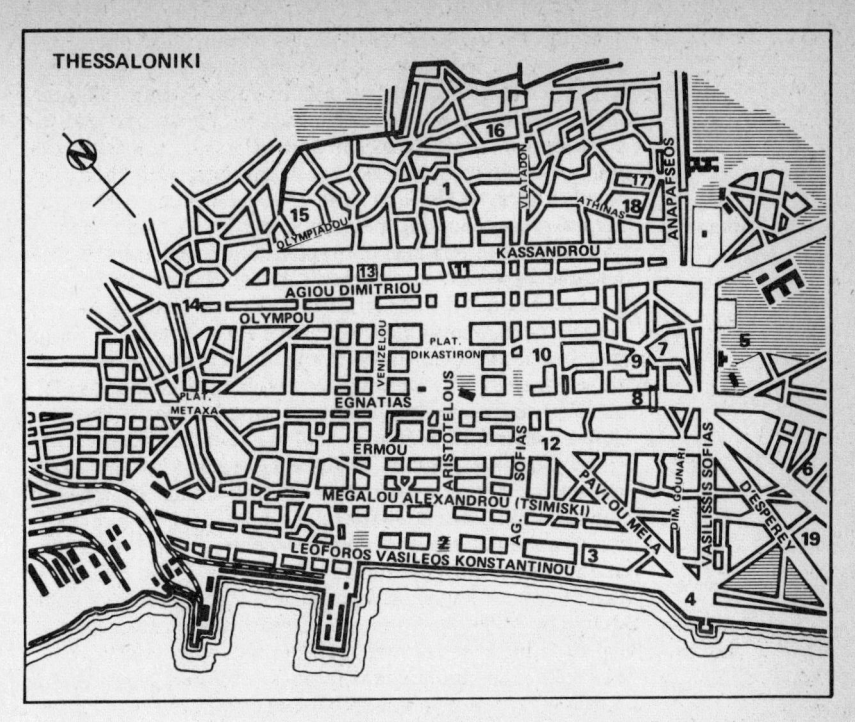

Plateia Aristotelous (2), facing the sea front, is a good place to sit and have an expensive cup of coffee before looking around: it is close to the banks and travel agents, and to the British, American and other consulates (to which a visit is necessary for those wanting to go to Mount Athos). Walking eastwards (strictly southeastwards, as the city is not quite on a north-south axis, but it will be described here as if it were, with the sea to the south) you pass the *Museum of Popular Art* (3) which has traditional local costumes, etc. At the farther end is the *White Tower* (4), built in about 1430 at the southeastern angle of the walls. From its top, you get a good view of the whole city: the walls enclosing the upper area are obvious to the north; the new city extends chiefly to the right (to the east). The boundary between old and new is roughly formed by the *University* (5), the *International Fair* (6) and the gardens below the White Tower, on the far side of which is the Archaeological Museum. One of the city's landmarks is *Agios Georgios* (7), identified by its tall minaret.

*

191

Touring Thessaloniki. Walking up Dimitriou Gounari towards Agios Georgios, you first encounter at the end of Egnatias the **Arch of Galerius** (8): this was a triumphal arch built by the Emperor Galerius in about AD 300 to commemorate his victories over the Persians, and has relief sculptures showing how he won them. Originally there was another arch to the east, and a dome rested on the four central pillars covering the crossroads. The Arch was central to a large development: in the southern part was the palace and the hippodrome (where in 390 the Christian convert Theodosios forgot himself to the extent of having 7000 or more citizens massacred in revenge for the lynching of his governor); to the north was the Rotunda, reached by a porticoed avenue. The Rotunda was probably designed as Galerius' mausoleum, but was never used as such and was converted into a Christian church at about the end of the 4th C AD, becoming known as **Agios Georgios** (7). The Turks converted it into a mosque, like most of the churches in Thessaloniki, and added the minaret. Now it is a museum. It has been temporarily closed for repairs owing to damage caused in the 1978 earthquake. In the dome and recesses it contains very fine *mosaics* against a background of gold, dating from its conversion to a church. The most interesting are the panels in the dome, of 8 saints in prayer portrayed in front of huge architectural facades, exemplifying a sort of baroque Hellenism not found elsewhere. The mosaics higher in the dome are fragmentary, and in parts restored by painting. Those in the recesses are of birds and flowers. To the left of the apse is a mosaic panel of St Andrew, while the apse has fragmentary 10th C frescoes.

Very near Agios Georgios, to the southwest, is the church of **Agios Pandeleimonos** (9), dating from the 12th or 13th C. From here a street leads westwards, in the direction of the central Plateia Dikastirion, to the church (10) of **Agia Parakevi** (or Panagia Acheiropoietos – so named after an ikon miraculously painted without hands). This is a basilica of the first half of the 5th C, with a narthex, a nave and two aisles; the columns within the arcades have fine *capitals* and inside the arches are elegant *mosaic decorations* of fruit, flowers and birds, together with various pictorial symbols like the Cross and the Book of Scriptures. The building is magnificently simple compared to the domes and decorations of the later churches.

From Agia Paraskevi, the famous churches of Agios Dimitrios and Agia Sophia lie in opposite directions; Agios Dimitrios to the north, on the other side of Agiou Dimitriou, and Agia Sophia to the south in an attractive garden at the end of Ermou.

Agios Dimitrios (11) is the earlier of the two, dating from the 5th C. St Demetrius was martyred in the reign of Galerius

(303), and in the early 4th C a church was built on the site of his martyrdom: this was superseded by the basilica in the 5th C, which was then partially rebuilt in the 7th C after a fire. The church has been very largely reconstructed again, after being badly damaged in the fire of 1917.

Agios Dimitrios, the largest church in Greece, is a double-aisled basilica with slighty projecting transepts giving a cruciform effect. Some of the pillars inside have very fine early *capitals*, but the church's main distinction is the remaining *mosaics*: in the corner to the left of the west door is a 5th C mosaic of St Demetrius, with angels hovering over him in a cloudy sky, but the most important mosaics are those on the piers of the choir. The right pier has three mosaics, including a 7th C mosaic of St Demetrius with an official and a bishop, who are described as the founders of the church, and were perhaps those responsible for the building of the basilica in the 5th C and the rebuilding in the 7th C, respectively. The subjects are treated more severely than in Agios Georgios, and Osbert Lancaster calls this 'the greatest remaining masterpiece of the pictorial art of the pre-ikonoclastic era in Greece'. But you might prefer the mosaic on the left pier, also from the 7th C, showing the saint with the two children of the donor of the mosaic, which was in effect a votive offering: the smaller child who shyly presses against the saint's white cloak is very appealing.

The church (12) of **Agia Sophia** (or Divine Wisdom) which was probably built in the 8th C represents the transition between an aisled basilica and a domed cross-in-square; the narthex is a feature common to both forms. The capitals of 'windblown acanthus' leaves are probably from an earlier building. The church was badly damaged by fire in 1890, when it was a mosque, and rather tastelessly restored. The *mosaics* mark the resumption of mosaic decoration after the ikonoclastic period (726–843): in the dome is a superb Ascension of Christ, with the Pantokrator (Almighty) and angels, below which are the Virgin Mary and 12 apostles. The inscription is the Greek original of 'ye men of Galilee, why stand ye gazing up into heaven'. In the apse is an enthroned Virgin and Child: you also see traces of a large cross, which was all that the ikonoclasts allowed in the way of representational art. The mosaics as a whole if a 'little uncouth' have an exciting directness in expression and composition.

Turkish baths and mosque

The Plateia Dikastirion (to the northwest) has at the bottom right corner a 15th C **Turkish bath-house** (still in use) and, opposite, the **Panagia Chalkeon** founded in 1028, a classic Greek cross-in-square church with a narthex: there are frescoes, mostly of the 11th C, in the dome, the apse and the narthex. Below the plateia is the market-area and south of this, across Ermou and Vasileos Irakliou, is a small square in the middle of which is another old Turkish bath-house now converted into a market: there is a taverna with tables on the pavement, where you can eat cheap, adequate food and look at the flower shops. The next street down, Megalou Alexandrou, is the main shopping area. This crosses Eleftheriou Venizelou, which then goes up, northwards, past a large Turkish building built in the 15th C, now a cinema but formerly a mosque, and continues across Olympou into a square in front of the Dioikitirion (13): here are the offices of the Ministry of Northern Greece – another place to visit if you wish to go to Athos.

If you follow Olympou westwards you come to a beautiful church in an old tumbledown square. This is **Agioi Apostoloi** (14), the Church of the Holy Apostles, built at the beginning of the 14th C and a good example of the artistic renaissance under the Palaeologue emperors. The cross-in-square church has two additional aisles to north and south, a narthex and exo-narthex: outside, the five *domes and elaborate brickwork*, particularly at the east end, give a very rich effect while inside there are fine 14th C *mosaics*, chiefly in the vaults under the drum.

The old quarter

The old quarter is now squeezed into the northern corner of the town: the small streets with their timber-framed houses and colourful gardens are a legacy from the Turks, and even if insanitary and inconvenient they are hardly inferior to the concrete tenements, the instant modern slums which crowd them out. The tiny streets are almost impossible to navigate by map or description: it is best just to wander and see where you arrive. Here are some possible starting points and objectives.

About a third of the way along Olympiados (from the west) is a street leading north to **Agia Ekaterini** (15), a little church rather similar to that of the Apostles, although slightly earlier (late 13th C); it has contemporary *frescoes*. **Profitis Ilias** (1) at the junction between Olympiados and Athinas, dates from the 14th C and was originally a monastic church; it has had to be heavily restored inside, but does retain rather a grand narthex. From Profitis Ilias you should be able to reach the small church of **Osios David** (16), by taking a left turn off Athinas, up Odos Vlatadon, and then the second on the left, and continuing northwards; but the church is difficult to find as it is tucked away in its own courtyard, and you may have to ask. Here we go back into time, to the 5th C. The church's unusual shape is because it has lost the nave and so only the top part of the Syrian cross remains. You enter by the south door and to the right, in the apse, is a remarkable 5th C *mosaic showing Christ appearing in a vision to two prophets*, Ezekiel (on the left) and Habbakuk, who both look a little uncertain. Once again the figures are static, archaic.

Byzantine walls

Not far above Osios David are the **Byzantine walls** which date from the 14th C AD although rebuilt or added to in places. The best preserved portion is that which also forms the *south wall of the acropolis* – it has several large towers, the one in the northeastern angle being contemporary with the White Tower. Within the acropolis is a *fortress*, now a prison, the central tower of which was built by the Turks in 1431. If you follow the line of the eastern ramparts back down, you should find yourself in Apostolou Pavlou: to its west reached by a parallel street is the charming 14th C church of **Agios Nikolaos** (17) with contemporary frescoes; almost at the bottom of Apostolou Pavlou is the *house* (18) where Mustapha Kemal – Ataturk – (1881–1938), first president of Turkey, was born.

Ataturk's house

The large **Archaeological Museum** (19) at the east end of town has the newly excavated treasures from the tomb of Philip II at Vergina including the superb *parade shield* which has now been restored. These are not to be missed. There is also a large room of finds from Macedonia, from the Neolithic to the Iron Age period, including pottery of the Sesklo style. The collection also includes the superb 4th C and Hellenistic grave goods found at Derveni and Neapolis respectively, and recent finds from the archaic cemetery at Sindos, including some fine gold jewellery.

Display of Macedonian treasures

From Thessaloniki you can drive part way up Mt Chortiatis to the small village of **Panórama** (9 kms) where there are some pleasant tavernas and you can enjoy a view of the area south, or go southwards to one of the seaside resorts on the Thermaic Gulf, such as **Agía Triáda** (23 kms) and **Néa Michanióna** (30 kms), the second of which has long shallow beaches to the east, and one or two good fish restaurants in the centre.

Excursions nearby

Chalcidici

East of Thessaloniki is Chalcidici (Halkidikí), a lump of land terminating in three peninsulas, like a jellyfish trailing thin tentacles through the sea. Its name derives from the colonies anciently sent to the area by Chalkis in Euboea, but it attracted many other colonies as well. Chalcidici appears also to have been inhabited at the earliest moments of human existence. At the **Petrálona Cave**, 15 kms beyond Nea Kallikrateia, a 400,000-year-old skeleton of a youth was found embedded in a stalagmite in 1976, as well as cooked animal remains at a level corresponding to a period of between 700,000 and 1,100,000 years ago – implying the earliest man-made fire in Europe.

Earliest European man

The middle of Chalcidici is mostly wooded hills, but a fertile coastal strip runs north of the three peninsulas, which are called (from the west) Kassandra, Sithonia and Athos. Of these, Kassandra and Sithonia with their many sandy beaches are being rapidly developed for tourism, and roads have now been built along virtually the entire coastline of both peninsulas. *Kassándra*, which is the most fertile of the three and therefore attracted many ancient colonies, has been developed in particular on the east coast, notably at **Kallithéa** (100 kms from Thessaloniki) and near **Palioúri** (132 kms). At the neck of the peninsula is Nea Potidaia which marks the site of the important ancient city of **Potidaea**, a Corinthian colony, later destroyed by Philip of Macedon; rebuilt by Kassander, it became the most important town in Macedonia, but was finally destroyed by the Huns. There are no very obvious remains of either Potidaea, or of the city of **Olynthos**, 15 kms to the northeast. Olynthos, of importance in the 5th and 4th C BC, was also destroyed by Philip (to the dismay of the Athenian orator Demosthenes who had encouraged its opposition to the Macedonians) but was never rebuilt: its excavation taught much about the ground-plan of a Greek city – chiefly, square houses laid out in streets crossing at right angles – but there is little left to see.

You reach *Sithonia* most easily via **Polígyros**, a picturesque small town (69 kms from Thessaloniki) in the interior of Chalcidici; it is the capital of the nome, and has an archaeological *museum* of finds from the area. Sithonia, the middle peninsula, is also midway in terms of appearance, more hilly than Kassandra and less wooded than Athos. At present it is comparatively unspoilt, but there is a grandiose new development on the west coast near Marmoras (130 kms), called **Porto Carras**, after the shipowner who has built it. On the opposite coast is **Sarti** (148 kms), a pleasant village built for Greek refugees from Asia Minor, after the exchange of populations in 1922. The single-storeyed houses, plastered with flowers, stand on the edge of the wide beach, and from here you have a wonderful view across the sand to the pale slopes of Mt Athos emerging from the haze.

The road through the middle of the Chalcidici via Arnaia passes near the birthplace of Aristotle at ancient **Stageira**, and then goes down the coast to the fishing town of **Ierissos** (129 kms), the site of ancient Akanthos. Beyond Nea Roda, Xerxes' canal you cross over a shallow ditch which marks the site of *Xerxes' canal*. This was dug in 480 BC to avoid the fate of a previous Persian fleet lost going round Athos in 491. The road ends at **Ouranópolis** (143 kms), another village built by refugees in 1922, and now a popular summer resort. Its small harbour serves the Holy Mountain of Athos, which stretches away to the southeast, and you often see the black habits of monks and (in greater numbers) the rucksacks of visitors, who are travelling to or from the mountain. Near the harbour there is a large tower on the sea-edge, built in the 13th C by the Emperor Andronikos II as an offering to the monastery of Vatopedi: in this tower 'on the doorstep of the Holy Mountain' lived a Scotsman, Sydney Loch, the author of *Athos:*

Holy Mountain, which perhaps best conveys the atmosphere of this extraordinary place.

The Holy Mountain

Athos is certainly one of the most beautiful places in Greece. A long central ridge runs the length of the peninsula to reach up to the bare shoulders of Mt Athos, which rises to 2033 metres before falling steeply into the sea. Except for the stark sides of Athos itself the entire peninsula is heavily wooded, and dripping with water. It is as if the old legend of the Giants piling Pelion on Ossa to reach Olympos has been changed, and Ossa piled on Pelion to reach a different God.

Mule paths thread through the trees and the scrub. 'It is on the rocky tracks, worked into paths by the hoofs of mule generations, that the note of this wild land sounds even more loudly than in the monasteries' (Loch). Little has changed since the first hermits arrived. As the path continues through the thickets, 'there increases a hope that round this approaching bend, or behind the rise ahead, a mystery will be revealed such as the early saints were allowed as medicine in their spiritual sicknesses'. No mystery is revealed to the humble modern visitor: the path leads on, past the crosses planted at the roadside, up shimmering slopes and down into shady gulleys where fountains pour cold streams of water; it passes decayed buildings of stone and slate hiding anonymously behind the trees, and finally arrives almost unexpectedly at the tall walls of a monastery, where for up to a thousand years Man has worshipped the Creator of this earthly paradise. It is said that the Virgin Mary declared the mountain hers, when she stopped here on the way to visit Lazarus in Cyprus. Her garden has since been jealously guarded.

Athos' History   The history of the monastic settlements begins with the advent of hermits in about the mid 9th C AD, roughly 100 years before the foundation of the first monastery. St Peter the Athonite was perhaps the earliest to arrive, after his ship had miraculously stopped still off the coast of Athos: he lived in a cave for 50 years. St Euthymios served his training in asceticism by moving about on his hands and knees eating grass for 40 days, and then living in a cave for three years, before he founded the first lavra or community of hermits on Athos. The first monastery, the Great Lavra, was founded by St Athanasios the Athonite in 963, and endowed by the Emperor Nikephoros Phocas. Before the saint's death, other monasteries had been founded, which like Lavra enjoyed independence from everyone except the emperor. By 1046 the Great Lavra had some 700 monks, and together with the other established monasteries controlled the general assembly of the monastic community at Karies. The monasteries were thus able to control or absorb the hermitages around them. The prohibition on any members of the female sex was put to the test towards the end of the 11th C after 300 Vlach families (who looked after the monastic flocks) had settled on Athos. Their eventual expulsion was only at the cost of the interference of the Patriarch of Constantinople, which has continued to a greater or lesser extent ever since.

At the beginning of the 13th C there were scores of monasteries on Athos. But they suffered greatly from being plundered by the Latins after the Fourth Crusade, and then by the Catalans about 100 years later. Only 25 monasteries survived into the 14th C. Towards the end of the century, a move began towards a more lax form of regimen, which in the following centuries led to many monasteries abandoning the coenobitic form (see below). In 1430 Athos prudently capitulated to the Turks after Thessaloniki had fallen, and secured both freedom from plunder and almost total independence. In the 16th C several monasteries were rebuilt, and this was also the period of the decoration of many of the churches with frescoes of the Cretan School. In the last quarter of that century the number of ruling monasteries was fixed at 20, as it remains today.

In 1821 the monks rose against the Turks but the Turks invaded, and imposed a heavy indemnity. From 6000 monks the numbers dropped to 1000, before reviving in the later 19th C. The mountain then suffered an invasion of a different kind, from Russian monks, which helped to restore flagging numbers, but also threatened to overrun Athos: by 1912, at the end of Turkish rule, the Russians had one monastery (Panteleimon) and many grandiose lesser establishments (like the skates of St Andrew and Profitis Ilias) and formed a majority of the monks. The Russian Revolution of 1917 removed this threat, by drying up the sources of manpower and finance. Under the 1927 constitution, agreed between the Greek state and the Athonite community, Athos is now part of the Greek state but has administrative autonomy in the form of a Holy Assembly, which has a representative from each of the 20 ruling monasteries; a committee of four representatives, the Epistasia, is the executive body. The Patriarchate exercises ecclesiastical jurisdiction. The Greekness of Athos is secured by the provision that all foreign monks become Greek subjects on entry. The representative of the Greek state on Athos is a governor at Karies who has a small police force.

Entry formalities The procedure for entering Athos is suitably Byzantine, and transport is also not without its difficulties. Details will be found in the *Practical Information* section following.

It is impossible in this Guide to describe all the monasteries and other items of interest on Athos. What follows are some general remarks about the monasteries, and a short itinerary involving a few of them, by way of example only. (In planning an itinerary you should not be too ambitious. First, time is limited, and it is better to see a few monasteries in a leisurely way, than rush about seeing as many as possible. Secondly, you may find that a few days' visit at a time is enough: there is a great temptation to flee paradise, to fall back into 'the world'.

Life on Athos Each monastery has a different character, a different history and usually its own stories of a miraculous ikon. Some monasteries are grand like Lavra, others are more modest while still possessing important features – Dochiariou, for example, is thought to have the finest church on Athos. Some are thriving like Philotheou, many like Panteleimon continue to dwindle in numbers. Some like Stavronikita are stricter than others. At present 12 of the monasteries are *coenobitic*, where there is strict obedience to the abbot, property is divided and meals are eaten in common in the *trapeza* or refectory: in the other *idiorrythmic* monasteries (which include the three largest, Lavra, Iviron and Vatopedi) there is no property in common, and each monk provides his own food and clothing, etc, from his own resources. All the monasteries are now Greek, except for the Russian Panteleimon, the Bulgarian Zographou and the Serbian Chilandari, and all except Vatopedi keep the old Julian calendar, 13 days behind the rest of us, and Byzantine hours which commence at sunset and so vary every day.

Every monk, who generally goes through the same three-year novitiate, should spend at least eight hours a day in prayer – much of it in the small hours. In the coenobia, on four days a week two meals are eaten, one after Litourgia or Mass in the morning and one in the late afternoon after Vespers (about 6pm in summer), while on fast days (Monday, Wednesday and Friday) only one meal is eaten – without olive oil, eggs, butter and cheese. Meat is never eaten in the coenobia, although fish sometimes is. In the idiorrythmic monasteries they do not fast on Mondays, and they eat meat. In addition there are special fasting periods before various feast days – in the case of Easter, seven weeks. If you go at the time of a major fast (for example in August, before the Feast of the Assumption on the 15th, which is celebrated on the 28th by our calendar) and you cannot stand beans, it might be wise to take something else with you.

Whatever else they are, the monasteries are incomparable Byzantine monuments. Most of them have exquisite churches, usually painted a dull red, cruciform with several cupolas. Inside, where there is generally a double narthex flanked by side chapels, they are completely covered with frescoes on a traditional plan. Their treasuries include important relics, such as fragments of the True Cross (Lavra), the Belt of the Virgin Mary (Vatopedi), the left hand of Mary Magdalen, which are usually enclosed in cases studded with precious stones. There are old crysobuls, gold chalices, colourful vestments and patriarchal crowns. The libraries possess beautifully illuminated early manuscripts, notably *evangelions* or gospels often encased in elaborate covers. The monastic buildings themselves, somewhat like a small walled town around the central church or *Katholicon*, are always intriguing in their variety, even if there is a certain drabness in the empty corridors, the black gowns and the builders' rubble. Some indeed of the monasteries seem dead, but there are many monks whose gentleness and spirituality are transparent on their pale, sleepless faces.

In fact the monasteries are only part of the picture. At present there is a population of between one and two thousand monks and laymen living permanently on Athos. About one half lives in the monasteries, the others are spread between Karies and the smaller monastic establishments, the skietes and kellia dotted about the peninsula. The skietes, like the kellia, are dependent on one of the 20 monasteries and with the exception of the large Russian skietes are monastic villages formed round a central church, for example the skete of St Anne's. The kellion or cell is a single building with a chapel inhabited by a small number of monks. There are also the hermits who carry on the tradition of St Peter the Athonite, living at the southern end of Athos, particularly on the cliffs at Karoulia. For everyone, money remains a problem: the monasteries have been dispossessed of their properties outside Athos, and much of their income now derives from the exploitation of the timber around them. The smaller communities often concentrate on ikon-painting and wood-carving. They nearly all grow their own food. There is a firm belief that somehow the Panagia will provide.

Touring the monasteries

Kariés, high on the central ridge, is full of block-like buildings amongst the trees, which look at best little used. Its central church, the 10th C *Protaton*, has important frescoes from the Macedonian School, most probably by Manuel Panselinos (early 14th C). Near Karies (to the north) is the amazing **skete of St Andrew**, a vast Russian foundation of onion-shaped domes built with imperial help about 100 years ago and now completely abandoned: there is one monk there, the Caretaker Father Athanasios, who also keeps a bookshop in Karies; he might entertain you with a banana liqueur as you sit in a large room on faded settees, under the proud countenance of a portrait of Czar Nicholas.

You can stay at one of the inns in Karies or go a short way through hazel trees to the attractive monastery of **Koutloumousíou** to the southeast. About two hours further on is **Philothéou**, which recently reverted to being a coenobitic monastery, and which has almost doubled the number of monks in the last few years: it now has over 60, many of them young. Situated amongst woods, it has the air of careful cultivation outside and good repair inside. This could provide a perfect introduction to monastic visiting: the loukoumi (Turkish delight) and coffee welcoming the visitor as you show your *diamonitirion* or permit, a wander around the courtyard, monks rushing to arrive at church after the beating of the simantra; following the service, a short visit to the church, and the embarrassed view of the relics being paraded for the Greek pilgrims, then supper of beansoup, some last talk with fellow guests on the terrace outside the monastery and finally after the gates have been closed at sunset, a hard dormitory bed and a night of little sleep.

One of the best walks in Greece

From Philotheou it is about six hours walk to Lavra, past the attractive monastery of **Karakállou**, then along the coast. It must be one of the best walks in Greece, with clouds of butterflies and lots of hoopoes, and Athos itself looming closer through the trees. The **Great Lavra**, which stands on a slope overlooking its harbour, is approached through a vaulted entrance: inside the crenallated walls every kind of building spills over into the courtyard, 'towers and storehouses, church and chapels, refectory, library, treasury, and guesthouse, fountains, shrines, trees, flowerbeds and endless rows of cells' (Sherrard). Built in the 10th C, alone of the monasteries it has not been damaged by fire. In the centre of the courtyard is the *refectory*, which has very fine frescoes of the Cretan School (16th C). Opposite its entrance is the church built by St Athanasios, who died after falling from the roof while building its dome. Between these buildings are two huge cypress trees, said to have been planted by Athanasios and his bursar Euthymios (who also founded Dochiariou): nearby is a beautiful 17th C *phiale*, a canopied basin used for blessing the holy water. The *Katholicon* was completed in the early 11th C, and is painted a dull red colour. The elaborate cruciform structure with three cupolas retains some of the features of a domed basilica, for example the arcades. An unattractive exonarthex, built in 1814 like a conservatory, leads through painted wood doors into the narthex. On entering the church you see two chapels to left and right, that of the 40 martyrs which contains the Tomb of Athanasios, and the chapel of St Nicolas which has 16th C frescoes by Frangos Kastellanos. The main part of the church is covered with 16th C frescoes by the Cretan Theophanes, but dark and difficult to see. In the nave there are portraits of the monastery's benefactors, the Emperors Nikephoros Phocas and his successor (and murderer) John I Tzimisces. The marble screen holds ikons heavily sheeted with silver, and elsewhere in the church there is a miraculous ikon of Christ which is said to have exuded blood when wounded by a Turkish bullet. The apsidal ends of the transept are covered with a frieze of Persian tiles, and nearby are fine ivory lecterns. The interior is thus immensely rich, but the chief impact is made by the soft, honey colour of the many objects of bronze and gold, the brazen doors and the huge chandeliers and the ceiling decorations which reflect the light until the whole area seems to vibrate with warmth.

The *Treasures* possessed by the monastery include a silver-gilt reliquary encrusted with jewels and containing a fragment of the True Cross, and the famous Bible, its cover of equal richness, both given to the monastery by Nikephoros Phocas. In the handsome *library* building, beyond the church, there are also many beautifully painted Evangelions, amongst numerous other early manuscripts.

It is another long walk by a difficult path round the extremity of Athos, through the desolate area inhabited by the hermits, to the **skete of St Anne's**. More comfortable will probably be an early morning boat ride to Iviron, as dawn dims the stars.

The impressive walls of **Iviron**, founded in 979, rise up to balconies above a pasture near the sea. Inside it has a neglected air, and there is little charm amongst the confusion of buildings. The *Katholicon*, dating from the 11th C, is similar to that of Lavra. The monastery possesses the miraculous 9th C *ikon of the Panagia Portaitissa* – Our Lady of the Gate. The story is that the ikon, having been committed to the sea at Nicaea to escape destruction by the ikonoclasts, sailed over the waves for 70 years until one day the monks at Iviron saw a pillar of fire rising from the sea: a voice from the ikon insisted that it would only come ashore if Gabriel, a hermit, came to fetch it. Gabriel was found, and eventually walked over the water to collect the ikon. The monks placed it in the Katholicon, but three times it moved back to the gate. The Virgin then appeared to Gabriel, and told him the ikon should be placed in a new chapel near the gate, where she could protect the monastery. There it still is, weighed down with sheets of gold and votive offerings.

Eastern Macedonia

From Ouranopolis you can reach the main road east from Thessaloniki to Kavala via the pleasant seaside resorts of **Olympiás** and **Stavrós**, on the northeast coast of the Chalacidici. This main road follows the Via Egnatia and at 104 kms from Thessaloniki crosses the river Strymon, guarded by a *Hellenistic lion*: on the other side of the Strymon are the ruins of the ancient town of **Amphipolis**, near the modern village (off the Serres road). This was an Athenian colony wealthy from the gold mines on Mt Pangaion, which surrendered to the Spartans early in the Peloponnesian War. It was taken by the Macedonians in 358, and became again of importance under the Romans largely owing to its position on the Via Egnatia which here turned north to go round Pangaion. The city was built on a hill above

Athenian colony

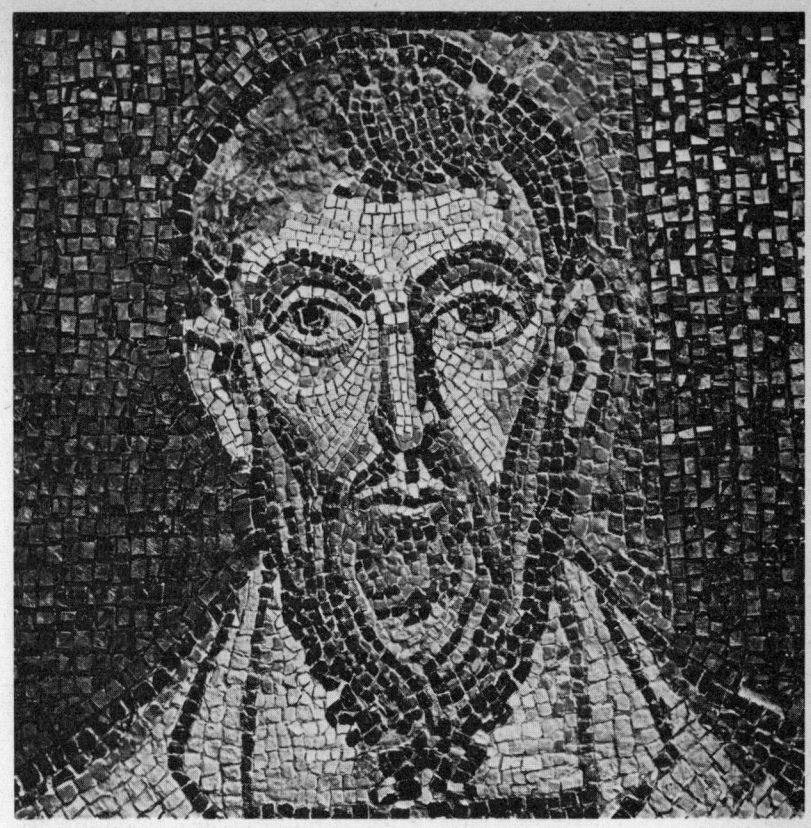

Mosaic in the church of Agios Georgios, Thessaloniki

the Strymon by which it was protected on three sides. The site is largely for the specialist although large stretches of the *city walls* have been uncovered (the archaeologists also discovered timbers from the ancient bridge across the Strymon) and there are also ruins of four *Christian basilicas* with fine mosaics which may now be on view. A small *museum* houses some of the less important finds; the rest have gone to Kavala.

The modern road passes south of Pangaion through a beautiful valley; and after Elevtheroupolis you cross a ridge with a fine view across to Thasos and beyond, before descending to Kavala (165 kms from Thessaloniki).

Byzantine and Turkish sights

Kavála is in a beautiful position, spreading over the hills which reach down to the harbour. Anciently, as Neapolis, it was the port of Philippi: now its harbour is used chiefly for the export of Macedonian tobacco, and it has become the second largest city in Macedonia and is the capital of its nome. Its

203

chief interest lies in the area of the *Turkish quarter*, within the Byzantine *walls*, on the promontory to the east of the harbour known as the Panagia district. The town remained under the Turks until 1912, although this was not the last of its foreign occupants – it has since also suffered from the Bulgarians. A 16th C *aqueduct* is clearly visible to the north of the ruined Byzantine *citadel*. On the west of the promontory is an *almshouse* (identified by its many towers) built by Mohammed Ali (1769–1849), later Khedive of Egypt, who was born at Kavala. His *house* is to be found on the south side of the promontory. The town's *museum* is on the west side of the harbour, and includes gold jewellery of the Hellenistic period and other finds from Amphipolis, also terracotta figures and other items of the 6th and 5th C BC from the *sanctuary of Parthenos* (excavated to the north of the almshouse).

Battle of Philippi

The ancient city of **Philippi**, 14 kms north of Kavala, lies on either side of the road to Drama. The modern road closely follows the old *Via Egnatia* at this point. The city was founded in the 4th C by Philip of Macedon, but gained in importance under the Romans. In the famous battle in the plain of Philippi, in 42 BC, Brutus and Cassius the republican assassins of Julius Caesar were defeated by Anthony and Octavian (later the Emperor Augustus): both committed suicide. After the battle, Octavian settled many of his veteran soldiers at Philippi. St Paul came here in AD 49, and was imprisoned. Later, the city became an important centre of Christianity, and only declined after the arrival of the Franks. Apart from the 10th C Byzantine defences, mostly built on Macedonian foundations, like the *acropolis with its three towers*, the ruins are mostly Roman or early Christian.

To the left of the road, along the line of the Via Egnatia, is the *forum*, which seems to date from the 2nd C AD in its present plan: it possessed porticoes on three sides, and flanking temples to east and west. Beyond the forum is perhaps the most interesting of the remains at Philippi, an *early Christian basilica* known as the *Direkler*. It was built in the 6th C AD but never completed, because the east end collapsed under the weight of a brick dome. It was thus an early attempt which failed to impose a dome on a basilical plan. (It was also to have had a cruciform appearance from the two apsidal buildings to north and south.) Parts of the dome are still visible on the ground. The tall pillars, a little forlorn, have capitals of the acanthus-leaf type. The only part of the church used as such was the narthex, converted in the 10th C. To the west of the basilica are the remains of a *palaestra*, most of which was removed when the church was built, and to the south, a large *public lavatory*, very well preserved.

To the east of the forum are the remains of an octagonal *church*, approached by a portico from the road. Across the road, on a terrace, is another large *basilica* in ruins, dating from the end of the 5th C AD. It was approached by steps, and then through a porticoed atrium. To the right of the steps a passage leads to a crypt of the Roman period, which it is said was *St Paul's prison*. To the northeast is the *theatre*, reached from the road: nearby is a tourist pavilion for the Ancient **Drama festival** Drama Festival held here in July and August. The theatre dates from the 4th C BC but was later remodelled by the Romans for gladiatorial shows, etc, and the bas-reliefs of Nemesis, Mars and Victory (on the left of the stage) are of this later period. Above the theatre, in the direction of the acropolis are numerous *votive reliefs* cut on the rocks, mostly dedicated to Bendis, a Thracian hunting goddess.

There is a new *museum* west of the basilicas.

Thásos

Thasos, the most widely appealing of the northern Aegean islands, lies close off Kavala. A new 90-kilometre road encircling the island gives easy access to its wonderful variety, especially the grand scenery of its southern coast, and makes it worthwhile bringing your car. Forests cover the slopes of the central mass, Mt Ipsarion, and in many places descend to the sea edge. There are several good beaches, and numerous villages (with ample accommodation) spread around the coast.

The capital is Thasos or **Limen**, a village of 2000 people whose houses, lying amongst the ruins of the ancient city, are somewhat overshadowed by this ancient rampart of Hellenism facing the barbarians of Thrace and the North. Gold mines, marble and good wine made ancient Thasos prosperous, and the construction of three safe harbours at this junction of trade between East and West, and between Greece and the Black Sea, caused Thasos to flourish over hundreds of years. A new importance has now been given to Thasos by the off-shore oil wells to the west.

Ancient Thasos The extensive remains of *ancient Thasos* include all the principal features of an ancient Greek city. In the centre is the *agora*. This was developed into its present plan over several centuries, much of it under the Romans, notably the porticoes (except that on the northwest, built in the 3rd C BC). The centre of the agora contained statues, altars, a sanctuary of Zeus and nearby a sacrificial hearth. On the northeast side, next to an intruding Christian basilica, are the ruins of ancient shops; behind the southeast portico there are houses facing onto an ancient street.

Stretching across the middle of the city were various *sanctuaries*: they included those of Dionysos (to the east) and Herakles (to the west), who were the city's guardians. The remains of the 4th C *theatre* are to be found against the city's east wall. It is the *city walls* that are of most interest. They descended from the acropolis and enclosed both the city and the naval harbour. The first circuit of about 494 BC had a unique feature, the gates being decorated with relief sculpture; these reliefs are still visible in places and lend charming detail to your walks about the ruins. The remaining walls however mainly date from rebuilding towards the end of the 5th C BC.

Walking eastwards from the modern quay you pass first the site of the *ancient naval port*, now occupied by a few caiques, and then encounter a stretch of *marble wall* remaining from the earliest circuit. It has two *gates*, both decorated with reliefs – the first, the better of the two, shows the goddess Artemis in a chariot.

Nearby is the *sanctuary of Poseidon*, in front of which remains a large altar to Hera. From here you can proceed directly south to the *acropolis*, which was built on the furthest east of three hilltops. The existing citadel dates from the 14th and 15th C AD, but there is on the outside wall an ancient relief of a funeral feast. The middle hill, to the southwest, has the foundations of a 5th C *temple of Athena*, while on the north of a third hill is a *sanctuary of Pan* with a Hellenistic relief. Following the line of the walls, beyond a tower, you see a rock carved with two eyes, to ward off evil (like on modern caiques). Near the southern angle, you pass the *Gate of Parmemon* (from a block nearby which says 'Parmemon made me'), and further on you reach the *Gate of Silenus*, slightly to the left of the road to the village of Panagia. This was a postern gate, and retains a very large relief of a naked Silenus holding a cup. Two towers away is the *Gate of Herakles and Dionysos* (identified from inscriptions, the reliefs having gone) and another two towers on is the *Gate of Zeus and Hera*, with reliefs.

The interesting **museum** includes many archaic pieces, and some good Roman imperial portraits.

Beaches

Two kms east of Thasos is a good beach at **Makri Ammos**, with tavernas; you reach this off the Panagia road, or by motor boat. **Panagía** (9 kms) and **Potamiá** beyond are both attractive villages, away from the sea, though below them are idyllic beaches. On the south of the island, again inland, is the village of **Theológos**, which was the medieval capital – nearby are the ruins of a castle.

Samothráki

The islands of Samothraki (Samothrace) and Lemnos are both part of the Eastern Sporades, but as these two can most easily be reached from northern Greece they are included here.

Panorama of the north Aegean

Samothraki rises magnificently from the sea, as much a mountain as an island, rugged and lonely. From the 1600-metre peak of Mt Saos, Poseidon surveyed the

The Sanctuary of the Great Gods

battlefield of Troy: Mt Ida distant beyond the Trojan plain returns the gaze; the coast of Thrace and Macedonia, the Chalacidici peninsula and Mt Athos are included in the grand panorama. The ascent of *Mt Saos* (also known as Phengari) is made in about five hours from the village of **Chóra** (Samothraki) on a crag in a fold of the hills overlooking the harbour.

The visitor is more often content to visit the *Sanctuary of the Great Gods* in a peaceful valley between the lower flanks of the mountain and ancient Palaiopolis on the northern coast. When the Greeks came to colonise the island in the 8th C they found a Thracian Mystery cult and grafted their Olympian gods onto the far older chthonic deities worshipped here. The local mother goddess Axieros became Demeter; the phallic fertility god Kadmilos became Hermes; the twin demons Dardanos and Aetion became the Dioskouroi (sons of Zeus); and the divinities of Nature and rebirth, Axiokersos and Axiokersa, were identified with Hades and Persephone. Hekate, Aphrodite, Kadmos and Harmonia were later introduced. From the 6th C onwards the cult drew pilgrims from all round the Aegean, including Herodotus and Philip of Macedon, father of Alexander, who first met his wife Olympias here.

The oldest part of the sanctuary is a Thracian rock altar from c1000 BC enclosed within the much later (c285 BC) *Rotunda of Queen Arsinoe* (the Arsinoeion) at the north end of the site (all the temples and buildings throughout the sanctuary are clearly labelled). Arsinoe was a Macedonian who married her brother Ptolemy II Philadelphus and ruled Egypt with him as Arsinoe II. With a diameter of 20 metres, this was the largest round building in ancient Greece, its cylindrical wall of Thasos marble elegantly crowned by a circular row of pilasters supporting a Doric entablature (a reconstruction is in the museum). It was here that the public sacrifices of the cult were performed before representatives of the Greek cities. The adjacent *Anaktoron* was a hall of initiation into the Mysteries, the Sacristy built onto its south end probably the place where initiates were enrolled.

The *Temenos*, an enclosed courtyard, was perhaps the scene of holy feasting; to its south is the *Hieron*, a long Doric structure used for the higher initiation ceremonies. Both date from the 4th C BC, but the Hieron was extensively restored in the 3rd C BC, and in 1956, five columns of the pronaos were re-erected, lending an imposing appearance to the ruins. Beyond the scant traces of the *theatre* is the *Nike Fountain*, its centrepiece once the famous Winged Nike of Samothrace, removed to the Louvre in 1863.

The well-arranged *museum* improves understanding of the site: in Hall A, sections of each building have been reconstructed. Sculpture, pottery and grave goods from the site and the ancient city are collected in the other halls.

The remains of the archaic and Hellenistic *city walls* of **Palaiopolis** are impressive.

Beaches
The Thracian sea is often rough and stormy, swept by the prevailing north winds – the climate on the island can be refreshingly bracing in the summer, in contrast to Thasos which is often humid, but then swimming, especially off the stony beach of Palaiopolis, is not good. Instead, and when the weather looks fine, you should take a small boat round the south side of the island to the beautiful and deserted beach of **Ammos**. There is no accommodation here; if you stay overnight it will be on the beach.

Lemnos

Lemnos (Límnos) is nearly bisected by inlets at the north and south, its isthmus barely more than 3 kms across. The east half of the island is sparsely cultivated plain; the west is rugged and hilly with a fine beach at **Mírina** (Kástron), the island capital and port of call for the ferry boats. Built under a rocky promontory surmounted by *Turkish walls*, a *Genoese castle*, and on its slopes the outlines of a prehistoric *Pelasgian city*, Mirina commands a superb view across to Athos, which, it is said, casts its shadow upon Lemnos twice each year.

From Mirina a road runs east across the isthmus to *Moúdros*, which overlooks the almost landlocked southern inlet which was the base for the disastrous British attack on the Dardenelles in 1915; there are two military cemeteries at **Moudros**. Further, near the village of Kiminia, is **Poliochni** where four cities have been found layered upon one another, the oldest going back to the 4th millenium BC, older than the most ancient remains at Troy and centre of the most advanced Neolithic civilisation in the Aegean. The *walls*, with gates and towers, of the third oldest of these cities (c2000 BC) stand nearly 5 metres high in places. On the north side of the island at **Ifestía** there are some remains of the ancient capital, including a theatre.

Savage Aphrodite
It was on Lemnos that Hephaistos fell when he was thrown from Olympos by his father Zeus. Hephaistos particularly, but also his wife Aphrodite, were the subjects of Lemnian cults. When Aphrodite committed adultery with Ares, the Lemnian women neglected her worship. In revenge, Aphrodite caused the men of Lemnos to neglect their women who in turn murdered every last one of them. Aphrodite, known for her savage aspect, must have been pleased and did not allow the women to suffer the consequences of their pique for long: Jason and his Argonauts chanced to put in here, and indeed found themselves putting in here for the next two years, until a future generation of Lemnians was assured.

PRACTICAL INFORMATION

TRAVEL TO NORTHERN GREECE AND ITS ISLANDS

Air: There are direct flights to Thessaloniki from many European cities including London with domestic connections to Lemnos and (see relevant chapters) Ioannina and Lesvos.

From Athens there are up to 9 flights a day to Thessaloniki, about 4 a week to Kastoria, 2 a day in summer to Kavala and 3 a day to Lemnos.

Bus: From Athens (100 Kifissou Street) there are 5 buses a day to Thessaloniki (in about 7½ hours), 3 a day to Edessa (8½ hours), one daily to Kastoria, 3 to Verria (8½ hours), and 2 to Kavala (11 hours). You can reach Thessaloniki from Volos 4 times a day (3½ hours); from Larissa buses depart hourly (2½ hours); from Ioannina and Kalambaka they go 4 times a day (3½ and 7 hours); and there are frequent buses from Kastoria.

Eastwards from Thessaloniki there are buses every hour to Kavala (3 hours), and at least one private bus a day to Istanbul. See under Thessaloniki for more local services.

Train: From Athens there are 7–8 trains a day to Thessaloniki (7½ hours), as well as an overnight sleeper, and about the same number from Larissa. Trains entering Greece from Europe all stop at Thessaloniki.

There is a service between Edessa and Thessaloniki via Verria about 7 to 8 times a day, and eastwards there are about 4 a day to Drama, Xanthi, Komotini and Alexandroupolis (up to 11 hours).

There is a daily train to Istanbul, leaving in the morning and arriving early the next day.

KASTORIA

Hotels: Xenia du Lac (centre of town) (A); Kastoria (by the lake) (C); Palladion (D).

Tourist Police: 25 Grammou Street, at the centre of town near the bus station.

There is a good *bus* service with Thessaloniki, some via Edessa.

The *Folk Museum* is situated in one of the old mansions, *archontika*, in Kapetan Lazarou Street.

EDESSA

Hotels: Xenia, Kataraktes (B); Alpha, Pella (D).

Restaurant: Omonia, Egnatias Street.

Trains 7–8 times a day from Thessaloniki via Verria.

Frequent *buses* from Thessaloniki; 4 daily to Kastoria; 6 daily to Verria.

VERRIA

Hotels: Villa Elia, Vassilis (C); Veroi (in main square, taverna nearby) (D).

Restaurant: Tourist Pavilion.

Verria is on the *train* line between Thessaloniki and Edessa (see above).

From the bus station in Odos Malakousi there are about 8 *buses* a day to Vergina (20 minutes), about 4 to Edessa and frequent buses to Thessaloniki.

VERGINA

Rooms to rent; *tavernas*.

Buses from Verria.

The *site* (Palace of Palatitsa and Tomb of Vergina) is open from 9am to 6pm daily, Sundays and holidays from 10am to 4pm, closed Tuesdays (ditto Tomb of Lefkadia).

PELLA

On the *bus* route between Edessa and Thessaloniki (frequent service); to get to Vergina you must change at Chalkidona.

The *site* is open from 8.30am to 6pm daily, 9am to 3pm on Sundays and holidays. The *museum* has the same hours but is closed Tuesdays.

THESSALONIKI

Accommodation

There are many *hotels* in the centre of town, not all expensive – many cheaper hotels can be found on Egnatias Street for example. Electra Palace (A); Palace, Astor, El Greco, Egnatia, Olympic (B); Delta (13 Egnatias; swimming pool), Rea, Esperia, Park, Amalia, Ariston, Aegeon (C); Tourist, Alexandria (D); Atlantis (E).

There is a *youth hostel* at 44 Principou Nikolaou Street. The XEN (*YWCA*) is in Agias Sophias Street; the XAN (*YMCA*) is opposite the Archaeological Museum.

There are *campgrounds* at Nea Krini and Agia Triada.

Eating and Entertainment
There are many restaurants and cafés along Vas. Konstantinou, the seafront; try Stratis at 19, and Olympos Naoussa at 5 (lunch only, weekdays). Otherwise there is Krikelas, 32 Gramou Vitsi (good selection of local wines), Soutzoukakia at 8 Venizelou, the Thomas Restaurant Taverna at 39 Iraklion, and at the cheaper end the City Self-Service Cafeteria in Komninon.

For a pastry shop try Tottis, both in Vas. Konstantinou and Plateia Aristotelous.

A lively part of town is the suburb of Nea Krini, particularly at weekends, where there are plenty of tavernas with music, etc. Take the No. 5 bus eastwards.

Travel
See also the general section for northern Greece, above.

Thessaloniki is the centre of bus and train services in the northeastern part of Greece, and it also has an airport (south of the city). There are buses within the city that also serve the suburbs and some of the nearby resorts, etc.

The *train station* is in the west of the city, in Monastiriou Street, the westward extension of the central street, Odos Egnatias. To get there take a bus along Egnatias. The *railway offices* (OSE) are at 18 Aristotelous Street.

The *bus stations* for many destinations also leave from the west of town: for Athens and Trikala from 67 Monastiriou, near the railway station where the similarly priced OSE buses depart; for Kastoria, Pella and Volos from Anagenniseos Street (the westward extension of Tsimiski); for Kalambaka and Ioannina from 19 Christoupipsou Street; and for Verria from 26 Oktovriou Street (near Anagenniseos). Buses for Chalcidici leave 68 Karakassi Street in the eastern part of the city (bus 10 from Egnatias). More locally, from Dikastirion Square buses go to Panorama, also to Aretsou beach (No. 23); from Plateia Eleftherias bus 22 or 23 takes you up to the Byzantine walls and bus 5 also to Aretsou; buses to Agia Triada beach go from Karolou Dil.

Boats: There is very little shipping now from Thessaloniki and surprisingly few ferries. In high summer there is a once-weekly service to Lemnos and Lesvos. Every weekend a boat goes to Lesvos, Chios and Piraeus. There is also a ferry every 6 days to Limassol (Cyprus) and Tartous (Syria). During summer small boats leave the quay near the White Tower for the beaches at Aretsou, Perea and Agia Triada.

Car hire: Hertz, 4 Venizelou Street, and at the airport; Doucas Tours, 8 Venizelou.

Bicycle hire: 66 Philippou.

Olympic Airways: 7 Vas. Konstantinou. Buses for the *airport* leave from near the Olympic office.

For up to date travel information consult the NTOG office at 8 Aristotelous.

Museums, Churches, etc.
Archaeological Museum: Open 9am to 6pm daily, 10am to 5pm Sundays and holidays, closed Tuesdays. Take buses 10 or 31 in Egnatias eastwards.

Folklore Museum, 68 Vas. Olgas (bus 3 or 5 eastwards): Open 9.30am to 2pm daily, closed Tuesdays.

Churches: As a general rule open 8am to 12pm and 4 to 7pm.

Ataturk's house: 9am to 1pm and 4 to 6pm, but you must ask at the consulate office nearby with identification.

Festivals
The *International Trade Fair* takes place in the permanent buildings each September, when Thessaloniki's hotels are usually full as a result. To visit it (open 10am to 2pm, 6 to 9pm) you get tickets from 154 Egnatias.

In October during the first week there is the *Film Festival* followed by the *Dimitria Festival* which continues to the end of November, with music, theatre, ballet, exhibitions, etc: information from the City Hall (Dimarchion) in Egnatias.

Other Things
Tourist Police: 10 Egnatias.

Bank of Greece: 12 Tsimiski, open 8am to 7pm for exchange (weekdays).

Central Post Office: 45 Tsimiski, open into weekday evenings.
OTE: 55 Vas. Irakliou.
British Consul-General: 39 Vas. Konstantinou.
American Consulate: 59 Vas. Konstantinou.
Athos permits: You must go to the Ministry of Northern Greece (Directorate of Foreign Affairs), Plateia Dioikitirion, open mornings only.
Shopping: The most elegant shops are along Tsimiski; for fruit and other food go to Komninon between Irakliou and Tsimiski.

CHALCIDICI

Buses leave the bus station at 68 Karakassi Street, Thessaloniki, almost hourly for Kallithea and Kassandria (on Kassandra); 4 times daily for Neos Marmaras and Sarti (on Sithonia); and 6 times daily for Ierissos and Ouranopolis (for Athos).

PETRALONA CAVE

Open 9am to 6pm. A *museum* with finds from the cave has been planned.

KASSANDRA

There are many large *campsites* around the coast, and the peninsula has spawned a large number of *hotel complexes* usually tied into the package holiday trade. Below are a couple of suggestions for places less affected by mass tourism. You can catch local buses in Kassandria and hire mopeds.

On the east coast **Chaniotis** has a long beach: for accommodation there is the Dionyssos (apartments) (B); several C class hotels and rent-rooms; tavernas on the square.
Nea Skioni, a fishing village on the west coast also with a pleasant beach, has the hotels Olympia and Skoni, both D, and rent rooms.
Gerakini, between Kassandra and Sithonia, has a campground, and the Gerakina Beach Hotel (B) has a waterski training centre and provides instruction in windsurfing.

SITHONIA

Travel: The Thessaloniki *bus* travels down the west coast and on to Sarti via the south. For the northeast coast (Vourvourou, for example) be sure to get a direct bus from Thessaloniki.

In general you should stick to the east coast which is less developed. There is a superb beach at **Vourvourou**: hotels Diaporos (B), Vourvourou (D). **Sarti** also has a good beach; there is the hotel Akti Sarti (B) with apartments, there are rooms, tavernas, etc, and a festival on 15 August. There is another excellent beach at **Kalamitsi**, where there is a campground.

Porto Carras has two huge hotels in the resort complex, Meliton Beach (L) and Sithonia Beach (A), with swimming pools, riding stables, a golf course, beach frontage of about 1 km, all in front of a huge manicured estate of olives and vines; depressing.

IERISSOS

Hotels: Mount Athos (B); Marcos (D); Akanthos (E). Also rent *rooms*.

OURANOPOLIS

Hotels: Xenia (B); Galini (D); Ouranopolis (E). Also *rooms*.

Pleasant *beach*; *tavernas*; *boats* to sail around the peninsula. Local carpet industry.
Note: There are zones for scuba-diving (which is generally very strictly controlled in Greece) on the east coast of Kassandra, the east coast of Sithonia, and the beginning of the Athos peninsula – enquire at an NTOG office or locally.

ATHOS

You must be male and you must get permission to visit either from the Ministry of Northern Greece (see Thessaloniki) or the Foreign Ministry (see Athens). To obtain permission you must first get a letter of recommendation from your embassy or consulate. In principle you need a good reason to go to Athos, be it academic or spritual or journalistic. After taking the letter to the Ministry you then go to the Foreign Police in 25a Tsimiski, Thessaloniki, for papers to give to the police on Athos. If you would prefer to make a brief visit and to avoid the bureaucratic hassle, Doucas Tours of 8 Venizelou, Thessaloniki, are said to arrange one-day tours with the necessary permits, etc.

There is a limit on the days allowed for a visit (usually 5); also in summer there is a queue to get in, so you will be given a date a week or more later. You must then present yourself, with the necessary papers and your passport, at Karies, the administrative centre of Athos, where you will be given a *diamonitirion* which enables you to stay in any one of the 20 monasteries, though usually only for one night at a time.

Karies is a long day's walk from the frontier. The most practical way is to go by sea. A caique runs, depending on the weather, from Ierissos to the monasteries of Vatopedi (2 hours walk to Karies) and Iviron (occasional bus to Karies or one hour's walk). More dependable is the motor boat from Ouranopolis to Daphni (the last one leaves mid-morning) from where there is a connecting bus to Karies.

The boat from Ierissos stops at most of the monasteries on the east coast, continuing to Lavra; the boat on the west coast does likewise, continuing to those monasteries beyond Daphni. With the bus from Daphni to Karies and Iviron and back, and a very occasional boat round the end of Athos, the options of assisted travel are exhausted, and otherwise you must walk between the monasteries.

Travelling on Athos is unusual, with its own rhythm and rules, and much of the most useful information will come from other travellers. The evening meal is eaten quite early, about 6pm in summer, and the conducted visits to the churches, treasuries, etc, are usually in the late afternoon or early evening, so do not arrive too late at a monastery. Also the monastery gates close at sunset.

KAVALA
Accommodation and Eating
Hotels: Galaxy, Philippi (B); Panorama, Acropolis (C); Attikon, Parthenon (D) – all in the immediate area behind the harbour. There are also *campgrounds* at Batis, Kalamitsa and Keramoti (see below).

There are many *tavernas* along the harbour; try Zafira-Panos.

Travel
Hourly *buses* from Thessaloniki arrive in the bus station near the waterfront in Mitropolitou Street. From here there are frequent buses to Philippi and to the beaches to the west of town.

For *ferries* to Thasos, see below under Thasos. There are also boats 3 times weekly to Lemnos (5 hours), once weekly continuing to Lesvos (12 hours); once weekly the *SS Kyklades* goes to the Eastern Sporades, and there is one boat a week to Samothraki. Another line goes about once a week in summer to Rhodes via Lemnos, Lesvos, Chios and Samos.

Activities
The *citadel* above the Byzantine walls is open most daylight hours.

The *museum* closes about mid-afternoon and on Tuesdays.

There are good *beaches* to the west of town at Kalamitsa, Batis beach (camping), Iraklitsa (Camping) and Nea Peramos.

The *festivals* at Philippi and Thasos stage ancient drama in the two ancient theatres at the weekends in July and August; tickets from the NTOG office. At Nea Peramos on 15 September there is a *Vintage Festival*.

Other Things
NTOG office: Plateia Elevtherias.
Tourist Police: 41 Omonias.

KERAMOTI
To the east of Kavala, where the shortest *ferry* for Thasos leaves. It has a *campground* and several cheap *hotels* (*bus* from Kavala).

PHILIPPI
Open daily 9am to 6pm, Sundays and holidays 9am to 3pm; the *museum* is closed Tuesdays.
Festival: see under Kavala.

THASOS
Travel to and on the Island
Ferries: frequent from Kavala both to Prinos and Limen (up to 15 a day) and from Keramoti to Limen. Note that Thasos is not on the ferry route to other islands; for Lemnos for example you must return to Kavala.

Inside the island several *buses* a day leave Limen for the villages around the circular coast road.

Limen
Hotels: Xenia, Timoleon (B); Angelika, Alkyon (C); Akti, Astir (D) – all near the waterfront except Xenia, a little to the west; further west, about 1 km, is the Glyfada (C) on a pleasant beach (much better than the town beach). Also *rooms* for rent, and *campgrounds* at **Rahoni** to the west and **Chrisi Ammoudia** to the east (and elsewhere; see below).
Tavernas: by the harbour; try Platanakia.
Information: Limenas Tours.
Tourist Police: on the waterfront.
Museum: 9am to 1pm, 4 to 6pm daily, 10am to 2pm Sundays and holidays, closed Tuesdays. The *agora* is reached from the square by the museum.
Festival: The drama festival at weekends in July and August takes place in the ancient theatre; for tickets enquire at the Tourist Police.

Around the Island
Makriamos has an adequate beach. Better is the large sandy bay of **Chrisi Ammoudia** below the attractive village of **Panagia** where there are small hotels and rooms. **Potamia** also has rooms and is the start for the climb of Mt Ipsari (about 2 hours); below there are many cheaper hotels at **Skala** on the coast.
  Aliki, the site of ancient marble quarries, has a good beach with a taverna. On the west coast there are several places with either rooms or hotels and good beaches including **Potos**, **Pefkari** and **Limenaria** (campgrounds at the latter two); Limenaria has a festival on the Tuesday after Easter. *Theologos* (worth a visit) has a festival on 3 July (ritual wedding).
Prinos, an unattractive place, has a campground.

SAMOTHRAKI
Travel to and on the Island
Ferries: There is the weekly boat from Kavala (4 hours) and in summer a daily boat from Alexandroupolis ($2\frac{1}{2}$ hours). The boats arrive at Kamaritossa, whence a bus goes fairly often to the main village of Chora and to Palaiopolis (sanctuary).

Around the Island
Kamariotissa has the Niki Beach hotel (C), rooms, tavernas, a pebbly beach. From here caiques go to the beach at **Ammos**. **Palaiopolis** has the hotel Xenia (B). The sanctuary is open for most of the daylight hours; the museum is closed Tuesdays. **Chora** has rooms, tavernas, a bank, telephones, and the Tourist Police.

LEMNOS
Travel to and on the Island
About 2 *flights* a day from Athens, one a day from Thessaloniki.
Boats: about 3 a week from Kavala (5 hours), connecting with Lesvos and the Northern Sporades and Kimi each once weekly; once a week from Agios Konstantinos (near Euboea), also weekly in summer from Thessaloniki. Another boat connects Lemnos with Lesvos, Chios and the Piraeus.
  On Lemnos there is a poor *bus* service from Mirina.

Mirina (also known as Kastron)
Hotels: Akti Mirinis (1 km out of town, with its own beach) (L); Serdalis, Lemnos (C); Aktaeon (D). Also *rooms*.
  Mirini has the Tourist Police, banks, etc. A museum with local finds is in the former house of a Turkish pasha. There is a sandy beach here, but better beaches to the south at Plati and Thanos (taverna) – walk or caique.

NORTHWEST GREECE

Adriatic ferries
The shortest passage between the south Italian ports (Bari, Brindisi and Otranto) and the mainland of Greece lands you at Igoumenitsa, not far from the Albanian frontier. The ferry will almost certainly have called in at Corfu first, and after Igoumenitsa most lines sail down the coast to Patras, linked to Athens by the fast National Highway. But **Igoumenítsa**, an insignificant village promoted to international transit point by the Adriatic ferry service, is the place where anyone less in a hurry should begin their adventure on Greek soil.

After the torpor of southern Italy, there is an alertness, a strength in the faces of the people here; after the domesticity of the Italian countryside and the lushness of Corfu, there is the hard, uncompromising and virile landscape. The road winds up from the bay and into the mountainous interior, wild and desolate, where silence hangs in the valleys like a crystal waiting to be shattered by the haunting music of sheep-bells and shepherds' pipes. It was this primitive and remote part of Greece that awakened a response in the 21-year old Byron; here that he felt the need and summoned the discipline to embark on his first major work:

> Childe Harold pass'd o'er many a mount sublime,
> Through lands scarce noticed in historic tales.

Geography and roads
Northwest Greece is cut off from the rest of the country by the great *Pindos* range running down from the Balkans to the Gulf of Corinth. So formidable a barrier are these mountains that they are traversed by only one major road, from Ioannina to Trikala over the 1707-metre Katara pass. And travel within the region is only really easy along the north-south valleys and gorges (the road from Ioannina all the way down to Messolongi is excellent), or along the new coast road from Igoumenitsa to Parga and Preveza.

The three provinces of the northwest are Epirus, Aitolia and Akarnania: geography denied them central roles in the 'historic tales' of classical times, though Pyrrhus and Antony passed dramatically across this side of the stage; and Byron's own visits, first (in 1809) to Ioannina, capital of the at once genial and monstrous Ali Pasha, later (in 1824) to Messolongi where he died in the cause of Greek freedom, puts this far side of Greece forever at the centre of Romantic lore.

From Igoumenítsa to Ioánnina

The 104-km road from Igoumenitsa to Ioannina replaces as the principal east–west route between Rome and Thessaloniki and Constantinople the ancient Via Egnatia which ran further north from coastal Dyrrhachium (Durazzo) in what is now not very transit-minded Albania. Readers of *Eleni* might want to follow the sign along here pointing north to the '*Villages of the Morgana: Lia, Litsa*'. It was in Epirus in November, 1940, that Greece humiliated Mussolini by driving back into Albania the invading Italian army and inflicting on the Axis its first land defeat.

At Klimatia, 81 kms east of Igoumenitsa, there is a turning north leading, in 5 kms, to **Zitza**, a small, picturesque town of paved streets and sturdy stone houses – legacies of prosperity under the Turks – with a now deserted monstery (Profitas Ilias) at which Byron stayed during his first visit to the country. The view is magnificent, and on the outer wall of the monastery are two lines of tribute from *Childe Harold:*

Monastic Zitza! from thy shady brow,
Thou small, but favoured spot of holy ground!

The Vikos Gorge There is a more awesome sight, the *Vikos Gorge* near Monodendri, about 40 kms north of Ioannina off the road towards Konitsa. Narrow, deep and dark, with the diminutive 15th C monastery of *Agia Paraskevi* perched on a rocky outcrop, there is the sound below, like distant thunder, of the boiling river fed by melting snow. Shepherds bring their flocks up to these high reaches of the Zagoria valley in summer, where the air intoxicates, the grass and trees grow springtime green, and the water gushes cold as ice from the living rock. The traditional villages in this area are known as the Zagorohoria.

The mountain road from Igoumenitsa debouches onto an upland plain where it joins the roads from Konitsa to the north and Metsovo, Kalambaka and the Meteora to the east.

The Katara pass **Métsovo** (58 kms) stands nearly astride the high *Katara pass* over the Pindos, the five great rivers of the mountain range having their sources within a few kilometres around. The houses are built of stone and exposed beams; the townspeople – many of them Vlachs, speaking a Latin dialect similar to Rumanian – still daily dress in their traditional dark blue costume, and are renowned for their attractive woollen rugs and embroidered textiles. A *museum* in the restored house of the Tositsa family displays the handicrafts of the region. Kalambaka is only another 67 kms, but the entire journey from Ioannina involves arduous and seemingly endless mountain driving (rewarded though by superb views when crossing the pass) for which half a day should be allowed.

From this crossroads on the upland plain you look down upon a long valley, well-cultivated with grain and tobacco, **Ioánnina** standing upon and behind a promontory projecting into Lake Pambotis opposite the bare and precipitous grey slopes of Mt Mitsikeli on the flank of the Pindos range. In summer when the mountains are bleakest, the virid fields and blue-green surface of the lake shimmer like a mirage. It can be oppressively humid then, and in winter bitter cold.

But as you descend through the busy streets of this pro-

A lurid past

vincial capital of Epirus, there is disappointment that so much of it is modern and ordinary, that so little atmosphere lingers from its lurid past. Appearing in books and on maps variously as Jannina, Yannina or Ioannina, its name is said by some to derive from the 6th C Byzantine Emperor Justinian, by others from an early monastery of St John the Baptist, though these claims of pedigree are without evidence and both name and founding remain buried in obscurity, though not antiquity: the existence of Ioannina can be documented only from the 11th C, and it has been a mongrel tale since then. After the sack by the Fourth Crusade of Constantinople in 1204, Ioannina filled with refugees and grew in importance, tempting Serb invasion a century and a half later: their leader Stefan Dusan proclaimed himself Emperor of Serbia and Greece here in 1346; and one of his successors, Thomas of Ioannina, 'possessed of the most unnatural and enormous vices', was fond of quartering and then chopping into pieces prominent clergymen, then turning their flesh on a spit. Ioannina perhaps gratefully surrendered to the army of Sultan Murad II in 1431, from that time until 1913 remaining part of the Ottoman Empire.

Approaching the town from above, there had been a glimpse of minarets, a touch of the Orient still, rising from the *frourion* or Byzantine fortress built upon the promontory. Here by the lakeside there is a thick sweet fragrance, perhaps of mountain herbs borne across Pambotis by sluggish currents of air. The fortress walls, restored by Ali Pasha in 1815, are extensive and encircled on their lakeward side by the pleasantly tree-shaded Leoforos Kosta Karamanlis, the townspeople promenading here on Sundays, or picnicking or boating; and there is a small seasonal fairground nearby. A cave in the cliffside traditionally marks the spot where Bishop Skylosophos, leader of a Greek uprising in 1611, was caught and skinned alive by the Turks. On the landward side, the walls were protected by a now filled-in moat.

It is here by the lake, down by the walls, that Ioannina is still haunted by its Moslem past. Ali Pasha, born in Albania in 1741, was a brilliant, ruthless and vindictive adventurer who deployed his talents on behalf of the Sultan against the Austrians and was rewarded with the pashalik of Trikala in 1788. But ability combined with ambition and treachery: in the same year Ali seized Ioannina and made it his headquarters, from then on allying himself with Napoleon or the British, or following whatever other policy that would augment his possessions and bolster his increasing independence from the Porte. Ioannina prospered for a time, became renowned for the filigree work of its silversmiths, and enjoyed a flowering of Greek culture; this, and his nose-thumbing at the Turks, have made Ali something of a Greek hero, though any regard he had for his Greek subjects was at best op-

'Since the days of our prophet the crescent ne'er saw / A chief ever glorious like Ali Pasha' – *Childe Harold*

portunist and transient. Peter Sheldon writes of 'Ali's massacre of the entire male population of Gardiki, over 700 men and boys, while the women had their clothes cut off below the waist, and thus indecently exposed were driven up the mountains to die from cold. This was Ali's long-delayed revenge for his mother's violation by a rather large number of Gardikiots'.

Byron's encounter with Ali

Ali was at the height of his power when Byron came to see him at Ioannina, and discovering that he was away to the north, in Tepelene, pursued the encounter over the mountains into Albania: 'He told me to consider him as a father', wrote the bisexual Byron to his mother, '. . . indeed he treated me like a child, sending me almonds & sugared sherbet, fruit & sweetmeats 20 times a day. . . . His Highness is 60 years old, very fat & not tall, but with a fine face, light blue eyes & a white beard. . . . He has the appearance of any thing but his real character, for he is a remorseless tyrant, guilty of the most horrible cruelties, very brave & so good a general, that they call him the Mahometan Buonaparte. . . . He has been a mighty warrior, but is as barbarous as he is successful, roasting rebels &c. &c.'.

Old Turkish houses crumble sadly within the fortress walls. Headstones stand broken or lie fallen in the long grass of the Moslem graveyard at the steps of the *Cami of Aslan Pasha*, an early 17th C mosque, moss- and lichen-covered like a tree stump. From the northwest corner of the frourion, the cami pleasantly overlooks the lake more like a gazebo built for whiling away a hot summer's evening, though the dome and soaring minaret (now closed to the public), and the recesses in its vestibule where the faithful once left their shoes before entering, remind you of its once religious purpose – it has been preserved against the creeping rot to which Greeks normally abandon anything of Turkish provenance because it has been pressed into service as the Municipal Museum. Its

Epirot costumes

rustic interior contains a fine collection of Epirot costumes, including brightly coloured village weaves, the black dresses and leggings of Sarakatsani nomad women, and the elegant streetwear of Greek merchants' wives from Ioannina's heyday. There is also a portrait of Ali, the 'Lion of Ioannina' himself, purring in the arms of his mistress, Kyra Vasiliki.

The murder of Kyra Phrosyne

But one beautiful woman, Kyra Phrosyne, was to fall victim to the Lion's claws. The wife of a rich Greek merchant, she would sleep with Ali's son while her husband was away. One night Ali invited her to his own lair but she declined the pleasure. Outraged, he raped her and then had her and 17 of her companions sewn up in sacks and tipped into the lake where it laps below the Aslan Pasha mosque.

At the southeast corner of the fourion is *Its-Kale*, a citadel within the citadel, now a Greek army confine (the public only sometimes admitted), with the graceful but decrepit *Fetichie*

Cami (Victory Mosque), Ali's restored palace where Byron sojourned, and Ali's tomb.

Ali's execution Ali had practised a lifetime of treachery yet was surprised by treachery at the end. Determined to crush this most dangerous of rebels before suppressing (as he hoped) the Greek uprising that had begun in 1821, the Sultan sent an army of 50,000 against Ioannina. By January 1822 it was besieging Ali in his citadel. The Sultan's general accepted Ali's offer to talk terms at a meeting to be held on the island in the lake, but when Ali arrived he found a firing squad waiting for him instead. Bullet marks in the floor of the 16th C *monastery of Pantaleimon* mark the spot where Ali fell. The guest room in the monastery is now a museum. His head was displayed about the provinces he had once ruled and was finally exposed outside the Seraglio at Constantinople. The leafy, reed-encircled *island* with its numerous monasteries can be reached by boats departing at least hourly from the town; the chief pleasure is to wander amidst the trees and flowers, whether purposefully visiting monasteries or not, and then enjoying a simple meal at the taverna here.

The island in the lake

Returning to the town, Odos Averof runs uphill from the landward wall of the frourion and is lined with *silversmiths*, all that remains of Ioannina's once flourishing bazaar. At the top of the street is a *museum* exhibiting archaeological finds of the region where you should not miss the small lead tablets excavated at Dodona inscribed with questions to the oracle. At the north end of the lake, 4 kms from town by Perama, are *caverns* bristling with stalactites and stalagmites. Guides will lead you through nearly a kilometre of electrically lit galleries.

Dodona and South

An increasingly rare delight in Greece is to visit a grandly situated archaeological site and to find hardly anyone there. An opportunity for that lies 22 kms distant from Ioannina, following first the Arta road. After 8 kms, take the turning on your right marked Dodoni. The road makes a sharply winding ascent with magnificent views of the Pindos along the eastern sky and of Lake Pambotis below, an astonishing, seemingly misplaced jigsaw piece of blue locked into the valley's pattern of greens. Then the crest of the ridge is reached and you descend into the isolation of **Dodona**, the oldest oracle in Greece. Robert Graves says that patrilineal invaders replaced Dodona's Earth Goddess with Zeus, but both men and women continued to deliver oracles, listening 'to the cooing of doves, or to the rustling of oak-leaves, or to the clanking of brazen vessels suspended from the branches'.

Oldest oracle in Greece

In August, the *theatre* is used for the annual drama festival; it was first built in the time of Pyrrhus (297–272 BC), but at the time of Augustus the Romans, typically, replaced the lowest rows of seats with a protective wall so that it could be used as an arena. The cavea is recessed into the acropolis hill and is supported by retaining walls 21 metres high and towers on either side.

Climbing above the highest rows of the theatre, you find a gate leading into the *acropolis*, its walls as much as 4.5 metres thick though now reduced to no more than 3 metres in height. From here a path descends to the sanctuary (which can be reached directly from the front of the theatre); the foundations of several buildings are evident and clearly labelled – the *Temenos of Zeus Naios* being the complex ruin that grew up round the site of the oracle. At first, going back to 1000 BC or more, there would have been only the sacred oak-tree itself. There are no oaks here now, and the sanctuary ruins are not impressive. But there is the rustling still of other trees, and puffy flocks of sheep wandering across the landscape, causing a constant clanking of their deep-toned bells.

What is marvellous, from the sanctuary or from the theatre, is the length of cultivated valley running off into the distance, a verdant river between grey slopes perenially dressed for the change of season in firs and stubbly bush. 'Wintry Dodona', Homer called it in his epics, and it is as though the hush of snow, like the rustling of the oak-leaves, might come at any time. From the upper rows of the theatre, the landscape must have overwhelmed any daylight drama on the stage. The cavea stands as audience to the whisperings of the sacred valley.

Rejoining the Arta road (Ioannina to Arta: 78 kms), a causeway carries you over marshy bottom land; the road then rises to over 600 metres and descends again into the beautiful **The Louros** *Louros Gorge* where it runs deep between the dark and **Gorge** densely tufted mountain walls, the river skittering fresh and cold over its smooth-worn bed of rocks, shaded by plane trees. Road and river pace one another nearly the whole distance to Arta. The valley broadens and is cultivated with bamboo, then narrows again, more ragged now, caves and spectacular stone arches at its heights. All too soon, for it is one of the most agreeable drives in Greece, you are out upon the Ambracian plain, a sea of orange groves. The Louros follows its own course towards the southwest while the road continues the last 8 kms southeastwards to where Arta sits encoiled within a great bend of the Arachthos which has run down through the Pindos from Metsovo.

The Coastal Route Through Epirus

Instead of heading for Ioannina and the alpine scenery of the interior, an alternative route through Epirus is to leave Igoumenitsa by the coast road, passing first through the village of **Platariá** (12 kms), with a good beach, then continuing inland to near Morfion (40 kms). Here the main road continues on to Preveza or Arta, while a turning to the right leads you down a spur road to the sea at Parga (51 kms from Igoumenitsa). Along the way in autumn during the olive harvest netting is looped round the trunks and branches of the trees like giant pythons.

Párga is a delightfully picturesque town and now that it is easily accessible is becoming a popular coastal resort. The old whitewashed houses, two and three storeys tall under gently sloping roofs of red tile, ascend amidst olive and orange trees from two coves either side of a rocky headland, *Norman battlements* at its crest. Parga came under Venetian protection at the beginning of the 15th C (accounting for the Lion of St Mark on the keep of the Norman fortress), passed in and out of French hands during the Napoleonic wars (from 1800 to 1807 even enjoying independent statehood under Russia's aegis), and in 1814 was taken by the British who promptly sold it for a song to Ali Pasha. The Pargiotes decamped with the ashes of their ancestors rather than live under Ali's rule and were replaced by Moslems who remained here until the exchange of populations between Greece and Turkey in 1924.

Steps and winding streets spill down to the small eastern cove, the waterfront lively here with numerous cafés and tavernas overhanging the water and looking out upon the rocks and islets close by, sailing boats and windsurfers gliding past. The larger western cove has a long sandy beach, a part of it taken over by the Club Mediterranée. A few tourist hotels are going up along an open bay to the east of Parga, but development is still modest.

The oracle of the dead

Back at the main road and travelling in the direction of Preveza, it is about 11 kms to the Acheron river. Immediately beforehand there is a turning left to the village of **Mesopótamo**. On a rocky hill overlooking the confluence of the Acheron and Kokitos is the **Nekromanteion of Ephyra**, sanctuary of Persephone and Hades and entrance to the underworld, where pilgrims came to communicate with the souls of their dead. Circe's description of the place to Odysseus is given by Homer (Book 10 of the *Odyssey*): when the North Wind 'has brought you across the River of Ocean, you will come to a wild coast and to Persephone's Grove, where the tall poplars grow and the willows that so quickly shed their seeds. Beach your boat there by Ocean's swirling stream and march on into Hades' Kingdom of Decay. There the River of Flaming Fire and the River of Lamentation, which is a branch of the Waters of Styx, unite round a pinnacle of rock to pour their thundering streams into Acheron'.

The Nekromanteion is a labyrinth of corridors and windowless rooms in fine polygonal masonry descending underground and dating from Hellenistic times, though the site is far older. The pilgrim would have been conducted on a disorientating tour within, then possibly given hallucinatory drugs before witnessing a spectacle involving mechanical trickery to produce the desired effect of a spiritual visitation. Today you work your way down into the dankness by metal steps with less the sensation of entering Hades than of visiting a public lavatory. Your ancient predecessors would have slipped more mysteriously into the depths by means of a precarious windlass mechanism (now in the Ioannina museum). Nevertheless it remains intriguing to visit this long vacant theatre of spiritual manipulation and to be reminded that it is not among stones but in the mind that the greatest adventures are realised.

If you continue south via Kanalaki, about 29 kms further on there is a turning left to the village of **Kamarína** (officially **Zálonga**), in the heart of Suliot country. The Suliots were a tribe of rugged mountain people, fierce resisters against Moslem encroachment. Ali Pasha cornered the greater number of Suliots at the *Monastery of Zalonga* here – the few who fought their way across country to Parga settled on Corfu, returning to the mainland again in 1824 as Byron's bodyguard. When the monastery was overrun, 60 Suliot women and their children escaped to the summit of the cliffs above and as Ali's soldiers relentlessly approached began to sing the old Suliot songs, dancing with their children in their arms ever closer to the edge, then one by one throwing themselves down the precipice in suicidal defiance. A monument commemorates the event.

Dance of the Suliot women

Close to the monastery on a ledge high over the Ambracian Gulf are the ruins of the ancient city of **Kassope**, only discovered in the early 1950s. Dating from the 4th C BC, it was burned by the Romans in 167 BC and finally abandoned with the founding of Nikopolis. Only walls and column bases remain, but you are alone here, no one comes, and Kassope commands a magnificent view towards Preveza, a perfect aerial map for Actium.

From Kamarina it is about 28 kms to Preveza. At 20 kms is Nikopolis from where you can head northeastwards round the Ambracian Gulf to Arta.

Antony and Cleopatra

Nikopolis was founded by Octavian, the future Augustus, to commemorate his victory over Antony and Cleopatra off **Aktion** (Actium in Latin) in the preceding year, 31 BC. The Ambracian Gulf narrows to a strait, barely a kilometre across, where it meets the sea: the ruins of Nikopolis and the modern town of Preveza are on the north side of the strait; at its south side is a sandy headland bearing the slight remains of the Temple of Apollo Aktios. Here Antony and Cleopatra camped with their 120,000 infantry and 12,000 cavalry they had massed for their invasion of Italy.

But in spring, Octavian's daring admiral, Marcus Agrippa, had captured Antony's vital supply station at Methoni in the

Peloponnese, and in summer had succeeded in blockading Antony and Cleopatra's combined fleet within the Ambracian Gulf. Antony's greatness was as a land commander; in Agrippa he was now facing perhaps the only Roman who ever understood naval strategy. As the blockade wore on throughout the hot month of August, time too turned against Antony: his men became restless, some (including Ahenobarbus) deserted to Octavian's side, while so many rowers died of fever that when finally battle was joined Antony could man only 230 ships to Octavian's 400.

The battle of Actium

Antony considered abandoning the fleet and striking across Greece with his army where twice before, at Philippi and Farsala, the fate of Rome had been decided. But abandoning the fleet meant abandoning Cleopatra's major contribution to his cause, and abandoning Cleopatra could mean losing Egypt and all its wealth. Antony instead decided to try and break through the blockade and return to Egypt with Cleopatra, leaving instructions for his army to cross Greece under his generals in preparation for a Macedonian campaign under Antony's direction the following spring.

What in fact happened was distorted by Roman propagandists to show Antony, supposedly feckless and un-Roman, deserting his fleet and his army to be with his treacherous Oriental queen. Far from intending to flee, Cleopatra and Antony were carrying out their plan to break through the Roman blockade. True, most of their fleet was captured or destroyed, but as one naval historian has written, 'to save even 60 ships out of 230 was a creditable achievement for a man embayed on a lee shore and vastly outnumbered'. The real disaster struck when Antony's army began marching towards Macedonia but was intercepted by Octavian's emissaries who offered them favourable terms, including the Roman soldier's traditional plot of land in Italy, if they would surrender. It was not that Antony lost the world in that one battle, nor that he lost it for a woman, but that over the course of a combined land and sea campaign, Octavian prudently avoided engagement by land, while Antony was checked and checked again by Agrippa at sea. It was morale that finally deserted Antony's waiting, onlooking army that September day – Antony only discovering the awful truth when it followed him to Egypt.

Settlement of Nikopolis

By the forced transfer of populations from towns over much of Aitolia and Akarnania, and adding veterans from the wars, Octavian settled his Roman city amidst a foreign land. The Vandals and Huns sacked it in the 5th and 6th C. Justinian rebuilt it, reducing the compass of its walls. Nikopolis fell once and for all to the Bulgars in 1040, and remains today abandoned, lonely and overgrown.

The southern sector of the site is encircled by the extensive though badly ruined *Augustan walls*; along their western stretch ran an aqueduct bringing water to the city from the Louros. Better preserved is the smaller circuit of *Byzantine walls* built by Justinian and broached by the great West Gate; within these is a *museum* – there is a Roman portrait of Marcus Agrippa. A small *odeion* lies outside the Byzantine gate, within the Augustan walls.

Within the Byzantine citadel are the ruins of three early *Christian basilicas*; a fourth lies outside the walls. The huge *church of Bishop Alkyson*, with five aisles and a threefold transept, lies at the centre of the Byzantine citadel. To find the other churches may require the services of the phylax: the *church of St Doumetios* possesses fine mosaics representing the Universe – earth, sea and air alive with beings; *Basilica D*, beyond the walls, contains a well-preserved peacock-design mosaic. Nikopolis was a hotbed of Christianity: peripatetic Paul wintered here in AD 64, and the 2nd C Pope Eleutherios was born here.

In the northern sector of the site there is a long depression, its outline picked out by the shrub that overgrows it. It is the *stadium*, rounded at both ends in the Roman way, and seeming like some sunken hulk – indeed the locals call it 'the ship'. This was the site of the Actian Games. At its eastern end is a *theatre*, built into a hillside in Greek fashion. A road running between theatre and stadium and up the hill past the village of Smyrtoula brings you to the remains of the *commemorative monument* erected by Octavian on the site where his tent had been pitched preceding the victory.

Préveza is 8 kms south, a town without interest, though nicely situated with the gulf on one side, the Ionian Sea (and some good beaches) on the other. The strait marked the border between Turkey and Greece from 1881 to 1912; a car ferry makes the brief crossing every half hour. Off to the right is the island of Lefkas, a surprising burst of mountain from the sea.

Árta to Messolóngi

The Turkish bridge across the Arachthos

Whether coming from Preveza or Nikopolis through the fragrant orange groves north of the Ambracian Gulf, or down the mountain road from Ioannina, you approach Arta from the northwest. Just before the modern road carries you over the Arachthos, there is a turning on the left signposted 'Old Arta Bridge', it perhaps sticking in Greek throats to identify it more precisely as a Turkish packhorse bridge, well paved with stone and gracefully arched across the river which loops about the town. There is an unmistakable Oriental artistry in the pleasingly irregular span placed against the backdrop of mountains behind. Constructed in the 17th C, the story goes that its completion had long been thwarted by the vagaries of the river until a bird revealed to the master builder that his wife would have to be immured in the foundations supporting its central span. This the builder did and the arches were joined, whereupon he committed suicide. The theme is found in many ballads sung about beautiful bridges throughout the Balkans.

Árta, or Ambracia as it was first known, was founded by Corinth around 625 BC. In the 3rd C BC, Pyrrhus, that king of Epirus who complained that his victories against the Romans were so costly they would ruin him, made Ambracia his capital. A century later the Romans did triumph and razed the city; whatever had been built up again was depopulated by Octavian when he founded Nikopolis. When Pausanias passed this way, he found nothing standing; and despite recent excavations, there is little of that period for the layman to appreciate today.

Byzantine Arta

But apart from its friendly atmosphere and river-beribboned situation (it is the ample presence of water that makes so much of the northwest delightful), Arta does offer the visitor several curiosities from its second period of greatness under the Byzantine despotate of the Angeli who established themselves here after the seizure of Constantinople by the Franks in 1204. The 13th C *frourion* with its crenellated walls in part constructed of reused classical blocks once enclosed the despot's palace and now provides a romantic river-view setting for the Xenia Hotel. The houses and little streets in this northeast salient of the town are full of character.

To the southwest, off Odos Pirrou, is the 14th C *church of Agios Vasilios*, its well-preserved exterior showing off the intricate and colourful brick and tile design for which this area is noted. In the same direction is the 13th C *church and convent of Agia Theodora*, similarly though less extensively decorated outside, lightened by numerous brickwork arches, and marvellously patterned within the domed narthex. On a rise behind the Plateia Skoufas is the high rectangular former metropolitan *church of Panagia Paragoritissa* (Virgin Mary the Consoler), looking something like an Italianate Texas School Book Depository – in fact 13th C Byzantine with a strong admixture of romanesque from the Angevin court on the nearby island of Kefallonia. There are six domes; within the gloomy interior the *central dome* can be seen to be supported by an extraordinary system of pillars, one atop the other, supporting projecting pendentives upon which the cupola seems uncertainly to rest. Original *mosaics* of Pantokrator and prophets tremble from on high.

The corniche

After passing through more orange groves across the Arta plain, the Ambracian Gulf is reached. There are beautiful and varied views, especially at evening, along the *corniche* that has been cut into the mountain ridge defining the eastern shores of the gulf, the 'Thermopylae of western Greece'. And there is the time-collapsing sensation, looking across the

A touch of the Orient still: the Aslan Pasha mosque, Ioannina

water to its narrow opening upon the sea, that Actium is still being fought in the silent distance.

The road from Preveza via the strait joins with that from Arta at **Amfilochía** deep within a narrow inlet at the southeast corner of the gulf. Continuing southwards over rolling landscape and along the shore of two lakes, the road skirts the village of **Strátos** (halfway between Amfilochia and Agrinion) on the left, sitting amidst the well-preserved *walls* (5th C BC) and scanty ruins of the ancient capital of Arkanania. The broad Acheloos flows by below. **Agrínion** (84 kms from Arta) is bypassed and there is no reason to object, though you can turn off here for one of the few roads across the Pindos, eventually reaching Lamia via Karpenision.

Lake and mountain sanctuary

Also from Agrinion you can follow the north shore of Lake Trichonis round to **Thermon**, the plateau sanctuary of the Aetolian League, its situation enhanced by the contrasting beauty of blue lake, snow-capped mountains and green fields dotted with agricultural villages. A 6th C *temple of Apollo* is identified by a few column drums; nearby are the substantial remains of a *prehistoric village*. A *museum* displays Bronze Age, Mycenaean and Geometric finds. Another road leads back to the Agrinion-Messolongi highway around the south side of the lake via the village of Kato Makrinou; or from the village you can follow a poor mountain road – though with lovely views as it rises from the lake – direct to Navpaktos.

The Klissoura Gorge

South of Agrinion, the main road soon slips between the towering sandstone sides of the *Klissoura Gorge*, eagles and hawks wheeling against the narrowed sky, until the walls fall away to reveal an olive-covered coastal plain, the medieval town of **Aitolikó** rising between an inner lagoon and the seaward Lagoon of Messolongi.

Defended by its shallow lagoon navigable only by flat-bottomed boats, its marshy ground, its walls and the cunning, courage and desperation of the fractious rabble within, **Messolongi** (Messolóngion) had fought off two sieges, in 1822 and again in 1823. In January 1824, when Byron landed for the second time in Greece, it was still the headquarters, albeit only a toe-hold, of the Greek forces on the mainland. The 'forces' were merely the bands of quarrelling brigand-captains who cared at least as much for their own welfare as for any national ideal; indeed, what nation there was barely existed beyond the imaginations of demoralised Greeks of western European education and a few broken Philhellenes: the Turks were reimposing their oppression on the chaos while Europe, after revolutions in France, Italy and Spain, and the long Napoleonic wars, was content to see the insurrection crushed.

Byron's death and his contribution to Greek freedom

Outside Greece, Byron was and remains the Romantic poet, the Satanic rebel, whose reputation rises and falls with the fashion and frustration of the times. In Greece, among these most infuriatingly inconsistent people, he has a constant value: national hero – because to Greece he came to fight and in Greece he died; and, curiously, because to Greece he came with fewer stars in his eyes than most travellers then or since. Byron detested hypocrisy in England; but for the factionalism and blatant larceny of the people for whose cause he was risking his life he showed patience. In his diary just before he died, he wrote: 'After all, one should not despair, though all the foreigners that I have hitherto met with amongst the Greeks are going or gone back disgusted'. And in one of his last letters from Messolongi: 'Of the Greeks I shall say nothing, till I can say something better – except that I am not discouraged. . . . I shall stay out as long as I can – and do all I can for these Greeks – but I cannot exaggerate – they must expect only the truth from me both of and to them'.

When he landed, Byron was greeted – more out of respect for the money he brought with him than for his literary reputation – with a 21-gun salute and made commander-in-chief of the Greek forces. His plan was to launch an attack on Navpaktos and to capture the fortresses at Rion and Andirrion, thereby establishing control over Greece's inland sea, the Gulf of Corinth. But in the miasmal airs of Messolongi he developed a fever and on 19 April 1824 he died. Messolongi, which then like today was a featureless, unhealthy and intrinsically uninteresting town, acquired a sudden world-wide fame, so that when finally it was taken by the Turks in 1826 its fall reverberated throughout Europe as though the infidel had sacked the second Jerusalem.

The main road from Agrinion (38 kms to the north) to Andirrion (41 kms to the south) bypasses Messolongi so that it requires a deliberate act of reverence, or at least curiosity, to see the few mementoes of the past. You enter through the Venetian walls by the *Gate of the Sortie*, so-named for the mass escape on the night of 22 April 1826 of 9000 of the townspeople after 12 months of siege by Turko-Egyptian forces. Betrayed to the enemy by a Bulgarian co-defender, 7200 of them were massacred on the slopes of nearby Mt Zygos, scene in mythology of the hunting of the Kalydonian boar. Those who remained within the walls blew up the powder magazines, and themselves and their enemies with them. The *Exodus* is solemnly commemorated each year. Beyond the gate, to the right, is the *Heroon*, the garden of heroes: on the left is a tumulus covering the bodies of unnamed defenders, to the right is the tomb of Botsaris who led the defence of Messolongi in 1823, and in the centre is a statue of Byron, beneath which is the poet's heart. At the central Plateia Botsari is the *Museum of the Revolution* containing Byron relics, while on Odos Levidou, at the bottom of Odos Trikoupis, is a memorial garden occupying the site of the *house where Byron died*, destroyed along with the rest of the town during the Turkish assault of 1826.

Mountains lie between Messolongi and **Andírrion** (ferry to Rion for the Patras-Athens highway) and you emerge on a corniche overlooking the Gulf of Patras, with fine views of Patras itself and of the mountains of the northern Peloponnese.

PRACTICAL INFORMATION

TRAVEL IN NORTHWEST GREECE
Air. There are airports at Ioannina (daily flights from Athens, twice weekly from Thessaloniki) and Preveza (4 flights a week from Athens).

Bus. From Athens (100 Kifissou Street) there are about 9 buses a day to Ioannina (7½ hours), 3 a day to Igoumenitsa (8½ hours), 3 daily to Preveza (7 hours), 8 to Arta (6 hours), and 11 to Messolongi (4 hours).

Within Epirus, Ioannina and Preveza are the main centres for transport (see below).

Igoumenitsa is of course a point of arrival for some visitors to Greece, and also a point of departure for Corfu, Kefallonia, Patras and the Italian ports (see below).

IGOUMENITSA
Hotels: Xenia (B); Tourist (C); Lux (D); Rhodos (E). There are *campgrounds* south of Igoumenitsa at Kalami Beach (10 kms) and Plataria (12 kms) with tavernas, etc.
Tourist Police: on the waterfront.

Ferries arrive from Italy in summer at least once a day; they continue to Patras in 8–9 hours, and one line stops at Kefallonia (5 hours). There is a similar traffic in the opposite direction, most boats calling at Corfu enroute. In addition throughout the day there is a (mostly) hourly ferry between Igoumenitsa and Corfu (in about 2 hours; cheap).

There are about 9 *buses* a day to Ioannina and 3 direct buses to Athens, though if you miss one of those you could go via Ioannina and pick up there one of the frequent buses to Athens (a longer route).

VIKOS GORGE
There is a daily *bus* to Monodendri from Ioannina, and there are a few buses to other villages in the Zagoria region. However there is very little *accommodation* for visitors, so you will probably have to sleep out if you are to explore the area at all, and with buses so limited you will have to be prepared to walk a good deal. There is a *trail* along the Vikos Gorge, starting near the Agia Paraskevi monastery, a difficult walk of about 8 hours, arriving at the road between Aristi and Papingo, where you may be able to pick up the afternoon bus back to Ioannina or go to Papingo, where if you are still keen you can climb Mt Timfi (2497 metres).

METSOVO
Hotels: Flokas (B); Galaxy, Egnatia (C); Acropolis, Athinae (E).
Taverna: Krifi Folia, in the plateia.
Festival: 26 July.

There are about 3 *buses* a day both to Ioannina and Trikala (via Kalambaka).

IOANNINA
Accommodation and Eating
Hotels: Xenia (B); and a wide range of hotels in or near the central square such as Acropole, Esperia, Tourist, Astoria, King Pyrrhos (all C); Brettania, Ilion (D); and by the old city gate, Elpis (E). On the island are 2 good cheap inns.
Tavernas: Pantheon by the city gate; To Nissaki and To Sarai on the island.

Travel
Apart from the 9 *buses* a day to Igoumenitsa and about the same number to Athens, there are about 5 daily to Arta, 3 to Trikala via Metsovo and Kalambaka, and also buses north to Konitsa. Four buses a day go to Thessaloniki and 2 to Patras. In addition there are services to more local destinations such as Dodoni and Zitsa.

The *bus station* for most destinations other than Athens is about 400 metres northwest of the central plateia behind Tsirigoti Street.

Other Things
NTOG office: 2 Napoleon Zerva Street (by Plateia Pirrou).
Municipal Museum: open mornings and late afternoons (except Sundays).
Archaeological Museum: open 8.30am to 12.30pm, 4 to 6pm daily, 10am to 4pm Sundays and holidays, closed Tuesdays.
Excursions: to the island in the lake (taverna), with frequent boats; and by bus 8 to the famous cave at Perama at the

north end of the lake (open during the day). Above all, to Dodona (below).

DODONA
Hotel: Andromachi (B). There is a Tourist Pavilion for *refreshments*.

The *site* is open 7.30am to 7.30pm daily, 10am to 6pm on Sundays and holidays. Once a year on one day in August there is a *drama festival* in the theatre: enquire at the NTOG, Ioannina.

Two buses a day, morning and afternoon, travel here from Ioannina but only stay about 20 minutes before returning; so if you do not want to stay all day or (better) all night you may be forced to take a *taxi*.

PARGA
Accommodation
Plenty of *hotels*, including Miltos (B); Avra (C); Agios Nektarios (D). At Chrissoyiali beach, Parga Beach hotel (B); at Lichnos beach, Lichnos Beach hotel (B).

There are several *campgrounds* including Parga Camping to the west of the harbour and on Lichnos beach.

Travel
Four *buses* daily from Preveza.

There are *excursions* to the island of Paxos, and also by boat along the Acheron to the Nekromanteion of Ephyra (below).

Beaches, etc
There is a sandy beach near the harbour; to the west there is a large sandy beach called Chrissoyiali, and there are more beaches to the south, at Ammoudia and at Lichnos. Also *windsurfing*.

NEKROMANTEION OF EPHYRA
Take the trip organised in Parga along the river Acheron to below the site.

KAMARINA (ZALONGA)
Two *buses* daily from Preveza.

NIKOPOLIS
Bus every 2 hours from Preveza.

There is an annual *festival of ancient drama* in August at the Roman odeon.

PREVEZA
Hotels: Zikas (B); Actaeon (C); Athinae (E). Also several *campgrounds* and *beaches* on the Ionian Sea.

Apart from the *buses* to Athens and Patras (both 3 times a day), there are buses to Ioannina, Parga (4 a day), Igoumenitsa (2), Zalonga (2), Nikopolis (see above), and also Arta and Lefkas.

Half-hourly *ferry* across the mouth of the Ambracian Gulf; cheap.

ARTA
Hotels: Xenia (in the castle) (B); Cronos (C); Hellas (D) – the last two by the main square, Plateia Kilkis, where you can find *buses* and *tavernas*.

Buses to Ioannina (5 daily), Preveza, Lefkas, Amfilochia, Agrinion and Messolongi.

THERMON (KEFALOVRISI)
Hotels: Aetolia, Hermes (D); also *rooms*. *Tavernas* in the plateia.

Infrequent *buses* from Agrinion.

The *site* is 1 km to the south of the village.

MESSOLONGI
Hotels: Liberty (B); Avra (D); Diethnes (E) – oddly there is not a hotel Byron. *Taverna:* Haravgi, 1 km on the Agrilia road.
Festival: Pentecost.

Several *buses* a day from Arta via Agrinion, also from Navpaktos and Patras.

ANDIRRION
See *The Road to Delphi* chapter.

THE IONIAN ISLANDS

The islands of the Ionian Sea run down the west coast of Greece like droplets. Green and lush throughout the year, forested with wildflowers in springtime, they are softer, even in the contour of their mellow landscapes, than the summer-dry, shimmering islands of the Aegean. In culture they are different too. Part of the Byzantine Empire, they fell prey to Frankish adventurers from the 11th C, and with the Ottoman sack of Constantinople became outposts of Christendom and **Western** the West against the encroaching East. Until 1913, the Turks **influence** stood on the mainland only 3 kms opposite Corfu. Of the islands' Western conquerors, Venice remained longest, her rule here more benevolent and serene than in the Aegean. When Napoleon put an end to the Venetian Republic in 1797, the islands passed to the French, later to the Russians, and finally, in 1815, to the British until they were united with an independent Greece in 1864. In the gentility of the people, the prosperity of their well-tended land, in the architecture of castles, churches, country houses and town arcades, the influence of the West has left its still visible mark.

In recent years the islands have become increasingly popular for tourists, and the Ionian Sea is now one of the great centres of flotilla sailing.

Corfu

Corfu (Kérkira) is the second largest, the most populous, and certainly the most popular island of the group. Brochures use feminine metaphors, 'soft, mysterious, yielding', which turn out to be correct, though in summer she is nearly raped by tourists in town and along most of the beaches and you have to press well in from the port to enjoy her in any intimacy. The green hills are like the folds of a dress, their slopes brocaded with olive groves, tassles of cypresses decorate the valleys. Odysseus wandered amorously here, and before the war this was the home of Lawrence Durrell (he describes the island in *Prospero's Cell*) before he retreated to the exclusivity of Provence.

The town of Corfu is almost un-Greek in the elegance of its main streets and squares, though the scores of backstreets serve as open theatres of Greek life: nearly every radio on, all broadcasting the same song, everywhere people nodding, tapping or singing to it; the sunlight on pink and yellow walls, cooking and talking going on behind closed shutters, cats stalking each other down alleyways, children and chickens running about, washing hung high across the streets as in Naples, arches, church bells, flowers growing out of paint buckets and glimpses of the sea and Albania beyond.

Layout of Corfu town. Adriatic ferries berth at the *new harbour* just to the west of town; the Igoumenitsa ferries dock a bit closer in. The *Neon Frourion* (New Fortress) of the Venetians rises above both the new and the old harbour which is fronted by the tree-shaded *Plateia Georgios B'* where carriages drawn by straw-hatted horses may be hired. Passing through the Porta Spilia brings you to *Odos Nikiforou Theotoki*, the principal pedestrian way through the town since Venetian times, lined with shops, confectioners (try *kum-kwat*, the local specialty of crystallised miniature oranges) and tavernas. Alternatively, you can follow the *sea road* out of the plateia, tall stately houses on your right, fine views of the mountains of Epirus off to your left, until you round the headland at the point of the *Archbishop's Palace* (on the site of Capodistria's birthplace) and first gain a view of the moated *Citadel*. Kerkira derives from *Corcyra*, the ancient name for the island. Corfu is a Venetian corruption of the Byzantine *Korypho*, meaning breasts, another tribute to the feminine, this time referring to the twin peaks on which the Citadel is built. Running north to south between the town and the Citadel is the *Esplanade*, a great open space once the Venetian parade ground. At its north end is the *Royal Palace* which overlooks that half of the Esplanade which now serves as a cricket pitch; a bandstand and an Ionic rotunda erected in memory of Sir Thomas Maitland, first Lord High Commissioner, are set on the grassy south half. *The Liston*, an arcaded row of tall houses along the north half of the Esplanade, was designed by the French after Napoleon's rue de Rivoli: local teams play cricket on Sunday afternoons, sometimes against the crews of visiting British warships, and you can sit here at one of the numerous cafés, soaking up an ouzo, applauding the play along with everyone else in a most restrained English manner. At night you can dine here, lights in the trees above you, Odos Georgiou a wide promenade of evening strollers fresh out of church and dressed to kill. Odos Nikiforou Theotoki emerges nearby, and along with the sea road and the Esplanade, forms a triangle, convenient for reference, around the heart of Corfu town.

Cricket, anyone?

Touring Corfu town. The **church of Agios Spirodon** lies within the triangle, on a street that runs into the Esplanade and bears the name of this patron saint of Corfu. Plain outside, the 16th C church is decked out High Renaissance inside and further graced by the presence of St Spirodon himself, standing tippy-toe in a gold-encrusted plankeen, face and feet visible through the glass cover, which is quite a goggle as he has been dead 1600 years. Born in Cyprus of humble origins, the Arian bishops of that island feared his influence at the Ecumenical Council of Nicaea (AD 325) and so per-

St Spirodon

suaded the governor to ban his passage on all ships off the island. But Spirodon took off his cloak and placed one half on the water, stood upon it, and attached the other half to his staff as a sail and pushed off to Nicaea, getting there *before* the Arian bishops who had left some days earlier. Clearly a man of formidable powers, when the Turks took Constantinople Spirodon's body was spirited away to Corfu where he has performed several posthumous miracles since. You may be fortunate enough to be here during a celebration in Spirodon's honour. Spirodon buttons, bearing a picture of his corpse, are on sale everywhere, some of them even with close-ups of his brown and wrinkly raisin face. The church is packed, but you push in, only to find out too late that you are on a queue to kiss old Spirodon's feet. It is probably to most visitors' liking to hail the saint at a more formal distance: he is carried about town four times a year, on Palm Sunday, Easter Saturday, 11 August and the first Sunday in November.

The **Royal Palace** at the head of the Esplanade was built by the British for the Lord High Commissioners and then from 1864 to 1913 served as a residence for the kings of the Hellenes. Its state rooms have been restored but are not open to the public, though by visiting the *library* and *museum* within you can get some idea of the interior. The palace and the **Maitland Rotunda** give Corfu a Regency flavour reminiscent of an English spa town. The English lived well here, tempering their autocratic rule with an unusual degree of eccentricity. 'King Tom' Maitland, for example, became so exasperated with frequent bearers of petitions that to one he bared his behind in turn. **Mon Repos**, the vast summer villa of the commissioners a mere 2 kms south of the town, continues the Regency theme. It was built by Sir Frederick Adam, the second Lord High Commissioner, at the instigation of his Corfiot wife whose tastes were as extravagant as her moustache. When the British left, the Greek royal family would summer here, and here in 1921 Prince Philip, Duke of Edinburgh, was born. That 'queer fish' Lord Guilford, as a colleague described him, established the **Ionian Academy** (now a school) at the bottom of the Esplanade to encourage a revival of Greek culture and promptly enacted his version of what that might be: 'Lord Guilford goes about dressed up like Plato, with a gold band round his mad pate and flowing drapery of a purple hue'.

English lords and loonies

Mon Repos is reached by following the pleasant promenade, backed with gardens, along the Bay of Garitsa (there is a beach beyond the point). Near its southern end, and a few streets landward, is the 12th C Byzantine **church of Saints Jason and Sosipater**, disciples of St Paul. You are in fact within the precincts now of **Palaiopolis**, or ancient Corcyra, which occupied the peninsula between the Bay of Garitsa and the lagoon of Kalikiopoulo, though almost all of what there is to see is found within the **Archaeological Museum** near the sea front at the southern end of the Esplanade beyond the Corfu Palace Hotel. Particularly striking is the archaic pediment of the *Temple of Artemis* (c580 BC), filled with a gorgon and panthers.

It is easy to walk to Mon Repos, and enjoyable to cover the entire distance to Kanoni at the point of the peninsula (4.5 kms from town) on foot; but there are buses. **Kanoni** was the site of a French gun emplacement but is visited for its familiar though still wonderful view of the two miniature islands of **Vlakerena** and **Pondikonisi** (Mouse Island), the first barely large enough to float a church and solitary cypress, the second just managing a chapel surrounded by trees.

Touring the Island. At **Gastoúri**, 8 kms south of Corfu town, is the pride and joy of the Empress Elisabeth of Austria and, later, of Kaiser Wilhelm – the ludicrous *Achilleion*. (The Kaiser dedicated the place 'to the greatest of the Greeks from the greatest of the Germans'.) Open year-round, it was completed in 1892 in a jumble of juxtaposed mock-classical styles including Pompeian rooms cluttered with fin-de-siècle Teutonic knicknackery and in the gardens nude gigolo statues passed off as Greek gods. In the evening the Achilleion is a casino, formerly (and perhaps still) run by Baron von Richthofen – black tie, no Snoopies. A further 3.5 kms southwards on the coast is **Benítses**, another kind of folly, which was once a real fishing village, picturesque and smelly, but is now a chic resort with a dozen or more hotels.

Paleokastrítsa (24 kms) lies on the west coast between Agios Gordis to the north and Ermones to the south. It has been a popular tourist spot since Sir Frederick Adam built a road to it in 1828; already in 1862 Edward Lear, the limericking landscape painter, wrote that although its beauty seemed to make him 'grow a year younger every hour' the pleasure could not last: 'Accursed picnic parties with miserable scores of asses male and female are coming tomorrow, and peace flies – as I shall too'. Well over a century on, the asses have multiplied.

After the shipwrecked Odysseus had washed and oiled himself and covered his nakedness with the cloak and tunic that had been given him, the Phaeacian princess Nausikaa 'gazed at him in admiration' and led him to her father's city, 'surrounded by high battlements' with 'an excellent harbour on each side . . . approached by a narrow causeway'. The promontory of Kattro below the town of **Lákones** happens to fit this description, with the bay of Agios Spirodon to the right, the bay of Alipa to the left, and here too the islet of Vigla like the fast Phaeacian ship that took Odysseus home to Ithaka and was turned to stone by vengeful Poseidon upon its

Teutonic modesty

Odysseus among the Phaeacians

233

return. As yet archaeologists have found no suitable Mycenaean remains in the Paleokastritsa area to justify this identification beyond geographical similarity, but on the other hand the substance and details of the Homeric epics are now accepted as having a solid basis in fact, however much embroidered by poetic imagination, and the possibility that this was King Alkinous' capital cannot be dismissed.

The journey to Kassiopi (37 kms) runs you up the east coast of the island, as far as Gouvia (9 kms) covering the same route as you follow to Paleokastritsa. There are hotels, camps that are suburbias of tents, and a youth hostel around Gouvia Bay, and then more campsites around Ipsos (16 kms) and Pirgi (18 kms) at either end of an inferior narrow beach. At Pirgi the road divides, the left fork leading to the 906-metre *Mt Pantokrator*, highest on the island, from the summit of which there are views clear down the length of Corfu and beyond as far as Lefkas, to Italy on the northwest horizon, and eastwards deep into Albania. The right fork continues to follow the coast, formed here by the bulk of Pantokrator pushing into the sea, and there is good swimming along the pebbly beach of Barbati Bay or in the coves just before **Nisáki** (22 kms). The loveliest part of the route is between Nisaki and **Kouloura** (30 kms) with prettily whitewashed houses set amidst luxuriant vegetation and Kouloura itself with its romantic cove where caiques call daily from Corfu town, Nisaki and Kassiopi. This was once the home of Lawrence and Gerald (*My Family and Other Animals*) Durrell. Larry has described a recent visit: 'Now it's a place of pilgrimage. The Club Méditerranée charged people enormous sums to go look at it as the Durrell residence and serve them Coca-Cola for even larger sums. I don't know how posthumous you can feel, but my brother and I put on dark glasses and funny hats and we went on one of these trips, and I've never heard so much misinformation about our family and in such strange French. I think they were all Syrians. Anyway, we drank Coca-Cola in our own honour and sneaked off back to town'.

Beyond here the landscape grows harsh and Corfu has a Cycladic aspect in keeping with Roman rather than English lunacies: Lawrence Durrell writes that at **Kassiópi** 'the mad flabby Nero sang and danced horribly at the ancient altar to Zeus'. By tradition the church stands on the site of the vanished temple and from here a path leads to the entrance of a 13th C *Angevin fortress*, haunt of owls who hoot throughout the summer nights.

Mountaintop view

Paxos

It is three hours' sailing time from Corfu to Paxos (or Paxí), the smallest of the main Ionian islands. Off its coast, so

Plutarch wrote, the Egyptian captain Thamus heard the cry, 'the great god Pan is dead', and carried the news to land where it was greeted with groans and laments.

The chief town, or rather village, of this 3 by 8 km island is **Gáio** (or Paxí), an amphitheatre of surprisingly handsome pink and whitewashed houses around a tiny inlet on the east coast. Numerous paths meander through the peaceful olive groves that cover the island; a road runs north to the still smaller port of **Lakka** where there is a sandy beach. Better yet, a caique will take you south to the satellite island of **Antipaxos** where you can complement your picnic with the local sparkling red wine and enjoy a swim at Voutoumi Bay, a quiet beach of fine white sand on the east coast where the water is the clearest blue.

Lefkás

Not quite an island

Thucydides reports that in 427 BC Lefkas (referred to often in the accusative, Lefkáda) was attached to the mainland, though centuries earlier Corinthian colonists had probably detached themselves by digging a canal which had silted up. Augustus built a new canal and the Venetians maintained it, but Lefkas today still has an ambiguous quality: ruled sometimes from the sea as an island, sometimes from the land as a peninsula, the result is partly Ionian, partly western Greek – shimmering olives, sandy beaches and the finery of Venetian costumes against timber-framed houses, lagoon fishing as at Messolongi, and the melancholy of Epirot music.

Lefkas is reached by chain ferry from Akarnania. Just on the mainland side of the crossing is *Agia Mavra Castle*, originally Frankish but given an Oriental caste by Turkish additions. A long sandspit, the *Yiro*, encloses the Sea Lake at its north end – an excellent sand beach extends all along its seaward side and beyond to the *Angevin chapel* at Agios Ioannis – but **Lefkás** town is approached over a more direct causeway. Its houses have a ramshackle look, the upper storeys often of sheet metal or hardboard designed to place the least burden on ground floor timber and masonry walls sometimes shaken by earth tremors. The whole shebang is given a slapdash of paint, white or lime, blue or apricot, and after all manages a Greek dignity. The one main street, Odos Zakka, runs like an Oriental bazaar through the heart of town, capillaries of sandy alleyways off to either side.

A road, now mostly paved, encircles the high wild interior of the island, and a road also penetrates the centre, taking you past Sfakiot villages settled by Cretan refugees in the 17th C as far as **Kariá** (15 kms), a hill-village overlooking the great sunken valley of Livadi. There are wonderful views of the Sea Lake and of the Arkarnanian ranges enroute.

The north and west coasts of Lefkas are barren, but along the east coast green valleys cultivated with orange and olive

Sappho's Leap

groves and dotted with attractive villages open out towards the mainland. Approaching the fjord-like *Vliko Bay* (21 kms) you can see offshore the island of **Skorpios**, owned by the late Aristotle Onassis. At southerly **Cape Doukato** where Childe Harold 'saw the evening star above Leucadia's far-projecting rock of woe', a temple of Apollo stood upon the 60-metre high cliffs. In annual sacrifice to the god a criminal was thrown down into the sea, wings, feathers and live birds attached to him so that their flutterings might lighten his fall. Waiting boats carried survivors away to where the evil banished with them could do the Lefkadians no harm. Sappho took the leap as a cure for unrequited love. It proved fatally effective.

Ithaka

Immortalised in the *Odyssey*, the spur to life's adventure in Cavafy's poem ('Without Ithaka you would not have set out . . . Poor though you find it, Ithaka has not cheated you.'), you wonder if you should not continue to leave Ithaka (Itháki) to your imagination, or at least to your old age. Odysseus described it as 'a rough land, a fit nurse for men', but Ithaka ruled a maritime empire; today its men try to eke a living from its stony soil and failing, they leave. But for the visitor there is no difficulty appreciating both the poetic and physical grandeur of this precipitous island lacerated by the sea.

From Patras and Kefallonia the boat beats along the wild and uninhabited eastern coast of Ithaka and rounds into the Gulf of Molo which almost separates the island into two halves. Empty mountains look down on you from all sides. Then an unsuspected bay opens to port, **Vathi**, sparkling white, cupped against its furthest end. Excursions about the southern, less 'Homeric', half of the island may easily be made from here: above Dexia Bay – where the Phaeacians left the sleeping Odysseus – is the *cave of the Naiads* where the returning hero supposedly hid his treasure; in the southeast of the island *Arethusa's fountain* (Perapigadi) is the spot – near a spring, a day's walk from the palace – that Eumaeus kept his swine. **Pisaetos** on the west coast was claimed by Schliemann as the palace site, but dating to only 700 BC disproved the theory.

Odysseus' palace

Stavrós (18 kms) towards the north of the island is a more fruitful centre for Homeric sleuthing. Overlooking Polis Bay on the northwest coast, Stavros may stand on the site of the Mycenaean town with *Odysseus' palace* 2 kms north at **Pelikáta** (some Mycenaean remains). The *Cave of Tripods* on the bay's north shore is the alternative to the Naiad cave near Vathi: at least here were found 12 bronze Geometric tripods (Odysseus had been given tripods by Alkinous on Corfu), later Greek shards dedicated 'To the Nymphs', and a votive mask of the 1st C AD bearing Odysseus' name – all suggesting that if this was not Odysseus' home at least people here 2000 years ago thought it was. Artefacts from the area, including the tripods, are in the *museum* at Pelikata.

Kefalloniá

Earthquakes Ithaka, Kefallonia and Zakinthos were all badly hit by earthquake in 1953; all have rebuilt, but on Kefallonia and more so Zakinthos entire Venetian towns have been lost. Kefallonia, once part of Odysseus' kingdom and lying spoon-in-spoon with Ithaka, is the largest and most mountainous island of the Ionian group. Forests of fir cover the slopes, giving them a sombre look, while peaks 1525 metres high burst incoming rain clouds, sudden thunderstorms watering the occasional meadowlands and valleys rich with flowers, fruit and shrubs in a landscape otherwise lacking the luxuriance of Corfu or Zakinthos.

During the Residency here of Sir Charles Napier, roads were built and the water supply improved – 'every hour not employed to do her good appears wasted'; he played host to his friend Byron who admired the island in those last months before crossing over to Messolongi.

Visitors arriving by boat will probably put in at **Sami**, on the channel separating Kefallonia from Ithaka. Here Don John of Austria's fleet lay at anchor before its triumph over the Turks at Lepanto. The town is entirely modern; a busy transit point rather than a congenial place to stay, its vast pebbly beach too impersonal. On the hills above the town are the remains of **ancient Sami**, capital of the island in classical times. Preferable is the modern capital of **Argostóli**, beautifully situated along an inlet within the great Bay of Livadi to the west, about 25 kms by road across the island. The *Archaeological Museum* has an extensive collection of Mycenaean finds; indeed only at Mycenae itself have greater treasures been found. In the *Koryalenios Public Library and Folk Museum* there are some fascinating photographs of 19th C Argostoli and of the 1953 earthquake.

The British-built causeway and bridge across the inlet have turned its inner reach into a lagoon, a walk of 5 kms all around; to the east of the lagoon are the considerable walls of ancient **Kranioi**. Another walk is to the north where inlet and bay become one – here near Katovothri there is a reconstructed *sea mill*. In 1835 an Englishman discovered that sea **The mysterious** water was rushing into a rock tunnel and disappearing under- **sea mill** ground, to rise again no one knew where. He built a corn-mill on the spot, but the mystery of the water was not solved until the 1960s when Austrian scientists dumped dye down the tunnel and to their astonishment found it appearing again 16 kms away in the semi-underground lake at Melissani near Sami, having plunged beneath the central mountain range.

Beaches

The 1953 earthquake has retarded the flow and the present mill turns by electricity. By bus from Plateia Valianos you can reach two of the finest beaches in these islands, **Platís Yialós** and **Makrís Yialós**, 3.5 kms south of town.

Castle of St George

On a hill outside the village of **Kastro** 8 kms southeast of Argostoli, soars the perfect phantom of the medieval past, the Venetian *Castle of St George*. Until the mid-18th C the island capital stood beneath its massive battlements from which there are splendid views. During the second half of 1823 Byron lived between here and the sea at Metaxata: 'Standing at the window of my apartment in this beautiful village, the calm though cool serenity of a beautiful and transparent Moonlight, showing the Islands, the Mountains, the Sea, with a distant outline of the Morea traced between the double Azure of the waves and the skies, has quieted me enough to be able to write'.

Napier's round-island road to the north is long and arduous, though to save making it a round-trip you can leave the island from Fiskardo, the Corfu-Patras ferry calling there once weekly. On the west coast, at the neck of a headland surmounted by a ruined Venetian *castle*, is the picturesque village of **Assos**, its colour-washed houses in gay relief to the stern grandeur of the sea and mountains around. A sand beach lies just to the south. Continuing to the extremity of the peninsula brings you to the only place on Kefallonia left undamaged by the 1953 earthquake: the 18th and 19th C *houses* at **Fiskárdo** are typical of the island's pre-concrete architecture. A *ruined church* on the nearby headland could be 11th C Norman – Fiskardo takes its name from the Norman conqueror of Sicily Robert Guiscard who died here in 1085. There is swimming from the rocks in the secluded coves to the north and south of the village.

Zákinthos

Zakinthos lies off the Peloponnese, the southernmost island of the Ionian crescent sheltering the entrance to the Gulf of Patras. It is reached by ferry from Killini. Topographically it is divided in two: spreading away from the port is a fertile plain described by Edward Lear as 'one unbroken continuance of future currant dumplings and plum puddings'; and beyond, rugged mountains, hilltop villages, stone-walled vineyards and, along the inhospitable west coast, cliffs dropping sheer into the sea. In springtime the plain is like a garden overrun with flowers; at the August harvest there is the remarkable sight of acres of currants spread out to dry in the shrivelling sun. To the Venetians the island was 'Zante, fior di Levante'.

Destruction of Zakinthos town

Zákinthos town was the finest monument to Venetian architecture in Greece – 'the Venice of the Ionian Sea'. At noon on 12 August 1953 it all came crashing down, a great fire ravaging even the broken remains. Only Agios Dionisios, church of the island's patron, and a bank and a school survived – and anyway they were all modern. A few lineaments of the Venetian town remain, in the street plan principally, the lemon-washed arcades nostalgically incorporated in new facades, the ikons in rebuilt churches.

The churches most worth visiting are *Agios Nikolaos sto Molo* in Plateia Solomou, the oldest in the town (1483), and *Kiria ton Angelon* (Our Lady of the Angels) north of the Xenia. Towards the south end of town, the *Panagia Faneromeni* was before 1953 the finest church; further on is *Agios Dionisios*, the church of the island's patron saint.

On Plateia Solomou is the *Neo-Byzantine Museum* displaying examples of the island's church art from the 12th to 19th C. Further back in the town towards the Castle Hill is the *Solomos Museum* containing manuscripts and mementoes of three great Zantiot poets, Ugo Foscolo, Andras Kalvos and Dionisios Solomos. Solomos (1798–1857), like Chaucer and Dante, chose to work in the vernacular, establishing demotic as the language of Greek literature. He and Kalvos lie in the mausoleum below. From the Venetian *kastro* atop the hill there is a sweeping view from Messolongi to Navarino.

View from Messolongi to Navarino

A circular excursion round the island can be made by crossing the plain to **Makerádo** (11 kms) where the *church* has an exceptionally sumptuous interior, then up into the hills and over a wild and rolling plateau to **Maríes** (32 kms), and back down again along the length of the plain, perhaps turning towards the sea for a swim off the sand beach at **Alikes** (16 kms from town). The closest beach to town is at **Tsilivi**, 5 kms to the north. The best swimming is at the tip of the Vasilikos peninsula (15 kms) – a pleasant enough excursion for its own sake – at **Porto Roma** or **Yerakes**. The long crescent of sand at **Lagana** (8 kms) on Keri Bay is crowded, especially at weekends.

PRACTICAL INFORMATION

TRAVEL TO THE IONIAN ISLANDS
Air. There are airports on Corfu, Kefallonia and Zakinthos. There are about 3 flights a day from Athens to Corfu (and direct flights from many European cities), daily flights in summer to Kefallonia, and several weekly to Zakinthos.

Sea. Corfu is on the main ferry route from Italy to Greece, giving daily connections with Igoumenitsa and Patras, and in addition there is the Corfu-Igoumenitsa boat every 2 hours during the day, the daily Corfu-Paxi boat, and the Ionian Sea Line boats running every other day between Corfu, Paxi, Kefallonia, Ithaka and Patras. Caiques run from Parga to Paxi. There is a daily Patras-Kefallonia-Ithaka ferry. Lefkas is not really an island and is reached by bus, while Kefallonia is served by boat not only from Patras but from Killini in the Peloponnese (twice daily) which is the only port for Zakinthos (7 daily).

Bus. From 100 Kifissou Street, Athens, buses leave 4 times a day for connections with Zakinthos (7 hours including ferry), 3 times a day for Lefkas (7 hours), and also for Kefallonia (8 hours including ferry) and Corfu (11 hours with ferry).

CORFU
The island has been very heavily developed, particularly on the coast to north and south of Corfu town and at traditionally popular and formerly unspoilt villages such as Kassiopi and Paleokastritsa. Around the island there are numerous hotels and complexes particularly in the more expensive categories, also campgrounds, etc, not necessarily suitable for the independent traveller. Many of the beaches, attractive enough in themselves, are simply too busy in summer. So what follows are some notes on Corfu town and a few other random suggestions, with the idea that you may prefer to stay in Corfu town a while and bus or bike around the island and find your own spot or maybe head off to one of the places mentioned.

Travel on the Island
Corfu town is the centre of public transport, and *buses* go all over the island which is now well served by roads. In general, buses leave the bus station at New Fortress Square for the north of the island, the one at San Rocco Square for the south, and the Esplanade for urban services including Mon Repos and Kanoni. You must enquire for details, but for example there are about 12 buses a day to Dassia, Ipsos and Pirgi, 8 to Kassiopi, then 6 a day across the island to Paleokastritsa, 8 to Pelekas, and 12 to Messongi and Kavos in the south.

Boats also leave from below the Esplanade for places on the coast north of Corfu town as far as Kassiopi, and on the south coast down to Kavos.

In Corfu town there is no shortage both of *car hire* firms (Avis, Hertz and Greek companies) and *moped rentals*.

Corfu Town
Accommodation
Hotels: all central: Cavalieri (Kapodistriou Street) (A); Astron (by the old harbour) (B); Arkadion (on Kapodistriou), Konstantinoupolis, Mitropolis (both by the old harbour) (D). There are several cheap hotels on Nikiforou Theotoki Street. A little out of town the hotel Ariti (A) at Kanoni has its own funicular railway down to its own beach.

There are many *rooms* to rent (you will be met by their owners off the boat; agree a price first).

There is a *youth hostel* at Kontokali to the north.

Campgrounds are found at Kontokali, also Komeno, Dassia, Ipso and Pirgi further north.

Eating and Entertainment
Aegli at 23 and Rex at 66 Kapodistriou, To Navtikon in Nikiforou Theotoki Street, Orestes in the suburb of Mandouki for fish, and further afield Gerekos in Kontokali (fish taverna), and south of town at Kinopiasta the Tripa Taverna for fun with folk dancing, etc.

There are several *discos* and *bouzouki clubs* on the road north.

Beaches
The nearest are Mon Repos beach 2 kms south and Alikes 5 kms north.

Museums, etc
Archaeological Museum: 8.30am to 12.30pm, 4 to 6pm daily, 9am to 3pm Sundays and holidays, closed Tuesdays.

The *Royal Palace* including the *Museum of Asiatic Art* is open the same hours as the Archaeological Museum.

Both the *New Fortress* and the *Old Fortress* (the moated Citadel) are open during the day; the Old Fortress has a sound and light show preceded by folk dancing each evening at 9pm from 15 May to 30 September.

Excursions
Bus or walk to *Kanoni*, take the causeway to *Vlakerena* and then a boat to *Ponidonisi*; visit the *Achilleion* during the day or have a night-time flutter (free bus service from the town; take identification); go to *Danilia Village* 8 kms to the northwest, a reconstructed Corfiot village from the medieval period with traditional craft-making, a museum and a great hall for jollies in the evening. For those who cannot miss their *golf*, there is a golf club with a very good 18-hole course in the Ropa Valley, near Ermones, which is open to visitors – it has a swimming pool too.

Other Things
The *NTOG* office is in the Governor's House (Diikitirion).
Tourist Police: 35 Arseniou Street.
Bank of Greece: opposite the Town Hall, Voulgareos Street.
Post Office: open to 8.30pm weekdays, next door to the NTOG office.
Emergencies: phone 100.
Shopping: Bombapiazza, Gilford and Nikandrou 18 (crafts boutique); a shop at 27 Philarmonikis for hand-carved olive wood; Poly's House and Kaki's Gallery for copper and pottery, and Sirena for hand-woven textiles.
Tennis: Courts for hire by the hour at the Corfu Tennis Club by the Corfu Palace Hotel.

Around the Island
North of Corfu town there is little to attract for most of the way. If you do like large hotels, but in single doses, the Nissaki Beach Hotel (A) at **Nissaki** is on an isolated site on a good beach, with windsurfing, etc. At **Kouloura** there is a delightful beach while at **Kalami** there is the famous White House taverna, formerly the Durrell home. **Kassiopi** has pensions and rooms, apart from A and B hotels, but is overdone. Along the north coast **Roda** has a lovely beach, but so has **Sidari** which is less busy with only a few small hotels, C and D class. From Kassiopi, Roda and Sidari there are motor boats to the 3 little **islands** to the northwest.

On the west coast of the island the beaches of Glyfada, Agios Gordis and Ermones are crowded. Between Ermones and Glyfada near Moni Myrtidion there is the less frequented and equally beautiful beach of **Myrtiotissa** (part nudist). **Pelekas** on top of a hill gives you superb views over the island and of sunset over the sea. Further north beyond Paleokastritsa there are also great views from the Byzantine castle of **Angelokastro**, a walk from Lakones or Krini; close to this, near the village of Makrades (bus from Corfu town) is the large sandy beach of **Agios Georgios** with rooms and tavernas. In the northwest corner of the island **Arilas** and **Agios Stephanos** both have sandy beaches, tavernas, windsurfing, etc, but remain at a midpoint in development, each with 2 C-class hotels and a good number of villas.

The southern part of the island is without the roads of the north and the southwest coast has yet to be developed, although here the island is not quite as spectacular. There is a large sandy beach at (another) **Agios Georgios**, and **Kavos** at the southern end with a few cheaper hotels and rooms would be a good base for exploration. It is possible to get a boat from Kavos to Paxos.

PAXOS
Gaio (or Paxi), the main harbour, has *rooms*. There are no *hotels* except the Paxi Beach Hotel (B), about 2 kms to the south. Gaio has a sandy *beach* nearby, though most beaches on Paxos are shingle.

The Corfu town-Paxi *boat* (daily) takes

3 hours and accommodation on Paxos is limited, so you may have to book rooms before you board (usually there is a man on the quayside). Paxos is also on the Ionian Sea Line route between Patras and Corfu. In high season boats cross from Parga (Parga Tours).

A *bus* is rumoured on the island, otherwise you *walk* or take a trip by *caique*. From Gaio there are caiques to Antipaxos. From Lakka boats go to the sea caves on the west coast.

Festival: 15 August on the islet of Panagia and at Gaio.

LEFKAS
Lefkas Town
Hotels: Nikos (on the Yiro), Lefkas (B); Byzantion (E).
There is a *campground* on the beach of Spasmeni Vrisi (3 kms).

The town has a *bank*, *post office* and a small *museum* in the library building.

Travel
Apart from the 3 daily *buses* from Athens and Patras, there are 4 daily from Preveza. There are periodic *boats* between Ithaka and Nidri on the east coast.

From Lefkas town *buses* travel regularly down to Nidri and Vliho on the east coast and to Vassiliki on the south coast.

Around the Island
On the east coast at **Nidri** you will find rooms, camping and many tavernas, and a reasonable beach, also boats to **Meganissi** and other islets. At **Vliho** there is a beach and rooms, with camping at Dessimi, while **Poros** has a beach and a campground. **Vassiliki** on the south coast is an attractive fishing village, with swimming, rooms, tavernas, etc, where you might be able to get a boat across to Kefallonia or Ithaka. From here you could take a long walk to **Cape Doukato**. On the northwest of the island **Agios Nikitas** has a sandy beach.

Festivals
Lefkas town has a festival for a fortnight each August, with folk dancing, theatre, etc. Karia has a 2-day festival on 11 and 12 August in honour of St Spiridon.

ITHAKA
In addition to the *boats* every other day on the Patras-Corfu run, there are boats between Vathi and Nidri (Lefkas) several times a week and daily boats from Sami (Kefallonia) and Patras.

Vathi
Hotels: Mentor (near town beach), Odysseus (B); Actaeon (E). *Rooms* also.

There are *tavernas*, a *bank* and *post office*.

The *museum*, behind the Mentor hotel, has a large collection of vases; open mornings.

There is a *music and theatre festival* at the end of August and through the first fortnight of September.

Buses run round the island to Stavros, Frikes and Kioni, leaving about 3 times a day. *Caiques* also go to Frikes and Kioni. *Mopeds* can be hired.

Around the Island
The **Cave of the Naiads** to the southwest is signposted 'Marmarospilia'; take a flashlight. **Perapigadi** is about one hour to the south from Vathi. There are beaches at **Pisaetos**, **Agios Ioannis** and **Polis Bay**. **Stavros** has some rooms to rent and some tavernas; if you take the short walk to **Pelikata**, you should make sure that the museum will be open (the schoolmaster in Stavros keeps the key). There are beaches and rooms both at **Frikes** and **Kioni**; from Frikes there are occasional boats to Vassiliki on Lefkas. None of the beaches on Ithaka is spectacular.

KEFALLONIA
All the *ferries* arrive at Sami except for the boat from Killini which goes to Poros. There is also the more expensive *hydrofoil* service in summer between Patras and Argostoli (3 hours compared to $3\frac{1}{2}$ hours on the ferry from Patras to Sami). Fiskardo has boats to Lefkas, Ithaka and Paxos (see below).

On the island there is a poor *bus* service, and on occasions you may be forced to use *taxis*; alternatively you can *hire your own transport*.

Sami
Hotels: Ionion (C); Kyma (on the square) (D). Also *rooms*. There is a *campground* at Karavomilos Beach.

There is a *bank* and *post office*.

There are about 3 *buses* a day from Sami to Argostoli, usually connecting with the ferries, and there is also a bus to Fiskardo. *Mopeds* can be hired.

From Sami you can visit *Drongarati cave* (4 kms) off the Argostoli road, or nearer and more dramatic the sea cave of *Melissani*, about half an hour's walk to the west. Both remain open all day.

Argostoli
Hotels: Xenia (B); and numerous C and D class hotels. Try also the accommodation on the beaches to the south.
Tavernas: Try Kalaphate by the market; also many on the waterfront. While on the island you should try the local Rombola wine.
NTOG, Plateia Metaxa; *Tourist Police* on the waterfront.

The *Archaeological Museum* is open 9am to 1pm, 4 to 6pm daily, 10.30am to 2.30pm Sundays and holidays, closed Tuesdays. The *Folk Museum* is open as above but is closed on Sundays.

Argostoli has a slightly better *bus* service than Sami, with buses to Platis Yialos, Poros, Assos and Fiskardo, apart from the 3 a day to Sami. You can hire *cars* and *mopeds*.

There are good *beaches* to the south, or take a caique across to the lovely beach of *Agios Georgios*. *Platis Yialos* has the White Rocks Hotel (A), tavernas, discos, etc. At *Agia Pelagi* there is the Irinna (B), and to the north at *Lassi* there is the Mediterranean (A) and a couple of C class hotels.

Around the Island
Lixouri is served by ferries from Argostoli. You can hire mopeds here. Hotels include the Ionios Avra (D). There is a small pebbly beach, but Agios Georgios to the south is a lovely sandy beach.

In the centre of the island apart from the Castle of St George you can visit near the village of Frangata the **Monastery of Agios Gerasimos** (closes over midday) which has the silver sarcophagus of the patron saint of the island. St Gerasimos has a feast day on 16 August. You can also drive to the summit of **Mt Ainos**, with wonderful views.

On the south coast there are good sandy beaches at **Afratos**, **Katelios** and **Nea Skala**. Nea Skala is a fishing village with the hotel Skala (C). There is a festival at **Makropoulou** on 15 August when some harmless snakes are coaxed into making an appearance.

Poros on the east coast has a good sandy beach also, and the hotels Hercules (B) and Atros Poros (C), rooms for rent and some good tavernas.

Assos, on the north coast, with the hotel Myrto (B), is near the superb beach of Myrto to the south, formerly unspoilt, but finally overrun by visitors in 1984. A ferry calls weekly at **Fiskardo** on the Patras-Kefallonia-Paxos-Corfu run. There are also local boats to Vassiliki on Lefkas and Stavros on Ithaka in summer. Fiskardo is one of the ports of call for the flotillas, and restaurants can get very crowded in the evenings. Try the hotel Panormos (B), and the Erodotos taverna (but go early).

North of Sami, **Agia Efthimia** with its little harbour may be preferable to Fiskardo or Sami; it has the hotel Pilaros (C).

ZAKINTHOS
In addition to the Killini *ferry* there is a daily *hydrofoil* from Patras.

Zakinthos Town
Hotels: Xenia, Strada Marina (B); Diana, Phoenix (C); Rezenta (D). Also *rooms*. There is a *hostel* and *camping* at the Turtle Bay Club.

For *tavernas* try Kallinikos or Kokkinos Vrahos. While on the island sample the local red wine. There are *discos* in town.

The *Tourist Police* are at 2 Lomvardou Street. There are *banks* and a *post office*.

The *Neo-Byzantine Museum* is open 9am to 1pm and 4 to 6pm, closed Tuesdays. The *Solomos Museum* has similar hours but is closed Mondays.

The town *beach* is poor; go elsewhere. You can get a caique to the north end of the island to see the *Blue Grotto*, worth the trip.

From the bus station on Philita Street there is a *bus* service to villages throughout the island, but usually once or twice a day at most.

There is an annual *theatre festival* in August, and there are processions on the feast days of St Dionysos on 24 August and 17 December.

Around the Island

At **Tsilivi** beach (Planos) there are several C class hotels (try the Tsilivi) and campgrounds. *Alikes* also has a number of small hotels; of these try Montreal (C). Also rooms. There is moped hire, and there are boats to the Blue Grotto. **Lagana** has some 25 hotels and is best avoided. **Argassi** south of Zakinthos town also has a sandy beach with a few mostly B class hotels, but quieter is **Vassilikos** near the sandy beach of Porto Roma, where there is hotel and room accommodation and a campground, or **Keri** which has a good beach with tavernas below it and rooms; 2 buses a day go from Zakinthos to both places.

THE CYCLADES

Islands of the Wine-Dark Sea

The Aegean

Greece is a country of two equal and intermingling parts, land and sea; and the Greek is as much at home when ploughing the blue Aegean as when growing vines among the high islands of his mountain villages. Obsidian from the island of Milos unearthed in a cave in the Argolid at a level corresponding to a date of 7000 BC is the earliest evidence of sea-borne trade anywhere in the world. By 2500 BC a fairly homogeneous culture extended over the length and breadth of the Aegean. Already the 'wine-dark sea' was at the heart of the Greek world.

Sea routes

One of the greatest pleasures of a visit to Greece is to sail these waters from island to island. Piraeus is usually your starting-point and you follow the sea routes like the spokes of a wheel. Often you have to double back to Piraeus to reach another group of islands on another spoke unless you can cut across on a wave-scudding caique. Or from Syros, Mykonos, Naxos and Rhodes you can set out on a lesser spin of radiations.

There are 1425 islands in the Aegean but only 166 are inhabited. Many are all but barren and rise from the sea like carved and sculptured rock; the withering light 'seems to melt, as if it were eating the islands; it lies heavy like the sheaves of a yellow harvest made of air, flattened into wide smooth circles like the sun' (Freya Stark). Where forests grew they have long since gone for triremes and caiques; the ubiquitous goat has reduced the land to desiccated steppe. That is not always true, but it is true often enough; and even where the inhabitants can stretch a living from their vineyards, their oil, their fishing, it may not be sufficient to dissuade them from their age-old recourse – emigration to the mainland cities or abroad. To counteract this, many islands are being scheduled for tourist development. Airports, extra shipping services, modern hotels and discotheques lure tourists who spend money which improves the islanders' standard of living. Sometimes it is done well – and it is often the larger islands that are able to absorb visitors without losing their Greek character; occasionally the result is disastrous. There are still many islands where the boat rarely calls, where life is traditional, where knowing some Greek would help, and where too the visitor should expect little in the way of amenities and, importantly, immediate medical help. There are benefits either way according to your circumstances and desires.

Traditional and tourist-developed islands

The Cyclades (Kýklades) in the central Aegean form a rough circle (*kýklos*) around sacred Delos upon which they were dependent in ancient times, though the islands more

Cycladic architecture

perfectly encircle Syros, capital of the modern nome. Neither uninhabited Delos nor Latin-flavoured Syros, however, offer examples of that sparkling white-cubed architecture for which the Cyclades are so well known. Houses are often linked together, forming blank fortress-like exterior walls, bastion after cubic bastion rising up the hillsides behind, a bewildering maze of narrow lanes within, defences in fact against the pirates who terrorised the Aegean until the early 19th C. Often the principal village or town of an island, Chora as it is locally called (though usually it officially takes the name of the island itself), was located well inland for this reason; only in the past century or so have the little island ports really come to life, leaving the old choras marooned on their heights.

The Northern Cyclades

Two of the Northern Cyclades can only be reached from ports in Attica: boats for Andros leave Rafina (which also serves other Cycladic islands) and for Kea they leave Lavrion (which also serves Kithnos). The others can be reached from Piraeus.

Ándros

Andros is an impressively mountainous and well-wooded extension of Euboea. It is the second largest of the Cyclades, the prosperous island home of many shipowning families who have built fine houses in Chora and villas scattered here and there on the sea-gazing slopes. Deep valleys deep in vegetation often shut out the sea though, and the island can seem still bigger than it is. It is an island for sailors and campers; its lack of sophistication, a near-absence of antiquities, also having first to go to Rafina to reach here, should protect it from the more strident forms of tourism. Those tourists who do come concentrate on **Batsí**, with its harbour and sandy beach, and its string of villas and hotels. Here and at **Gávrion**, the other and major port (8 kms north), is gathered such fast life as there is; ignore it and strike inland for the many unspoilt villages, **Arni** is one, or to **Agios Petros** (45 minutes' walk from Gavrion or Batsi) with its strange *Hellenic tower*, 20 metres high.

A road climbs south from Batsi between mountain and sea and at 8 kms overhangs the scant but superbly sited remains of **Paleopolis**; you come not to ruin-hunt but to enjoy what must have been one of the finest harbour settings of the ancient world. The road continues inland and runs high above the beautiful valley of Messaria, thick with the sizzle of cicadas in summer, in spring the snows still capping Mt Kovari and the fields full of flowers, and then descend to the far (east) side of the island where (at 24 kms) **Chora**

(Andros), mansioned and picturesque, presides over beaches facing the cooling northern breezes of the open sea.

Kéa

Despite its proximity to Attica, Kea was until recently one of the least visited of the Cyclades. Much of the land is idle, and the hillsides are carved with defunct terraces. You land in the northwest, in the attractive small port of **Livádi** (classical Korissia). Round the bay to the east is the fishing village of **Vourkári** (beaches both here and by the port), opposite which on a promontory a *Minoan-type palace* (known as Agia Irini) is being excavated. About 5 kms above the port is the **Chóra**. This was ancient Ioulis and vestiges of an ancient temple are visible in the ruined *Venetian kastro*. Ten minutes walk to the east, amongst mulberry trees, there is a large *lion*, carved out of the rock.

But the charming little Cycladic town is a relic of a more recent age, of a time before the drift from the land. Paved mule tracks wind between the fields in the surprisingly rich interior, making for pleasant walks – to ancient *Poiessa* (modern Pisses) on the west coast via the deserted monastery of *Agia Marina*, built into a fine Hellenic tower; or to **Karthaía** on the east coast where there is an ancient acropolis, with ruins of a Doric *temple of Apollo* beautifully situated on a platform overlooking the sandy shore.

Sýros

Until the growth of Piraeus early this century, **Ermoúpolis** on Syros was the major port of the Aegean and is still the largest town in the Cyclades. Mills and tanneries around the bay, dry docks opened in the last two decades or so, and the sight of several large freighters awaiting the welder's torch are all signs of a modest revival and pleasing for their unexpectedness and incongruity. The town is handsomely 19th C, with much neo-classical and Italianate architecture. The quayside is lined with lively cafés and tavernas, and with shops selling loukoumi (Turkish Delight), a speciality of the island. But going up Odos Ermou to the grandiose *Plateia Miaouli* with its public buildings, its arcaded cafés, its opera house where no opera has been performed since 1914 – these are the rouge on cheeks that have lost their bloom.

Centre of Catholicism
The double breasts of *Ano-Sýros* (on the left) and *Vrontado*, each surmounted by a large church, rise behind the lower town; the latter is the Orthodox quarter, the former the Roman Catholic – Syros and Tinos are the centres of Catholicism in Greece, a legacy of Venetian domination and, on Syros, later French protection as well.

Galissás, **Fínikas** and **Delagrátsia**, all to the southwest, have good beaches – their names recall, as does the island

itself, what is probably the most popular of Greek songs, *Frankosiriani* (Frankosyrian Girl), by Markos Vamvakaris:
> A spark, a flame inside my heart –
> It's as if you've bewitched me, sweet Frankosyrian girl.
> I'll come to meet you again on the shore,
> I'd like to gorge myself on caresses and kisses.
> I'll take you around Finikas, Parakopi,
> Galissas and Delagratsia until I drop dead.
> To Pateli, to Neochori, we'd enjoy Alithini
> And find romance at Biskopo, my sweet Frankosyrian girl.

The edge is that *frankosiriani* means a Catholic girl of Syros; there is a suggestion of exotic if not quite forbidden fruit.

Tínos

On 25 March and 15 August, lame and sick pilgrims from all over Greece come to the *church of the Panagia Evangelistria* on Tinos with its wonder-working ikon in hope of a cure. There is nothing lame or sick about the inhabitants who with miraculous alacrity accost their visitors with all manner of religious gee-gaws – causing other islanders to warn, 'They will rob you of all you possess'. The town has some traces of Venetian architecture and an ordered, relentless whiteness. The interior is more interesting, with its compact Cycladic hamlets picked out in white upon the green hillsides and – as on Andros – the intricate lace-like designs of the many Venetian dovecotes, the local expression of an imported Italian mania for building towers. The best swimming, protected from the meltemi, is in the quiet bay of **Agios Nikitas** on the west coast of the island.

Mýkonos

The Cycladic town *par excellence*

The impact of Mykonos is only felt once you get within it. From the boat deck you see it built upon a barely sloping crescent projecting from the featureless hills behind: it lacks the drama of Hydra's climbing amphitheatre with its harbour as the stage. But Mykonos' defence against marauding pirates – and in 1822 the Turkish navy – was to construct a casbah closed to the sea, a confusing maze of narrow cobbled streets where sounds carry with crystal clarity, where whitewashed houses are almost painfully dazzling. Architecturally, the town is best appreciated during the sauna-heat of siesta, or well past midnight at full moon when its cubes and cupolas seem lit by an interior radiance – during those few hours, that is, of asbestos silence when Mykonos retires into its shell and is no longer playing the role of Cycladic Carnaby Street, filled with funfair noises and funfair people.

Only one of the famous windmills still flutters – flour is ground on the mainland and imported; Mykonos has found easier ways of making money. The international set comes in

Fleshpots droves, the nightlife is wild and rock and roll rampages from the stereo speakers of alleyway discotheques. Uncountable boutiques sell souvenirs, jewellery and the strikingly coloured weaves for which Mykonos has always been noted. A quiet kafeneion is hard to find and the tavernas are scenes, even for Greece, of exceptional pandemonium. If it is a party you want, this is it, especially if you are gay.

There is respite, however, at the unvisited *Archaeological Museum* at the north end of the harbour. The prize is a 7th C BC pithos depicting the Trojan war in archaic comic-strip form. Achaean warriors, faintly conscious of seeming ridiculous, peer from hatches in the flanks of their wooden horse-on-wheels.

Beaches on the exposed north coast are badly hit by the meltemi; better to head south. Crossing the island, bright white little churches, especially gay with their red-painted roofs, illuminate the parched fields and stony hillsides. A bus runs to **Platís Yialós**; from there you walk or take a boat **Nude beaches** (boats also from town) to the nude beaches beyond (**Paradise, Super Paradise, Elia**), all excellent, with good sand and superb crystal clear water.

Délos

On mornings when the meltemi is not blowing too strongly, several small boats set out on the 30-minute crossing to Delos. You are usually given three hours to scoot through it all, which can just be enough, otherwise a second visit is necessary. (It would be nice to stay at the Xenia here but its four rooms seem always to be taken by archaeologists.) The problem is that everyone comes to the island at once and you have little time to linger, little opportunity to feel the place. Maybe that is why you might think Delos overrated: in summer its extensive tracts of foundations and sculptureless pedestals – particularly in the area of the sacred and public buildings – lay about like burnt sliced onions on this small dry brown frying pan of an island. In springtime it is different, with bright red poppies and the white and delicate blues of anemones bobbing about on the green waves of long-stemmed grasses. Holy places impress themselves upon you through all your senses and it might be better not to rush about but to touch the stones – 'The modest stones of **The Sacred Isle** Greeks,/ Who gravely interrupted death by pleasure.' (Durrell) – and catch the fragrance of the season, for here the radiant Apollo was born and 'all Delos was immeasurably filled with ambrosial perfume; and the vast earth laughed, and the deeps of the grey sea did rejoice' (Theognis of Megara).

Pregnant by Zeus and rejected by every spot of earth at **Birth of** jealous Hera's bidding, Leto finally found humble refuge **Apollo** where Poseidon had fixed floating Delos to the sea-bed. Here

249

on Mt Kynthos according to one version of the myth, by the Sacred Lake according to another, Leto in her labour stood grasping a date palm while Artemis, born to her the day before, assisted at her brother's birth.

History of the island

Enrichment of the island began after the Persian wars when the treasury of Athens' maritime league was located here until removed to the imperial city in 454 BC. Following the plague that killed Pericles and thousands of others at Athens in the early years of her war with Sparta, the Athenians, at the command of an oracle, in 426 BC purified Delos, disinterring its dead and decreeing that no-one must ever die or be born here again.

At that time the Delian Festival in honour of Artemis and Apollo was restored and the Delian Games instituted, taking place every four years. But in Hellenistic and Roman times the festival became no more than an excuse for international trade fairs; Syrian, Egyptian and other merchants founded important trading houses at Delos; the population swelled to 20,000; and the island became the largest slave market in Greece, as many as 10,000 slaves sold here in a single day. In 88 BC, during the First Mithridatic War, the Parthian general Menophanes, by way of striking against Rome, seized the island, killed every man on it, and sold all its women and children into slavery in turn. The city was razed to the ground, never to recover; in the 2nd C AD Pausanias observed that if the temple guard were withdrawn the island would be uninhabited.

Depredations

Turks and Venetians worked the marble ruins as a quarry; nearby islanders and classically-minded English aristocrats embellished their homes with fragments of sculpture bought or looted; and the colossal Apollo, cut base and figure from a single block of Naxian marble, still recognisably intact when sketched by the Dutch painter Segur de Vries in 1672, was soon after reduced to the near-formless torso that you see today, the rest having been hacked away and taken to the lime kilns. Since 1873 Delos has been excavated by the French School; the finest sculpture has been removed to Athens, the shattered remainder exhibited in the island's museum.

Touring the site. A selection of guide books to the site can be obtained at the tourist pavilion. The highlights of the visit are the dismembered Apollo, the Lions and the Sacred Lake, the residential and theatre quarter, and the climb up Mt Kynthos.

Except in rough weather, you land at a point between the **Sacred Harbour** on the left, the **maritime quarter** with its warehouses on the right, and ascend to the wide, paved **Sacred Way** leading off to your left. At its far end, to the right, is a vast precinct, the **Sanctuary of Apollo**, enclosing

The sacred precincts

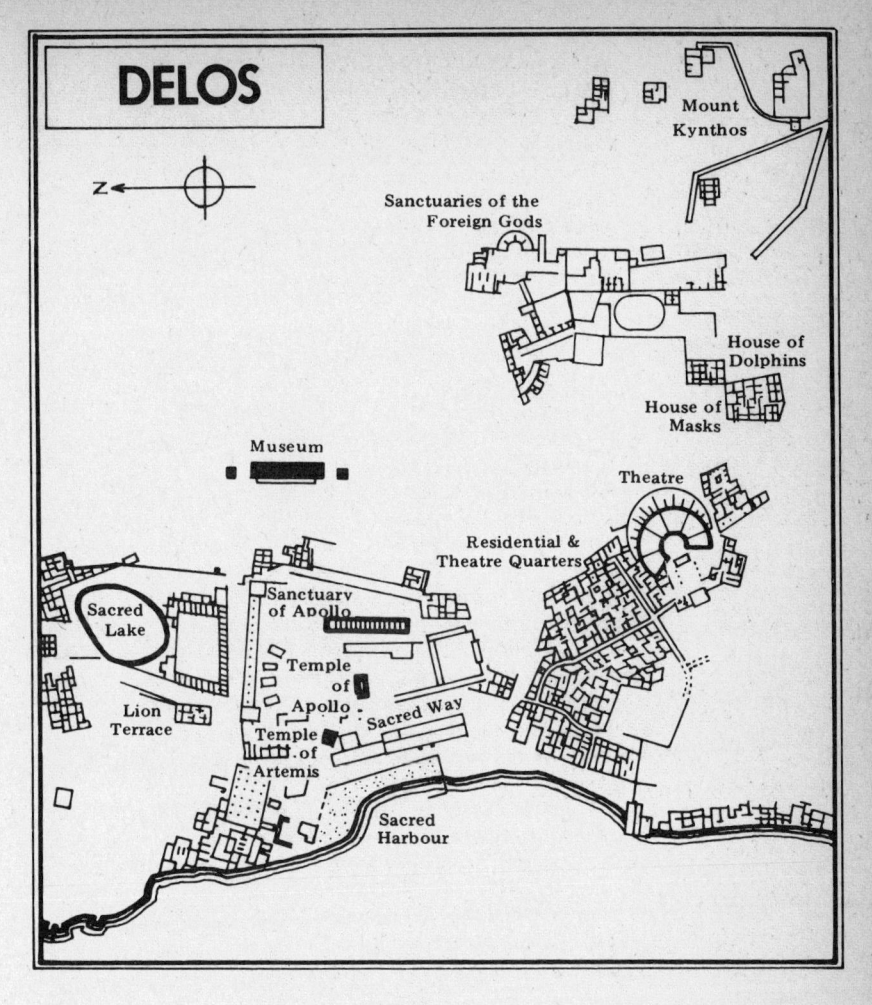

temples, altars and other vestiges of 1000 years of worship.

The *Great Temple of Apollo* is here, and in front of it the *base* on which the colossos stood. Left of the Sacred Way, by the *Temple of Artemis*, you will find the *colossos Apollo* lying broken out in the sun where the Venetians left it – so cool to the touch, even where the sun strikes it directly. Its mass is impressive and burgeoning still with an inner power – it really ought to be reassembled on its base.

Further on is the **Terrace of the Lions**, five lean beasts with eternity in their jaws; they survey the dried-up **Sacred Lake**, an evocative palm tree growing at its centre, planted by a French lady archaeologist in commemoration of Leto's labour.

The view from Mt Kynthos

Circling round the lake you come to the **museum** and the **tourist pavilion**, a short distance in front of which is the small **Sanctuary of Dionysos**, sporting several choregic monuments in the shape of huge phalluses. Passing through the **Sanctuaries of Foreign Gods** you begin the stepped ascent of **Mt Kynthos** (only 112 metres) where Apollo and Artemis were worshipped in archaic times and Cycladic dwellings of the late 3rd millenium have been found. But the reason for the climb is the sweeping view of the Cyclades. 'It is the most perfect imaginable island scenery, just as the mountain scenery of Apollo's other great shrine at Delphi is, as mountain scenery, the most perfect imaginable' (Robert Liddell) – it is a matter of luck: on a summer's day the haze can reduce Paros and Naxos to shadows and make Syros entirely invisible.

The ancient city

Between the foot of Mt Kynthos and the maritime quarter, Delos is like Pompeii. There is a fine view of the excavated city from the upper tiers of the **theatre**, abutting which is a three-storey **hotel** where visitors to the festival may have stayed. Further uphill is the **House of the Masks**, named after its *mosaic pavement*, perhaps a hostel for actors. The paved street descending from the theatre is lined with Hellenistic and Roman workshops and expansive villas set around open courtyards such as the **House of Dionysos** and the **House of the Trident**, again named after their vividly coloured *mosaics*. There is a sense of bustle only temporarily absent, the long centuries of silence a passing siesta.

The Eastern Cyclades

Barren landscapes and declining populations mark **Kíthnos** and **Kímolos**, two islands served on the eastern Cyclades run (see the *Practical Information* section for details on these).

Sérifos

On Serifos, at least, the rocky and mountainous terrain achieves some character and from the hot landlocked harbour hard-worked terraces rise against a bony crag, the **Chóra** like a wave breaking on its edge. It is rewarding to make the steep walk up, and then back for a swim in the sand-rimmed bay. In summer usually one boat calls here daily enroute for Sifnos and Milos.

Sífnos

The landing at Sifnos is made at the unattractive Bay of Kamares; this whole west coast is bare and unappealing and to the traveller merely sailing by conveys an erroneous impression of the island. You must take the bus the 5 kms up to the Cycladic villages of **Apollonía** or **Artemónas** which undulate along the island's spine; individually, their houses are as fine as those on Mykonos, though the composition suffers from lack of compression. Artemonas has several good tavernas and a lively nightlife. The eastern slopes of the island dropping down below are well-watered and green; **Kástro**, on the coast, turns out to be one of the loveliest villages in the Aegean with a delightfully medieval air with arches and projecting wooden balconies, its crumbling Venetian houses hugged against the hillside by 14th C walls, built perhaps from the stones of the island's ancient capital here. The longest beach in the Cyclades is on the south coast, at **Platís Yialós**, now developing as a resort.

Mílos

Volcanic Milos, its mountains encircling a great gouging bay, was once a pirate haven where the pasha was paid to turn a blind eye while the inhabitants prospered through the disposal of booty. It has always benefited from the mining of its volcanic rocks, and in the prehistoric period the island produced obsidian. The port of **Adámas** is unremarkable, but there is the strange sight of purple-blossomed brine trees watered by the sea, and along the bay's encircling peaks the glittering sentinels of shrines and chapels; Adamas remains, probably, the best place to stay.

    A winding road ascends to the island's capital, **Plaka** (4 kms), burning white against the volcanic soil. It spreads across the acropolis of the ancient city where near the walls the *Venus de Milo* was found in 1820 and spirited off to the Louvre. Nearby are extensive early *Christian catacombs*. Thucydides dramatically presents that moment of arrogance, with Nemesis standing in the wings, when the Athenian envoys argue that might has given them the right to dictate to the Melians. Only after months of siege did the Melians surrender, the men put to death, the women and children sold into slavery.

    You can also stay at the fishing village of **Apollónia**, opposite Kimolos, about 2 kms from **Phylokopé** where excavations have revealed at Minoan/Mycenaean city. There is a good beach here.

The Venus de Milo

Minoan colony

The Central and Southern Cyclades

Daily boats from Piraeus, often calling at Syros enroute, serve the central and southern Cyclades – in particular Paros, Naxos, los and Thera (Santorini). (The *Practical Information* section contains details on both these major and some of the minor islands.)

Páros

The symmetry of Profitas Ilias (771 metres) and the gentle contour of its slopes already from a distance establish the coherence and harmony that make Paros the most endearing island of the Cyclades. The island is this single mountain, its skirts the flaring coastal plain, treeless but cultivated with wheat and barley and the vineyards that produce the island's dark red wine. The genial impression is confirmed as you enter its broad bay, sand beaches and a scattering of villas and farmsteads around it, the island's main village, **Paroikía**, running over a slight rise in the shoreline to the right – a rhythm of white houses and blue domes, a ruined 13th C *Venetian kastro* (incorporating the remains of a temple of Demeter) and a few windmills – a visual iambic recalling Archilochos, the 8th C BC lyric poet who was the first to write in that metre and was born on Paros.

Paroikia has the architecture if not the size of Mykonos – nor has it been transformed by a surfeit of tourist-minded shops and tavernas. The main street soon establishes its own Greek tempo, past small fruit shops and grocers to whitewashed walls cascading with bougainvillea and houses large and small of modest grandeur, graceful arches decorating some, outside staircases on others leading to upper-storey balconies. A solitary bell suspended from its tower leads you round another corner in search of its hidden chapel. Though only three or four streets in depth, it is possible to get lost altogether.

Finest church in the Aegean

Paroikia's cathedral, the *Panagia Ekatontapiliani* ('of the hundred doors', though more likely a corruption of *katapoliani*, 'on lower ground'), is the finest in the Aegean. Said to have been founded by St Helena, mother of Constantine, on the spot where she had her vision of the True Cross, the existing church was built two centuries later at the behest of Justinian by the same architects of the great Agia Sophia in Constantinople. Not that you should expect magnificence; interest lies in its peculiarities, for it is really three churches in one: the main cruciform structure with a patterned interior of green, purple and yellow stone; the basilica of Agios Nikolaos, its columns from a 6th C BC Doric temple, to the left of the apse; and a baptistry off the south transept with a font for total immersion. There is an *archaeological museum* behind the church.

Paros assisted the Persians at Marathon, so that Miltiades later led an expedition against the island and while failing to take it broke his leg and died of gangrene. After the defeat of Xerxes, Paros became subject to Athens and her marble preferred for sculpture. The *quarries* lie about 8 kms east of Paroikia – abandoned for centuries, marble was again taken from them in 1844 for Napoleon's tomb.

Following a lovely green valley to the north coast you come to the fishing village of **Náoussa** (10 kms) with its tiny caique harbour, half-submerged kastro and good beaches freshened by breakers rolling in past the headland. The building of half a dozen big hotels here, however, is fast destroying all charm. The *Valley of the Butterflies* is 10 kms in the other direction – in fact an area of ivy-covered trees at the foot of a slope, with many bright orange moths. There is another such valley on Rhodes, where the tourists nearly outnumber the moths – at least that is not the case here. A caique from Paroikia takes you to the islet of **Antíparos** where in a vast cavern, seemingly supported by stalagmite columns, the French Ambassador to the Porte celebrated midnight mass on Christmas 1673, illuminating the cave with hundreds of torches, and paying 500 bemused Parians to attend.

Náxos

Naxos is the largest of the Cyclades, the gauntness of its interior relieved by fertile and well-watered valleys beyond sight or salt of the sea where the air is sweet with an earthy fragrance. Lemons and oranges, figs and pomegranates provide the islanders with a healthy income, which along with their traditional coolness towards visitors adds up to a reluctance to compromise with modern tourism. Byron liked it. The main road winds through a graceful valley, dividing the northern from the southern ranges, to the olive-covered plain of Tragaias where **Chalkí**, a Cycladic village interspersed with Venetian towerhouses and Byzantine churches, sits below medieval walls; it then continues to **Filóti**, on the north flank of Mt Zia (1003 metres – highest in the Cyclades), the largest village on the island, and to **Apíranthos**, a decaying though beautiful white village towards the far side of the island. The road descends to the coast at **Apóllonas** where a *colossal unfinished kouros* lies in the quarry and the beach is covered with smooth-worn marble stones.

The Dukes of Naxos From 1207 until 1566 when the Turks took the island, **Náxos town** was the capital of the Venetian dukes whose feudal sway extended over the entire Cyclades. Their memory is preserved by the occasional coat of arms over house-fronts along the handsome streets of the upper town within the medieval *walls*, in the middle of which stands their 13th C *cathedral*. On an islet connected to the town by a causeway is a great marble rectangle, the *portal to a temple of Apollo* (c530 BC), framing Delos in the distance – though **Ariadne and Dionysos** some, recalling how 'gently and sweetly, Dionysos, with his merry train of satyrs and maenads, came to Ariadne's rescue' (Robert Graves) after Theseus abandoned her here on his way home to Athens from Knossos, ascribe the temple to the god of wine. Naxian wine is good, but you should make a point of pausing along the quayside to enjoy a citron, the local liqueur, a distillation of the sweetness, bite and fragrance of the lemon's flesh and peel.

There are excellent sandy beaches south of Agia Anna, but

no road to them – you need good feet for the daily walk, or should take a tent and water for a longer stay.

Amorgós
The most easterly of the Cyclades, primitive and unspoilt Amorgos rises like a wall from the sea, three mountain peaks along its narrow spine, precipitous cliffs along its south coast. Sheer walls guard the entrance to the harbour at **Katápola**, too, at the centre of the island, a lively place considering its small size, and with good beaches. The ruins of ancient **Minoa** lie above, and an hour's steep climb beyond is the **Chóra**, wonderful mountain scenery all around; and finally, built into a cliffside across the island is possibly the most magnificently situated monastery in Greece, the **Hozoviotíssa**, pendent over the blue.

Íos
Ios derives its name from the Ionians who with their unfailing sense for the graceful settled on this beautiful island. Homer is said to have died here, though the tomb claimed as his at Plakotos, at the north tip, is a much earlier prehistoric grave. Arrival is through a winding bay, the Chora clinging to the first of three symmetrical hills, charming at a distance. You imagine it inviolate, belonging to another world. It has in fact been ruined over the past decade or so by a plague of locusts who pack snack bars, boutiques and discotheques, appreciating nothing, giving nothing, taking everything. It is better to sail on.

Armpit of the Aegean

Síkinos and **Folégandros** to the west are the two driest islands of the Cyclades and barely populated. Their Choras, and what cultivation there is, are set well back from the coasts – remarkably precipitous in the case of Folegandros. Of the two, only Folegandros has begun to be developed for tourism.

Théra
At the change of seasons, spring and autumn, the Aegean can suddenly rise to violence. Battering hailstones and gale force winds drive you through the Naxos channel. Against the wet watercolour sky of mingling black and grey, Thera's odd abrupt outline, a smashed asteroid flung from the cosmos by some mightier-than-Olympian god, defies the furious waves. By night, pressed against the cathedral wall at clifftop Phira, listening to the shrieking wind which tears at corners and at rooftops, watching incandescent talons ripping through the black curtains of the horizon, it seems the entire island might yet crack and tumble into the sea. You have never so much doubted the ground on which you stand. Your arrival may not be so atmospheric – but any will do.

Thera (Santoríni) is the most extraordinary island in the

Aegean, extraordinary for its beauty, its history, its tragedy and the legends of a lost world which have struck a chord of wonder and yearning over thousands of years. Only 96 kms north of Crete, this was a highly sophisticated outpost of Minoan civilisation built, unwittingly, upon one of the greatest volcanoes on earth. Around 1450 BC the island was torn apart by an explosion unequalled by man or nature since, and as its greater part was hurled through the sky or sank beneath the sea, so also, some believe, a gigantic tsunami broke upon the shores of Minoan Crete, mortally wounding that most graceful of civilisations. The memory of the event may have entered the mythology of Mediterranean man, surviving in the legend of Atlantis.

Sailing into the caldera

Today you sail into the great *caldera* of the shattered volcano, its ribboned pumice walls rising hundreds of metres sheer above you. These are the cliffs of crescent **Thera**; the circular outline is continued to the west by **Therasia**, 9 kms distant. Floating islands of gathered pumice chunks roll within this inland sea, the black jagged lava dome of **Kaimeni** island, the new volcano which last seriously erupted in 1938–41, at its centre. The boat calls first below Oia at the northwest horn of Thera, and then either berths at Ormos Athinios (buses and taxis to Phira), weather permitting, or anchors off Skala Phira from where you make the 30-minute zig-zag climb (205 metres) on foot or mule (or use the new cable car) to Phira running high along the cliff edge. From up here, Kaimeni sits like a gigantic black octopus within the lagoon, still active, sometimes smoking, and as a prelude to further eruptions or earthquakes usually discolouring the water around it. Kaimeni can be visited by motorboat from Skala Phira.

Dovecote on Tinos

Half **Phirá** was destroyed by earthquake in 1956. Some houses have been abandoned, others built further along, but all still hang upon the precipice, staring into the abyss which sooner or later will shrug or yawn and bring them down again. Why do these people do it? Every observation suggests that the land is used more extensively, more productively on Thera than anywhere else in Greece. Perhaps they don't want to build upon any of their usable soil. Despite its sterile appearance late in summer, the soil produces an abundance of tomatoes, wheat (there are numerous threshing-floors around the island) – and excellent grapes for wine. In this case tourism is complementary to the staple product, since it is the tourists who consume most of the wine.

The 2½ hour walk to **Oía**, a smaller, run-down version of Phira, takes you after a short distance through **Skaros**, the ruined medieval capital built by the Naxian dukes. In spring musk thistles grow from the castle walls, a delicate pink stock clings to the cliffs, and as you walk on there are beautiful views down the intricately-terraced slopes, bright red and yellow with corn poppies and Bermuda buttercups, with Anafi, Amorgos and Ios across the blue. Another excursion, southeast, is to the *monastery* on Megalos Agios Ilias, the highest point on the island (566 metres), from where you can see the mountains of Crete. At its base is **Pírgos**, with many fine old Cycladic houses and a blank-walled ruined Venetian kastro. **Ancient Thera** (signposted) is another hour's walk (or by bus or taxi). The ruins are strikingly situated on the rocky spine of Mesa Vouno, the black sand beaches of **Kamari** (the ancient port) to the north, **Perissa** to the south. No one building is particularly well-preserved; the site is more important for its position and its extent. The ruins are mostly Ptolemaic – Kamari was an Egyptian naval station – but the site was inhabited from the 9th C BC through Byzantine times.

The Minoan settlement at Akrotiri

On the southwest horn of the island, 1 km beyond the village of **Akrotíri** (12 kms), are the excavations of the *Minoan settlement* that have turned up the magnificent frescoes now in Athens. Reproductions, as at Knossos, would enhance the visitor's appreciation of the site, but still it is fascinating. Banks of ash have been pushed back around the buildings, some of them two and three storeys high. They were first damaged by earthquake and then two to three years later buried by the great eruption of c1450 BC. Professor Marinatos, who led the excavations from 1967, is buried within one of the buildings he uncovered, opposite where he was killed in 1974 by a collapsing wall.

Back in Phira the *museum* contains mostly Geometric through Roman artefacts, though a new museum for the Akrotiri frescoes, etc, should be completed soon – an extraordinary intention considering the geological possibilities.

PRACTICAL INFORMATION

TRAVEL TO AND WITHIN THE CYCLADES
Air. From *Athens* there are up to 9 flights daily to Mykonos, and 1 to 2 a day both to Milos and Thera (Santorini).
Sea. There is now a good service from *Rafina* in Attica. There is an average of 3 ferries a day to Andros in 3 hours (*note:* this is the only ferry route to the island); about 2 a day to Tinos (4 hours) and Mykonos (5 hours); usually one a day to Syros (3½ hours), Paros (5 hours) and Naxos (6½ hours).

From *Lavrion* in Attica there are 1 to 2 boats a day to Kea in 2½ hours (*note:* this is the only ferry route to Kea) and about 2 weekly to Kithnos (4 hours).

For these services and all the many boats from Piraeus the best advice is to get an *up-to-date* timetable from the NTOG office in Syntagma or elsewhere.

Some general points about the boats from *Piraeus*. The popular islands have boats at least once a day. Most boats leave early in the morning between 7 and 9am. Many of the trips last most of the day, so be prepared with food (not always available on board, though there should be at least drinks; to be sure, bring your own water supply) and reading material

The following are the principal routes from *Piraeus*, though they are not completely self-contained. Brackets indicate places less frequently served on that route.
1. Syros (4 hours), Tinos (5 hours), Mykonos (5½ hours).
2. (Syros), Paros (7 hours), Naxos (8 hours), (Amorgos), Ios (11 hours), Thera/Santorini (12 hours), (Folegandros), (Sikinos).
3. Kithnos (4 hours), Serifos (5 hours), Sifnos (6 hours), Milos (8 hours), (Kimolos), (Ios), (Thera).

Each island will have signs outside the agencies advertising boats, so it is easy enough to plan the next step.

In addition to these main routes there are boats which for example continue on to Crete or link the Cyclades with say Rhodes or Samos. Some reference is made to these possibilities under the islands concerned.

Finally there is the hydrofoil service which runs several times a day between the central islands of Syros, Tinos, Mykonos, Paros, Naxos, and Ios. Remember that if your schedule is tight the hydrofoils do not run in rough weather.

ANDROS
The *ferry* arrives at Gavrio on the west coast, and *buses* run from Gavrio to Andros town (Chora) via Batsi, usually connecting with the ferries.

Andros town
Hotels: Paradissos (near beach), Xenia (B); Aegli (C). There are *rooms* to rent but few of them and they tend to be booked up. *Campground.*
Tavernas: try O Frangouris, and the Exochikon (by the beach).
Disco. Bank, post office, OTE, Tourist Police.

Reasonable sandy *beach* to the south, but the beaches on this side of the island are exposed.

The Archaeological Museum and Goulandris Museum (modern art) both close in the middle of the day and on Tuesdays.

Nearby **Apikia**, well-known for its mineral water, has 2 C class hotels (buses from Andros). **Korthio**, south of Chora (about 3 buses a day), has the hotel Korthio (C), rooms, tavernas, etc, and a small beach. There is a festival on 15 August.

Gavrio
Hotels: Aphrodite (B); Galaxias (D). Also *rooms*.
Taverna: Yiannoulis Valmas.
    Beach to the northwest.
    From Gavrio you can walk in about ¾ hour to the *ancient tower* of Agios Petros.

Batsi
Hotels: Lykion (B); of the several C class hotels try Chryssi Akti. Also *rooms*. *Tavernas, discos*, good sandy *beach*.

KEA
The Lavrion *ferry* is the only boat to Kea.

Buses run infrequently from Livadi (Korissia) to the Chora and to Vourkari.

Livadi
Hotel: Karthea (C). *Rooms.*

Many *tavernas* along the quay. *Disco* at the motel I Tzia Mas (B).

Tourist Police on the quayside.

Beyond **Vourkari** (tavernas and a few rooms) at the bay of **Otzias** there is a good beach with tavernas and rooms but it gets crowded in summer.

Chora
Hotel: Ioulis (B). A few *rooms*. *Bank, post office, OTE,* several *tavernas*.

There is a temporary display of finds from Agia Irini in the small *archaeological museum*.

There are swimming *beaches* with hotels at **Pisses** and at **Koundouro** on the west coast.

When on Kea you should try the local red wine called Mavriti.

KITHNOS
This quiet island, reached both from Piraeus and Lavrion, has several fine beaches.

Boats arrive either at **Loutra**, a spa on the northeast coast, or at **Merihas** on the west coast, depending on the weather. A bus runs across the island between Loutra and Merihas via **Kithnos (Chora)**.

There are beaches, rooms, tavernas, etc, at both ports; **Loutra** has the hotel Xenia (C), and **Merihas** the hotel Possidonion (C). There is little accommodation at the **Chora**, which possesses a number of churches with early ikons and frescoes. There are good beaches at **Driopis** (tavernas), **Kolona** and **Kanala**.

SYROS
Ermoupolis
Buses go from the waterfront to villages on the island like Galissas, Finikas and Possidonia (Delagratsia). There is a bus up to Ano-Syros. *Moped* hire.

Hotels: Hermes (near ferries) (B); Nissaki, Cycladikon (on Plateia Miaouli) (C). Some *rooms*; try the Elmot pension behind the harbour.

Restaurants: many along the quay (try the Forty Dragons for fish), also the Tembelis Taverna on Vrontado.

The *museum* next to the Town Hall has antiquities from Syros and some other islands; it closes at midday and on Tuesdays.

The *Tourist Police* are on the quay and the NTOG has an office in the main street. *Banks, post office, OTE* in and around the Plateia Miaouli.

There are good *beaches* at several places around the island: at **Kini**, **Galissas** (hotel Francoise, C), **Finikas** (several hotels, try Olympia C), and **Possidonia/Delagratsia** (which has hotels Delagratsia (B); Possidonion (C); and 1 or 2 others; several *tavernas*). **Vari** on the east coast is becoming a beach resort with half-a-dozen or more hotels; the beach at **Megas Yialos** (hotel Alexandra, C) is less busy. You should be able to find *rooms* at most of these places.

TINOS
Apart from the normal *ferry* run there are also daily *excursions* to Mykonos and Delos.

Tinos Town
Buses from the quay serve the island.

The town has many *hotels* and *rooms* to cater for the huge number of visitors to the Panagia, but accommodation is very difficult to find at the major festivals on 25 March and (especially) 15th August. Of the hotels away from these dates you might try the Poseidonion (C); and the Aegli (with restaurant) (D). Also *Tinos Camping.*

Numerous *tavernas* and *cafés* along the waterfront. Otherwise try To Koutouki.

The *church of the Panagia* is open 8.30am to 8.30pm, as are the adjacent Byzantine and sculpture *museums* and picture *gallery*.

The street parallel to the pilgrims' way up to the church has the *post office*, *OTE* and the *Archaeology Museum* (closed over midday and Tuesdays). The *Tourist Police* are at 5 L. Sohou Street. *Bank* on the quay.

Near the town there are *beaches* at **Kionia** to the west (Tinos Beach Hotel (A), with swimming pool, tennis courts, etc) and less far **Agios Fokas** to the east. There are good beaches at **Kolimpidra** and **Ormos Panormou** (rooms, tavernas) on the north coast and at **Agios Nikitas** (same) on the west.

One *excursion* from Tinos town would be to climb to the ruins of the Venetian castle at **Xombourgo**; there is a fine view. The ancient city lay below. For this take the bus for Pyrgos, and descend for Xinara. Excursions are arranged by Tinos Tours around the island.

MYKONOS

Apart from the normal *ferry* routes there is a boat twice a week for Patmos-Leros-Kalymnos-Kos-Rhodes, and one a week to Samos and Ikaria.

Mykonos Town

Daily boats at 9am to Delos, returning about 12.30.

Buses go regularly to Agios Stephanos, Ornos, Platis Yialos and Ano Mera, all from outside the Leto except for Platis Yialos which go from the square to the northeast of town. There are also boats to Paradise Beach, etc.

Car and *Moped* hire.

Hotels are usually booked in high season so any selection is probably academic, but you could try Leto (A); Theoxenia (B); Manto (C); and Philippi (D). You will be met by *room-renters* off the boat, but be prepared to bargain; otherwise try the back streets for *rooms*. In August you cannot be too choosy; take what you can. There is a *youth hostel*, and there is *camping* at Paradise Beach (best reached by boat).

There is an almost unlimited choice of restaurants and tavernas from chic to (almost) Greek, but try Spiro's on the harbour, the Fisherman's Taverna for seafood, and Marco Polo's. Prices on Mykonos are usually higher than elsewhere.

There are numerous *bars* and *discos* catering for all tastes and sexes. For *Greek dancing* there is Baboulas.

Banks, post office, OTE and *Tourist Police* are along the waterfront.

Archaeological Museum: 9am to 1pm, 6 to 8pm daily, 10am to 2pm Sundays and holidays. The *Museum of Folk Art*, open early evenings, is near the church of the Paraportiani (itself worth a visit), behind the OTE.

The town *beach* is bettered by many around the island. Beaches, all with tavernas, include **Agios Stephanos** to the north (hotel Alkistis (B) and others cheaper; rooms), **Megali Ammos**, a 15-minute walk to the south (hotels, including Mykonos Beach (C), also rooms), **Ornos** (hotel Paralos Beach (C) and others), and **Platis Yialos** (2 C class hotels, also rooms; windsurfing). From the only other village on the island, **Ano Mera**, where you could visit the **Tourliani monastery**, you can reach **Panormos Bay** or **Kalafati Beach** (hotel Afroditi (B)). Ano Mera has an A class hotel of the same name and rooms to rent.

DELOS

Apart from the *morning trips by boat* there are more expensive *private tours* usually in the afternoon (advertised).

You can *camp* overnight behind the museum (check this though before you go in case it has changed), or of course you can try the *hotel* Xenia (B).

There are *refreshments* at the Tourist Pavilion, but if you camp you should take your own food.

The *museum*, which should be visited if time allows (it has a particularly good collection of 6th C BC kouroi and korae, statues of young men and women in the archaic style) should now be open to visitors after being closed temporarily in 1983.

SERIFOS

The *boat* lands you at Livadi, whence there is an hourly *bus* to Chora.

Livadi

Several small *hotels* and *pensions* including Perseus (B); Maistrali and Serifos Beach (C). Also *rooms* to rent. Unofficial *camping* at Karavi Beach nearby.

The best *taverna* is the Perseus.

You can hire *motorbikes* at the 100 Pipers disco on the road to Chora.

Chora has little accommodation and two tavernas. There is a very good sandy beach at **Psili Ammos** (taverna), a 1-hour walk northeast of Livadi. Boats go in high season to beaches at **Mega Livadi** and **Koutalas** on the west coast (tavernas). Bike to the **Monastery of the Taxiarchon** to the north of Chora, where Father Nektarios may welcome you. Below the monastery is a large beach at **Plati Yiali** (taverna).

SIFNOS
From Kamares there is a *bus* to the capital Apollonia, and from there buses continue to Artemonas, Kastro, Faros and Platis Yialos.

Kamares
Two reasonable *hotels*, Kamari (B); Stavros (C). Also *rooms* to rent.

Beach, *tavernas*, etc, *disco* in high season.

Apollonia
Hotels: Apollonia (B); Signos (restaurant with superb view) (C); and other adequate small hotels. Rent *rooms*.

Restaurants (the Sifnians have a good reputation for their cooking): Niko's, Cyprus, Kalliope's. Several *discos*.

Bank, *post office*, *OTE*, *Tourist Police*.

There is a *folk museum* in the square by the buses, open early mornings only.

Kastro
Rooms to rent.

Try the Alexis-Zorba *taverna*.

Swimming below off the rocks.

Artemonas
The *hotel* Artemon (C), and *rooms*.

Platis Yialos
There is a *boat* to Paros several times a week.

Hotels: Platis Yialos (B); Panorama (D). *Rooms*.

There are also good *beaches* at **Faros** (rooms, tavernas) and **Vathi** (same) which you can reach by caique from Kamares and where you can also visit the 16th C **monastery of Taxiarchos**.

Festival: Profitis Ilias, 20 July.

MILOS
Several *buses* a day leave the square at Adamas for Plaka, Apollonia and Zephyria.

Adamas
Hotels: Venus Village (B); Corali (C); amongst others including several D class hotels. Rent *rooms*. Unofficial *camping* at Bombarda beach to the west.

Several *tavernas* (though many close over midday); *discos*.

Bank, *post office*, *OTE*.

The *churches* of Agios Charalambos and Agia Triada both have fine Cretan ikons (Adamas was founded by Cretan refugees).

There are sandy *beaches* to either side of the village. You can also take a caique from Adamas to the beaches at **Emborios** (tavernas) across the bay. Another good beach is **Palaiochora** (taverna) on the south coast beyond Zephyria (bus).

Plaka
A few *rooms*.

The small *archaeological museum* by the bus stop has finds from the island back to the neolithic period (closes over midday and on Tuesdays). Plaka also has an interesting *folk museum*.

Occasional *performances* in the Roman theatre in August. The *catacombs* have been closed for several years; enquire.

Apollonia
There are *rooms* to rent, also you can *camp* on the beach.

Several *tavernas*.

There are boats to **Kimolos**, where the village of Kimolos above the harbour of Psathi has some rooms and tavernas and where there are some good beaches.

Festival: Agios Ioannis Theologos on the west coast of Milos, 7 May.

PAROS
About 3 times a week you can catch a *boat* that goes beyond Thera to Crete and then on to Rhodes.

Paroikia
The *buses* leave from the windmill with the Tourist Office by the quayside (schedule displayed), approximately hourly to Naoussa ($\frac{1}{2}$ hour), regularly on another route to Lefkes-Marpissa-Piso Livadi-Dryos (about 1 hour), and thirdly to Pounda and Aliki. Daily at about 5pm there is a bus to the Valley of the Butterflies.

There are *boats to the beaches* to the north of Paroikia such as Krios and (best) Agios Fokas. Also daily boats to Antiparos (below).

Car and *moped* hire.

Hotels: many in Paroikia, often full in high season: try Xenia (B); Oasis, near harbour (C); Argo, Alkyon, both near the beach to the north of the harbour (C); Kontes, near harbour (D); Dina, in town (E). Many *rooms*: either bargain at the quayside or aim for the kastro and look among the streets behind. *Campground* to the north near Argo beach (Livadi).

Tavernas: numerous both along the waterfront and among the streets in town, best to look around yourself – but look out for Vassilis on the waterfront and Klimataria, Pandrosos and To Tamarisko.

Many *discos*, especially along the waterfront to the south.

The *OTE* is on the waterfront near the harbour; the post office and a bank are in the main street.

The town *beaches* reasonable, either to the north (Argo beach) or about a 10-minute stroll along the waterfront south, but the beaches reached by boat are better.

The *Church of the Panagia* closes over midday and to enter you should be respectably dressed. There is a big festival on 15 August.

The *museum* is open 9am to 1pm and 4 to 6pm, and is closed on Tuesdays.

There are some travel agencies that arrange *tours*.

The *petaloudes* (butterflies) are beyond the monastery of **Christou Dasous** and you can walk there in under 2 hours; you follow the road to Pounda for 5 kms, then find a track to the left. Beware: unless it is early summer, the migratory moths may not be there.

There are daily boats across to **Antiparos** from Paroikia, and tours are also arranged to visit the famous cave; you can stay in the village of Antiparos, which has some small hotels, rent-rooms, tavernas, etc, and there are good beaches nearby, one of which has camping.

To reach the *marble quarries* you get off the Marpissa bus at **Marathi**, and you walk onto the hills to the right; there are at least 2 long shafts into the ground, open at all times. Take a flashlight. A ½ hour walk further on is the 16th C fortified **monastery of Agios Minas**, in lovely country.

Naoussa
The bus passes by **Kolimbithres** which has a good beach, with tavernas, also camping. Naoussa itself has a lot of *hotels*, some 10 C class: try Naoussa (B); Calypso (C) in particular; also *rooms* to rent.

Some good *tavernas* by the little harbour. Also Christo's (expensive) and Meltemi (moderate).

Boats go to some of the *beaches* nearby. You can walk along the coast from Naoussa to Marpissa via **Ambelas** (beach, taverna) in about 3 hours.

Marmara and **Marpissa** are both attractive villages.

Piso Livadi has about 10 hotels, rooms, a good beach with windsurfing, camping, etc. The beaches to the south are quieter, so stay on the bus to **Chrysi Akti**, one of the best on the island, with tavernas. **Dryos**, further on, has been spoilt.

On the west coast there are beaches at **Pounda** (boats also go from here in summer to Antiparos) and **Aliki** (several hotels and fish tavernas).

Festivals: Panagia, in Paroikia on 15 August and in Naoussa on 23 August.

NAXOS
In addition to the very frequent *boats* between Piraeus and Naxos via Paros, some boats continue to Crete and eventually Rhodes, and there are several boats a week to Amorgos, 1 or 2 stopping at the smaller islands in between (Iraklia, Shinousa, etc.).

Naxos Town
Buses leave the quay (schedule posted) about hourly to Agia Anna, 5 times daily to Apollonas via Chalki and Filoti (in about 2 hours), and for Kastraki, Aliko and Pyrgaki on the west coast via Tripodes. In summer buses get full, so be there early.

Boats go regularly, except in rough weather, to Agia Anna.

You can hire *jeeps* and *mopeds* to get to the otherwise inaccessible northwest and east coasts; remember the distances on Naxos are quite large.

Hotels: Ariadne (B); Koronis (C) – both towards Agios Georgios beach; Hermes, Aegeon (both along waterfront, near the bank), Apollon (below Kastro) (all C); Okeanis (near quay) (D); Anna (near Apollo) (E). No problem with *rooms* even in high season; look in streets below the kastro or beyond the Ariadne hotel.

There is a *youth hostel* below the Hotel Dionysos (near the kastro). Unofficial *camping* beyond Agia Anna.

There are many *tavernas* both in the lanes in town (try Manolis) and on the waterfront – here try O Nikos and Symposium.

The *National Bank* is along the waterfront to the right; the *OTE* is nearby; the *post office* is up the street opposite the bank (which also has some of the better souvenir shops) and first right.

Information, etc, is obtainable from travel agencies along the front.

The *Archaeological Museum* is on the kastro: 8.30am to 12.30pm, 4 to 6pm daily; 9am to 3pm Sundays and holidays; closed Tuesdays.

The best town *beach* is Agios Georgios to the south, with many tavernas (try the Meltemi), windsurfing, etc, busy in high season; along this beach is Naxos' night life: several *discos* and *bars*.

Festival: Agios Nikodimos, 14 July.

Agia Anna
Some of the best *beaches* in the Aegean are to the south of this little harbour (tavernas, rooms). The further you walk along the dunes the fewer the people (and the fewer the clothes). Tavernas along the way.

Flerio
In this area to the east of Naxos town lies another large *kouros* figure, in someone's garden! Take a taxi, then walk back in about 2 hours.

Sangri (off the road to Chalki).
Folk-art festival in mid-August.

Chalki
The *Panagia Protothronis* opposite the bus stop has early wall-paintings. One hour walk northwest to the Venetian castle of *Pano Kastro*.

Filoti
Rooms, restaurants.

Long walk south to the huge *Hellenistic tower* of Pyrgos Chimarou.

Apollonas
Small *hotels* and *rooms* available; several *tavernas*.

The *kouros* is about a 15-minute walk on the hill behind (signposts off the road into village).

Tripodes (on the bus route to Pyrgaki).
You can walk from this pleasant village in about 2 hours down to the long *beach* south of Agia Anna.

There are good *beaches* at **Kastraki**, **Aliko** and **Pyrgaki**; Kastraki, a short walk off the bus route, is the quietest and has a taverna with rooms.

AMORGOS
Infrequent *boats*, mostly local from Naxos, call both at Katapola and Egiali (at northern end) and are the only means of transport between the two parts of the island, except for *caiques* in summer.

Katapola
A *bus* runs up to Chora and on down to the beach at Agia Anna about 4 times a day.

No hotels as such but *pensions* and *rooms*.

Of the *tavernas* try O Gavalas.

Chora
The *rooms* and few *tavernas* no longer meet demand in high summer, otherwise a pleasant place to stay.

The **Hozoviotissa** is open for visitors during mornings and late afternoons. **Arkessini** (Kastri) to the south is reached by daily truck from Chora; there are good beaches nearby. **Agia Anna** (bus from Chora) has a good pebble beach, but no taverna as yet. **Egiali** is about a 5 hour walk from the Chora. Hotel Mike (C), and rooms along the beach (sandy). Tavernas, etc.

IOS
Boats go on to Crete 3 times a week. Also daily *excursions* to neighbouring islands.

Harbour (Yialos)
Buses run frequently up to Chora and on to Milopotamos. *Boats* to Manganari in morning.

Hotels: many, including Corali, Sea Breeze, Homer's Inn (on hill) (all C); Actaeon (D); Helena (E). *Rooms*, particularly on the beach to the left, and up the hill to Chora. *Camping*.

Tavernas near the quay and along the beach.

Sandy *beach, windsurfing*.

Chora
Hotels: try Philippou (C); Afroditi (to-

wards Milopotamos) (D). Otherwise many *rooms* and *pensions*.
Tavernas: many, crowded into the main street (go early though). Try the Pithan opposite the Philippou.
Discos, bars galore (after all it is the poor man's Mykonos): the best remains the Ios Club on the way to the harbour, sip the sunset to Mozart, then hot stuff after; for Greek music (!) go to Zorba's.
OTE, bank, post office, police are all here.

Milopotamos
Hotels include the Delfini (C); Nissos Ios (D).
Rent-rooms. Campgrounds. Tavernas.
Frequent bus from Chora.
Sandy *beach, windsurfing.*

From Chora you can take a wonderful *walk* in about 2½ hours across the island to undeveloped **Agios Theodotis** bay. **Manganari** is reached by caique from Yialos; it has a sandy beach and a bungaloid hotel.

SIKINOS AND FOLEGANDROS
In addition to the several *boats* a week that call at these islands on the Santorini run to and from Piraeus, there are *local boats* daily between the islands and to Ios.

From the port of **Sikinos** (taverna) you walk up to the **Chora** with rooms and tavernas. There is a good beach at **Spilia**.

Folegandros is more developed. The harbour of **Karavostassis** has accommodation (rooms) and some good beaches. There is now a bus up to **Chora** which has a couple of hotels and rooms.

THERA (SANTORINI)
In addition to the normal Piraeus-Paros-Ios-Thera *boat* (with variations), there are frequent boats to/from Crete and also boats to Mykonos.

Phira
There is a good *bus* service throughout the island from the main square, Theotokopoulou, where the *tourist offices* are mostly situated also. There are frequent buses (times are posted) to Oia, Messaria, Pirgos, Kamari, Perissa, Emborion and Akrotiri. There are also buses to the port of Athinios, not always at times helpful for the ferries; it may be worth a *taxi* (similarly on arrival). *Moped* hire is available.

The tourist offices on Theotokopoulou Square will help with *information* and they arrange *tours*; Damigos Tours are often the most useful.
Accommodation can be a problem in high season and you may just have to take what is on offer, within reason; it is worth considering (if you are early enough) taking a bus out of town to a place such as Messaria (inland, see below) or Perissa (by the sea, below) where space may be easier to find, or if you are arriving by a late ferry then getting off at Oia (below).
Hotels include Atlantis (superb view, good restaurant, and the best disco – definitely A class); Kavalari, Panorama, Theoxenia (C); Tataki (D); Lygnos (E).
Rent-rooms include many overlooking the sea at the top of the cliffs (if you can get one!).
There is a *youth hostel* just on the way to Oia.
Tavernas: great choice; try Camille Stephani or Kastro at the top end of the market; more moderate are Babis and Leschi, both with good views though.
Many *discos* and *bars*.
Bank, post office, OTE – all near the main square. The *police* are in the square.
Archaeological museum: 9am to 1pm, 4 to 6pm daily, 10am to 2pm Sundays and holidays. Closed Tuesdays.

Therasia/Kaimeni:
excursion trips are arranged from Phira to both Therasia and Nea Kaimeni (where you can walk over to the crater). There are ordinary boats also just to Kaimeni from Phira giving you a couple of hours before returning, and similarly boats cross to Therasia from Oia. The village of Manolas on Therasia has rooms and food, but there seems little point in staying on the island.

Oia
Hotels include the Fregada (D) with a fine view; and *rent-rooms*; you could try the NTOG office in the main street since they now rent out a number of *traditional houses* which they have restored recently.
Taverna: try the Kyblos to the west.
Moped hire.
You can climb down to the small *beaches* below the cliffs.
There is a small *maritime museum*.
In the middle of the island there are

several hotels in **Messaria** and there is a beach with a hotel at **Monolithos**. The **Monastery of Prophitis Ilias** (closed Sundays) has a museum of monastic crafts open 8am to 1pm and 3 to 6pm. There is no public bus, so it is either a long walk from Pirgos or take a taxi or join one of the tours (which usually include the monastery with the visit to Akrotiri). **Ancient Thera** (which you walk to from the monastery in about one hour) is open 9am to 1pm and 3 to 6pm, Sundays and holidays 10am to 2pm (check the times however before setting out). **Kamari** is quite a lively place with several hotels (try Kamari (C)), rooms, tavernas, a disco, etc; **Perissa** is slightly quieter with one good hotel with an excellent restaurant (Christina (C)), rooms, tavernas, a youth hostel and a small campground. **Emborion** has a D class hotel and rooms to rent.

The site of **Akrotiri** is open all day except Sundays (then 10am to 2pm), but check first in case it closes now over midday. In any event there is a beach nearby with a taverna.

Finally . . . there is the island of **Anafi** to the east. A boat goes from Thera about twice a week but apart from leaving the tourists behind there is little to be gained; it has one village with few facilities.

THE EASTERN SPORADES

The Eastern Sporades, more fertile than the Cyclades, are scattered down the coast of Asia Minor. Samothraki and Lemnos have been included in the chapter on northern Greece from where they are most easily reached.

Sámos

From Piraeus the boat passes under the long, high island of **Ikaria** (see the *Practical Information* section for details), and in the distance, at the western end of Samos, you can already see 1445 metre Mt Kerkis, mantelled in forests that have survived – so rare on Aegean Islands – since ancient times. Eastwards there is a pass, but then the mountain backbone arches again, with great spurs falling away from Ambelos (1140 metres), precipitous along the north coast, but enclosing a series of plains and good beaches along the south. On Samos the friendly sound of splashing streams reminds you of the island's richness, where even the birds gave milk, so Menander said. Today wines, tobacco and olives are exported all over the world, sustaining a large population in scattered mountain villages and in the island's three ports.

Karlóvassi, along the north coast, is uninteresting, but now the boat thrums along the beautiful mountain coastline to **Vathy** (or Samos). From **Ano Vathy**, above, with its red tiled roofs and timbered houses reminiscent of northern Greece or Turkey, you look down upon the deep-cut bay and sense a Levantine mood. Across the island you can see Turkey, only 3 kms of blue water marking the divide. On the south coast of the island, with a wonderful view down the Dodecanese and across the Strait of Mykale to Turkey is the lazy seafront village and port of **Pithagórion**, named for the great mathematician born in ancient Samos on which the present village in part stands. Pithagorion is for many reasons the best place to stay. To the west there are several good beaches, some sandy, some pebbly, all protected from the northern meltemi. There are the Turkish mountains running down to Cape Kanapitza, indolently viewed from a café table. And nearby are the formidable remains of the ancient city.

Aesop and Epicurus, as well as Pythagoras, once lived in ancient Samos. So did Aristarchos, the first to state that the earth revolved around the sun, and also the explorer Kolais who around 650 BC made his name and fortune by sailing to the Pillars of Hercules. The *walls* of the city climb steeply over the hill of Astypalaea, its towers and central sections in good condition at the crest. But it was under the rule of Polykrates, says Herodotus, that three of the greatest building and engineering feats in the Greek world were carried out. The first was the *harbour mole* on whose founda-

Wonders of the ancient world

tions its modern counterpart still projects far out from the coastline. The second was the kilometre-long *Tunnel of Eupalinos* cut through Astypalaea, a guarantee of water supply at times of siege, an escape route too if necessary. The tunnel took 15 years to dig and was completed in 524 BC; it has recently been repaired and electricity installed, so that it is possible to walk all the way through it. The third – and this was sometimes ranked among the seven wonders of the world – was the *Temple of Hera*, 8 kms along the coast and past the airport at a place called **Kolonna** after the single skew column rising now from the vast limestone foundations. According to legend, Hera, Queen of Olympos, was born along the torrent Imbrasos here, and since c1000 BC there has been a sanctuary on this spot dedicated to her. In the early 8th C BC a megaron surrounded by a peristyle of columns was constructed here, the earliest example of a true Greek temple. A later temple, already the largest in Greece, was destroyed by fire in 525 BC; Polykrates at once ordered the construction of the yet larger one whose ruins you now see. Comparable in size to the Olympeion in Athens which was to take 700 years to complete, Polykrates' temple had progressed to its still astonishing dimensions within three years when, in 522 BC, he was tricked, captured and crucified on the mainland by the Persians, and construction ceased. What you might most regret, however, is the loss of Kolaios' little ship, which like some space capsule was long exhibited on the site.

Samian wine   While on Samos you should certainly try some of the Samian wines which are among the best in Greece.

Chíos

Like Samos, Chíos enjoys fertility and a good climate. The island was famous for its wine in antiquity (and for the Chian's enjoyment of it). With Samos and several mainland cities including Ephesus and Miletus, it was a member of the Ionic Confederation that succumbed first to Croesus of Lydia, then to Cyrus of Persia. The confederation's unsuccessful revolt against Persian domination was assisted by Athens and decided Darius on his punitive expedition against the Greek mainlanders in 490 BC. The island's richness has always attracted foreigners. For 300 years until 1566, when the Turks captured the island, Chios prospered under the Genoese and, unusual for Greece, developed a native aristocracy whose country houses set within gardens surrounded by high mud-brick walls remain typical of Kambos, the fertile plain abounding in citrus groves extending south of Chios town. Under the Turks its prosperity was largely based upon the production of mastic, particularly the south of the island.

Unlike Samos, however, Chios has suffered horribly from

natural and man-wrought devastation. In 1822 the islanders rose against the Turks. It is said that the ladies of Constantinople were furious at losing their source of mastic (used for making a liqueur and a sweetmeat, as the basis for chewing gum and, most importantly for the ladies, as a breath sweetener). A Turkish force landed on Chios, murdering and abducting the largely unarmed population. These regulars were soon joined by every armed, greedy and vicious Turk who could cross over from the mainland. In the end, 25,000 Chiots were killed, 41,000 taken to Constantinople for sale as slaves – along with sacks of human heads, noses and ears that were strewn around the streets where the putrefying flesh was left to be trampled into the mire. The massacre shocked Europe and led Delacroix to paint his famous if insufficiently grisly *Scenes from the Massacres of Scio*, now hanging in the Louvre (a copy of which hangs in the Chios town museum). The island's social structure was destroyed, and in 1881 a further 5000 Chiots were killed by earthquake. Many Chiots were forced to make their lives elsewhere, including a number of well-known shipowners.

The massacre

Facing Turkey's Karaburnu peninsula 8 kms distant, **Chíos town** has a nondescript commercial air relieved only occasionally by a projecting Turkish balcony and by the inevitable kastro, this time Genoese, with crumbling towers, gates and gun embrasures, some of them bearing the arms of the Giustianini, and with the old Turkish quarter huddled within. The modern town almost entirely obscures ancient Chios. Twelve kms west is the *convent of Nea Moni*, founded in the 11th C to house a miraculous ikon and visited for its fine mosaics which are comparable with those of Osios Loukas, although they were damaged by the Turks in 1822. Though there is no evidence for the claim, **Kardámila**, 27 kms to the north, is touted as Homer's birthplace. The upper town is picturesque and there's good swimming nearby. **Volissos**, 46 kms to the northwest, was once the home of a clan claiming descent from Homer and is promoted as the place where he lived and worked.

Homer's home town

Pirgí, 24 kms south of Chios town, is certainly the most unusual and attractive spot on the island. Round-roofed houses line narrow streets spanned by arches as a protection against earthquakes, and the houses are strangely decorated with geometric patterns cut into plaster and coloured – sgraffito it is called, an Italian fashion, but executed here during the Turkish occupation and strongly Islamic in character. This is a medieval fortress town in the heart of the mastic growing region, the fortifications necessary against the Turks who came, raiding for women. Though lacking any sgraffito, the best example of a fortified town is **Mestá** to the west, no streets, but alleyways, dark and tunnel-like with no windows on the ground floors. At **Emborió**, on a promontory along the southeast coast, a Bronze Age settlement, thought to be a rival to Troy, has been unearthed. There is good swimming off the black pebble beach here.

Lésvos

Sappho's island Lesvos (Lesbos) is visited less for its antiquities than for its beauty and its literary associations. Aesop came from Lesvos, while the landscape between Mytilene and Methymna provided the setting for Longus' erotic pastoral *Daphnis and Chloe*; but most importantly this was Sappho's isle – 'I love delicacy, and the bright and the beautiful belong for me to the desire of the sunlight': *the* poetess the ancients called her, in the same way that Homer was *the* poet. In Sappho's time (7th/6th C BC), this third largest Aegean island after Crete and Euboea was a major trading and cultural centre renowned for its high standard of education and its comparative freedom for women – two attributes it retains today. Its capital, Mytilene, was an important ally of the Athenians during the Peloponnesian War until its oligarchs attempted to join with the Spartans. Outraged and embittered by the betrayal the Athenian assembly despatched a galley with orders to put every citizen to death. It is one of the more dramatic moments in Thucydides, for the following day brought a change of heart and a second galley was sent racing across the Aegean, its crew sleeping in turns, eating and drinking at their oars, sweeping into Mytilene just as the death sentence was being read out.

Mountainous and rugged, with strange forests of petrified conifers and sequoias in the largely barren west, green with olive, pine, oak and chestnut trees in the east, Lesvos contains some of the wildest and also the most romantic, idyllic scenery in Greece. The weather is mild, the beaches are good, and there is an agreeable lingering of Turkish influence – here at least they ruled with restraint.

Probably the finest thing about sailing into what was the ancient harbour of Mytilene (modern **Mitilíni**) is imagining that moment of reprieve 2400 years ago; the waterfront is lively enough, and this is the place to enjoy some of the best ouzo and olives in Greece, but the town is without particular interest. There are good views, however, along the coast and across to Turkey from the Kastro, and all about the landscape is superb, especially across the peninsula along the shores of Yera Bay where also there is excellent swimming.

Mólivos (anciently Methymna), 60 kms distant on the beautiful northern coast, is built against a headland surmounted by a Genoese castle. Its towerhouses, fishing harbour and a long beach make it the most appealing place to spend some time. **Skala Eressou**, at the southwest end of Lesvos, has a long beach beneath the rocky acropolis of the ancient city where Sappho was born.

PRACTICAL INFORMATION

TRAVEL TO THE EASTERN SPORADES
Air. From Athens there are 2 to 3 flights a day to Samos (also direct flights from Europe), the same to Chios, and 3 to 4 a day to Lesvos (also served from Thessaloniki).

Sea. From Piraeus almost daily to Ikaria (8 hours) and Samos (10 hours), and on a different route weekdays only to Chios (10 hours) and Lesvos (14 hours). There is also a boat from Rafina to Chios (see below). There are in addition connections with other islands; some are mentioned below.

IKARIA
Boats from Piraeus call at either Evdilos on the fertile north coast or Agios Kirikos along the steep and rocky south coast, enroute to Samos. From the island there are boats to Patmos.

Once noted for its enormous production of wine (it was commonly known as Oenoe, wine island), it is now better known for its therapeutic springs at Therma and Therma Lefkadas near Agios Kirikos; there is also excellent raki and honey. It is not yet on the main tourist beat.

Agios Kirikos has a few hotels, also rooms and tavernas. Here there is the Tourist Police, post office, OTE and the island's only bank. The best swimming is off the rocks to the east, towards Therma. Both **Therma** and **Therma Lefkadas** have a good number of hotels; at Therma Lefkadas the Toula (B) has a disco.

From Agios Kirikos there are boats to **Fanari** to the north, which has a sandy beach and from where you can visit the large Hellenistic tower at the north tip of the island, and also to the island of **Fourni** where the Chora has rooms and fish tavernas.

A bus crosses the island to **Evidilos** (continuing to Armenistis) a pretty little port with the odd hotel, rooms to rent, tavernas and good swimming. At nearby **Kambos** there are some remains of the ancient city of Oenoe and also of a Byzantine palace; there is a small museum. **Kosikia** to the south of Evdilos has a 10th C Byzantine fortress.

Most people head for the superb sandy beach at **Armenistis**, where there are rooms and tavernas, also unofficial camping.

Festival: island festival on 17 July; among many village festivals one of the biggest is at Christos on 6 August.

SAMOS
Boats from Piraeus usually call both at Karlovassi and Vathy. There are also connections with Patmos, Rhodes, Lesvos, Lemnos and other islands (some from the port of Pithagorion). Boats to Turkey (Kusadasi, near Ephesus) leave daily from either Vathy or Pithagorion: you must make your passport available some time before departure, there is a good deal of paperwork (and therefore hanging about) involved in Turkey and it is expensive (but it is still worth going!).

Vathy
There is a reasonably good *bus* service from Plateia Nicolaou: fairly frequently to Pithagorion (some via Mitilini) and westwards to Karlovassi, and 2 to 3 buses daily to places such as Posidoni, Psili Ammos, Iraio and Pirgos.

Moped hire (and Samos is an ideal place for your own transport).

Hotels: Xenia (waterfront) (B); Samos (waterfront) (C); Hera (Plateia Nicolaou) (D); Poleos (harbour) (E). Also *pensions* and *rent-rooms*.

Tavernas along waterfront: try the Samian, near the Xenia.

Banks along the waterfront; *Tourist Police, post office* and *OTE* are all further along in the area behind the city gardens.

Samos Tours, on the waterfront both at Vathy and Pithagorion, are helpful.

Archaeological Museum (near the Tourist Police): 9am to 1pm, 4 to 6pm; Sundays and holiday 10am to 2pm; closed Tuesdays. It has finds from ancient Samos and the Hera temple.

Swimming at Gagou Beach about 1 km to the north (bus); rent-rooms enroute, tavernas, etc. West of Vathy there are several good swimming beaches. **Kokkari** has several hotels including the Venus and Tsamadou (C), rent rooms, tavernas; to the west is Tsamadou Beach, with a taverna. **Avlakia** has a hotel and a small pebble beach, possibly less busy than Kokkari. There is another beach at **Agios Konstantinos**.

Pithagorion

Accommodation: very crowded in the high season, otherwise a good choice of *hotels* including the Pithagoras and Polyxeni (C) and *rooms*.

Tavernas along waterfront. *Disco*.

The main street down to the harbour (Odos Lykourgou) has the *bus station* (frequent *buses* to Vathy, about 3 a day to the Temple of Hera, etc), *moped* hire, *bank, post office* and *Tourist Police*. OTE on the waterfront.

The *Archaeological Museum* is in Metaxa Square, behind the waterfront.

The fortress to the west is the *Castle of Logothetis* built by the Samians in 1824.

To reach the **Tunnel of Eupalinos** (open 10am–1pm, Monday, Thursday and Saturday) you take a road to the left off the Vathy road as you are about to leave town; then the road branches, left to the tunnel, right to the Monastery of **Panagia Spiliani** (in front of a large cave, fine view).

There are boats to the fine *beaches* of Psili Ammos and Possidoni (both with tavernas) to the east, and also to the island of Samiopoula (beach, taverna).

Temple of Hera

Reached by *bus* from both Vathy and Pithagorion (or about an hour's *walk* from the latter), the Heraion is open during the day, though check in case it closes over midday. The nearby village of **Iraion** has 2 to 3 hotels and a beach. The beaches between Iraion and Pithagorion with some hotels, tavernas, etc, are good but a bit close to the airport.

Karlovassi is not a place to stay, though there are about 5 hotels (the best is the Meropa (B) at Pefkakia beach) and good pebble beaches nearby. If you get off the boat here you can bus along the north coast or go south to **Ormos Marathokambou, Votsalakia** or **Chrysi Ammos** (all sandy beaches with rooms, tavernas); 2 buses a day leave Karlovassi for these places and also to the pretty inland village of **Platanos** (hotel). There is also moped hire at Karlovassi.

With your own transport you can more easily reach the many monasteries on Samos, for example the 16th century foundations of **Timiou Stavrou** and **Megalis Panagias** (west of Chora), the oldest on the island the **Panagia Vrontiani** built in 1566 (near Vourliotes on the north coast), and **Agia Triada** (just north of Pithagorion).

Another stop could be at the Palaeontological Museum at the Town Hall, **Mitilini** (open Monday to Friday 9am to 2pm); the animal fossils found in parts of Greece such as Samos may have inspired many of the creatures of mythology.

Festival: Agios Panteleimonos at Kokarri, 27 July.

CHIOS

Apart from the Piraeus-Lesvos route, there are *boats* to Samos, Patmos, Kos and Rhodes. There is also a ferry-route between Rafina and Passa-Limani.

From the port of Chios in summer there are several boats a week to Cesme in Turkey (see under Samos above).

Chios (Chora)

Buses leave the main square along the 3 asphalted roads through the island, north to Marmaro, northwest to Volissos and southwards to Pirgi. There is also a bus service part of the way to Nea Moni going as far as Karies (with an occasional direct bus on Sunday).

Car and *moped* hire.

Hotels: no shortage, including Xenia, Chandris Chios (on the waterfront near the town beach) (B); Kyma (on the waterfront) (C); Philoxenia (D).

Tavernas, discos (including one at the Xenia).

Tourist Police; also helpful *Tourism Office* at the corner of the harbour. A *bank* and the *OTE* are in the main square; the *post office* is on the waterfront.

The *Archaeological Museum* is on the waterfront, with local finds. The *Town Museum*, at one time housed in a former mosque in the main square, is said to have moved near the Chandris Hotel: open 9am to 1pm, 4 to 6pm daily; Sundays and holidays 10am to 2pm; closed Tuesdays.

The town *beach* is nothing special; much better is the sandy beach 13 kms south at **Karfas** where there is a D class hotel, rooms to rent, and good fish tavernas.

One of the big mansions in **Kambos** has become a museum with paintings, costumes, etc, of the former Chiot aristocracy (*Philip Argenti Museum*, open Monday to Saturday, mornings).

Nea Moni
There is a *bus* all the way Thursdays and perhaps Sundays, otherwise take a *taxi*. Open 8am to 12, 5 to 8pm.

To the north, **Langada** is a fishing village; there is a B class hotel at **Kardamila** of the same name with an excellent beach at nearby **Marmaro**, and another good beach at **Nago** (tavernas). Two kms south of **Volissos** there is a large undeveloped beach at **Limnia**.

Southwards, **Pirgi** has a pension and a few rent-rooms; here you should visit the frescoed church of Agioi Apostoloi off the main square. At **Mesta** some of the houses have been converted for tourist use under the NTOG scheme.

Two sea excursions: to the **Inousses Islands** to the northeast, reached by daily boat from Chora, where on the principal island you can find sandy beaches, tavernas and a hotel; and to **Psara** to the west, reached by boat from Volissos, also with some rooms and a taverna. Psara was also the subject of a dreadful massacre in 1824, from which it has never recovered.

Festival: Agia Markella, Volissos, 22 July.

LESVOS
Additional connections: by *air* daily with Thessaloniki, and by *boat* with Thessaloniki, Kavala, Lemnos, Samos and islands to Rhodes.

All during the summer season several boats weekly to Ayvalik, Turkey (see Samos and Chios above).

Mitilini
The *bus station* in the middle of the harbour serves the villages nearby; the *main bus station* is near the southern end of the harbour. Service is not overfrequent, about 3 daily to Mandamados, 4 to Molivos, 2 to Eressos and Sigri, and 5 to Plomari in the south.

Lesvos is another island for your own transport if possible: *car* and *moped* hire available.

Accommodation: can be difficult in high season, with hotels often booked and comparatively few rent rooms. Of *hotels* Xenia (B), 3 kms south on the coast, has a swimming-pool, otherwise try Blue Sea (B); Sappho (C); Megali Brettania (E) – all on the waterfront.

Many *restaurants* on the harbour, Several *discos* and *Bazouki clubs*.

Tourist Police, banks, OTE, post office – all on or near the waterfront, as is the *Archaeological Museum* (9am to 1pm, 4 to 6pm, closed Tuesdays).

The *Hellenistic Theatre* is to left of road leaving town northwards to Thermi.

The town *beach* is poor. A slightly better beach is north of the north harbour, at Tsamakia, and some people camp on the wooded hill behind. Otherwise there are places to swim along the coast to the north on the way to **Mandamados**, and there are sandy beaches at **Kratigos** and **Agios Ermogenis** to the south.

Nearby *excursions* include the Roman aqueduct at *Moria* (north) and *Varia*, 3 kms south, where the primitive painter Theophilos Hadjimichael was born (died 1934) and there is a museum of his paintings.

Northern half of island
Past Kalloni Bay, where you can swim at **Skala Kalloni** (tavernas with sardines caught in the bay), **Petra** (hotel Petra (C), rent-rooms, tavernas) on the north coast has a good swimming beach; the village is named after a rock on which stands the 18th C Church of the Panagia Glykofiloussa (sweet-kissing!), and there are frescoes in the 16th C church of Agios Nikolaos. **Molivos** (or Mithymna) has a helpful Tourist Office near the bus stop which can arrange accommodation. The hotels are expensive (of these the Sea Horse (B) on the harbour is the best) but there are plenty of rooms. There are some good restaurants on the main square, and there is a disco on the beach. Moped hire is available. In the kastro, occasionally there are theatre performances. The town

beach is rocky; there is a better pebble beach to the south by the Delphinia hotel (B), and Eftalou Beach, 3 kms east, is sandy with tavernas.

Westwards of Kalloni, **Eressos** has an archaeological museum of local finds; ancient Eressos (birth place of Sappho) was at **Skala Eressou** which has the hotel Sappho (C) and rooms.

About 5 kms west of Vatoussa the 16th C **Perivoli monastery** has good frescoes. **Sigri**, below a Turkish kastro, has a good beach; hotel Nisiopi (B) and rooms. The remains of the famous petrified forest is scant; some can be seen to the southeast in the direction of Eressos. North of Antissa there is a fine beach with tavernas at **Gavatha**.

Southern half of the island

Agiassos is a charming inland village, with rooms and tavernas, and a large festival on 15 August. You can cross the Gulf of Yera by a passenger boat from Kountourdia to **Perma**, which has a sandy beach. **Plomari** on the south coast, the home of an ouzo distillery, has the hotel Oceanis (C), rooms and tavernas, and beaches both to west and east; a few kms to the east there is a very good pebble beach at **Agios Issidoros. Vatera**, some distance west, reached from Polichnitos, has a sandy beach and tavernas.

Festivals: Apart from the festival on 15 August at Agiassos (Koimisis), the most remarkable are those at Mandamados and Agia Paraskevi (near Kalloni) during May when bulls are sacrificed in honour of Agios Charalambos. On 6 and 7 July there is the festival of Agia Kiriaki at Petra.

THE DODECANESE

Like the Eastern Sporades, the Dodecanese closely follow the Turkish coastline, their extremities sometimes embraced by the headlands of Asia. The islands themselves are often indented, usually mountainous and, the more so as you head south, blessed with a warm and sunny climate the year round. They are also undeniably Greek in character, though they were part of the Ottoman Empire until 1912, governed with increasing harshness by the Italians until the British occupation in the closing years of the Second World War, and only united with Greece in 1947. Nevertheless, part of the pleasure of the Dodecanese is the varying degree to which classical, Byzantine, Crusader, Turkish and Italian influences make themselves felt on each island. They may be reached by sea from Piraeus (via the Cyclades or Crete), while there are air services from Athens to Kos, Rhodes and Karpathos.

Pátmos

Island of the Apocalypse

If Delos is the holy island of classical Greece then Patmos is the holy island of Christianity where St John the Divine received his vision of the Apocalypse and wrote *Revelations*. Patmos is suitably an island of extremes, the most northern of its group, the most arid, one of the smallest and perhaps the most beautiful with a wildly undulating coastline of coves and headlands, hidden beaches which require a boat to reach, a lively port and, high above, the atmospheric medieval Chora helmeted by the fortified Monastery of St John.

The boat ties up at **Skála**, deep within a lovely, almost entirely enclosed bay, a narrow beach extending northwards along the waterfront. The houses are white, their doors and shutters painted ochre and in muted blues and greens. The impression is bright, pleasant and friendly, and there are some good kafeneions by the arcaded plateia – an Italian legacy – where breakfast or an evening drink is attended by the gentle rocking of sailboats and caiques at their moorings. After Rhodes and Kos, Patmos is the most visited of the Dodecanese, but mostly by cruise ships which come and go again within a few hours; otherwise, even at the height of summer, it is a peaceful and relaxing place.

A donkey path climbs steeply up towards Chora, or you can follow the more gradual, winding road. There are buses and taxis. Halfway up is the **Grotto of the Apocalypse** (signposted), which you enter via the chapel of Agia Anna built over its yawning opening. Rock ledges are identified as the saint's desk and bed, and ikons vividly depict the moment of cosmic revelation which enroute from God to St John blasted a three-way fissure near the mouth of the cave – odd, that; as though the Word could not be bothered to go in by the very obvious front door.

Climbing towards Chora

Continuing upwards, the views are spectacular. You see that Skala is built on a narrow isthmus, the bay on one side, the open Aegean on the other. The arid island landscape is so deeply incised by coves and bays that from here the sea sometimes seems a stunning blue lake amidst the rolling slopes of brown and dun-green. Though often shuttered, and quiet except for the meltemi whistling across its narrow streets, **Chóra** is beautiful – substantial 16th and 17th C houses of several storeys with marvellous wooden doors and elaborately wrought knockers. And rising above them are the crenelated battlements of the **Monastery of St John**, founded in 1088 with the permission of the Byzantine emperor by the Blessed Christodoulous, a monastery with teeth, to fend off pirates and foreign powers and preserve the most important monastic collection in Greece outside of Mt Athos. Inside, all is white and angular, arcades, terraces and patios open to the sun. The view finally from the rooftops is of gleaming, burning whiteness; tiled Byzantine cupolas; glittering sea; Naxos, Paros, Kos in the far distance like basking whales. It is far more superb a view than that from stunted Delos. Below, the *Library* contains hundreds of parchments and hand-written books, many of them exquisitely illuminated, and 33 leaves from a 6th C *Gospel of St Mark*. In the *Treasury* are jewellery, church furniture, embroidered stoles and numerous ikons, the most interesting being one of St Nicholas in mosaic, no piece greater than one-tenth of a centimetre across. There are 17th C frescoes in the *main church*, and the *Chapel of the Theotokos* has frescoes from the early 13th C.

Aegean panorama

Roads from both Chora and Skala (boats from Skala, too) take you to **Grikou** beach, 3.5 kms south of Skala, with a few tavernas, a couple of hotels, good swimming in a lagoon-like bay, and out at the tip of a spit of sand a great rock, its cave inhabited in prehistoric times. The alternative is **Kambos**, 8 kms to the north by road or boat, some rooms to let, better sand than Grikou, but not nearly as attractive a situation.

Léros

Leros is remarkably similar to Patmos in configuration, but with none of its interest and not so much of its charm. **Lakkí**, at the head of a vast, still bay on the west coast, was a major Italian naval base and will be your likely port of call. It is a dreary, crumbling place. **Plátanos**, on the east coast, is livelier and there are some fine views from the Byzantine kastro. A peculiarity of Leros is that property is inherited through the female line, nearly all land and houses belonging to women.

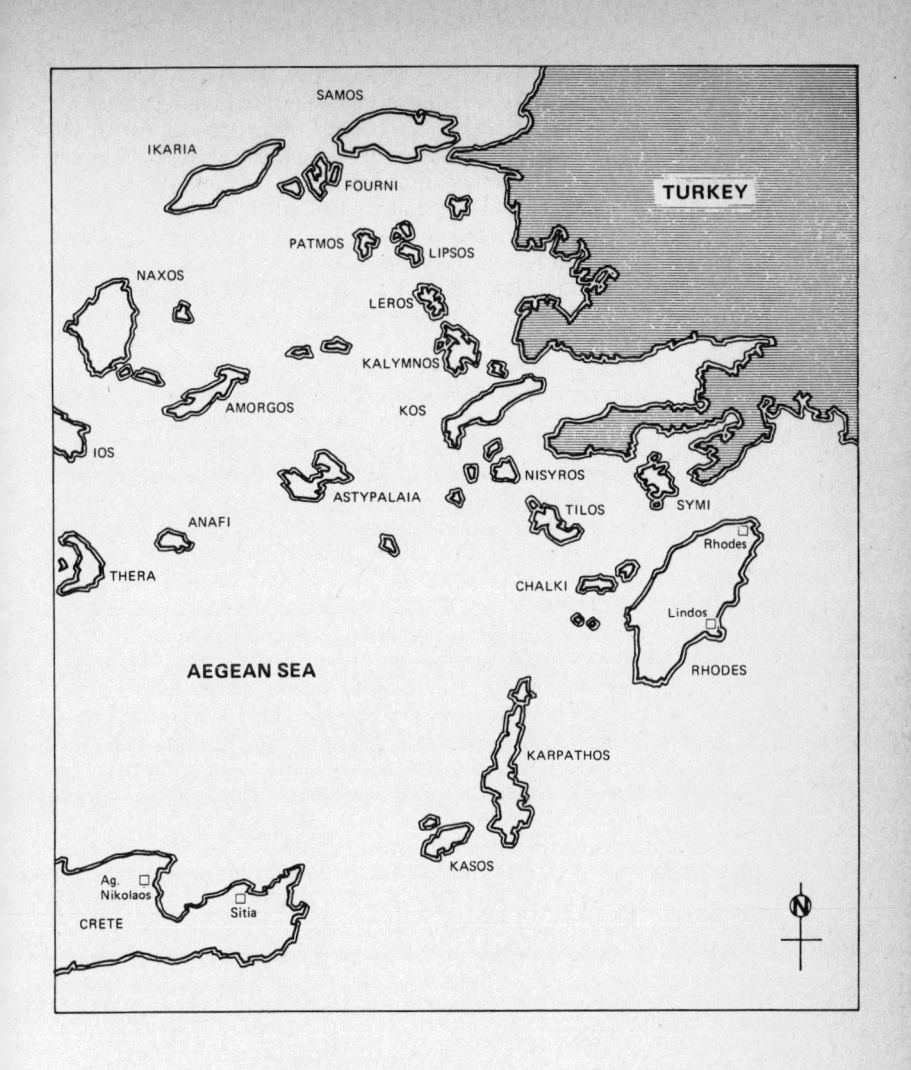

Kálymnos

Sponge diving

Only 2 kms of sea separate Leros and Kalymnos an imposingly mountainous island whose inhabitants rely on fishing and the declining rewards of sponge diving for their livelihood. The Aegean's depleted sponge beds oblige the divers to search along the North African coast; they are gone from Easter until summer's end and only when they return does the island really come to life. **Kálymnos town**, looking southeastwards towards Kos, presents to the arriving visitor an ascending flight of predominantly blue-and white-painted houses, a display of the Greek national colours calculated in decades past to annoy the Italians. There are several interesting neo-Byzantine churches, the finest being *Agios Christos* in the clock tower square by the waterfront.

Kalymnos' once extensive tree-cover was stripped by the Turks, though between the bony mountain ranges running east to west are two beautiful valleys rich in fruit: the village of **Vathý** lies where one valley meets the east coast and oranges and tangerines grow succulent in the volcanic soil; the other valley runs westwards from Kalymnos town, the old **Chóra** with medieval castle lying 3 kms along the way, to **Lineariá Bay** (5.5 kms). From here northwards to **Myrtíes** (7.5 kms) and **Masouri** (8.5 kms) there are many good sandy beaches backed by groves of cypress, pine, lemon, fig, tangerine and oleander. Small boats from Myrties cross in 10 minutes to the islet of **Télendos** rising 400 metres from the sea, a small fishing village with a simple taverna on its shore. There are ruins of a monastery and castle to explore, solitude and beautiful views, especially by morning light, of the Kalymnian mountains to enjoy.

Kos

Second in size to Rhodes in the Dodecanese, the long low profile of Kos is interrupted only once by a mountain of any height. Well-irrigated and green, this is a garden island of lemons and oranges, grapes, melons, almonds and honey inhabited by farming people, not fishermen. There is a significant Moslem community. Kos is ringed by miles of lovely sand beaches, though those on the north coast (Tigaki, Marmari, Mastichari) are exposed to the meltemi: Kardamena on the south coast is more sheltered, and **Ágios Stéfanos**, near Kefalos towards the southern tip of the island, is the best of all (perhaps the best in the entire Dodecanese), although it is now being developed. Bicycles are a favourite form of transport over this gentle landscape.

Kos attracts fewer visitors than Rhodes, though its appeal amongst the cognoscenti goes back at least as far as Ptolemaic Egypt when vacationing pharaohs spent the odd fortnight here.

Hippocrates   Hippocrates, 'father of medicine', taught and healed in a sacred grove on high ground 3 kms behind what is now the harbour of Kos town. The views of verdant hillsides, the Aegean and the shores of Asia Minor cannot be much less therapeutic now than they were then, in the late 5th, early 4th C BC. Proximity to Asia, also to Egypt, was no accident, for there medicine of a sort had been practised for centuries before, though it had been inextricably bound up with magic and religious mumbo-jumbo. The Hippocratic method was rational and based on observation, with the course of illnesses recorded – an approach adopted and advanced by the Arabs following their conquest of Greek Alexandria and only accepted again in Europe 2000 years after Hippocrates' time. A Hellenistic sanctuary, the **Asklepieion**, was built upon the site after Hippocrates' death, now an uncertain assortment of picturesque ruins worth visiting mostly for the pleasantness of its situation.

Back in **Kos town**, on Plateia Eleftherias, is a *museum* containing a 4th C BC statue of Hippocrates himself, plus many other Greek and Roman marbles displayed in rooms surrounding an open courtyard decorated with a Roman mosaic floor. Hippocrates is said to have lectured under a spreading plane tree and the locals claim their *Platanos Ippokratou* is it. Certainly it is a venerable tree and Plateia Platanou is pleasingly cool, green and shaded, bordered by a Turkish mosque and with a refreshing fountain. The nearby excavations have revealed a layered jumble of medieval, Greek and Roman ruins, once the *agora* area.

Further back in town, at the end of Vasileos Pavlou there are the ruins of *Roman baths* and a large Roman house with mosaics called the *Casa Romana*. Near the ancient acropolis there is a Hellenistic *theatre*, the restored colonnade from the gymnasium, and a section of paved *Roman road* lined with houses à la Pompeii, some with mosaics, further along which there are more baths and mosaics. Jutting out into the sea is the *Castle of the Knights of St John*, 15th C, its battlements crumbling, wildflowers waving across the stones and views of infidel Turkey through the embrasures.

Lesser Islands

Astipalaia lies furthest west of the Dodecanese, too far back from the front line for the Knights of St John to bother with it; all Western influence on the island is Venetian. It is mountainous, though not dramatically so; the most attractive village is **Livádi**, southwest of **Chóra** with its Venetian castle. The boat serving Astipalaia from Piraeus via the southern Cyclades also calls at Nisyros, Tilos and Simi, lying between Kos and Rhodes.

Volcanic island

Nísyros is thought once to have been attached to Kos and separated by a volcanic explosion. It is itself a volcano, circular and rising towards a 4-km wide crater at its centre, a further and still warm volcanic cone within that. The best views are from **Nikiá**, on the crater's rim, especially when the island's many almond trees blossom in February.

As on Astipalaia, the women of **Tílos** still wear traditional costume. Much of the small population is engaged in agriculture.

Nearly enclosed by two mountainous peninsulas of Turkey, **Sími** itself is as impressively mountainous as Kalymnos. Not the soil, but shipbuilding, sponge diving and trade provided a bounteous living for the islanders, reflected in the 19th C mansions of **Yialós** around the harbour and leading up to the older **Chorió** where a more Cycladic style of architecture dominates, the interiors often beautifully woodcarved. Suliman the Magnificent (see Rhodes) so prized Simi's fast ships that he encouraged the island's prosperity and under the indulgence of his successors small barren Simi ranked with Kos and Rhodes as one of the three most important islands of the Dodecanese until the close of the last century. The Italian occupation, loss of the sponge beds and competition from steel-hulled steamships broke Simi and much of its population left. Today it is reviving again on tourism: day-trippers over from Rhodes to admire its architecture. When the last tourist boat leaves at evening it can be a quiet and lovely place to be.

Rhodes (Ródos)

As you sail into Rhodes the walled, medieval town rises honey-coloured from the sea, a romantic spectacle of turrets, towers and battlements built by the Knights of St John to defend the island against the Infidel, but conquered in 1523 by Suleiman the Magnificent and made still more exotic by the domes and minarets of Turkish mosques. (The siege, which held the attention of all Europe for six months, was only won when the Sultan's 100,000 troops persuaded the 180 surviving Knights – out of an original complement of 650, aided by 200 Genoese, 50 Venetians, 400 Cretans and 600 inhabitants – to accept honourable terms.) The island is green and wooded. A range of hills runs from north to south, Mt Ataviros down the west coast exceptionally rising to 1215 metres. In contrast to the starkness of many other Aegean landscapes Rhodes can be unusually verdant and gentle. The island, however, has been ruined by its popularity – the northern half, anyway, with ugly hotel strips along its coastlines and vast swarms of package holiday locusts fresh from their depredations on Majorca.

The **city of Rhodes** is divided into the New and Old Towns. Apart from the usual urban and touristic facilities, the **New Town** is of no interest except for the buildings of the Italian occupation standing by the mouth of *Mandraki Harbour*. These are of the fascist period, overlarge and proclaiming their importance to the point of buffoonery, utterly out of place in Greece. The most entertaining among these is the former *Governor's Palace*, now the Nomarchia (administrative headquarters), patterned in Venetian Gothic style with an arcaded facade.

The Colossus of Rhodes

You are here standing by the site of one of the ancient world's Seven Wonders, the *Colossus of Rhodes*. The belief that this gigantic bronze statue (27 metres high) of Helios, the sun-god protector of Rhodes, once bestrode the entrance to the harbour so that ships passed between his legs lacks evidence, but at any rate here he stood for a brief 60 or 70 years before being toppled by an earthquake in 225 BC. Out of superstition, his broken form was left undisturbed for eight centuries until Arab pirates shipped the pieces to Tyre and there sold them to Jewish traders who on 900 camels carried them away to be melted down and sold. Mandraki Harbour, today guarded by a pair of small bronze deer (replacing on the seaward side the Italian she-wolf), is now a yacht anchorage. The *Commercial Harbour* lies beyond the mole and south; this is where all but the smallest inter-island ships tie up. Behind it rise the walls of the **Old Town** which you enter through one of its gates.

The Knights of St John   When the Knights of St John retreated from Asia Minor and the Holy Land they based themselves in Rhodes. Their architecture borrowed heavily from the Gothic of their native lands – principally France and Spain – and combined both military and religious styles. The *Street of the Knights* (Odos Ippoton), narrow and cobbled, is lined with the inns of the various nationalities making up the Order. Of these the *Inn of the Tongue of France*, on the right, about halfway up from the port, is architecturally the most distinguished. The street is silent, severe, broken only by the splashing of water from a Turkish fountain, the details of escutcheons on the solid walls and stone traceries around the doorways and windows. The street runs gently upwards towards the *Palace of the Grand Masters*, residence of the head of the Order and meeting place for senior knights. The Palace contains many splendid Roman and early Christian mosaics.

From here you can see the pink dome and minaret of the *Mosque of Suleiman*, built immediately after the Turks had driven the Knights from the island. The Knights were probably the most formidable opponents of Islam in the Eastern Mediterranean, conflict caused not only by religion but by trade. Rhodes was a flourishing commercial outpost of the West and a threat to Turkish shipping. So the Knights defended themselves with massive *walls and gates* which you can tour twice a week.

At the bottom of the Street of the Knights are the Museums of Archaeology and of the Decorative Arts, the former once the *Hospital of the Knights*, the latter an *arsenal*. The Hospital is the the most important medieval building in the Old Town, in excellent condition and witness to the original function of the Order: the care of the ill and needy. In this respect, the coutyard and, up the steps and to your left, the infirmary which could bed 100 patients, are of interest. Beyond the infirmary and passing the refectory are three rooms containing sculpture: in the first is a *head of Helios*, the sun-god represented in the famous Colossus; in the second is the 1st C BC *Aphrodite of Rhodes* emerging from **The Marine Venus** the sea; in the third is the 3rd C BC *Aprhodite Thalassia* – 'The seawater had sucked at her for centuries till she was like some white stone jujube, with hardly a feature sharp as the burin must originally have left it. Yet such was the grace of her composition – the slender neck and breasts on that richly modelled torso, the supple line of arm and thigh – that the absence of firm outline only lent her a soft and confusing grace. Instead of sharp classical features she had been given something infinitely more adolescent, unformed. The ripeness of her body was offset by the face, not of a Greek matron, but of a young girl.' – made famous by Lawrence Durrell in his *Reflections on a Marine Venus*.

Around the island

At the beginning of the first millenium BC the Dorians replaced the early Minoan and Mycenaean colonists and built three cities: Ialisos, Kamiros and Lindos. Only later did they federate and build the town of Rhodes as their capital. **Ialisos** lies nearest to Rhodes, about 15 kms down the west coast route, and has hardly been excavated. But the view from Mt Philerimos – its acropolis – is marvellous and there is a church and ruined castle of the Knights and a Byzantine monastery. 36 kms from Rhodes along the same coastal route is **Kamiros**, the entire groundplan of the ancient city excavated. If you turn inland about halfway between Rhodes town and Kamiros you come to **Petaloudes**, the wooded gorge where thousands of 'butterflies' gather from June through September – though unlike the flocking tourists they are usually camouflaged against the trees, leaves and rocks.

But the place most people want to visit is **Líndos**, 55 kms down the east coast – and unfortunately they do, all at the same time. This was once considered the Aegean's most perfect blend of nature, antiquity and the Middle Ages, but unless you visit well out of season it is improbable that Lindos will hold for you that particular kind of romance.

A place to avoid

There is a panorama from the clifftop *acropolis* hovering 116 metres above the sea; it is of course dramatic because it is high, but it is working with a second-rate landscape, lacking the spectacle of mountains or a varied coastline, the surprising shifts between luxuriance and barrenness that can be found elsewhere; here the shapes are doughy, in summer the colour a monotonous brown; even the blue of the water is flat. The acropolis was fortified by the Knights, and earlier it was occupied by the *Sanctuary of Athena Lindia*, a surviving temple sited at the edge of the cliff at the southernmost point of the acropolis. The *temple*, its setting apart, is entirely uninspired, of poor stone, the arrangement highly formalistic – Mussolini's Italians did better at Mandraki harbour. After this, and the prissiness of Sounion, the Temple of Aphaia on Aegina with its energy and originality of form stands out as the greatest of the sea-staring temples.

There is a long sandy beach below (St Paul is said to have landed here on his way to Rome) and a village of many *15th C houses* combining Gothic, Byzantine and Oriental features which might be lovely if you did not have to fight your way through the crowds. On some of the houses are cute little enamelled tiles set into the wall by the door announcing the name of the package holiday company that has taken a long lease on the place – what the trade would call a sensitive echo of Lindos' age-old renown for pottery and ceramics. The tour operators have made Lindos a dormitory.

Kásos

Some undiscovered islands

The sea approach to Rhodes from Piraeus via Crete takes you to Kasos, Karpathos and Chalki enroute.

Kasos is a small island inhabited by barely more than 1000 people, ravaged and depopulated by the Egyptians acting for the Turks during the War of Independence, later resettled by families who had the enterprise to take the lead in the switch from sail to steam. There are Kasiot shipping families living in London today. Many Kasiots emigrated to Egypt and were employed in cutting the Suez Canal; the pilots of the first ships through both the Suez and Panama canals were Kasiots. The island is mountainous, little visited, traditional; its few villages are all within walking distance of **Ophrys** (or Phry), the port on the north coast.

Kárpathos

Karpathos is about the size of Kos, but unlike that gentle and abundant island, which is sheltered within a fold of the Turkish mainland, it is a rugged mountain spine standing picket on the outer perimeter of the Aegean. Although it bestrides the sea lanes between Rhodes and Crete, the waves of Roman, Venetian and Ottoman conquests that swept over those larger neighbours were barely felt against its precipitous coastline. Tourism has similarly failed to impress itself, on the northern half of the island at least, and the mountain villagers of Olimbos still utter Dorian words among their local dialect and fit their houses with wooden locks and keys similar to those described by Homer.

The highest peak is Kalilimini, 1220 metres at the centre of the island. To the south is 'European' Karpathos, traced with streams and fertile, where orchards and olive groves flourish on the high Lastos Plain and round the port of **Pigádia**. The port itself is dull, but the outlying villages are pretty and there are several good beaches round the southern coast. But Karpathos is far more interesting north of Kalilimini, severely beautiful and thinly populated, and linked to the south only by ancient paths and a dirt road cut a few years ago.

Otherwise the two halves of the island are connected by caiques which sail along the eastern coast, landing at coves like **Apella**, a solitary crescent of sand shielded within a mountain fold; the lovely hamlet of **Kíri Panagía** with its seaside shrine to the Virgin; the fishing village of **Ágios**

Traditional mountain village

Nikoláos; and then on up to the northern port of **Diafáni**, a strip of bleak shingle with a concrete quay.

There are several hotels at Diafani and there is even a recent road winding up to **Ólimbos**. A taxi will cover the distance in a quarter of an hour. But it seems a sacrilege to favour modern contrivances for your entry into this medieval mountain world. And so you follow the old way through wooded gullies, over scrub ridges and finally, after an hour and a half, along a walled path with a sudden wonderful panorama of a high fertile valley and the village like a Tibetan lamesery clinging to the flank of Mt Profitis Ilias. Women wearing full white dresses embroidered in red, long black cassocks and high leather boots, hoe the furrows and gather fruit from the orchards. They drive their donkeys laden with sheaves of wheat up the steep lanes to the row of windmills along the ridge. A banner of cloud streams from the summit of Profitis Ilias and beneath it Olimbos climbs like Jacob's Ladder, one house growing out of the top of another. Chimney pots bulge like vases encircled with geometric designs, balustrades and cornices are carved with demiurges of the vine or sea, and balconies bear the double-headed eagle of Byzantium.

At night men gather at a kafeneion and sit rigid against the walls to listen to the tsabouna, a goat-skin bagpipe, and the three-stringed lyra. Miniature cymbals strung along the bridge of the bow clash at the end of each stroke, counterpointing with their varied timing the high wail of the strings. Bagpipe, strings and cymbals weave in unexpected Eastern patterns, and in this mountain village 'European' Karpathos on the other side of the island seems a continent away.

Chálki

Chalki suffered rapid depopulation after a sponge blight and synthetic substitutes killed the trade. There was emigration to Australia and to Florida, hence Leoforos Tarpon Springs which runs up from **Emborió**, the harbour, to Chorio, which was finally abandoned around 1950 and left to crumble. In Skala shops closed, owners emigrated, houses were shuttered and the population fell to less than 400 from several thousand. Skala has the look of a run-down Symi, in need of a pastel paint job, and the houses are anyway less elegant. Though a day-trip boat putts over from Kamiros on Rhodes (16 kms eastwards), hardly anyone comes; when you decide to stay overnight you discover nobody knows what to do with you. In the evening when the few tavernas put out their tables and chairs and switch on their lights in the trees it becomes a lively but still pin-prick world. The church of Agios Nikolaos possesses the highest bell tower in the Dodecanese, but that belongs to the bravado of the past; if you have been looking for an island to yourself, this is it; if you can survive three days here, you get a medal.

But it is very beautiful to walk about this island, first up the green and silent valley to **Chorió** in half an hour, a miniscule Mistra clinging to a flank of a jagged ancient acropolis. There is a *church* here built of Hellenic materials with a few frescoes inside, while atop the mountain is what seems from a distance some gothic fantasy painting, **Kástello**, the crenellated *Castle of the Knights* from where there is a wonderful view of the island and the sheer cliffs of the lower western coast of Rhodes. There are isolated monasteries further over the island, and where the paved road peters out beyond Choria someone has inscribed in the concrete: FULL MOON RISING OVER RODOS. QUICK! WRITE CONCRETE POEM BEFORE IT SETS.

Gothic castle

Kastellórizo (Megísti)

Kastellorizo is the most remote of the Greek islands, six hours eastwards from Rhodes, the mountains of Asia Minor looming like storm clouds against the phosphorescent night. A village glimmers, a minaret is faintly illuminated; this is the Turkish village of Kas, and across from it, separated only by 2 kms of water, Kastellorizo rises like a Greek Gibraltar from the sea. The boat steers between the mountains and the rock, rounds the headland of Agios Stefanos, and is suddenly embraced by a magnificent harbour sparkling with lights.

Once this was the busiest port between the Aegean and Beirut. At the turn of the century as many as 300 merchant schooners anchored here at a time, and during the 1930s the harbour was crowded with seaplanes from Paris – Air France

Seaplanes and schooners

Kastellorizo harbour from the headland of Agios Stefanos

might land eight flights a day here, enroute to the Levant. In 1900, 15,000 people lived on Kastellorizo; now there are only 250 and they survive on a subsidy from Athens. The island's schooners lost their trade to steam, the Turks bombarded the town from Kas during the First World War, an earthquake struck in 1927 and British occupation in 1943 invited German air attacks. Not that Kastellorizo is in any way forlorn. Fig trees grow among the levelled houses as though they had always been planted in terraces, so that without looking at the old photographs in the *museum* you would never guess how much has been lost. Though only a small harbour village now, you sense its cosmopolitan soul, and like a twilight glow this warms the simple pleasures of your stay.

The harbour is lined not with island village homes but noble town houses, tall and narrow. There is a touch of Anatolia about them, with wooden balconies overhanging shaded passageways. Taverna tables are set on the waterfront, braziers grilling octopus soaked in ouzo, or fish, caught fresh that morning. You can snorkel around any of the numerous islets beyond the harbour, watching schools of colourful fish playing among pieces of ancient amphorae, the only litter along this stretch of the Mediterranean. There are no beaches, but a path climbs through the spare landscape to the white *chapel of Agios Stefanos* on the headland, where there is a cove and you can dive off the rocks and sun yourself on them afterwards.

Luminous sea cave

It is worthwhile making the risky journey round the serrated coast to **Fokiali**, a *sea cave* more vast and beautiful than the famous Blue Grotto of Capri. Timing is everything: you must set out early to catch the morning angle of the light, and the sea must be calm, for the opening is barely a metre high and your rowing boat squeezes through between swells as you crouch low to avoid banging your head. For a moment it seems an ill-advised passage out of daylight into darkness, but heads up and you are floating on water of such luminous blue brilliance that it floods with colour the great dome of rock overhead. The effect is caused by sunlight passing through the submarine entrance and suffusing the remarkably translucent water. A family of seals lives here, and they break the stillness with their barks.

The island is named for the *castle* of red stone, Chastel Roux, built by the Knights of St John to the east of the harbour; three towers and a section of wall survive. An enormous Greek flag waves from the highest tower, large enough, you guess, suspecting the defiant intention, to be seen from Turkey. Many flags have flown over Kastellorizo, but the population has always been Greek. Homer mentions the fleet they sent to Troy, and an old and beautifully made mule *path* switches up the mountain behind the town where you might find the ruins of the *Dorian acropolis*.

PRACTICAL INFORMATION

TRAVEL TO AND WITHIN THE DODECANESE
Air. From Athens there are about 2 flights daily to Kos, some 6 to 7 a day to Rhodes, and 1 to 2 a day to Karpathos. There are direct flights to Kos and Rhodes from many European cities, mostly chartered. In addition you can fly to Rhodes from several Greek islands: from Kos (about 2 a day), Karpathos (3), Crete (1), Mykonos (about 4 weekly) and Thera (3 weekly).

Sea. From Piraeus the principal service is daily except Sundays along the route Patmos-Leros-Kalymnos-Kos-Rhodes (8, 10, 12, 14 and 18 hours); there is a boat on Sundays too just to Kos and Rhodes. The islands of Kasos, Karpathos and Chalki are principally served by the Piraeus-Crete-Rhodes ferries, a lengthy route. The islands of Astipalaia and Simi have about two boats a week from Piraeus, and Nisyros and Tilos just one. There are other connections between some of the islands and these are indicated below. One particular boat, the *SS Panormitis*, goes each week northwards from Rhodes up through the Dodecanese as far as Samos, southwards to Kasos and eastwards to Kastellorizo. There are three boats a week to Kastellorizo from Rhodes, including one originating in the Piraeus. Since 1984, passage from Rhodes to Kastellorizo has been *free*.

PATMOS
The Piraeus boat goes on to Rhodes via Leros, Kalymnos and Kos. Other connections include Samos, Ikaria and Chios. In summer there are excursion boats to Lipsi to the east (see below).

Skala
Bus and boat *timetables* are posted opposite the ferry. *Buses* run up to Chora about 8 times a day; they go to Kambos and Grikou about 4 times a day. Boats go to various beaches around the island including Meloi, Kambos, Lambi, Psili Ammos, and Grikou. *Excursion* trips can be arranged around the north of the island as far as Levkes.
Moped hire.
Accommodation: Demand sometimes exceeds supply, particularly of hotel rooms in high summer, so get a *rent-room* early if possible. Of the *hotels*, try Patmion (B); Astoria, Chris (C); Rex (D) – all on the harbour; or Rodon (D). *Campground* at Meloi beach to north (20 minutes walk to north or boat).
Restaurants: sometimes too many mouths to feed; go early, try the Avra behind the harbour. There is virtually no nightlife.
Post office, banks in the main square; *OTE* on the waterfront.
Health food shop on the road to Kambos.
The town *beach* is small, so bus or boat (as appropriate) to one of the beaches mentioned above: *Grikou* with a sandy beach is the most developed with a couple of hotels including a Xenia (B), several pensions, etc, and there are also rooms and tavernas at *Kambos* and *Lambi*.

Chora
An E *hotel* (Neon) and a few *rooms*; not many tavernas either (the best is the Patmion).
Apart from the Monastery of St John, there are many interesting churches in the town, though they are usually locked; you will have to ask about for the key.
Monastery of St John: Open usually about 8am to 12, 3 to 6pm, but it closes some afternoons. Dress appropriately.

LIPSI
Reached by caique both from Patmos and from Agia Marina, Leros; also on the route of the weekly ferry from Rhodes to Samos.
It is quiet, with good beaches; there are rooms and tavernas.

LEROS
Apart from the frequent ferries between Piraeus and Rhodes via Leros and the other islands of the Dodecanese, there are connections with Samos and Ikaria and other islands to the north, also about once a week with Mykonos and Tinos. In addition there are frequent excursions to Kalymnos (from Xirokambos in the south), and less frequently to Patmos.

Lakki
A *bus* runs between Platanos and Xirokambos via Lakki about 6 times a day, and half as often between Platanos and Partheni (in the north) via Alinda. Otherwise you can hire *mopeds* or *bicycles*, or indeed *walk* many of the distances.

Hotels: about half a dozen hotels in the C to E classes, of which try the Leros (C) on the waterfront; otherwise there is a good pension some distance inland, Xenon Angelou (B). Also *rooms*. There is *camping* about 10 minutes walk to the south on a beach with tavernas.

Swimming also at Koulouki beach 2 kms to the west (taverna).

Post Office, OTE.

Platanos has various pensions and rooms, as does **Agia Marina** (its harbour), and neighbouring **Panteli** (also 1 to 2 cheaper hotels). **Panteli** has some good restaurants by the beach, and a disco.

Further north on the east coast, **Alinda** has a good beach (with windsurfing, etc) and accommodation including the Maleas Beach (B) by the beach. At nearby **Krithoni** there is a new hotel by the sea, the Athena (C).

At the north end of the island **Partheni** has a secluded beach a few minutes walk away at Blefouti Bay (taverna). At **Gournas** in the middle of the island there is a beach with rooms and tavernas. Similarly at **Xirokambos** in the south, where you can also camp.

KALYMNOS
Additional connections include Samos, and there are excursions to Leros and Patmos from Myrties.

Kalymnos town (Pothia)
A *bus* runs quite frequently from Pothia to the beaches on the west coast, continuing to Arginonta twice a day; 4 times a day a bus runs between Pothia and Vathy. Otherwise there are *taxi-buses* on these routes, or you can hire a *car* or *moped*.

Hotels: several C to E class, but try Olympic (C); or Crystal (D) – both on the harbour. Also *rent-rooms*.

Restaurants by the harbour. *Discos*.

Bank, *post office*, OTE, *Archaeological museum*.

The town *beach* is small; best to go to one of the beaches on the west coast (below).

Boat excursions to the cave of Kephalas in south, also to Pserimos island (beach).

On the west coast there are beaches with accommodation at **Panormos** (several hotels including Drosos (C)), **Linaria** (rooms), **Platis Yialos** (rooms), **Myrties** (hotels including Delfini (C), rooms and some good restaurants, though a shingle beach) and **Masouri** (best of these beaches, sandy; with hotels including Masouri Beach (C), and Ioanna (D); rooms and also some good restaurants). Further north there are beaches at **Arginonta** and **Emporios** (tavernas) but nowhere to stay.

Telendos has 2 sandy beaches and a couple of pensions.

Vathy has no beach and nowhere to stay, but there are some places to eat and you can swim from the harbour to the large sea-cave of Daskalios.

Festival: Sponge Week (Ipogros) after Easter when the sponge diving boats leave.

KOS
Apart from the Piraeus-Rhodes ferry, there are connections with other islands like Astipalaia, Amorgos, Nisiros, Tilos and Simi. Also daily hydrofoil service with Rhodes in summer. Several times a week in summer there is a boat to Bodrum in Turkey (see Samos). There are also excursion trips to Kalymnos, Pserimos and Nisiros from Kos town, and to Pserimos from Mastichari from where there is also a daily caique to Kalymnos.

Kos town
Buses serve Tigaki and Mastichari on the north coast, also the resorts of Kardamena and Kephalos on the south, as well as the inland villages like Asfendiou, but only 2 to 3 times a day as a rule. A good island to hire your own transport: a *bicycle* is quite adequate, though *jeeps* and *mopeds* are available also. The *bus station* is in the middle of town at the junction of Kleopatras and Pisandrou.

Accommodation: Kos can be very crowded in high season despite about 70 hotels in the area of Kos town; it can be wise to take the offer of a room off the boat, at least for the first night, though a good area to look around for *rooms* is to the north of the harbour, behind Averoff Street.

The *hotels* spread out of town along the beaches to west and east, but all the following except the first 2 listed are in town: Atlantis (at Lambi), Ramira Beach (3 kms to the east) (both A, with pools); Alexandra (B); Koulias (C); Helena (D); Kalymnos (E) – all 4 near the harbour; there are several adequate C class hotels in Artemisias and Venizelou Streets which run, east-west across the town, and at either end of Venizelou there is the Oscar (with pool) and the Elizabeth; then there are the hotels Theoxenia, Kos (B); Zephyros (C) – all on the pebble beach to the east. Apart from the Atlantis, Lambi (2 kms to the northwest) has a few cheaper C class hotels, also a relatively quiet beach.

Camping-ground at Psalidi beach, 2½ kms east of town.

Good fish *restaurants* on the harbour. *Discos, Bazoukia* (best bazouki club is the Hellas in Lambi).

NTOG and the *Tourist Police* are both on harbour (at castle end).

National Bank on harbour; *post office* in Venizelou, *OTE* nearby.

Castle, Museum, and *Casa Romana* all have the same hours; approximately 9am to 1pm, 4 to 6pm; Sundays and holidays 9am to 3pm; closed Tuesdays.

Asklepieion
There is no public bus, so use your bicycle, etc, or take a taxi – it is a hot walk (via Platani). Same hours as for the Castle, etc, above.

Probably owing to the seasonal meltemi wind along the north coast the *beaches* there are less developed than on the south. With a windbrake **Tigaki** and **Mastichari** are the best places to go: both have the usual facilities of tavernas and rent-rooms; Tigari has a B class pension and a C class hotel, while Mastichari has the Mastichari Beach (B). **Kardamena** on the south coast with a hotel bungalow complex, and many other hotels and pensions, hosts many package tours, and **Kamari** will probably go the same way, although the long beach to the east which extends to the area of the ruins of the basilica Agios Stephanos allows some seclusion.

ASTIPALAIA
Though on the Piraeus-Rhodes ferry route it is still relatively quiet.

Astipalaia town has 3 D class hotels, also rent-rooms, a sandy beach and the usual facilities (OTE, etc). From here the best form of transport is by caique along the south coast. **Livadi**, a short distance west, has a couple of beaches, also rooms and tavernas. **Analipsi**, a fishing village to the east, is smaller still, with a beach, a few rooms and a taverna.

NISYROS
Connections with Kos and Rhodes, Tilos, Symi and Astypalaia about twice weekly; also excursions from Kos and Rhodes (including hydrofoil).

Accommodation at **Mandraki**, the port and capital, includes about 3 hotels, pensions and rooms; there is a good sandy beach about 10 minutes away (Miramare). A bus meets the tourist boats (otherwise very infrequent) and goes around the island past **Pali** (beach, a few rooms, tavernas) to **Emborio** and **Nikia**, where from both places you can descend to the crater. It is 2 to 3 hours walk from Mandraki to the crater.

TILOS
Similar connections as Nisyros

There are few facilities for tourists and no public transport. The port of **Livadia** has an E class hotel, some bungalows to rent by the beach (you get the key from the mayor) and a few restaurants. 7 kms away, the capital **Megalo Chorio** ('large village', an exaggeration!) has some expensive apartments and a few rooms which are available when the apartments are taken. There are good beaches nearby, especially at **Nausica** on the west coast (taverna). The island runs short of fresh fruit and vegetables, so you should bring some with you.

SIMI
Connections by ferry with Rhodes, Kos and other nearby islands; daily tourist trips to and from Rhodes.

Yialos and Chorio

The port of Yialos and the upper town of Chorio are connected principally by some 400 steps, though there is a route by road with a taxi service. There is no public transport system and no vehicles to hire for the one road; you go by *taxi* or *by foot* or take a *boat* along the coast.

Accommodation consists of 1 or 2 *hotels* and *pensions* on the harbour (best is the Aliki (A)), a couple of cheaper hotels in the square behind the waterfront, and *flats* and *rooms* in the town, many of which are in the restored mansions of Chorio. In high season Simi gets full; if necessary try Simi Tours. At that time too showering gets limited owing to a shortage of water.

There are many tavernas on the waterfront; try Les Katerinettes (where the Italians formally surrendered the Dodecanese in May 1945).

Post office, OTE, banks – all in Yialos.

Swimming is mostly off the rocks in the port area; also *windsurfing; waterskiing*. Otherwise there is Nos Beach, 10 minutes walk (taverna and disco), and a beach at **Pedi**, with rooms available, best reached by caique from Yialos.

There is a tiny *museum* in Chorio; you should certainly wander around the upper town. In the medieval *castle* the church of the Panagia has frescoes.

Many of the excursion trips stop at the **Monastery of Panormitis**; you can also get a boat from Yialos. The monastery has a magnificent ikonostasis. There is a small beach nearby.

If you like *walking* an Engishman called Hugo conducts walks over the island.

RHODES

Rhodes is a centre of communications at the eastern end of Greece, and in addition to the connections by air and the frequent ferries to and from Piraeus via Kos (see above), there are connections three times a week with Kastellorizo, at least twice weekly with Chalki, Karpathos, Kasos and Crete, also Simi, Tilos, Nisyros, Astipalaia and Mykonos, and once weekly with Samos, Chios, Lesvos and Kavala, also Cyprus, Syria, Israel and Egypt. Excursions by boat include daily to Simi and Chalki (the latter from Skala Kamirou). There is also a daily hydrofoil between Rhodes and Kos. In summer there is a daily boat to Marmaris in Turkey (see Samos).

City of Rhodes

There is a fairly frequent *bus* service both along the east coast of the island as far as Lindos (from Papagou Street, near the area of the Sound and Light show) and along the west coast down to Monolithos (from Averof Street nearby).

Car, moped and *bicycle* hire is widely available.

Excursion trips include the city itself, Lindos, Kamiros and Petaloudes. Triton Tours is one of the best agencies.

There are about 100 or so *hotels* to choose from, L to E, though most will be booked solid with tours in high season. The following are all on or close to the waterfront by the beaches around the New Town, unless otherwise mentioned: Grand Hotel Astir Palace (L); Belvedere, Hibiscus, Siravast (A); Cactus, Alexia, Spartalis (behind Mandraki harbour) (B); Carina, Marie, Astoria (Vass. Sofias) (C); Alkyon, Rhodiakon (D); Ialyssos, Sidney (Apellou Street, Old Town) (E).

If you do not snap up a room off the boat or perhaps go to the Tourist Police for a list of rooms the best place to head for is in fact about the best place to be, namely within the walls of the Old Town, best entered by the New Gate to the south of Mandraki Harbour. Here there are plenty of *pensions* and *rooms* to rent; try especially in and around Pithagora and Omirou Streets.

There is an immense variety of *restaurants* including a Chinese one owned by Mandy Rice-Davies! In the Old Town, try Casa Castelana, in a 15th C building at 33 Aristotelous (expensive) or Corali, 13 Ippodamou, for reasonably priced sea food; in general for cheaper places avoid the main area of Socratous and look around Omirou and Pithagora. The Kon Tiki in Mandraki Harbour serves good seafood, and the New Market has several cheap places to eat. Elsewhere in the New Town there is Restaurant 13, Kos Street, and the Snack Bar Hermes, 5 Plastira, both good value, or if you want to be Scandinavian like most people there is the Dania, 3 Iroon Polytechniou, where on

Sunday nights you can have a traditional smoerrebroed.

Any number of *discos*, *bars*, etc. For Greek music go to Zorba's at 4 Iroon Polytechniou (by the Dania). The *Casino* at the Grand Hotel stays open to 4am.

The *NTOG* office and *Tourist Police* are next door to each other at the junction of Makariou and Papagou Streets (get your detailed travel information from there).

The *post office* on Mandraki Harbour and the *National Bank* on Vas. Sophias both stay open to about 8pm weekdays; the *OTE* on 25 Martiou is open to midnight.

The *beaches* on either side of the New Town are all right if you do not mind crowds; alternatively you can take boats down the east coast as far as Lindos and go to beaches such as Zephyros, Kalithea, Falikari, Afandou, Kolimbia, Tsambika, and Charaki, all of which will be quieter.

Each evening, at different times according to the language used, there are *Sound and Light* shows outside the walls of the Castle of the Knights. Also each evening at 9.15pm there are performances of *traditional Greek dancing* at the Theatre in Andronikou Street in the Old Town.

Palace of the Masters: 8.30am to 12.30pm, 4 to 6pm; Sundays and holidays 9am to 3pm. Closed Tuesdays.

Museum of Archaeology: 8am to 7pm; Sundays and holidays 10am to 6pm. Closed Tuesdays.

Museum of Decorative Arts: 9am to 1pm on Mondays, Wednesdays and Fridays.

Mosque of Suleiman: open mornings and late afternoons (similarly the *Turkish library* nearby).

Tour of the Walls: on Mondays and Saturdays at 3pm from the courtyard of the Palace.

The partially restored *Temple of Apollo*, *Theatre* and *Stadium* at the ancient acropolis on Mt Smith are open 8.30am to 12.30pm, 4 to 6pm; Sundays and holidays 9am to 3pm.

Children might be interested in the *Aquarium* and collection of preserved marine animals, open all day, at the north tip of the town.

Places to visit could include the park at **Rhodini**, 3 kms away (bus), where there is a wine festival every evening during the summer (as at Daphni the ticket allows free bibing); **Petaloudes**, or the 'Valley of the Butterflies', where during the summer a large area is covered with moths (compare Paros) – 2 buses daily or excursion; **Epta Piges** inland of Kolimbia, an attractive wooded area near springs, with a restaurant; and the ruins of **Kamiros** on the west coast, open 8.30am to 12.30pm, 4 to 6pm; Sundays 9am to 3pm; with a beach and tavernas below (bus). If you are a golfer there is an 18-hole golf course at **Afandou** which is open to visitors and where you can hire clubs (Tel: 0241.51129).

Further along the east coast, below the *Castle of Feraklos*, also built by the Knights, is **Charaki**, about 36 kms from Rhodes town; some may find the quiet shingle beach, with a few tavernas and rooms to rent, preferable to the action in Lindos. The best and the worst of it is that there is no bus, so you have to walk the few kms from the bus route on the main road, if you do not have your own transport.

Lindos
Frequent *buses* from Rhodes (crowded in summer) or *boat* from Rhodes.
Accommodation: one *hotel*, the Lindos Bay (A), a *complex* near Vliha Bay to the north; otherwise *pensions* and *rooms* – but anywhere will be very difficult to find in high season. You could try Pallas Travel Agency for help.

Usual facilities include *car* and *moped* hire.

For a *taverna* try the Triton down on the beach. *Discos* in the village.

The town *beach* has windsurfing; boats go to nearby beaches.

The *acropolis* is open 8.30a.m. to 12.30pm, 4 to 6pm; Sundays 9am to 3pm.

Further south the crowds thin out and there are some secluded beaches. Beyond Lardos, **Genadi** (1 bus a day) has a fine shingle beach, some tavernas and a few rooms. At **Plimiri** there is a restaurant where you may get a room, and there are some rooms at **Katavia**. On the southwest coast there are long, almost empty beaches. Higher up there is the superb

Castle of **Monolithos**, built by the Grand Master d'Aubusson, inside which is the frescoed church of Agios Pantelimon. Back in more familiar tourist country is the village of **Embonas**, where a couple of tavernas put on traditional Greek dancing in the evenings and there are some rooms; from here you can climb to the summit of Mt Ataviros, 1215 metres once topped by a temple, in about 2 hours.

Festivals: 29 and 30 July, Agia Soula at Soronis; 14 to 23 August at Kremasti.
Wines: try the red Chevalier de Rhodes and the white Ilios.

KASOS
Ophrys, the capital, has 2 C class hotels, some rooms and tavernas. There is a beach at **Ammousa**, 15 minutes' walk away, or you can take a boat to the beach on the islet of **Armathia**. Every 7 July a ceremony remembers the massacre of the islanders by Ibrahim Pasha in 1824. You can walk across the island to **Chelatros**, a lovely cove with good swimming.

KARPATHOS
The ferries mostly call both at Pigadia in the south and Diafani in the north. Caiques go between the two also.

Pigadia
There is a sketchy *bus* service to Arkasa, also Piles via Aperi, and to the beach at Amopi. There is a very poor road to Olimbos in the north, with a bus a few times a week – but priority goes to villagers, so you may not get a ride. Try *hitching* or a *taxi*. *Car* and *moped* hire.
Hotels: several in the C to E class; try Porphyris of Atlantis, both C. Also *rooms*.
Restaurant: the Porphyris is the best in town.
  Disco. Long sandy *beach* in the Bay.
  OTE, post office, exchange.

Amopi, ½ hour walk to the south (also bus), has a long beach, with tavernas and rooms. Otherwise there are rooms at **Arkasa** which has a beach (near the site of ancient Arkessia and the ruins of Byzantine churches with mosaics) and further north at **Lefkos** (beach, tavernas, no bus). Between these 2 places the small harbour of **Finiki** has a beach and a restaurant, but nowhere to stay.

Diafani
Several small *hotels*, also *rooms* available.
  Good fish *restaurants*.
  Beaches to north and south; Vanada beach, ½ hour north, has *camping*.

Olimbos
You can *walk* here in a couple of days from the south, or in about 1½ hours from Diafani, from which you can also take a small *bus* or a *taxi*.
  The village has some *pensions* and *rooms* and 2 to 3 tavernas.
Festival: Panagia, August 15 at Olimbos.

CHALKI
Apart from the ferry from Rhodes there is a daily boat from Skala Kamirou on Rhodes.
  The port of Skala may have rooms to rent if you persist, some tavernas and a small sandy beach about 10 minutes away.

KASTELLORIZO
The port has a *hotel*, Xenon Dimou Meghistis (B), also *rooms*, and some good seafood tavernas. Usual facilities of *OTE*, etc.
  A new *museum* has been opened in a rebuilt house above the harbour and contains photographs of the town as it once was. Following a path round the seaward side of the castle you come to a fine *Lycian tomb* cut out of the rock and facing Anatolia.
  There is good swimming off the rocks; otherwise there are boats to one or two beaches like the islet of Agios Georgios.
  Excursions can be made by boat to the sea cave on the east coast, and to Kas on the Turkish coast opposite.

CRETE

In size, diversity, beauty and history Crete (Kríti) is an island apart, a world of its own. It is the largest of the Greek islands and, after Sicily, Sardinia and Cyprus, the fourth largest island in the Mediterranean. Over its length of 257 kms and its width which varies from 12 to 61 kms is a compression of landscapes of continental variety: palm-lined beaches, 2500-metre mountains capped with snow, cliffs, caves, coves, lowland plains and alpine meadows and a magnificent gorge which is the deepest in Europe. Even the simplest bus ride from A to B is an absorbing adventure.

Crete sets the southern limit of the Aegean and lies on the same latitude as Sousse in Tunisia or Palmyra in Syria. Equidistant from Athens and the coasts of Turkey and Libya, it combines the blazing summer climate of North Africa with the cool breezes of the open Mediterranean, and its people and culture too, though fundamentally European, display the spontaneity yet mystery of African and Asian influences. The island has been in the hands of Rome, Byzantium, the Arabs, Venice and the Ottoman Empire. Only in 1898 were the Turks tossed out, and only in 1913 was Crete officially united with Greece. Centuries of struggle have shaped the Cretans into a rugged, rebellious and proud people, their character described in the novels of Nikos Kazantzakis. But like the early Cretan spring there is the gentler spirit of the brilliant Minoan civilisation which flourished here 4000 years ago with its luxurious palaces, joyful frescoes, the first and possibly finest civilisation in Europe.

Heraklion (Iráklion)

Most people who come to Crete arrive in the early morning at Heraklion. The ship ties up near the old orange harbour walls of the Venetians. This is the major commercial and tourist drop-off town on the island. It is not very pretty and has almost the dusty disorder of a Wild West town, though some of the side streets are charming, there is a Venetian fountain and loggia, a small park with a bust of El Greco (alias Dominikos Theotokopoulos, a native son) and the Archaeological Museum with its Minoan collection, which if nothing else would make the visit more than worth while.

Venetian sights At the centre of the town is the Plateia Venizelou, more commonly known as *Fountain Square* for its 17th C Venetian fountain around which are several cafés where you can enjoy a pastry and get your bearings. Facing north towards Odos 25 Avgoustou, lined with banks and travel offices and running north down to the old harbour, you can see on its right the reconstructed *loggia* and behind it the *Venetian armoury*, now the town hall. Wander into the narrow streets here for some delightful glimpses of old balconied houses softly pasteled. On your immediate right, on the corner of Odos Daidalou, is the 14th C Venetian *Church of St Mark*, now housing copies of frescoes from churches around the island – helpful in planning your tour. Behind you, across the traffic lights, is Odos 1866, an outdoor *market* and excellent place to see and meet people under the guise of buying a tomato. The older Cretans come down from the mountains wearing their knee-high leather boots which protect them from the thorny hillsides (in summer the slopes are grey and brittle with thorns, but in spring the spurge is still green and fresh and flowering).

East from the traffic lights is Plateia Eleftherias (Liberty Square) where you will find the *Archaeological Museum*. From here you can begin a circuit of the *walls* (4 kms). The strongest of their day anywhere in the Mediterranean, for 22 years (1648–69) they withstood the final Turkish siege. Embedded in the most southerly bastion is the *grave of Nikos Kazantzakis*, author of *Zorba the Greek*, *Christ Recrucified*, etc. He was buried here when the Orthodox Church refused him sacred ground. The inscription on his stone replies, 'I hope for nothing. I fear nothing. I am free.' A reconstruction of the study of Kazantzakis, with his furniture, belongings and books, is in the *Historical Museum* opposite the Xenia hotel on the seafront. The museum also contains a collection of art, handicrafts and historical mementoes dating from the early Christian era to the present.

Minoan Civilisation

Before going to Knossos and the other sites, and again afterwards, you should visit the *Archaeological Museum*, for nearly everything removed from the sites and used to build up our picture of Minoan civilisation is here, including sealstones, Linear B tablets and all the original frescoes. Also there is a scale reconstruction of Knossos. The rooms are arranged chronologically and geographically, and many of the labels are in English, so that the visitor with a limited schedule may move through fairly quickly yet still grasp in outline the development of Minoan civilisation and appreciate the museum's highlights. For a more detailed study of the collection, a guide book in English by the museum's director, Dr Alexiou, with an introduction by Professor Platon, is available in the entrance hall.

Myth and history In that way that legend has of collapsing centuries of hazily recalled events into one good story, King Minos (Minos was in fact probably the title of all kings from 2000 BC onwards) was born the son of Zeus by Europa, while his wife Pasiphae, developing an uncontrollable lust for bulls, gave birth to the Minotaur. It was this creature who dwelt in the labyrinth designed by Daedalus beneath Knossos, and to whom Greek youths were sacrificed until Theseus, with the help of Ariadne, put an end to it. (Mary Renault's novel *The King Must Die*, tells the story.) Minoan defence and power lay in controlling the sea. Their cities and palaces were absolutely secure and so developed like grand terraced villa complexes, stone foundations supporting wooden pillars and floors upon floors of rooms decorated with brilliantly coloured fescoes. Everything, their palaces, their frescoes, their pottery showed an exuberance in life expressed with a graceful insouciance prefiguring millenia later the Provence of the Middle Ages and perhaps the Paris of the Third Republic.

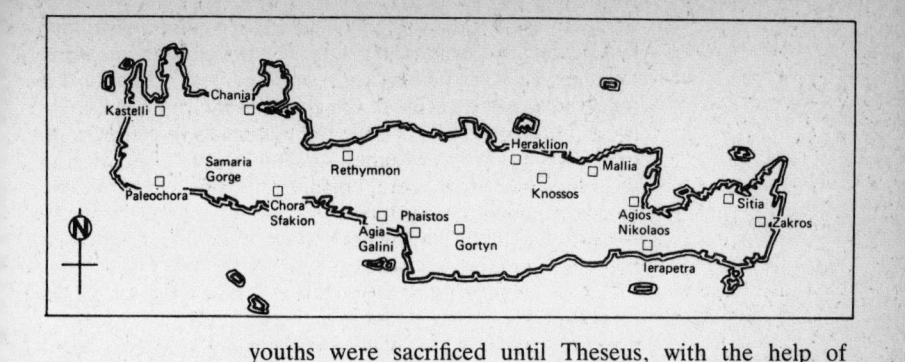

The destruction of Minoan civilisation

But the bull lurked sinisterly beneath the palace. Bulls' horns, like crenellations, decorated the walls of Knossos. Every Minoan palace had its bull arena, and frescoes depict men and women leaping over bulls in a ritualised bull-dance that makes modern bullfighting look like a sport for sissies. The Minoans had an obsession with bulls, or rather with what the image of the bull symbolised. It has been conjectured that the bull and its roar was linked to the roar of the earthquakes which flattened Minoan cities every century or so. The Minoans were supreme on the sea, extending their influence over the whole of the Aegean and even to Libya and Egypt, but they lived in terror of the land and eventually, perhaps with the massive and unequalled explosion of volcanic Thera (c1450 BC) and the consequent tidal wave, their civilisation was washed out. In fact the cause of Minoan civilisation's seemingly sudden end is hotly debated. Some argue that invading mainland Mycenaeans – or Dorians later on – burnt the palaces; others, while accepting some theory of natural catastrophe, argue that Thera's tidal wave or its ejection of volcanic ash were of insufficient magnitude to account for Minoan collapse. At any rate, Minoan civilisation has been in a way resurrected at Knossos.

Knossos

The Palace of Knossos is 5 kms east of Heraklion, an easy pilgrimage on foot for some, otherwise quickly reached by local bus. Initial poking about was done by Schliemann, but the full work of excavation was undertaken from 1900 by the English archaeologist Sir Arthur Evans and paid for out of his own pocket. Evans' idea was to help the imagination of the amateur by partly reconstructing the palace, using the original materials where possible, but resorting to concrete as well. This has been welcomed by some people and criticised by others, but since the other palaces, like Phaestos, have not been reconstructed, you can learn about palace design at Knossos and then vividly imagine rooms and grand staircases rising up from the barer excavations elsewhere.

A tour of the palace

A tour of the palace is conveniently begun at the **West Court** (1) where there is a bronze bust of Sir Arthur Evans. The west facade of the palace would have been perhaps 12 to 14 metres high; from the direction of smoke stains here Evans deduced that it was springtime when the final fire consumed the palace; a south wind is common in spring. The **West Porch** (2) was the ceremonial entrance; visitors would then have passed through the **Corridor of the Procession** (3) where the Procession fresco and the Cup Bearer were found. The southwest corner of the palace has fallen down the slope, so it is by cutting through intervening rooms that you come to the spot where the *Priest King* or *Prince of the Lilies* fresco (4) was discovered. (In fact the feathered crown was found separately from the human figure and it is more likely that it adorned a sphinx led by the man.) The **Central Court** (5), where bull-dancing might have been performed lies before you, its original paving in place. On the left is the **Throne Room complex** (6), an *antechamber* leading to the Throne Room itself, at the left of which down a flight of steps is a *lustral basin*. The *Throne Room* when excavated was decorated with a river scene (not preserved); this has been replaced by two *griffins*, a complete fantasy of Evans' and painted for effect in AD 1930. The *'throne'* – for so it was called, being the fanciest piece of furniture discovered at Knossos – at least was found where you see it.

Off the northwest corner of the Central Court a passage leads to the **Corridor of the Magazines** (7); the north magazines were apparently for storing textiles, those to the south, with their large pithoi, for storing liquids. *Marks of burning* are evident at the entrances of some of the magazines. Beyond the northwest corner of the palace is the **Theatral Area** (8) and the **Royal Road** (9), thought to be the oldest road in Europe. Returning via the **North Pillar Hall** (10) and the **north entrance passage** (11) with the *relief of the Charging Bull*, you cross to the **domestic quarters** to the east of the Central Court. Here is one of the most impressive monuments of Minoan architecture, the **Grand Staircase** (12) which received light from the open **Hall of the Colonnades** (13). The magnificent **King's Room** or **Hall of the Double Axes** (14) could be partitioned by folding doors (note the

PALACE OF KNOSSOS

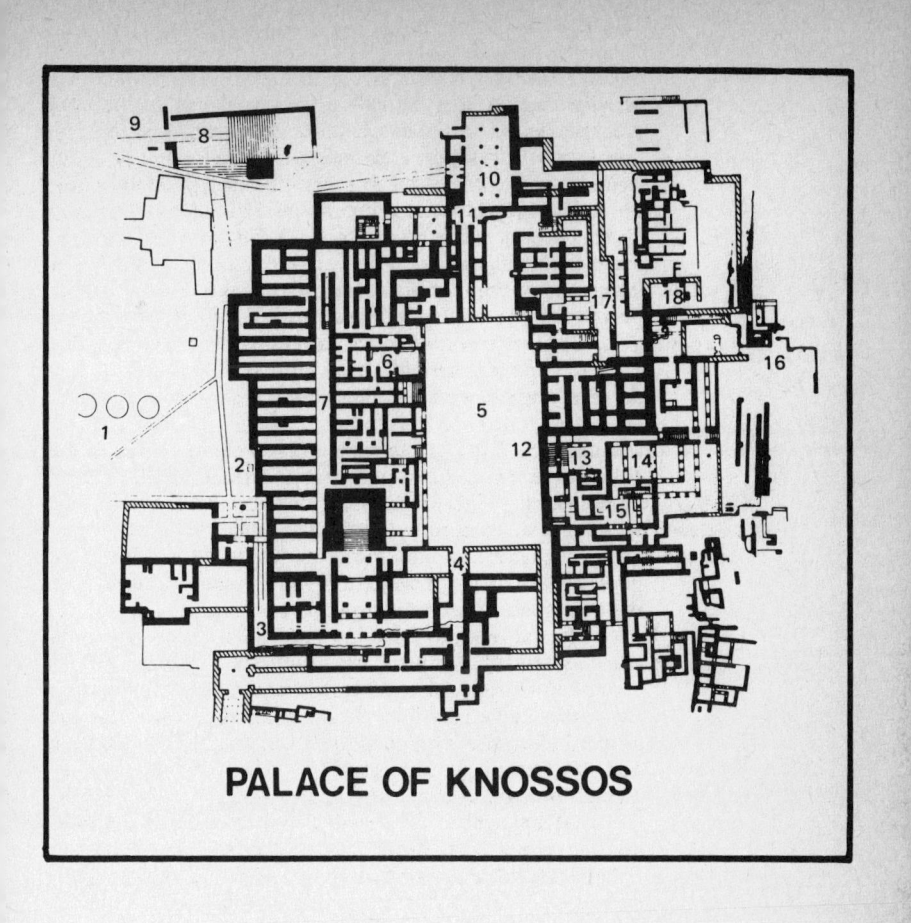

pivots in the floor). The **Queen's Megaron** (15) is graced by the *Dolphin fresco* and there is evidence nearby of the Minoans' amazing plumbing system: drainage of fresh water pipes in the floor and the famous *flush toilet*. Even the method of controlling the speed and direction of water which had to run from one storey down to another shows an appreciation of hydrodynamics; at the **east bastion** (16) you can observe how the water would have flowed through its courses, its speed checked by a series of parabolic curves. Below the **Corridor of the Draughtboard** (17) where Evans found a beautiful inlaid ivory and crystal gaming board you can see *terracotta pipes* so designed and fitted as to resist the pressure of fresh water introduced to the palace system. Near here (18), *giant pithoi* indicate another storage area.

Near the palace is the Villa Ariadne, originally Evans' home, around which Dilys Powell has written her book about Crete ancient and modern, *The Villa Ariadne*.

South from Heraklion

Shortly after leaving Heraklion the bus grinds up the road that crosses the mountains running like a backbone through the centre of Crete, the great mass of Mt Ida looming on your right, and at 45 kms stops by a 7th C basilica of Agios Titos, the ruins of **Gortyn**, the Roman capital of the island, spread about on either side of the road. A *temple of Apollo* and another of *Isis and Serapis* lie across the road along with the *museum*; on the right-hand side is a small *theatre* and an *odeion* into which the Romans built the 2500-year old Law Code of Gortyn inscribed in 'ox-plough' writing – one line running from left to right, the next from right to left, and so on. But impatience calls: Phaestos lies only 16 kms further on.

The last paradise on earth

From where the bus lets you off you climb a bluff to the pavilion, and there below on the level terrace are the ruins of Phaestos, the hillside rolling down behind them into the vast Messara Plain ringed by distant mountains. The panorama itself is magnificent and you think what fine and beautiful people these Minoans were, to build a palace and city here, their frescoes of birds and flowers matching opaque walls to open terrace views of fields beyond. The ruins are unreconstructed, mostly at foundation level, yet especially after a visit to Knossos, easy to trace and understand. What is far more impressive here than at Knossos is the situation of the palace, described by Henry Miller as 'the last Paradise on earth'. Several writers and travellers have compared the masculine, and sometimes forboding, sense of Knossos to the feminine and serene atmosphere of Phaestos. It is certainly equal to Knossos in design, but probably held a secondary political position allowing its populace, known for their wit, to lead more relaxed lives.

The bus can drop you off a further 2 kms beyond Phaestos where there is a turning on the left and a ½ km walk to **Agía Triáda**; alternatively you can follow the pleasant path west along the ridge from Phaestos, a 45-minute walk, to this Minoan site which probably stood by the sea when the water level was higher. It is conventional to think of Agia Triada as a summer palace, but it may have had a primarily religious function in view of the extent of cult practice found in the building.

After Phaestos the road divides, the left fork going off to **Mátala**, that stretch of fine beach and cave-riddled cliffs made famous aeons ago by troglodytic hippies. Following the right fork, the road descends to the village of **Agía Galíni** (75 kms from Heraklion), which looks uninspiring at first approach, never becomes especially lovely even when you get to know it well, but which once at least was a delightful place to spend some time. Then as now in spring the mountains rising up behind the beaches were still glistening with snow at their peaks and there was the pervading fragrance of thyme and lentisk. Fishing boats went out at night with lights shining from their sterns, and if you were up when they returned and they had had a good catch, a taverna suddenly re-opened under the star-thick sky, bottles of wine were passed around, fish were fried up on the grills and you shared freely in the good fortune. Donkeys guffawed explosively in the midnight fields, reminding you how quiet the village could be and you could hear the waves lapping outside your window, the cocks crowing to the dawn. And on Saturday nights half the village carried chairs down to the harbour-front for the mobile picture show. The generator cranked up, someone threw a sheet over a balcony, and you sat stupefied watching John Wayne killing Indians who spoke only dubbed Greek. But with the opening now of snack bar/discotheques like Bozo's and Zorba's the village is fast sacrificing its simplicity to its rapacity. Zorba's tries to create 'atmosphere' with photos on the wall of Agia Galini the way it was before Zorba's and Bozo's and their mindless clientele began to disfigure it. Come out of season and you may recapture its old simplicity still.

The road from here to Rethymnon (52 kms) carries you through high mountains capped with snow into May, their lower slopes covered with flowers, valleys rolling with green wheat and lovely white mountain villages all along the way. The first stretch, where it climbs high above the cliff-coast, provides spectacular views. At Koxares you can instead return to the south coast and head west for Chora Sfakion.

West from Heraklion

The new National Highway runs west along the north coast from Heraklion to Rethymnon (79 kms) and Chania (137 kms), though by first following the old inland road you can detour to the attractive village of **Týlissos** (13 kms) with excavated Minoan villas. Another detour, this time off the new road, is to **Fódele** (26 kms), thought to be the birthplace of El Greco who never lost his feeling for Byzantine style and the Cretan landscape.

El Greco's birthplace

On a narrow point of land surrounded by the sea, with slender minarets rising from narrow streets, **Réthymnon** is the most Oriental of Cretan towns. Although severely damaged during the Second World War, it is still strongly marked by its Venetian and Turkish past.

For colour go to the tiny *Venetian harbour*, a neglected area, houses crumbling, paint peeling off, but full of charm. Standing here with your back to the fishing boats looking up at the small semicircle of narrow houses with wrought-iron balconies (Turkish houses have wooden balconies, supported by angular stays), you could imagine this was all there was to a sleepy and forgotten village, no hint of Rethymnon crouching behind. In the *fortress* there is a mosque and solitary date-palm. On Odos Man. Bernardo, off Plateia Titou Petuchaki, is another *mosque* now used as a theatre; you can climb the spiral stone steps to the top of its minaret for a good view over the rooftops. Nearby is a *Venetian fountain*; and there is also a small *Archaeological Museum*, nicely laid out, with a collection of small bronzes from a Roman shipwreck off Agia Galini, and coins covering every period on Crete. In July the Cretan Wine Festival is held in the Public Garden. Kafeneions and tavernas liven the Venetian harbour, and there is a wide sandy beach to the east.

Freedom or death   It is a 22-km excursion to the **Monastery of Arkádi**, symbol of Crete's ageless dilemma, freedom or death. On 9 November 1866, hundreds of rebels, men, women and children, blew themselves up here rather than surrender to the besieging Turks. The ornate 17th C Venetian church combining classical, Renaissance and Baroque elements is defiantly at odds with the wild landscape.

Soúda Bay, a major Greek and NATO naval base, is the alternative port of arrival for visitors to Crete, and the best if you want to concentrate on the wilder western end of the island. **Chaniá**, 6.5 kms to the west, is the capital of Crete, a distinction it has retained from the 19th C when the Pasha installed his seraglio here. There are two Chanias, the modern town on the plain where the bus stations, market (modelled on the one in Marseille) and cinemas are, and the *old Venetian town* of narrow streets clustered around the horseshoe harbour, the 17th C *Mosque of the Janissaries* on the right, reconditioned to house the National Tourist Organisation. Tall Venetian houses of pink, ochre, green and much cream with brilliantly contrasting shutters line the promenade; all the roofs red tiled, balconies and outside staircases in elaborate ironwork. With the mosque as your view, people strolling by and in the late afternoon fishermen repairing their nets, this is the place to park yourself at a café or taverna. Then go for a walk through the narrow streets behind, one side in cool shadow, the other bleached in sunlight, with curiosities like the church at 51 Odos Zambeliou which is now a coal cellar where blackfaced Beelzebubs load up the sacks. To the east on the delightful Plateia 1821 is the *Church of Agios Nikolaos*, its Venetian campanile and beautiful Turkish minaret witnesses to its conversions. The *Archaeological Museum* on Odos Halidon occupies the vaulted Venetian Church of San Francesco, a Turkish fountain in the adjoining garden. The collection includes several graceful Minoan sarcophagi.

West of Chania, past a string of disgusting or unsafe beaches, is **Maleme** (16 kms); at the airport here the Germans staged their massive parachute invasion of Crete in 1941. Subdued **Kastélli** (43 kms) is the port for twice-weekly arrivals from Piraeus via Monemvasia and Gytheion. From here you can go directly down to **Palaiochóra** on the south coast, a small village with a 13th C Venetian fort and a large sandy beach, though now overcrowded.

Into the mountains

The bus ride from Chania to Omalos is another intoxicating mountain adventure. In the high cool air the village people are cheerful and redfaced, the moon floats bright in the clear blue afternoon sky, and nobody takes any notice of the hairpin turns and precipitous drops. In fact, riding the bus is a social occasion during which everyone chatters and the driver divides his time between looking at the road and acting as master of ceremonies. Finally the road levels off and the round Omalos plain spreads before you, mysterious and beautiful, like a lost world.

And down the gorge

From a lodge on the far side you descend into the **Gorge of Samaria**, the largest in Europe, with sheer walls rising 600 metres in some places, at the *Iron Gates* closing to only 5 metres across. From the lodge to Agia Roumeli on the coast the distance is about 19 kms and the walk can be comfortably done in 6–7 hours. The gorge has been gouged out by torrents of rain down from the White Mountains and during the rainy season and after the thaw a sizeable stream runs its length. In the summertime much of the bed is dry which makes passage easy, but May is the best time to make the walk – the stream is low enough to let you through and the vegetation is still at its height of fullness and beauty. There was an oracle of Apollo here and various nymphs and nereids are said to have inhabited the region. Certainly the presence of the gods and goddesses of nature is powerfully with you as you walk along.

The gorge opens up into a valley, the afternoon sunlight refreshing after the recent shadows. High stone-walled lanes snake past occasional cottages, flowers and grass on the walls, chicks along the lane, goats in the gardens. Fresh, idyllic, absolutely quiet except for a goat bell or a child calling 'kalispera'. This is **Agía Roúmeli**; the mountains quickly deflate to low hills and you can smell the salt breeze in your face. A gigantic fan of stones spreads out towards the sea.

The compleat angler

At night there are flashes of light on the water, followed by dull thuds. Pavlos is drinking ouzo and retsina; he is missing his right hand and some fingers on his left. That is from fishing, he says; he dynamites the fish at night and sometimes does not throw soon enough. Singing and laughing and drunk, Pavlos goes off fishing again, blowing up fish with boisterous enthusiasm.

Along the South Coast to Chora Sfakion

The Sfakia region is mountainous and largely inaccessible except on foot or by looping along the coast in a boat. Its centre is Chora Sfakion which can be reached by road from the north coast. The land is rugged, stark and magnificent;

Rebels and brigands

the people have become legendary as fighters and brigands. Their origins are unknown: some say they are pure Dorians, others that they are Saracens, but their fearlessness and independence is not doubted. This is the one part of Crete that the Venetians and Turks were never able to subdue, and from their mountain strongholds the Sfakians led the resistance against the German occupation during the Second World War. To this day, there are areas of Sfakia where the writ of Athens does not run.

The land of Sfakia is covered with blood and tales of battles both with outsiders and amongst themselves. Family feelings are strong, vendettas are common, traditions are preserved. But the visitor gets only a hint of this now and again, perhaps a terrific fight or the sight of a gun or just a story told in a village. Treat the Sfakians with respect and respect will be returned.

Instead of going direct from Agia Roumeli to Chora Sfakion, put in at **Loutro**. You sail into a beautiful cove of crystal green and turquoise water, some houses round the pebbly beach and palms. For all the world a South Pacific lagoon. Many of the houses stand empty. Some are derelict, others uninhabited for the moment as families move up into the mountains with their goats and sheep. Mountains climb behind the village and following a steep path you can reach **Anapolis** (also bus from Chora Sfakion), a village now but once a town of 70,000 which flourished in Roman and Byzantine times. The ruins of its giant *walls* remain. Another path, a bit dangerous, clutches its way along the coast to Chora Sfakion.

The Cretan hero, Daskalogiannis

Until recently at Loutro the pace of days was measured by the chickens and turkeys running in and out of doorways, and the nights were illuminated only by the rising moon across the harbour waters. Now there is electricity and the hiring-out of windsurfing boards and kayaks. Just at the jetty where the boat ties up was a café run by friendly, toothless, stubble-chinned old Andreas. He made you a coffee on his single burner inside, and you asked him about Daskalogiannis. Andreas spoke no English and you might have known only a dozen words in Greek, but like all Greeks Andreas could convey anything vividly with his gestures, expression and tone. So this old man sat over the coffee he had made for you and told you about his great-great-grandfather, Daskalogiannis, national hero and leader of the Cretan uprising against the Turks at the end of the 18th C. The Pasha invites Daskalogiannis to Heraklion to talk. The Turks cannot subdue Sfakia and ask only that the Sfakians pay a tax. Daskalogiannis says no and the Pasha has him skinned alive and thrown into the sea. Using his hand like a knife, Andreas cut the flesh off his face. He did not flinch, to let you know Daskalogiannis did not flinch. Only the women, before Daskalogiannis goes to Heraklion, cry no, do not go, but Daskalogiannis says it is his duty and he is not afraid. Dear old Andreas with his kafeneion and that picture on his wall inside of bearded Daskalogiannis and his wife.

The heyday of **Chóra Sfakíon** has passed and now it is small and dull, merely a transit point in your travels. From here the British and Commonwealth forces were evacuated after the fall of Crete to the Germans, though many could not be got off in time and had to surrender. After putting down their arms, some were killed by straffing Luftwaffe planes who were unaware of the capitulation. For all that, the situation is excellent, with mountains dropping into the sea to the west, and to the east a littoral between the mountainsides and the coast and 9 kms along **Frangokastello**, a Venetian fortress emblazoned with the Lion of St Mark. Cretans claim that on 18 May, at dawn, you can see the ghosts of warrior Sfakians dancing round the castle. The road out of Chora Sfakion loops and winds against the bare rising hills as though, when viewed from high up, it had been laid solely for some grand aesthetic purpose, a tentacle unwound from a Minoan vase to decorate the land.

The phantoms of Frangokastello

East from Heraklion

You should not miss a visit to eastern Crete. If it cannot boast the largest Minoan palaces, it does possess three major Minoan sites at Mallia, Gournia and Zakros, as well as several lesser ones. There is also the most beautiful of the upland plains on Crete, Lasithi; the best known of the frescoed churches, at Kritsa; and the only town of any size on the south coast, Ierapetra. Unfortunately, the beaches on the north coast have attracted a number of large hotels, but the Cretan landscape, although less severe at this end of the island, is sufficiently spectacular to withstand almost the worst excesses.

If you take the old road (not the highway) from Heraklion towards Agios Nikolaos (67 kms) you pass, about 1 km east of the airport, **Karteros Beach**. Before the road starts to climb again over Kakon Oros (Bad Mountain) there is a turning on the left to the Minoan site of **Amnisos**, suggested as one of the ports of Knossos. The *House of the Lilies* (from its fresco) has been excavated to the east of a prominent rock; to the west are some remains of what might be *harbour installations*. **Limín Chersonísou** (27 kms) is an old village grown into a busy resort with many new hotels. Pine-shaded tavernas look over the water, beneath which – when it is not too windy, often a problem on Crete – you can see shapes indicating the line of the *ancient harbour for Lyttos*, an all but vanished classical city to the south.

About 9 kms eastwards is the Minoan **Palace of Mallia**. The modern village is strung along the road; a little way north are several large hotels by a very good beach. Finally there is the site, about 3 kms further to the east of the village (buses to Mállia terminate at the site). At this point the narrow coastal strip has opened out and in a particularly satisfying position between the mountains and the sea is the palace, ranking in size after Knossos and Phaestos. Dating from the Neo-Palatial period as do the principal remains at the other two sites, it has the same general layout, but inevitably more of the feel of Phaestos, little restored and the pithoi as tall as most of the remains.

About 2 kms west of Limin Chersonisou a turning to the right leads up through olive groves and several pretty villages: in **Potamiés** the monastic *church of the Panagia* has some good 14th C frescoes (key from the village priest), as does the *Church of Agios Antonios* in **Avdóu**. Finally you go through a pass, guarded by derelict stone windmills, into the **Lasithi Plain**, which lies in a bowl of mountains, the highest of which is Mt Dikti to the south (2149 metres). The plain spreads before you like a garden, almost completely flat, with countless windmills to irrigate the rich land; dotted around its edges are several small villages. The area produces a lot of grain (also fruit and potatoes) and, although machinery now does much of the harvesting, in August you can still see cattle pulling laden sleighs around the earth threshing-floors, and the villagers winnowing the wheat with large olive wood prongs. You should try to see the first operation: a woman perches uncomfortably on top of a large stone on a wooden sled driving two yoked cows in front of her around one of these circular floors, separating the wheat from the straw. The air is full of swallows diving after the countless insects, but the best moments come when she produces a large plate and has to juggle with an avalanche of dung from one of the animals, to prevent the grain being fouled, before depositing it in a neat pile to one side.

On the far side of the plain is the pleasant village of **Psychró**, a good base for walks around Lasithi and up to the

The 'Diktaion Cave'

'Diktaion Cave', the alleged birthplace of Zeus, about half an hour to the west. This cave is worth a visit, although it may not be the one which the ancients associated with Zeus (according to Robert Graves it definitely is not). It descends steeply, with numerous stalagmites and stalactites at the bottom, the daylight above distressingly remote. Hereabouts the guide will point to the exact spot where Zeus was born, whereas the ancient legend only speaks of the infant being hidden in the 'Diktaion Cave' by Mother Earth after his birth in Arcadia, to prevent him being eaten by his father, Kronos. As the poet Kallimachos said of the Cretan claim that Zeus was also buried on the island, 'the Cretans are always liars' –

Worship of the Earth Goddess

or perhaps they are just developing the myth. In any event, there is no doubt that the Earth Goddess was worshipped here from the Minoan through to the archaic period, since many votive offerings have been found, and in the upper part of the cave there was a sacred enclosure.

Outside again, the plain seen in the evening light is like an enormous tapestry, or a Brueghel painting, with ant-like humans coming home from the fields after the day's harvesting.

Less than two decades ago, **Ágios Nikólaos** was just an attractive small port, and the only development was the Minos Beach complex in the bay on the west. Now it could be a resort on the Costa Brava: if that is what you like, it is ideal – large hotels, discos, bars, boutiques – but it has not got much to do with Crete. However, the swimming is good, off rocks into clear turquoise water, and owing to the nearby mountains the town enjoys a superb position. Other features are the 'bottomless pool', an inner harbour where quite often in summer there is outdoor music, and a small *museum* in the west of town with finds from Lasithi nome of which Agios Nikolaos is the capital.

<small>The finest frescoed church on Crete</small>

Kritsá, 12 kms to the southwest, is an attractive village with probably the finest frescoed church on Crete – the *Panagia Kera*, situated amongst olive groves on the right of the road 2 kms before the village. The whitewashed church has three aisles with powerful frescoes of the 14th and 15th C. The south aisle shows scenes from the life of the Virgin Mary and her mother, St Anne. The middle aisle shows the life of Christ – the Last Supper is particularly fine. The north aisle depicts aspects of Paradise. There are also panels of saints and martyrs and in the north aisle you can see the founders of the church. The Cretan church is an imitation, in symbol, of the Cosmos, a microcosm of the whole universe, create and uncreate – from Christ in his cupola representing heaven, down to the church founders on the lowest, earthly level.

Eastern Crete

From Agios Nikolaos to Sitia (73 kms) the scenery is very beautiful. Initially, there are several villages in fertile pockets of land on the Gulf of Mirabello, and the Sitia mountains can be seen ahead. At 19 kms you pass the site of **Gourniá**, which lies on a hillock on the right hand side of the road, indicated by a small sign. Gournia is the best preserved Minoan town yet excavated. It was in an important position at the northern end of the shortest and easiest north–south trade route across the island, and possessed a harbour in the cove below. You can walk around the narrow, stepped streets between the small houses of this Minoan township as you might do in a Greek hill village like Arachova or the Chora of a Cycladic island such as Kea or Ios. There is a knowledgeable but garrulous guide who can quickly point out the obvious features.

<small>Minoan town</small>

Travel writers are perhaps a little too kind to **Sitía**, an unremarkable small port. The Venetians who made Sitia one of the four capitals of the island were disappointed enough by the outcome to remove the cannons from the fortress to go elsewhere. Below the decayed Venetian kastro, the houses straggle down the hill to the harbour, which is now largely concerned with the export of raisins. Little to enthuse over, but it is a quiet place and has several good tavernas along the quay.

East of Sitia the road passes over one of the most satisfying stretches of country in eastern Crete – villages of one-storey houses with outside ovens and amphoras for chimneys, and (in August at least) hills covered with purple thyme. After about 15 kms there is a left turn to the isolated **monastery of Toploú**, which is worth a detour of 4 kms. It looks like a castle, and has long had a reputation as a centre of resistance (Toplou means 'cannon' in Turkish) and for hospitality to refugees and travellers alike. After an earthquake in the early 17th C had destroyed the original 14th C foundation, the monastery was rebuilt in a style showing Venetian influence. Its most famous possession is an ikon called 'O Lord Thou Art Great', painted in 1770 by Ioannis Kornaros, a great masterpiece of Cretan art. The main road continues to **Palaíkastro** (overgrown excavations of a Minoan town nearby); 3.5 kms to the north is the long sand beach and tall palms of **Vai**, so often praised for its seclusion that now it has become an open air dormitory in summer.

Áno Zákros (37 kms from Sitia) is a large village, like a modern Gournia, clinging to the hillside above a green valley, and nurtured by a gushing spring. It is pleasant to walk up to the spring, through the narrow streets, past plots of vines, and flowers and jolly women, and along the open, concrete ducts full of freshwater crabs. About 1 km out of Ano Zakros, on either side of the road to **Káto Zákros**, the remains of a *Minoan villa* of the Neo-Palatial period have been found: there was a wine-press in the building, although olive oil must have been at least as important a product to the Minoans of the region. You continue through the olive groves, then along the ridge above a huge gorge known as the Valley of the Dead (from the number of caves which were there used for Minoan burials) until the road descends to the beautiful bay of Zakros. Two headlands enclose the bay which has a good beach lined with a dozen or so buildings and a banana grove behind. In the north corner of the bay, near the mouth of the gorge, is the **Palace of Zákros**, perhaps the most romantically situated of all the Cretan palaces.

Zakros seems to have been an important centre for the import into Crete of rich materials from the East; though similar to the other Neo-Palatial palaces and, like them, destroyed c1450 BC, it was never reoccupied or plundered so that excavations since 1962 under Professor Platon have turned

Bull figurines at the Archaeological Museum, Heraklion

Palace treasures up some superb treasures: over 50 stone vessels of diverse style and decoration, many bronze saws and swords, chalices, a rock crystal rhyton, countless vases, bronze ingots from Cyprus and tusks of ivory from Syria – the best of these can be seen in Room VIII of the Archaeological Museum in Heraklion. Possibly the most famous find from Zakros is the Mountain Shrine Rhyton, which has reliefs of goats romping around the hillside and was originally covered with gold leaf.

From Pachia Ammos back at the Gulf of Mirabello you can turn south for **Ierápetra** (18 kms) through a plain which stretches from coast to coast, full of olive trees. No substantial Minoan remains have been found at Ierapetra, which is surprising in view of the apparent trade link across the island to Gournia. Hellenistic and Roman *ruins* lie just outside of town, but there is little to see. The Venetians or Genoese left a fine *fort* by the sea and the Turks a *minaret* and a charming *fountain* in the bazaar area in the west of town, but Ierapetra's attraction does not lie chiefly in these relics. The town faces across the Libyan Sea to Africa (you know it too, when the hot sirocco blows) and an easy-going atmosphere pervades the idle seafront: there, men sleep in the afternoon shade as if nothing other than the arrival of a long forgotten vessel from Africa or the East could stir them. But that trade has long gone, and Ierapetra's prosperity depends now largely on the olives, tomatoes and other vegetables grown in the region. There are also plenty of tavernas, pastry shops, and even discotheques to accept the money of the travellers and idlers who have come in increasing numbers recently to **End of the** this lazy coast, but the Ierapetrans take the invasion easily as **line** if they have seen it all before.

PRACTICAL INFORMATION

TRAVEL TO CRETE
Air. From Athens there are 7 to 8 flights daily to Heraklion and 4 to 5 a day to Chania. There are many direct flights to Heraklion from other European cities. In addition there is a flight almost every day between Rhodes and Heraklion, and 3 flights a week from Thera.

Sea. From Piraeus there are 2 ships every day to Heraklion, leaving early evening (12-hour trip), and there is also an evening ship every day to Chania (11 hours). There are 3 ships a week to Agios Nikolaos and Sitia (continuing to Rhodes), and at the other end of Crete the port of Kastelli has 2 boats a week from Piraeus via Monemvasia and Kithera. There are frequent connections from Crete with Thera, Ios, Naxos, Paros, and Syros; less frequent with Milos, Kimolos, Sifnos, Serifos and Mykonos. In the summer there are day trips by both boat and hydrofoil to Thera. Further afield, there are weekly boats to Haifa via Cyprus and to Alexandria.

TRAVEL AROUND CRETE
There is a good *bus* service throughout most of the island, and it is particularly good along the north coast. There is no comparable road along the south coast (in fact there is seldom a road at all) so that sometimes you may be forced to return to one of the major towns in the north, in reality no great hardship, before catching another bus southwards. One drawback is that the last buses tend to be in the late afternoon or early evening.

If you can afford it, *hiring your own transport* is probably the best solution, it being possible to see most of the island that way within the time of a normal holiday period.

For those with more time to spare there is almost a tradition of *walking* on Crete (here one remembers Pendlebury), more so than elsewhere in Greece, something of a paradox since Crete and particularly the south coast is inhospitable to walkers. If you do go walking you will obviously need a pair of very good boots, you must take plenty of water and some food, and you really should travel with at least one other person.

HERAKLION
Accommodation
Hotels: Astoria (Plateia Eleftherias), Xenia (scafront, west of harbour), both with pools (A); the following are all reasonably central: Daidalos (15 Daidalou), Knossos (25 Avgustou), Olympic (Plateia Kornarou), Park (El Greco Park), Selena (near Plateia Venizelou) (C); Palladion (Chandakos Street) (D); Ionia (Evans Street) (E). There are several cheap hotels on or near Chandakos and Evans Streets. A walk or taxi-ride away to the eastern suburb of Poros is the C class Possidon (46 Possidonos), which is said to be worth the trouble.

Also *pensions* and *rooms* available in the usual way.

Youth hostel, 24 Chandakos.

A *camping ground* is 5 kms west; take bus No. 1 from Eleftherias Square.

Eating and Entertainment
Tavernas: Knossos, opposite the Morosini fountain; Maxim's, El Greco Park; Klimataria, 8 Daidalou; Psaria, at the bottom of 25 Avgustou. For cheaper meals go to Dirty Alley between 1866 Street and Evans Street. A *pastry shop*, Averoff, is in Dikaiosinis Street.

Discos are found in and around Plateia Eleftherias; for *Cretan music* go to Erotokritos.

Travel
Car and *moped* rentals: start looking around El Greco Park.

Tours all over Crete are arranged by Creta Tours, 25 Avgustou Street.

Alas, there are 5 *bus stations* in Heraklion serving different parts of the island; getting the right bus or changing buses can be a complicated affair. For *eastern Crete* (Agios Nikolaos, Lassithi, Ierapetra, etc) go to Bus Terminal A, on the waterfront east of the harbour; turn left as you disembark or take bus 2, 3 or 5 from Eleftherias Square. For the *northwest coast* go to the Chania/Rethymnon Terminal next to the

Historical Museum on the waterfront (turn right as you disembark). For *Phaestos, Matala, Agia Galini*, etc, go to the Chania Gate Bus Station (Bus Terminal C), by the Venetian gate in the western wall of Heraklion. For destinations to the *southwest of Heraklion* (Tylissos, Anogia, Fodele, etc) go to Bus Terminal D to the north of Chania Gate station, a short distance along the wall. For the *southeast of Heraklion* go to the Oasis Bus Station (Bus Terminal B) at the end of Evans Street and just outside the wall at Kainouria Gate.

Buses serving *Heraklion and vicinity* usually leave from Eleftherias or Venizelou Squares.

Museums and Sights
The *Archaeological Museum* is open from 8am to 7pm daily, with reduced hours on Sundays and holidays.

The *Historical Museum* (including early Christian, Byzantine and Venetian periods, also the transplanted study of Nikos Kazantzakis, and photographs of the Battle of Crete) is to the west of the harbour by the Xenia hotel, and is open from 9am to 1pm, 3 to 6pm daily, closed Sundays.

The *harbour fortress* is open mornings and late afternoons.

The *Church of Agia Aikaterini* in the square of the same name just south of Kalokairiou, contains a collection of ikons; open usually in the mornings and late afternoons. Six ikons by Michael Damaskinos (16th C) are in the *Cathedral of Agios Menas*, in the same square.

Beaches
The best option near Heraklion is the beach at *Amnisos*, 8 kms to the east, reached by bus 6 from Eleftherias Square; you can keep away from the large hotels to the west, and there are places to eat; there is also a campground nearby.

Other Things
Tourist Police: Konstantinou Street, parallel to Daidalou.
NTOG office: opposite the Archaeological Museum, by Plateia Eleftherias.
National Bank: on 25 Avgustou; open to 7pm weekdays.
Post office: Plateia Daskalyiannis, just west of Plateia Eleftherias; open to 8pm weekdays.
OTE: El Greco Park; open till midnight.

KNOSSOS
Bus 2 from Eleftherias Square.
Open 8am to 7pm; shorter hours on Sundays and holidays.
You can find *rooms* in the village, and *tavernas*.

GORTYN
The *bus* to Phaestos stops at Gortyn; open all day to about 7pm.
It is possible to find *rooms* in tavernas in the nearby village of Agii Deka.

PHAESTOS
Open 8am to 7pm; Sundays and holidays 9am to 6pm. Xenia (D) by the site has a few *rooms*; you can also find rooms a few kms east at the Olympic Pension (C) in Mires.
From Phaestos you can pick up *buses* to Matala and to Agia Galini.

AGIA TRIADA
No *bus*. Open 10am to 4pm; Sundays and holidays 9am to 2pm. Closed Fridays.

MATALA
Accommodation: hotels and pensions are relatively expensive – a cheaper option would be to find *rooms* at Pitsidia, 3 kms inland, and to enjoy the beaches, etc, from there. Otherwise try the Matala Bay (C) or the Zaphyria pension. There is a *campsite* behind the beach.
Tavernas along the waterfront; *discos*.
You can hire a *car* or *moped*.
There are *beaches* (though less nice than those at Matala) with rooms at both **Limenes** and **Lendas** to the east (Lendas can be reached by bus from Heraklion).

AGIA GALINI
In addition to the *bus* service to and from Heraklion there are several buses a day to and from Rethymnon. (On the latter route the lush inland village of **Spili** is an attractive place to stop, with rooms and a C class hotel, To Prasino – 'The Green').
From Agia Galini there are buses to Phaestos, and it is worth checking if it is now possible to get a bus to Chora Sfakion

309

to the west via Koxares, whence you can certainly go as far as Plakias.

This former fishing village now boasts some 25 *hotels* and any number of *pensions* and *rent-rooms*, and is to be avoided in high season when anyway it can be difficult to get a room. If you have any choice in the matter try the Astoria, Candia (C); Livyi (D); Aktaeon (E) – the latter 2 looking over the harbour. *Camping* 2kms east.

Several good inexpensive *tavernas* on the street leading from the harbour; *disco* on beach.

WEST OF HERAKLION
There are 5 *buses* a day to **Tylissos** and **Anogia**. The Minoan ruins at Tylissos are open from 10am to 4pm daily; 9am to 2pm Sundays and holidays; closed Mondays. There are *rooms* in the village. At Anogia there are 2 E class *hotels*. From here it is a 4 hour walk to the **cave of Idha**, where there was a post-Minoan cult.

RETHYMNON
Accommodation
Hotels: Xenia (by the town beach), Ideon (Plastira Square, behind the old harbour) (B); Valari (on Kountouriotou) (C); Acropol (Iroon Square, near the beach), Minoa (Arkadiou, behind the waterfront) (D).

Pensions and *rooms* are plentiful out of high season, especially in the area along and behind the waterfront to the east of the old harbour (Arkadiou, etc).

There is a *youth hostel* at 7 Pavlou Vlastou. *Campgrounds* are to the east and west of town; about 3 kms east there are 2 (bus to Platanes).

Eating and Entertainment
There are several good fish *tavernas* on the old harbour, with *discos* nearby.

Travel
In addition to the frequent *buses* along the north coast to Heraklion and Chania, from the bus stations in Iroon Square and south of Kountouriotou at Moatsou Street (junction with Dimokratias) you can reach the Arkadi monastery (3 buses daily), Spili and Agia Galini (4 daily), Plakias (2 daily), and there is a daily bus at about midday to Chora Sfakion.

Car hire, mopeds.

Museum, etc
The *Archaeological Museum* is in a 16th C Venetian loggia at the western end of Arkadiou Street; open 8.30am to 12.30pm, 4 to 6pm; Sundays and holidays 9am to 3pm; closed Tuesdays.

The *Venetian fortress* is open from 9am to 7.30pm, Sundays and holidays from 9am to 4pm.

Other Things
The *Tourist Police* are next to the museum in Arkadiou.

The *NTOG* office is at 100 Kountouriotou; the *post office* is next door, and the OTE is along the same street to the west.

The *National Bank of Greece* is on Antistaseos, going down to the harbour. The town has a wide sandy *beach* on its eastern side. There is a *wine festival* during the last 2 weeks in July in the park west of Kountouriou; a ticket entitles you to unlimited wine, and there is Cretan music and dancing.

MONASTERY OF ARKADI
Open all day, though the small historical *museum* closes over midday. There is a *Tourist Pavilion* and some *rooms*.

GEORGIOUPOLIS
23 kms to the west of Rethymnon; there is a good *beach* and 1 C, 3 E class *hotels*, plus *rooms*.

CHANIA
Accommodation
Hotels: Xenia (at the northwest end of the Venetian walls around the harbour), with pool (A); Samaria (near bus station) (B); El Greco (near Xenia), Lucia, Manos, Plaza (above Kavouria restaurant) – all these are on the harbour, Dictynna (Betollo Street, near the market), Chania (1866 Square) (C); Phidias (near the cathedral) (D); Averoff (1866 Square) (E).

There are numerous *pensions* (try looking in Zambeliou Street behind the harbour waterfront), and *rooms* for rent.

There is a *youth hostel* at 33 Drakonianou Street (a bus journey away from the market in a southeast suburb). Camping at Agia Marina beach 7 kms west (bus).

Eating and Entertainment
Tavernas: Kavouria, Faros, both on the

harbour where there are many other cheaper places; for wine from the barrel, Taverna Annitsaki in Hadzimichali Yiannari Street; Asposperida, 37 Kondylaki Street, though this may be closed in high season.

Discos on the harbour.

Travel
Buses about every $\frac{1}{4}$ hour to and from Souda, arriving in Chania at the market. Buses to most local destinations depart from Plateia 1866 just south of the top of Halidon Street. The long-distance bus station is in Kidonias, a block further south, although buses for Rethymnon and Heraklion leave from near 1897 Square to the east. There are about 12 buses a day to Kastelli (about hourly, in about $1\frac{1}{4}$ hours), 3 to Omalos and the Gorge of Samaria, about the same number to Chora Sfakion and Palaiochora, and two daily to Sougia.

Car and *moped* rentals available.

Canea Travel Bureau, 46 Karaiskaki Street, arrange *tours* to the Samaria Gorge and elsewhere.

Museums
The *Archaeological Museum* is in the 13th C church of San Francesco in Halidon Street, open 9am to 1pm, 4 to 6pm; Sundays and holidays 9am to 3pm; closed Tuesdays.

The *Naval Museum of Crete* to the left of the harbour is open 10am to noon, 5 to 8pm, and has models of ships, etc.

Excursions and Beaches
There are several beaches to the west, the nearest being Nea Chora (bus from 1866 Square) with tavernas. Further away is Agia Marina and Platanias. An alternative is to go into the Akrotiri peninsula: Stavros for example has a good beach, rooms and tavernas; you can visit the **monastery of Agia Triada** which has a fine Renaissance church, and on the hill of Profitis Ilias there is the **grave of Eleftherios Venizelos** (1864–1936), the Greek statesman, who was born just south of Chania at Mournies.

Other Things
NTOG office: in a tarted up mosque on the right of the harbour.
Tourist Police: 44 Karaiskaki Street.
Post office: 3 Tzanakaki, south of the market, open weekdays to 8pm.
OTE: next to the post office, open to midnight.
National Bank: next to the bus station in Kidonias Street.

Chania is well known for its *leather goods*, particularly footwear, and you can have shoes, etc, made relatively cheaply (go to the street behind the hotel Dictynna).

The *Chania Festival*, from mid-May to mid-June, includes folk dancing on the harbour.

KASTELLI
Accommodation: about 3 *hotels*, of which Kastron (C) is the best; otherwise several reasonable *pensions* along the beach. Better than the rocky beach here, however, is the sandy *beach* at **Falassarna**, about 15 kms to the west, provided it is not being polluted by engine-oil from fishing-boats; you catch a bus to Platanos and walk 5 kms north – there are a couple of tavernas with rooms by the beach.

PALAIOCHORA
Buses from Kastelli and Chania; in high summer there is a daily *boat* along the south coast to Chora Sfakion.
Accommodation: 2 D class *hotels*, many *pensions* and *rent-rooms*. Campground 1 km east of village.
Tavernas, disco.

Sougia, to the east, reached by the boat from Palaiochora or bus from Chania, is quieter and has a long pebble beach, with tavernas and rooms. It is possible to walk from Palaiochora to Sougia, but not recommended.

GORGE OF SAMARIA
The gorge is open to walkers from 1 May to 31 October, and you cannot set out to walk through it after 3pm. There are 3 buses a day from Chania to the top of the gorge: the first 2, at about 6 and 9am, allow you to get through the gorge in time to get the boat to Chora Sfakion at the bottom (the last boat is about 5pm) which should in turn connect with a bus back to Chania, so that you can do it all in one day. However apart from the rush involved you should allow 2 days in any event since the boats can be unreliable and the bus at Chora Sfakion is often full.

At the top of the gorge, Xiloskalo, there is a Xenia with refreshments and 3 *rooms* (Tel: 93237 to reserve), and you can also stay at one of the tavernas at Omalos, 6 kms away, but any of these rooms will be hard to get in high season. In the gorge you will find water, but you should take some anyway and a little food.

Agia Roumeli has a B class *pension*, many *rooms* and several tavernas, though these can scarcely cope with the traffic in August. In July and August there are 3 *boats* daily to Loutro and Chora Sfakion, and 1 daily to Sougia and Palaiochora.

From Agia Roumeli it is possible in 5 hours to *walk* along the coast to Loutro; but it is more interesting to walk from Agia Roumeli to **Anapolis**, above Loutro (about 6 hours), though it is hard going.

LOUTRO
Pensions, rooms, tavernas.

Apart from the regular *boat* service to Chora Sfakion and Agia Roumeli, there is a beautiful coastal *path* to Chora Sfakion (about 2 hours).

There is also a taverna and rooms at **Finix** to the west.

CHORA SFAKION
Xenia *hotel* (B); also *pensions* and *rooms*. Small *beach* by the harbour.

Buses back to Chania soon fill up, so hang about to grab a seat when it arrives. One of the buses goes up to **Anapolis** (see above), where there is a lovely upland area and the taverna you first come to at the top has rooms.

FRANGOKASTELLO
One *bus* a day passes by the fortress; nearby there is a sandy *beach* with a couple of tavernas and a few *rooms*.

Further east **Plakias** (bus from Rethymnon) has good beaches, though one has been colonised by a hotel-bungalow complex with the incongruous name of Calypso Cretan Village. Plakias has a good B class *pension* (Lamon), 2 C class *hotels*, *rooms*, a *youth hostel* (there is another youth hostel at nearby **Mirthios**) and a *camping-ground*. The monastery of **Preveli** (St John Theologos) is open to visitors from 8am to 1pm, 5 to 8pm; the nearest bus is to Asomatos, about 6 kms away. Enquire at the monastery how to get to the beach below.

LIMIN CHERSONISOU
Now has 36 *hotels*, including 1 luxury, 3 A class and 12 B! Outside this range you could try the C class hotels Nefeli or Palmera Beach (disco), both by the sea, or the Iro on the main street. There is also the D class Crystal and the E class Samanthia and 1 or 2 pensions. There is a *camping-ground* 1½ kms east.

MALLIA
About as appealing as Limin Chersonisou to stay at, though if you must there is a better choice with about a dozen *hotels* in the D to E categories (mostly behind the main street). *Youth hostel* to the east of town; 2 *camping-grounds*, one near the beach with a restaurant, disco, etc, and the other 5 kms east.

LASITHI
About 2 *buses* daily both from Heraklion and Agios Nikolaos.

You can find places to *eat* and *accommodation* at **Tzermiadon** (Kourites (B); Kri-Kri (E)), **Agios Georgios** (3 E class hotels) and **Psychro** (Zeus (D); and 2 E class hotels).

The **Diktaion Cave** has a Tourist Pavilion nearby; there are guides, mules, etc, available, but you can do it all yourself with a flashlight or some candles though you may miss seeing exactly where Zeus was born. Psychro has a *festival* over 29 to 31 August, including the celebration of a traditional Cretan wedding.

It is possible to *walk* in about 8 hours from Lasithi to **Kritsa** via the Katharo plateau (better that way round than uphill from Kritsa), a beautiful but very tiring trek.

AGIOS NIKOLAOS
From the bus station on the waterfront to the south at Atlantidos Square there are in addition to the frequent *buses* to Heraklion about 9 departures a day for Sitia (via Gournia) and for Ierapetra, and hourly buses to Kritsa and Elounda. *Car hire*, etc, available. There are also *boat trips* to Elounda and Spinalonga. *Tours* are arranged by Buzz Travel.

Accommodation: some 70 *hotels*, also *pensions*. The famous Minos Beach Hotel (L) is some way out of town. Nearer the action and probably your purse are the El Greco (overlooking the sea) (B); Acratos, Du Lac (both near the lake on 28 Oktovriou) and Pergola (quiet) (all C); Lato (D); Egeon (E). There are 2 B class hotels and 1 C class in Minos Square, near the bus station and convenient for the beach, but in reality you will have to take what is available in high season (if anything). If necessary, go to the Tourist Police by the lake for help. There is a *youth hostel*, at 3 Stratigou Koraka (near the harbour).

Restaurants: tend to be expensive especially by the lake and harbour; 2 of the best are Avra and Rififi on Akti Koundourou. Numerous *bars* and *discos* in the harbour area.

Usual facilities of *bank*, *post office* and *OTE*.

The *museum* is open during the mornings except for Tuesday.

Swimming: apart from off the rocks there are small beaches either side of the town, and a good sandy beach at Almiros, 2 kms to the east.

ELOUNDA

Frequent *caique trips* to the Venetian fortress on Spinalonga.

Hotels: Elounda Beach (L); Aristaea (C); Olous (E).

Taverna: Delfini.

Beyond Elounda, **Plaka** has a good pebble beach with tavernas.

KRITSA

Pensions and *rooms*; tavernas.

Panagia Kera: open 9am to 12, 2 to 5pm.

Festival on 15 August.

GOURNIA

The *site* is open 8.30am to 12.30pm, 4 to 6pm; Sundays and holidays 9am to 3pm.

There is a good *beach* at **Pachia Ammos**, 20 minutes walk to the east, with one C, one D Class *hotel* and *rooms*.

SITIA

Apart from the frequent *buses* to Agios Nikolaos and Heraklion there are 4 buses a day to Ierapetra and to Palaikastro and Vai, and 2 daily to Zakros. *Car hire*, etc.

Hotels: among the 15 or so, try the Denis (B); Itanos, Crystal (C); Flisvos (D) – all on or near the harbour. Also *pensions* and some *rent-rooms*. *Youth hostel:* 4 Therissou Street.

Good fish *restaurants* on the waterfront, also *discos*.

Post office, OTE, bank.

Big sandy *beach* on the eastern side of the harbour, with watersports.

Raisin Festival: local dancing, etc, mid-August.

MONASTERY OF TOPLOU

No bus, but you can *walk* the 4 kms from the turning off the bus route to Vai.

PALAIKASTRO

Hotels, pensions and *rooms*.

VAI

Nowhere to stay (except on the beach); a couple of *tavernas*.

ANO ZAKROS

Hotel: Zakros (C). *Tavernas*.

KATO ZAKROS

No bus – an 8 km *walk* or *taxi* ride.

Several *pensions* and a few *rent-rooms*. *Tavernas* with limited menus.

IERAPETRA

In addition to the 9 daily *buses* to Agios Nikolaos (and Heraklion) there are about 7 buses a day westwards to Mirtos, 2 of which continue to Heraklion, and about 5 to Sitia via Koutsouras and Makriyialos. *Moped* hire.

Hotels: some 16, mostly C to D category, of which you might try Creta (near the bus station at Venizelou Square), Cretan Villa (quiet), El Greco (on the seafront), Atlantis (2 kms to the east, by beach).

Also *pensions*. There is a *youth hostel* near the hotel Atlantis, 2 kms east. *Camping-ground*.

A long sandy *beach* stretches to the east.

The small *museum* is near the post office at Kothri Square. There is also an *OTE* and *bank*.

EASTWARDS OF IERAPETRA

Agia Fotia has a sandy beach, with rooms. There is accommodation at the village of **Koutsouras** which has been restored in traditional fashion, but it may all be taken up by the tour operators. **Makriyialos** also has a good sandy beach with windsurfing, etc; there are several pensions, a few rooms and any number of tavernas.

WESTWARDS OF IERAPETRA

Myrtos has a sandy beach and 2 C class hotels. **Arvi** too has a good beach, with the hotel Ariadni (C) by the sea, pensions, rooms and the usual tavernas, but the bus only comes as near as Ano Viannos, 10 kms away; however it is worth the walk.

INDEX

Athens (Athínai)	36	Adámas	253
Acropolis	38	Aegina (Aígina)	84
Agios Eleftherios	57	Agía Galíni	298
Agora	51	Agía Roúmeli	301
Anafiòtika	57	Agía Triáda	298
Archaeological Museum	65	Agía Triáda	195
Ardettos	69	Agia Lavra, Monastery of	113
Areopagus	51	Agia Pelagía	130
Athena Nike, Temple of	44	Agios Nikitas	248
Benaki Museum	61	Ágios Nikólaos (Crete)	305
Byzantine Museum	69	Ágios Nikólaos (Karpathos)	283
Erechtheion	50	Agios Petros	246
Fetichie Mosque	57	Ágios Stéfanos	278
Greek Popular Art, Museum of	56	Agrínion	225
Hadrian's Arch	59	Aigosthena	136
Hadrian's Library	56	Aitolikó	225
Hephaisteion (Theseion)	53	Akmetaga	165
Kanellopoulos Museum	57	Akrotíri	258
Kerameikos	54	Aktion (Actium)	221
Kolonaki	62	Alikes	239
Long Walls	65	Alónissos	168
Lykavittós	37	Amárinthos	166
Lysikrates, Monument of	58	Amfilochía	225
Mendreses	57	Ammos	207
Monastiraki	54	Amnisos	303
Munychia	66	Amorgós	256
National Archaeological Museum	62	Amphipolis	202
National Gardens	58	Amfissa	159
Naval Museum of Greece	65	Anapolis	302
Odeon of Herodes Atticus	47	Ándros	246
Olympian Zeus, Temple of	59	Andírrion	161, 227
Parliament	58	Andrítsaina	108
Parthenon	47	Anghístri	85
Philopappou	47	Ano Vathy	267
Piraeus	65	Áno Zákros	306
Plaka	55	Antipaxos	235
Pnyx	51	Antíparos	255
Propylaia	43	Apella	283
Proto Nekrotafeion Athinon	69	Apóllonas	255
Roman Forum	56	Apollonía	252, 253
Royal Palace	69	Apíranthos	255
Stoa of Attalos	52	Aráchova	148
Stadium	69	Areópolis	125
Theatre of Dionysos	47	Argive Heraion	100
Theseion	53	Argolid	95
Tower of the Winds	56	Árgos	101
Turkolimano	66	Argo-Saronic	84
War Museum	61	Argostóli	237
Zappeion	59	Arkádi, Monastery of	300
Zea	66	Arni	246
		Árta	224
Acro-corinth	96	Artemision	165

315

Artemónas	252	Dístomo	145
Asine	102	Dystos	166
Asklepieion	279	Eastern Sporades	267
Assos	238	Édessa	187
Astipalaia	279	Eléfsis	78
Athos	197	Eleutherai	136
Attica	76	Emborió (Chalki)	285
Aulis	164	Emborió (Chios)	269
Avdóu	304	Epídavros	103
Bassae	108	Erétria	165
Batsí	246	Ermoúpolis	247
Benítses	233	Euboea (Évvia)	164
Chaironeia	142	Fársala	179
Chalcidici (Halkidikí)	195	Filóti	255
Chalkí (Naxos)	255	Fiskárdo	238
Chálki	284	Fínikas	247
Chalkís	164	Fódele	299
Chaniá	300	Fokiali	286
Chlemoútsi	113	Folégandros	256
Chóra (Alonissos)	168	Frangokastello	303
Chóra (Amorgos)	256	Gáio	235
Chóra (Andros)	246	Galata	88
Chóra (Aspalaia)	279	Galaxídi	160
Chóra (Kalymnos)	278	Galissás	247
Chóra (Kea)	247	Gastoúri	233
Chóra (Kithera)	131	Gávrion	246
Chóra (Patmos)	276	Géfira	127
Chóra (Samothraki)	207	Gerolimín	126
Chóra (Serifos)	252	Geronthrai	127
Chóra Sfakíon	303	Gla	142
Chorió (Chalki)	285	Glóssa	168
Chorió (Simi)	279	Gortyn	298
Chíos	268	Gourniá	305
Chíos town	269	Grikou	276
Chrisó	159	Gýtheion	126
Corfu (Kérkira)	230	Helos	127
Corfu town	231	Heraklion (Iráklion)	293
Corinth Canal	95	Hozoviotíssa Monastery	256
Corinth (Kórinthos)	96	Hydra (Ídra)	88
Crete (Kríti)	293	Ialisos	282
Cyclades (Kýklades)	245	Ierápetra	307
Dáphni	76	Ierissos	196
Daulis	144	Ifestía	208
Dávlia	144	Igoumenítsa	214
Delagrátsia	247	Ikaria	267
Délos	249	Ioánnina	215
Delphi	149	Iolkos	175
Desfína	159	Ionian Islands	230
Diafáni	284	Íos	256
Diakoftó	112	Ipáti	173
'Diktaion Cave'	304	Itéa	159
Dimini	175	Ithaka	236
Diros	125	Ithome	121
Dodecanese	275	Jerusalem, Monastery of	144
Dodona	218	Kaimeni	257
Doukato, Cape	236	Kaisarianí	76

Kalamáta	121
Kalambáka	180
Kalávrita	112
Kallithéa	196
Kálymnos	277
Kálymnos town	277
Kamari	258
Kamarína (officially Zálonga)	221
Kambos	276
Kámbos	123
Kamiros	282
Kanoni	233
Kapsáli	131
Kardámila	269
Kardamýli	124
Kardítsa	179
Kariá	235
Kariés	200
Karlóvassi	267
Kárpathos	283
Karpenísi	173
Karítaina	107
Karteros Beach	303
Karthaía	247
Kárystos	166
Kásas	283
Kassándra	196
Kassiópi	234
Kassope	221
Kastélli	300
Kástello	285
Kastellórizo (Megísti)	285
Kastoría	187
Kastro	238
Kástro	253
Kástro	167
Katápola	256
Káto Zákros	306
Kavála	203
Kéa	247
Kefallonía	237
Kirrha	159
Kími	166
Kímolos	252
Knossos	295
Kolonna	268
Koróni	122
Kos	278
Kos town	279
Koíta	125
Koukounaries	167
Kouloura	234
Kranioi	237
Krannon	178
Kíri Panagía	283
Kritsá	305
Kíthera	129
Kíthnos	252
Lábia	112
Lagana	239
Lakkí	276
Lakka	235
Lákones	233
Lamía	173
Langáda	125
Lárissa	177
Lasithi Plain	304
Lavrion	80
Lefkás	235
Lefkás town	235
Lemnos (Límnos)	207
Léros	276
Lésvos	270
Levádia	139
Lévktron	124
Lia	215
Limen	204
Limeníon	125
Limín Chersonísou	303
Limni	165
Linariá	167
Linariá Bay	278
Litóchoron	178
Litsa	215
Livádi	279
Livádi	247
Líndos	282
Loutrá Aidipsoú	165
Loutráki	96
Loutro	302
Maina, Castle of	126
Makerádo	239
Makri Ammos	206
Makrinítsa	176
Makrís Yialós	238
Máleme	300
Mállia	303
Mani	123
Mantinea	106
Marathón	80
Maríes	239
Masouri	278
Mátala	298
Matapan	126
Megalópolis	107
Megaspeleion, Monastery of	112
Mesopótamo	220
Messene	121
Messolongi (Messolóngion)	225
Mestá	269
Metéora	180
Méthana	88

Methóni	122	Párga	220
Métsovo	215	Parnassos	147
Milíes	177	Paroikía	254
Milopotámos	130	Páros	253
Minoa	256	Patatíri	168
Mistrá	119	Pátmos	275
Mitilíni	270	Patras (Pátrai)	113
Mílos	253	Paxos (Paxí)	234
Mólivos	270	Pelikáta	236
Monemvasía	127	Pelion (Pílion)	175
Morgana villages	214	Pella	188
Moúdros	207	Peloponnese	95, 106, 117
Mírina (Kástron)	207	Perachóra	96
Mycenae (Mikínai)	98	Perissa	258
Mýkonos	248	Petaloudes	282
Myrtíes	278	Petrálona Cave	195
Náfplion (Nauplia)	102	Phaestos	298
Náoussa	254	Philippi	203
Navarino	122	Phirá	257
Návpaktos	160	Phylokopé	253
Náxos	255	Pigádia	283
Náxos town	255	Piraeus	65
Néa Michanióna	195	Pirgí	269
Néa Stíra	166	Pisaetos	236
Nekromanteion of Ephyra	220	Pithagórion	267
Nemea	97	Plaka (Milos)	253
Nestor's Palace	122	Plataea	137
Nikiá	279	Plátanos	276
Nikopolis	221	Platariá	219
Nisáki	234	Platís Yialós	238, 249, 253
Nómia	125	Píli	179
Northern Sporades	166	Polígyros	196
Nísyros	279	Poliochni	207
Oía	257	Pondikonisi	233
Ólimbos (Kárpathos)	284	Póros	88
Olympia (Olimbía)	108	Porto Carras	196
Olympias	202	Porto Germano	136
Olympos (Ólimbos)	178	Porto Roma	239
Olynthos	196	Potamiá	206
Ophrys	283	Potamiés	304
Orchomenós	141	Potamós	130
Oreoí	165	Potidaea	196
Ósios Loukás	145	Préveza	223
Oítilon	125	Pírgos	258
Ouranópolis	196	Pírgos	113
Pagasae-Demetrias	175	Pírgos	125
Palaiochóra	301	Psychró	304
Palaiopolis	207	Pýlos	122
Palaíkastro	306	Réthymnon	299
Paleochóra	130	Rhamnous	81
Paleokastrítsa	233	Rhodes, city of	280
Paleopolis	246	Rhodes (Ródos)	280
Palioúri	196	Ríon	114
Panagía	206	Salamis	85
Panopeos	143	Samaria Gorge	301
Panórama	195	Sami	237

Sámos	267
Samothráki	206
Sarti	196
Sérifos	252
Sesklo	175
Sífnos	252
Sikyon	114
Sími	279
Sitía	305
Sithonia	196
Skála (Lakonia)	127
Skála (Patmos)	275
Skala Eressou	270
Skaros	257
Skiáthos	167
Skiathos town	167
Síkinos	256
Skópelos	167
Skópelos town	167
Skorpios	236
Skýros	166, 167
Smokovo	179
Soúda Bay	300
Soúnion	79
Sparta (Spárti)	117
Spétsai	91
St John, Monastery of	276
Stageira	196
Stavrí	125
Stavrós	236
Stavrós	202
Stoúpa	124
Stíra	166
Strátos	225
Sýros	247
Tegea	106
Télendos	278
Thásos	204
Thebes	137
Theológos	206
Thera (Santoríni)	256
Therasia	257
Thermon	225
Thermopylae	172
Thessaloníki	189
Tithorea	145
Tílos	279
Tínos	248
Tolón	102
Toploú, Monastery of	306
Tríkala	179
Troezen	88
Trípolis	106
Trís Boúkes	166
Tsangaráda	176
Tséria	123
Tsilivi	239
Týlissos	299
Vai	306
Vale of Tempe	178
Vássai (Bassae)	108
Vátheia	126
Vathi	236
Vathy	267
Vathý	268
Vergína	188
Vérria	188
Vlakerena	233
Volissos	269
Vólos	174
Vourkári	247
Vravrón	80
Xerxes' canal	196
Xilókastro	114
Yerakes	239
Yialós	279
Zákinthos	238
Zákinthos town	238
Zákros, Palace of	306
Zálonga	221
Zitza	215